G·L·O·B·A·L S·T·U·D·I·E·S

INDIA AND SOUTH ASIA

FIFTH EDITION

Dr. James H. K. Norton

OTHER BOOKS IN THE GLOBAL STUDIES SERIES

- Africa
- China
- Europe
- Japan and the Pacific Rim
- Latin America
- The Middle East
- Russia, the Eurasian Republics, and Central/Eastern Europe

McGraw-Hill/Dushkin Company
530 Old Whitfield Street, Guilford, Connecticut 06437
Visit us on the Internet—http://www.dushkin.com

STAFF

Ian A. Nielsen	Publisher
Brenda S. Filley	Director of Production
Lisa M. Clyde	Developmental Editor
Roberta Monaco	Editor
Charles Vitelli	Designer
Robin Zarnetske	Permissions Coordinator
Joseph Offredi	Permissions Assistant
Lisa Holmes-Doebrick	Administrative Coordinator
Laura Levine	Graphics
Michael Campbell	Graphics/Cover Design
Tom Goddard	Graphics
Eldis Lima	Graphics
Nancy Norton	Graphics
Juliana Arbo	Typesetting Supervisor

Library of Congress Cataloging in Publication Data
Main Entry under title: Global Studies: India and South Asia.
    1. India—History—20th–21st centuries. 2. India—Politics and government—1947–.
    3. Asia, Southeastern—History—20th century. 4. Asia—History—20th–21st centuries.
I. Title: India and South Asia. II. Norton, James H. K., *comp.*
ISBN 0–07–243298–5   954   91–71258

Fifth Edition

Printed in the United States of America   1234567890BAHBAH54321   Printed on Recycled Paper

India and South Asia

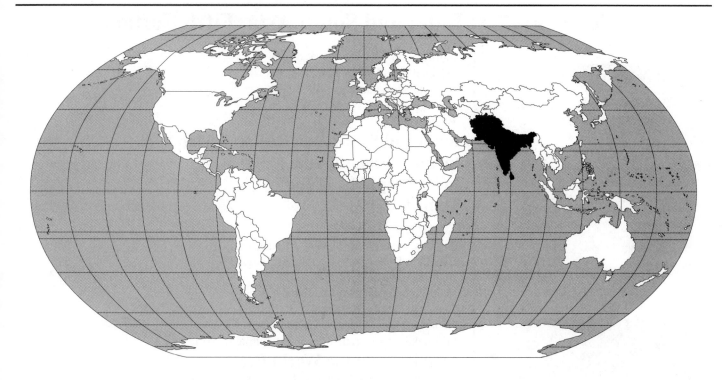

AUTHOR/EDITOR
Dr. James H. K. Norton

The author/editor of *Global Studies: India and South Asia, Fifth Edition,* received a B.S. degree from Yale University, B.A. and M.A. degrees in Sanskrit from Oxford University, and a Ph.D. in Indian philosophy from the University of Madras in India. He taught for 10 years at the College of Wooster, where he was associate professor of religion and chairman of the Department of Indian Studies. While at Wooster, Dr. Norton initiated a junior-year study program for college students in Madurai University, India, now part of the University of Wisconsin College Year in India program. He has also taught at Madurai University, Boston University, and Oberlin College. He is currently farming in Massachusetts, conducting continuing-education courses, and serving on the school committee for Martha's Vineyard. Dr. Norton spent five years in India as a Ford Foundation scholar while doing graduate work at the University of Madras as a teacher and as a senior research fellow of the American Institute of Indian Studies. He is a member of the American Academy of Religion, the Association for Asian Studies, and the Conference on Religion in South India, and he has served on the executive committee of the Society for South Indian Studies. His articles on Indian philosophy and on comparisons of Eastern and Western thought appear in a number of books and journals.

SERIES CONSULTANT
H. Thomas Collins
PROJECT LINKS
George Washington University

Contents

Global Studies: India and South Asia, Fifth Edition

South Asia Page 9

South Asia Page 14

India Page 33

Bangladesh Page 59

India Page 38

Nepal Page 69

Using Global Studies: India and South Asia

THE GLOBAL STUDIES SERIES

The Global Studies series was created to help readers acquire a basic knowledge and understanding of the regions and countries in the world. Each volume provides a foundation of information—geographic, cultural, economic, political, historical, artistic, and religious—that will allow readers to better assess the current and future problems within these countries and regions and to comprehend how events there might affect their own well-being. In short, these volumes present the background information necessary to respond to the realities of our global age.

Each of the volumes in the Global Studies series is crafted under the careful direction of an author/editor—an expert in the area under study. The author/editors teach and conduct research and have traveled extensively through the regions about which they are writing.

In this *India and South Asia* edition, the author/editor has written introductory essays on the South Asia region and country reports for each of the countries included.

MAJOR FEATURES OF
THE GLOBAL STUDIES SERIES

The Global Studies volumes are organized to provide concise information on the regions and countries within those areas under study. The major sections and features of the books are described here.

Regional Essays

For *Global Studies: India and South Asia,* the author/editor has written an essay, "Images of South Asia," focusing on the religious, cultural, sociopolitical, and economic differences and similarities of the countries and peoples in the region. A detailed map accompanies the essay.

Country Reports

Concise reports are written for each of the countries within the region under study. These reports are the heart of each Global Studies volume. *Global Studies: India and South Asia, Fifth Edition,* contains eight country reports, including India.

The country reports are composed of five standard elements. Each report contains a detailed map visually positioning the country among its neighboring states; a summary of statistical information; a current essay providing important historical, geographical, political, cultural, and economic information; a historical timeline, offering a convenient visual survey of a few key historical events; and four "graphic indicators," with summary statements about the country in terms of development, freedom, health/welfare, and achievements.

A Note on the Statistical Reports

The statistical information provided for each country has been drawn from a wide range of sources. (The most frequently referenced are listed on page 204.) Every effort has been made to provide the most current and accurate information available. However, occasionally the information cited by these sources differs to some extent; and, all too often, the most current information available for some countries is dated. Aside from these difficulties, the statistical summary of each country is generally quite complete and up to date. Care should be taken, however, in using these statistics (or, for that matter, any published statistics) in making hard comparisons among countries. We have also provided comparable statistics for the United States and Canada, which can be found on pages viii and ix.

World Press Articles

Within each Global Studies volume is reprinted a number of articles carefully selected by our editorial staff and the author/editor from a broad range of international periodicals and newspapers. The articles have been chosen for currency, interest, and their differing perspectives on the subject countries. There are 33 articles in *Global Studies: India and South Asia, Fifth Edition.*

The articles section is preceded by an annotated table of contents as well as a topic guide. The annotated table of contents offers a brief summary of each article, while the topic guide indicates the main theme(s) of each article. Thus, readers desiring to focus on articles dealing with a particular theme, say, the environment, may refer to the topic guide to find those articles.

WWW Sites

An extensive annotated list of selected World Wide Web sites can be found on the facing page (vii) in this edition of *Global Studies: India and South Asia.* In addition, the URL addresses for country-specific Web sites are provided on the statistics page of most countries. All of the Web site addresses were correct and operational at press time. Instructors and students alike are urged to refer to those sites often to enhance their understanding of the region and to keep up with current events.

Glossary, Bibliography, Index

At the back of each Global Studies volume, readers will find a glossary of terms and abbreviations, which provides a quick reference to the specialized vocabulary of the area under study and to the standard abbreviations used throughout the volume.

Following the glossary is a bibliography, which lists general works, national histories, and current-events publications and periodicals that provide regular coverage on India and South Asia.

The index at the end of the volume provides reference to the contents of the volume. Readers seeking specific information and citations should consult this standard index.

Currency and Usefulness

Global Studies: India and South Asia, like the other Global Studies volumes, is intended to provide the most current and useful information available necessary to understand the events that are shaping the cultures of the region today.

This volume is revised on a regular basis. The statistics are updated, regional essays and country reports revised, and world press articles replaced. In order to accomplish this task, we turn to our author/editor, our advisory boards, and—hopefully—to you, the users of this volume. Your comments are more than welcome. If you have an idea that you think will make the next edition more useful, an article or bit of information that will make it more current, or a general comment on its organization, content, or features that you would like to share with us, please send it in for serious consideration.

Selected World Wide Web Sites for India and South Asia

(Some Web sites continually change their structure and content, so the information listed here may not always be available. Check our Web site at: http://www.dushkin.com/online/—Ed.)

GENERAL SITES

1. BBC World Service—**http://www.bbc.co.uk/worldservice/sasia/**—The BBC, one of the world's most successful radio networks, provides the latest news from around the world and in South Asia at this site. It is possible to access the news in several languages.

2. CNN Online Page—**http://www.cnn.com**—U.S. 24-hour video news channel. News, updated every few hours, includes text, pictures, and film. Good external links.

3. C-SPAN ONLINE—**http://www.c-span.org**—See especially C-SPAN International on the Web for International Programming Highlights and archived C-Span programs.

4. International Network Information Center at University of Texas—**http://inic.utexas.edu**—Gateway has pointers to international sites, including South Asia.

5. Penn Library: Resources by Subject—**http://www.library.upenn.edu/resources/subject/subject.html**—This vast site is rich in links to information about Asian studies, including population and demography.

6. Political Science RESOURCES—**http://www.psr.keele.ac.uk**—Dynamic gateway to sources available via European addresses. Listed by country name.

7. ReliefWeb—**http://www.reliefweb.int**—UN's Department of Humanitarian Affairs clearinghouse for international humanitarian emergencies.

8. Social Science Information Gateway (SOSIG)—**http://sosig.esrc.bris.ac.uk**—Project of the Economic and Social Research Council (ESRC). It catalogs 22 subjects and lists developing countries' URL addresses.

9. Speech and Transcript Center—**http://gwis2.circ.gwu.edu/~gprice/speech.htm**—This unusual site is the repository of transcripts of every kind, from radio and television, of speeches by world government leaders, and the proceedings of groups like the United Nations, NATO, and the World Bank.

10. United Nations System—**http://www.unsystem.org**—This is the official Web site for the United Nations system of organizations. Everything is listed alphabetically. Offers: UNICC; Food and Agriculture Organization.

11. UN Development Programme (UNDP)—**http://www.undp.org**—Publications and current information on world poverty, Mission Statement, UN Development Fund for Women, and more. Be sure to see Poverty Clock.

12. U.S. Agency for International Development (USAID)—**http://www.info.usaid.gov**—U.S. policy toward assistance to Asian countries is available at this site.

13. U.S. Central Intelligence Agency Home Page—**http://www.cia.gov/**—This site includes publications of the CIA, such as the World Factbook, Factbook on Intelligence, Handbook of International Economic Statistics, and CIA Maps.

14. U.S. Department of State Home Page—**http://www.state.gov/index.cfm**—Organized alphabetically: Country Reports, Human Rights, International Organizations, etc.

15. World Bank Group—**http://www.worldbank.org**—News (press releases, summary of new projects, speeches), publications, topics in development, countries and regions. Links to other financial organizations.

16. World Health Organization (WHO)—**http://www.who.int**—Maintained by WHO's headquarters in Geneva, Switzerland, this comprehensive site includes a search engine.

17. World Trade Organization (WTO)—**http://www.wto.org**—Topics include foundation of world trade systems, data on textiles, intellectual property rights, legal frameworks, trade and environmental policies, recent agreements, and others.

GENERAL INDIA AND SOUTH ASIA SITES

18. ASEANWEB—**http://www.asean.or.id**—This official site of the Association of South East Asian Nations provides an overview of Asian Web sources, Summits, Economic and World Affairs, Publications, Political Foundations, Regional Cooperation.

19. Asia Web Watch—**http://www.ciolek.com/Asia-Web-Watch/main-page.html**—Here is a register of statistical data that can be accessed alphabetically. Data includes Asian Online Materials Statistics and Appendices about Asian cyberspace.

20. Asian Arts—**http://asianart.com**—Here is an online journal for the study and exhibition of the arts of Asia, which includes exhibitions, articles, and galleries.

21. Asian Studies WWW Virtual Library—**http://coombs.anu.edu.au/WWWVL-AsianStudies.html**—Australia National University maintains these sites, which link to many other Web sources, available at each country's location.

22. Asia-Yahoo—**http://www.yahoo.com/Regional/Regions/Asia/**—Specialized Yahoo search site permits keyword searches on Asian events, countries, and topics.

23. History of the Indian Sub-Continent—**http://loki.stockon.edu/~gilmorew/consorti/1aindia.htm**—As part of Stockton's World Wide Web Global History Research Institute, the history of the Indian subcontinent has been arranged chronologically at this site. This excellent resource contains maps, pictures, short writings, and scholarly writings.

24. South Asia Resources—**http://www.lib.berkeley.edu/SSEAL/SouthAsia/**—From this University of Berkeley Library site there is quick access to online resources in Asian studies as well as to South Asian specialists and other special features.

See individual country report pages for additional Web sites.

The United States (United States of America)

GEOGRAPHY

Area in Square Miles (Kilometers):
3,618,770 (9,578,626) (about ½ the size of Russia)

Capital (Population): Washington, D.C. (568,000)

Environmental Concerns: air and water pollution; limited freshwater resources; desertification; loss of habitat; waste disposal

Geographical Features: vast central plain, mountains in the west, hills and low mountains in the east; rugged mountains and broad river valleys in Alaska; volcanic topography in Hawaii.

Climate: mostly temperate

PEOPLE

Population
Total: 276,000,000
Annual Growth Rate: 0.91%
Rural/Urban Population Ratio: 24/76
Major Languages: predominantly English; a sizable Spanish-speaking minority; many others
Ethnic Makeup: 69.1% white; 12.5% Latino; 12.1% black or African American; 3.6% Asian; 0.7% Amerindian

Religions: 56% Protestant; 28% Roman Catholic; 2% Jewish; 4% others; 10% none or unaffiliated

Health
Life Expectancy at Birth: 74 years (male); 80 years (female)
Infant Mortality Rate (Ratio): 6.82/1,000
Physicians Available (Ratio): 1/365

Education
Adult Literacy Rate: 97% (official; estimates vary widely)
Compulsory (Ages): 7–16; free

COMMUNICATION
Telephones: 173,000,000 main lines
Daily Newspaper Circulation: 238 per 1,000 people
Televisions: 776 per 1,000 people
Internet Service Providers: 7,600 (1999 est.)

TRANSPORTATION
Highways in Miles (Kilometers): 3,906,960 (6,261,154)
Railroads in Miles (Kilometers): 149,161 (240,000)
Usable Airfields: 13,387
Motor Vehicles in Use: 206,000,000

GOVERNMENT
Type: federal republic

Independence Date: July 4, 1776
Head of State: President George W. Bush
Political Parties: Democratic Party; Republican Party; others of minor political significance
Suffrage: universal at 18

MILITARY
Military Expenditures (% of GDP): 3.8%
Current Disputes: none

ECONOMY
Per Capita Income/GDP: $33,900/$9.25 trillion
GDP Growth Rate: 4.1%
Inflation Rate: 2.2%
Unemployment Rate: 4.2%
Labor Force: 13,943,000
Natural Resources: minerals; precious metals; petroleum; coal; copper; timber; arable land
Agriculture: food grains; feed crops; fruits and vegetables; oil-bearing crops; livestock; dairy products
Industry: diversified in both capital- and consumer-goods industries
Exports: $663 billion (primary partners Canada, Mexico, Japan)
Imports: $912 billion (primary partners Canada, Japan, Mexico)

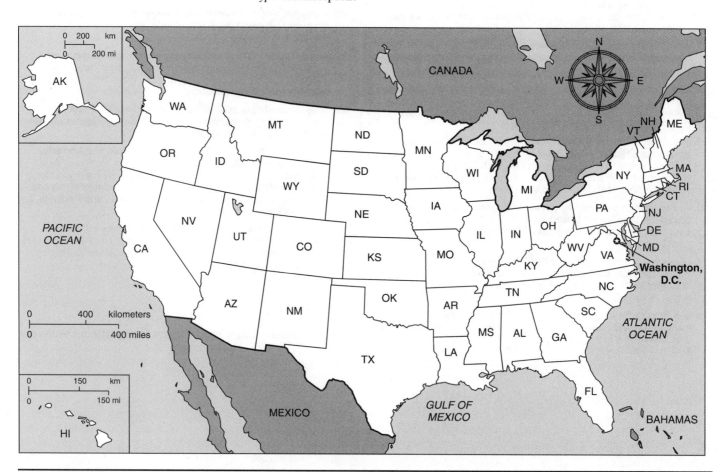

Canada

GEOGRAPHY

Area in Square Miles (Kilometers):
3,850,790 (9,976,140) (slightly larger than the United States)

Capital (Population): Ottawa (1,000,000)

Environmental Concerns: air pollution and resulting acid rain severely affecting lakes and damaging forests; water pollution; industrial damage to agriculture and forest productivity

Geographical Features: permafrost in the north hinders development, mountains in the west, central plains, and a maritime culture in the east

Climate: from temperate in south to subarctic and arctic in north

PEOPLE

Population

Total: 31,300,000

Annual Growth Rate: 1.02%

Rural/Urban Population Ratio: 23/77

Major Languages: both English and French are official

Ethnic Makeup: 28% British Isles origin; 23% French origin; 15% other European; 6% others; 2% indigenous; 26% mixed

Religions: 46% Roman Catholic; 16% United Church; 10% Anglican; 28% others

Health

Life Expectancy at Birth: 76 years (male); 83 years (female)

Infant Mortality Rate (Ratio): 5.08/1,000

Physicians Available (Ratio): 1/534

Education

Adult Literacy Rate: 97%

Compulsory (Ages): primary school

COMMUNICATION

Telephones: 18,500,000 main lines

Daily Newspaper Circulation: 215 per 1,000 people

Televisions: 647 per 1,000 people

Internet Service Providers: 750 (1999 est.)

TRANSPORTATION

Highways in Miles (Kilometers): 559,240 (902,000)

Railroads in Miles (Kilometers): 22,320 (36,000)

Usable Airfields: 1,411

Motor Vehicles in Use: 16,800,000

GOVERNMENT

Type: confederation with parliamentary democracy

Independence Date: July 1, 1867

Head of State/Government: Queen Elizabeth II; Prime Minister Jean Chrétien

Political Parties: Progressive Conservative Party; Liberal Party; New Democratic Party; Reform Party; Bloc Québécois

Suffrage: universal at 18

MILITARY

Military Expenditures (% of GDP): 1.2%

Current Disputes: none

ECONOMY

Currency ($U.S. Equivalent): 1.53 Canadian dollars = $1

Per Capita Income/GDP: $23,300/$722.3 billion

GDP Growth Rate: 3.6%

Inflation Rate: 1.7%

Labor Force: 15.1 million

Natural Resources: petroleum; natural gas; fish; minerals; cement; forestry products; wildlife; hydropower

Agriculture: grains; livestock; dairy products; potatoes; hogs; poultry and eggs; tobacco; fruits and vegetables

Industry: oil production and refining; natural-gas development; fish products; wood and paper products; chemicals; transportation equipment

Exports: $277 billion (primary partners United States, Japan, United Kingdom)

Imports: $259.3 billion (primary partners United States, Japan, United Kingdom)

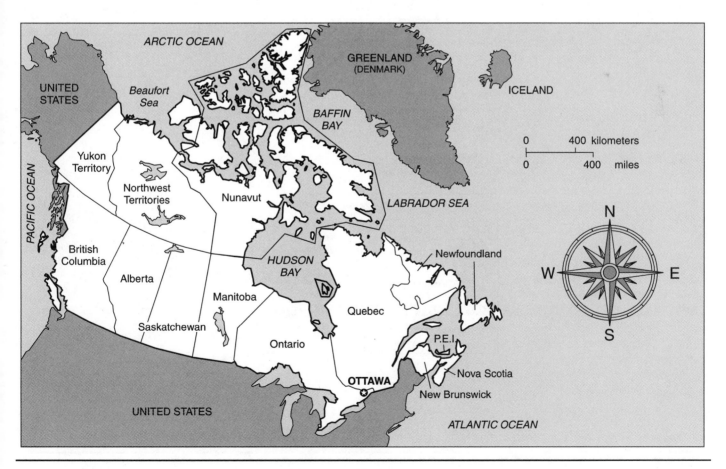

This map is provided to give you a graphic picture of where the countries of the world are located, the relationship they have with their region and neighbors, and their positions relative to the superpowers and power blocs. We have focused on certain areas to illustrate these crowded regions more clearly.

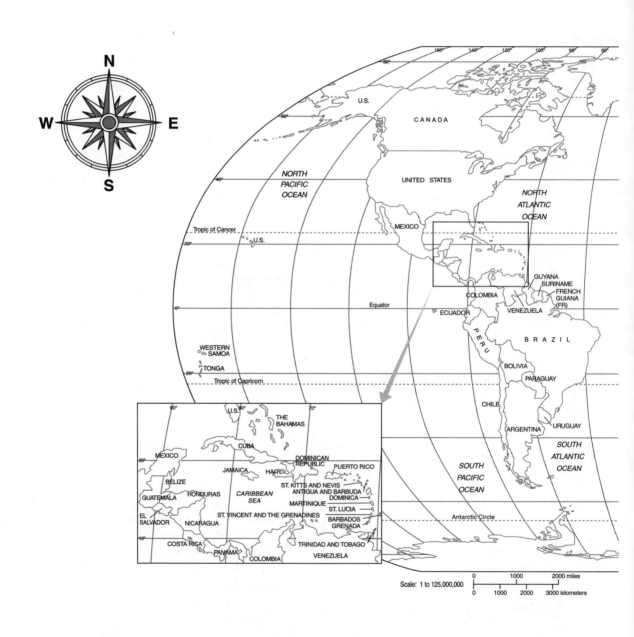

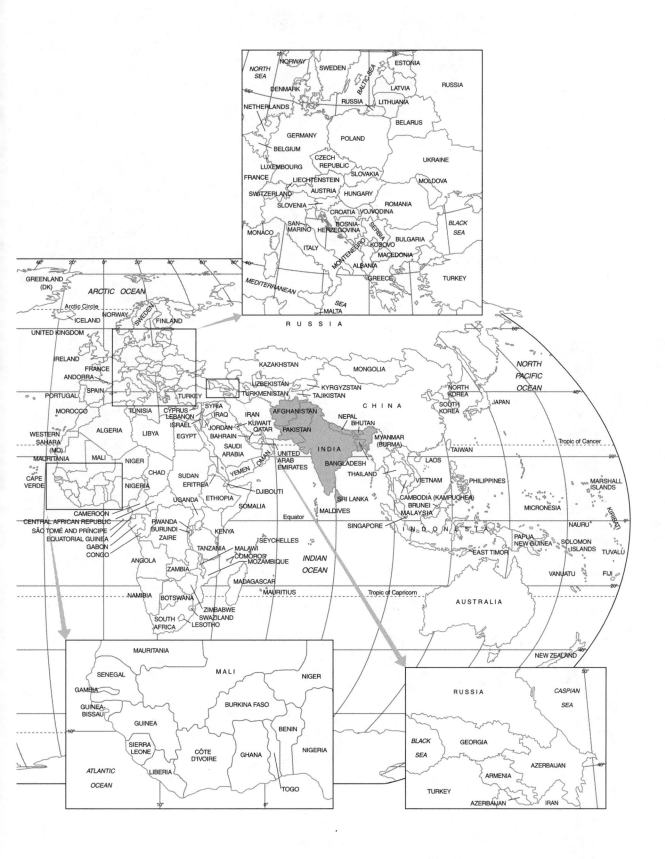

India and South Asia

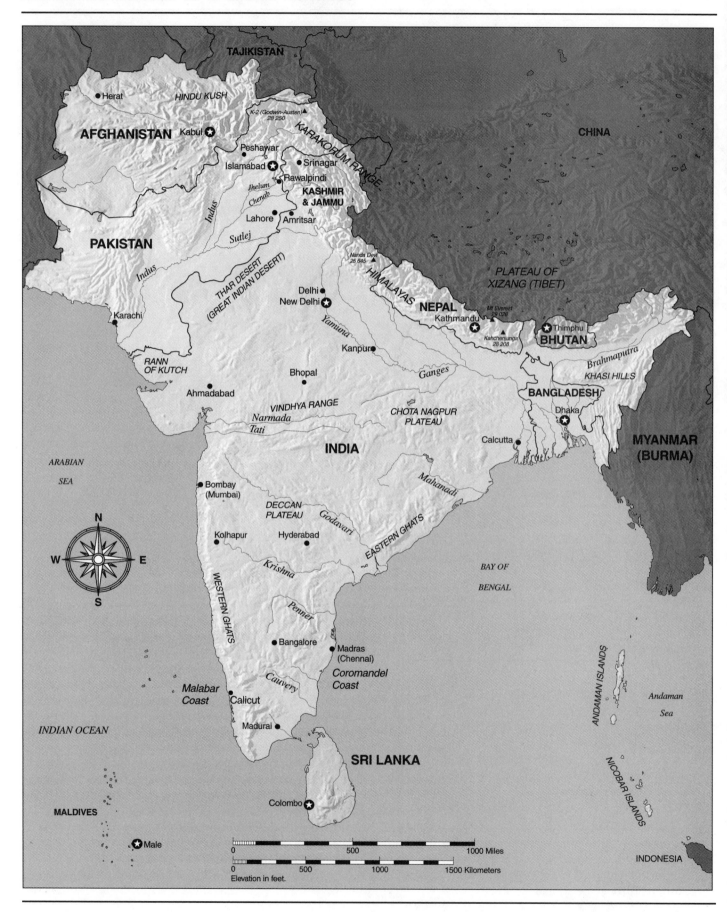

TAJIKISTAN

Herat
HINDU KUSH
AFGHANISTAN
Kabul ★
K-2 (Godwin-Austen) 28 250
KARAKORUM RANGE
CHINA
Peshawar
Islamabad ★
Srinagar
Rawalpindi
Jhelum
KASHMIR & JAMMU
Chenab
Lahore
Amritsar
PAKISTAN
Indus
Sutlej
Nanda Devi 25 645
HIMALAYAS
PLATEAU OF XIZANG (TIBET)
Karachi
Indus
THAR DESERT (GREAT INDIAN DESERT)
Delhi
New Delhi ★
NEPAL
Kathmandu ★
Mt Everest 29 028
Kahchenjunga 28 208
Thimphu ★
BHUTAN
Yamuna
Kanpur
Brahmaputra
KHASI HILLS
RANN OF KUTCH
Bhopal
Ganges
BANGLADESH
Ahmadabad
VINDHYA RANGE
Narmada
Tati
CHOTA NAGPUR PLATEAU
Dhaka ★
MYANMAR (BURMA)
INDIA
Calcutta
ARABIAN SEA
Bombay (Mumbai)
DECCAN PLATEAU
Mahanadi
Godavari
Kolhapur
Hyderabad
EASTERN GHATS
BAY OF BENGAL
N
W E
S
Krishna
Penner
INDIAN OCEAN
WESTERN GHATS
Bangalore
Madras (Chennai)
Cauvery
Coromandel Coast
ANDAMAN ISLANDS
Andaman Sea
Malabar Coast
Calicut
Madurai
MALDIVES
★ Male
SRI LANKA
Colombo ★
NICOBAR ISLANDS
0   500   1000 Miles
0   500   1000   1500 Kilometers
Elevation in feet.
INDONESIA

2

Images of South Asia

South Asia is a unique part of the world. We recognize South Asian women because of their distinctive dress, called *saris* or *salwar-chemises*, and the cosmetic red mark called *bindu* on their foreheads. Men might wear *dhotis, jodhpurs,* or sometimes trousers and notched-collar Nehru jackets. Some men wrap turbans about their heads. Indian cooking, with its delightfully spicy curries, has a flavor all its own. And Indian music, played on the *sitar, vina,* or *sharod,* has tonal scales called *ragas* and follows rhythm patterns that are different from Western styles of music. These experiences identify what is normal for a people whose native place and culture, languages and traditions are distinct. Even South Asians' attitudes and assumptions about such elemental realities as truth, life, time, and life-after-death are different from those held in other parts of the world.

Some contributions that the world has received from the subcontinent identify the uniqueness of South Asia. Zero, the most symbolic and elusive of all numbers, was added to the traditional ways of counting in the West only after Arab traders brought it from South Asia in a system known, for that reason as Arabic numbers. Linguistics, the study of the structure of language, also had its origin in South Asia. *Yoga,* a spiritual discipline increasingly pursued in the West, has been practiced in South Asia since ancient times. And *satyagraha* (nonviolent resistance) was developed in the twentieth century by India's "Mahatma" Gandhi as an alternative to power politics. These contributions reveal the extent and variety of creative ideas that evolved in the unique cultural environment of South Asia for the benefit of all humankind.

There are also some common challenges that the peoples of this region share with other parts of the world. Population density and growth, environmental degradation, national identity, economic development, social equality and women's rights, child labor, illiteracy, poverty, and disease (among which is an alarming increase in the cases of HIV/AIDS) are all issues that affect the well-being of everyone in the world. How the peoples of South Asia respond to these challenges is important, not only for their own well-being but also toward assuring a future for us all.

OUT OF MANY VIEWS, A PORTRAIT

This essay focuses on five images of South Asia. These images are not definitive. Rather, they intend to point to a comprehensive picture of what we can learn from this immensely varied part of the world.

The first image is that South Asia is a distinct geographical and cultural region inhabited by more than 1.3 billion people, one fifth of the total population of the world. These people live in a clearly defined space, about a quarter of the size of North America, set apart from the rest of the world by high mountains and ocean waters. In this space a unique and ancient history has shaped the cultures, languages, social patterns, institutions, and religious traditions in ways that are quite different from those found anywhere else.

Study of the setting of the lives and traditions of the peoples of South Asia provides a basis for mutual respect and understanding, where a lack of such awareness may lead to stereotyping and mistrust. In an increasingly interconnected world, ignorance of such a significant portion of the world's population is not only deplorable, but it can also be dangerous. A recent example is the portrayal in the Western press of India as war-mongering and violent because of its nuclar testing in May 1999 and its refusal to sign the Comprehensive (Nuclear) Test Ban Treaty passed by the United Nations in September 1996. This characterization of India, at the very least, does not take adequate account of the security risks that India faces in its unsettled disputes over its 2,800-mile border with China.

The second image is that South Asia is an incredibly diverse as well as crowded multicultural environment. The large population·is currently divided among eight countries: Afghanistan, Bangladesh, Bhutan, Maldives, Nepal, India, Pakistan, and Sri Lanka. As islands, the borders of Maldives and Sri Lanka are defined by geography. But the borders of Sri Lanka and all the other countries of the region, with the exception of Bangladesh, do not enclose peoples of common language and ethnic origin. The countries are all multicultural, with a wide diversity of social groups who speak different languages and follow distinct customs and separate religious traditions.

Their boundaries also separate peoples of shared ethnicity, language, and religion into different nationalities. The Pathans, for example, were divided by the border established between British India and Afghanistan in 1907. In 1979, at the time of the Soviet invasion of Afghanistan, about 6 million Pathans—more than a third of the total population of Afghanistan—lived on the Afghan side. Another 10 million lived on the other side of the border, constituting the dominant population in the Northwest Frontier Province of Pakistan.

India, by far the largest country in South Asia, with more than 75 percent of the total population and occupying 64 percent of the land of the subcontinent, is socially and linguistically the most diverse. Seventeen distinct, indigenous languages, each with innumerable dialects, are recognized in the Constitution of India. Each is dominant in a different part of the country, and none is spoken by a majority of the population. Only English, although foreign in origin and spoken by less than 6 percent of the people, serves as the "link language" among all the many distinct linguistic regions of India.

People living in the same place who all speak the same language are also divided into extended kinship groups called caste (*jati*) communities. These communities sustain accepted norms of behavior, dress, and diet for all of their members. They are also endogamous, which means that families are expected to find marriage partners for their children among other families within the group. Many are identified by a traditional occupation, from which each derives its name, such as *dhobi* (washerman community), *gujar* (goat herder community), and *jat* (farmer community). There are hundreds of thousands of such kinship groups throughout the country. In a normal village setting, individuals will interact on a daily basis with others from about 20 different jatis. The locally accepted position of their jatis in a social hierarchy, generally termed the *caste system,* will determine the expected social norms of their daily interactions. One's position in the immediate family is also highly proscribed by traditional expectations, maintained in most instances by the patriarchal structure of the family.

Another significant division in all of the countries of the subcontinent is between the urban and the rural populations. Rural dwellers outnumber city dwellers three to one. Those who live in villages also contrast vividly in maintaining more traditional customs and lifestyles than those in the cities. Another striking contrast, in both the cities and villages, is between those who are wealthy and the multitude of the very poor.

That such a diverse population lives in such crowded circumstances, with everyone drawing upon limited resources, is a great achievement—and a constant challenge. There is no shortage of causes for altercation among socially distinct groups. Extensive outbursts, rampaging, and rioting do occur among competitive factions and differing religious communities, as well as outright warfare among militant nationalist organizations and between nation-states. Yet for most of the subcontinent, there is a heritage of accommodation and an expectation of tolerance among peoples of differing customs, languages, and religious faiths. To understand something of the complex patterns of social interaction that exist in South Asia, to see how it does and doesn't work, should be helpful to other peoples as they become more multiculturally conscious.

The next two images amplify the first two images of South Asia as a distinct, diverse, and crowded cultural region of the world. The third image looks toward the past, at the classical heritage of the peoples of the subcontinent, known as the "Great Tradition," to see how it underlies and sustains the complex and persistent social diversity in South Asia. The fourth image looks at the impact of democracy in the subcontinent today, especially among peoples whose primary sense of identity is ethnic, religious, and linguistic, as sustained by one's jati community—rather than political, as a nation.

The third image, of the Great Tradition of South Asia, has its earliest discernible roots in two vastly different sources. One is the Harappan city culture. Archeological remains of this ancient urban culture reveal organizational and commercial skills developed in these Indus River Valley cities more than 4,500 years ago. Another source is the Vedic tradition, recorded in a sacred literature that contains the religious musings of a robust, cow-herding people, called Aryans. They drove their horse-drawn war chariots into the subcontinent from Central Asia a thousand years later. Over the course of many centuries, these two heritages were coalesced, elabo-

(UN Photo 153428/John Isaac)

The sheer multitude of people who live in South Asia is mind-boggling: More than 1.3 billion crowd the subcontinent, and despite some successes in family planning, that number is climbing rapidly.

rated, appended, and refined into classical forms that became normative for the way civilized people in that region of the world should perceive and participate in life. These forms provided the structure for immense intellectual and artistic creativity, which produced many outstanding works of thought and art.

Because of the skill, discipline, and depth of insight achieved by South Asia's classical thinkers and artisans, their accumulated works are intellectually challenging and inspiring. The tradition that they created reveals an enduring perspective on our world that can be broadening and self-affirming for us, as well as giving some definition to the uniqueness of South Asian cultures. An awareness of this Great Tradition also provides a context for understanding the introduction of democracy as a political force among the nations of South Asia. In addition, it offers alternative paths to realize the goals of democracy in a world torn by ethnic violence and warfare.

The fourth image of South Asia looks at the introduction of democracy into the subcontinent as a primary instrument of political modernization. Democracy is having a profound impact not only on the form and goals of governments in the countries of South Asia; it is also changing the bases of people's interaction with one another. Democratically elected representative government is a modern Western institution, introduced by the British colonial government during the nineteenth and early twentieth centuries. Its introduction has brought about a number of far-reaching issues. All of the countries have had to deal with challenges of national identity, of the relation of religion to nationalism, of refugees, and of political stability. These issues have produced unanticipated, sometimes traumatic, consequences for many millions of people. Yet today, more people live under democratic rule in South Asia than in any other part of the world. There is much that we can learn about democracy by examining the various ways that it has come to function in the South Asian cultural setting.

Finally, in a fifth image, we focus attention on Mohandas Karamchand Gandhi, called the *Mahatma,* the "Great-Souled One." During the early 1900s, Gandhi evolved an effective process of nonviolent political resistance. He also developed a style of leadership that drew upon a unique combination of the classical norms and modern aspirations described in the previous two images of South Asia. He articulated, in enviable simplicity, the profound perspective of the classical tradition in committing himself not just to the removal of colonial domination, to political independence, but to true freedom for an oppressed people. He thus empowered those who today are citizens of India, Sri Lanka, Bangladesh, and Nepal to participate in the destiny of new, democratically ruled nations in the modern world.

To understand Gandhi and his leadership role is to realize how much he embodied what is distinct about the peoples of South Asia. Yet it is in his uniqueness as an individual among a specific people that he speaks to us all. No one else in the twentieth century had so wide and positive an impact on the political awareness and empowerment of oppressed peoples all over the world.

IMAGE 1: SOUTH ASIA, A DISTINCT LAND AND AN ANCIENT CIVILIZATION

A. K. Ramanujan used to tell the story of a Mongolian conqueror who had a certain species of nightingale brought to him from Kashmir because he had heard that this bird sang the most beautiful song in the world. But when the bird arrived, it did not sing. It was explained to the enraged conqueror that the bird sang only when perched on the branch of a chinar tree, and that the chinar tree grows only on the hillsides of Kashmir. Ramanujan concluded this story of what the conqueror needed to do to get his captured nightingale to sing, with these words of St.-John Perse:

> We know the story of that Mongolian conqueror, taker of a bird in its nest, and of the nest in its tree, who brought back with the bird and nest and song the whole natal tree itself, torn from its place with its multitude of roots, its ball of earth and its border of soil, a remnant of home territory evoking a field, a province, a country, and an empire. . . .
>
> —St.-John Perse, *Birds*
> (cited in A. K. Ramanujan, *Poems of Love and War*)

A DISTINCT LAND

The land on which the people of South Asia live is clearly set apart from the rest of Asia as a geographical area. Geologically speaking, it is a recent addition to the continent. About 100 million years ago, it broke away from the east coast of Africa and drifted slowly on a separate geological plate east and north, until it collided, about 28 million years ago, with the southern edge of the continental landmass of Asia. The immense power of this impact scrunched up the south coast of Asia. It pushed the Tibetan Plateau more than three miles into the air and created a high ridge of snow-clad peaks, which today mark the line of impact. This mountain range, the Himalayas, is the highest in the world, and it is still rising (at a rate of about 10 inches per century) as a result of the massive collision that occurred so many millions of years ago.

The perimeters of the subcontinent are still clearly delineated by nature—on the north, by the high, forbidding Himalayas; on the south, by the vast expanse of the Arabian Sea, the Bay of Bengal, and the Indian Ocean. The high mountain peaks and vast ocean waters dominate the landscape. They also produce the annual monsoons, the seasonal torrents of rain upon which the livelihood of the people of South Asia depends.

Within these natural borders is a wide range of geographical conditions, of topography and climate, that divide into four distinct regions. First, farthest to the north, are the frigid, arctic heights of the south face of the Himalayan Mountains. All of Afghanistan and Bhutan, most of Nepal, and small portions of India and Pakistan fall within this region.

These mountainous Himalayan lands fall precipitously and dramatically toward the south into the second region—the wide, alluvial river valleys that stretch across the north-central portion of the subcontinent. Three river systems—the Indus, the Jumna-Ganges, and the Brahmaputra—all begin within 100 miles of one another in the Himalayas, but flow in three different directions through the mountains and down into the expanse of the north-central plains. The Indus flows to the west, through Pakistan to the Arabian Sea. The Jumna-Ganges Rivers flow to the south, and then join to flow east across the great northern plain, to where they merge with the Brahmaputra River. The Brahmaputra flows to the east from its Himalayan source, and then south into Bangladesh. Both river systems then flow together, through many tributaries, into the Bay of Bengal.

All three river systems provide the north-central plains with a steady, if uneven, flow of melting snow. Because of this flow through the temperate northern plains, this region is the most widely irrigated and has the most productive agricultural lands of the subcontinent.

To the south of the northern plains region, entirely in India, are the highlands of the peninsula, which project out into the Indian Ocean. The highlands rise to a wide plateau, called the Deccan, which is bordered to the east and west by smaller, but older, mountains than the Himalayas. The central portion of Sri Lanka also rises to highlands, which, together with the Deccan, form the third geographically distinct region of the subcontinent. Because these highlands are not high enough to be snow-covered, farmers in this region are entirely dependent upon the seasonal monsoonal rains for sufficient water to cultivate the land.

From these highlands, the land slopes down into the fourth region, the coastal plains and tropical beaches of India, Pakistan, Bangladesh, Sri Lanka, and Maldives. Most of South Asia's largest cities, which developed as trading posts during the seventeenth century and are now great centers of commerce, fall within this coastal region.

These four distinct regions, which also include desert and rain forest, present as wide a range of topography and climate as exists anywhere in the world. Together, appended to the southern side of Asia, they form a varied and isolated geographical space.

AN ANCIENT CIVILIZATION

Maritime Commerce

The earliest evidence of a distinctive South Asian culture is found in the archeological sites of the world's earliest known urban civilization. This Harappan city culture flourished in the Indus River Valley, in the northwestern portion of the subcontinent, from 3000 to 1500 B.C. Excavations of these ancient Harappan sites have revealed that the early city dwellers produced enough surplus, primarily in cotton and grains, to carry on trade well beyond their own region. Their commercial activity extended into the developing civilizations in the Fertile Crescent, Africa and Europe to the west, and Southeast Asia and China to the east.

This trading shows that from earliest times, the ocean waters into which the subcontinent projects have been not so much a barrier as a vital concourse. Maritime commerce has continued to be a major activity along the shores of the subcontinent, from the days of Harappan mercantile enterprise, through the era of silk trade, to the fiercely competitive activity of European trading companies in the seventeenth and eighteenth centuries, into the present day.

As a result of this crucial location on international trade routes, the peoples of South Asia have interacted with the major currents of human civilization since very ancient times. This interaction brought peacocks out of the subcontinent to embellish the throne of King Solomon in ancient Israel, the number zero to Europe during the Renaissance to change the way mathematical computations are done in the West, and Buddhism to become a major religious faith in East Asia and the rest of the world.

AN ANCIENT CIVILIZATION

What He Said

As a little white snake
with lovely stripes on its young body
troubles the jungle elephant

　this slip of a girl

　her teeth like sprouts of new rice

　her wrists stacked with bangles

　troubles me.

—*Catti Natana r Kur 119*
(translated by A. K. Ramanujan)

This small statue of a girl was cast in bronze more than 4,000 years ago in Mohenjo Daro, the ancient city of the Harappan civilization in the Indus River Valley. Lost in the sands that buried that city so long ago, her image was captured 2,000 years later by a south Indian poet at the other end of the subcontinent, some 2,000 miles away, in this love poem found in the classical Tamil Sangam anthology called the *Kuruntokai*. Recovered in the twentieth century from the excavations of the ancient city and in the translations of the classical Sangam poetry, we, too, are tantalized by this tiny yet enduring image from South Asia.

Because of the extent and intensity of this interaction, it is difficult to trace the origin of many of the concepts and practices that came the other way—that entered the subcontinent from other regions and now form a part of South Asian daily life. We do not know, for example, the origin of the Harappan city builders, whose layout of streets and water use reveal a clear understanding of urban planning. We have no earlier instances of city dwelling to learn how or where these skills were developed. The practice of spiritual discipline called *yoga* is also of unknown origin, as is the Dravidian culture of south India. Both are old enough to have developed within the Harappan city culture, and attempts have been made to establish demonstrable links between them. But they could have arisen out of totally separate interactions that have been lost, and of which they are the only trace.

Adding to the difficulty in understanding the impact of this interactivity is the persistence of so many different indigenous cultural threads, which have continued to evolve into such a variety of patterns. So much has been added—yet nothing ever appears to be thrown away. Large slabs and rolling stones, termed *saddle-querns,* were used more than 6,000 years ago by the earliest agrarians known to live on the subcontinent to grind grain into flour. Even though that grinding is now done in mills, saddle-querns are still used in village kitchens to pulverize condiments to season food. Many old traditions, sometimes intertwined in a variety of ways with other traditions, or appearing in new garb, are still recognizable as significant elements in the heritage of this distinct region of the world. In the Western world of planned obsolescence, such tenacity is hard to imagine. Geeta Mehta, in *Snakes and Ladders,* describes this contrast in a slightly different way: Whereas Westerners have a great struggle to recover their past, the problem for Indians is to discover their present.

The Aryan Migration
In contrast to the more elusive impact of maritime commerce, migrations of peoples from other parts of the world are a clear source of new life and perspective in South Asia. They have come for the most part overland, across the Central Asian trade routes between China and the Middle East, down into the northwestern approach to the north-central plains region of the subcontinent.

Of the many migrations over the centuries, the two of greatest impact were the Aryan settlement, beginning around 1500 B.C., and the Moghul invasion, which began in the sixteenth century A.D. The Aryans—tribal, martial, and pastoral in background—brought with them into the subcontinent an Indo-European language. This later evolved into Sanskrit, the classical language of ancient India, and the many contemporary languages that are spoken throughout the northern portion of the subcontinent and on Sri Lanka and Maldives. They also brought collections of religious songs, which formed the basis of a tenth century B.C. anthology of

1,028 poems called the *Rg Veda,* the oldest-surviving religious literature in the world. The *Veda* is still considered *sruti*—that is, inspired; literally, "heard by ancient seers"—the most sacred of all Hindu religious texts. And the Aryans either brought or soon developed a mythic understanding of the world as a sacred reality: that everything is part of a universal, cosmic sacrifice. This perspective blossomed as Vedic culture during the time of their settlement in the subcontinent.

During the era of the Aryan settlement, Brahmin priests were responsible for developing, celebrating, and interpreting Vedic sacrifices as expressive of the total sanctity of all being. They asserted a dominant role in restructuring Aryan society around their religious activity. One of the later Vedic hymns

(United Nations/MB/jr)

Hinduism has evolved over the millennia in many different ways, and today it is intricately woven into the social fabric. Shaivism is one of the two main sects of Hinduism tracing its roots back to the ancient Harappan cities in the Indus River Valley. Pictured above is the gateway of a Siva temple in Tanjore, in the state of Tamil Nadu. The huge *gopuram,* or ornamental tower, is characteristic of south Indian temple architecture.

sets forward the earliest celebration of the *varna,* or classical, model of the caste system:

> When they divided the Man [in the primordial sacrifice], into how many parts did they apportion him? What do they call his mouth, his two arms and thighs and feet?
>
> His mouth became the Brahmin; his arms were made into the Warrior, his thighs the People, and from his feet the Servants were born.
>
> —*Rg Veda* 10.90,11–12
> (O'Flaherty translation)

This hierarchical structuring of society divided people into those four groups (Brahmins, Warriors, People, and Servants). Significantly, it placed the *Brahmins,* the priests, at the top. Next in order of preference on the scale were *Kshatriya,* warriors, or rulers by might; then the *Vaisya,* citizens, with landholding or commercial status; and *Sudra,* laborers or craftspeople. Grouping of people on this scale was done primarily on the basis of an extended family's, community's, or tribe's inherited occupation. The ranking was based on a combination of the ritually purifying–polluting status in a sacrifice of a group's traditional occupation, as determined by the priesthood, and the ability of that social group to maintain social order. Maintaining social order was everyone's responsibility, but the priests held a specific and elevating prerogative because they had unique recourse to sacred power, which emanated from their performance of sacrificial rites. This scale clearly envisioned a Brahmin-dominated society.

Subsequent periods in South Asian history and literature do not show general acceptance of this dominant role for the priesthood. In the period from 500 B.C. to A.D. 200, the Sanskrit epics (the *Mahabharata* and the *Ramayana*) and early Buddhist literature gave more prominence to the warrior, or princely community, to which the heroes of the epics and the Buddha belonged. Social and world orders were not based on the rite of sacrifice, nor were they maintained by the Brahmin priests. They were based, rather, upon princes' strict adherence to their chivalrous obligations, called *dharma.* Rama, the hero of the *Ramayana,* is portrayed as a prince who is severely righteous in order to assure the peace and well-being of the people over whom he is called to govern. In that same tradition, Siddharta Gautama, who was to become the *Buddha*— the "Enlightened One"—taught to his religious community an eight-fold path of righteousness, which he called *Dhamma,* the "Way," to lead them to realize their Buddha nature and, ultimately, attain the transcendent state of *nirvana.*

The high point of Buddhist expansion came upon the conversion of the Mauryan emperor Asoka to the Buddha's Way in the third century B.C. In the eighth year of his reign, Asoka was deeply moved by the devastation caused by his military defeat of a neighboring kingdom. He then determined to add any further conquests to his realm by moral force rather than by military might. His new policy, which he proclaimed on a series of pillars erected throughout his kingdom, was to shun aggression and to seek "safety, self control, justice and happiness for all beings." He thus gave a wide legitimacy across the span of his empire in the northern plains region to the Buddhist Dhamma, upon which his policy was based. Also during his reign, Asoka sent his son, Mahinda, to bring the teachings of the Buddha to Sri Lanka. Mahinda's arrival in 246 B.C. marked the beginning of the Theravada Buddhist tradition on that island.

Brahmin religious authority continued to spread and to be recognized through the northern plains and peninsular regions of South Asia. But its full cultural impact was not realized until the beginning of the Gupta imperial dynasty, in the fourth century A.D. Sanskrit, the sacred language of the priesthood, had by then become accepted as appropriate for the royal court, and for all of the intellectual and artistic endeavors that the court supported. Also by that time, the influence of other religious communities (such as Jainism and Buddhism), and especially a great surge of popular religious lore, long practiced but unrecognized in courtly circles, infused courtly life with new perspectives and theistic fervor. The austere righteousness and the intricate, sacrificial purity of the earlier eras were augmented by a sense of divine playfulness spun out in recitations of exemplary cosmic exploits of unnumbered gods and goddesses, heroes and heroines from a mythic past. The Gupta era, from A.D. 300 to 650, was a time of great creative activity, drawing upon and affirming enhanced Sanskritized models devised by the Brahmin priesthood. The poetic works of Kalidasa, the philosophical writings of Shankara, and the artistic creations found at Ajanta, Ellora, and Elephanta all portray the imaginative insight, excitement, and refinement achieved in that eclectic, yet highly disciplined and politically stable, era.

In the centuries following the Gupta era, the Brahmin community gained economic dominance in addition to its intellectual and religious authority, which had increased during that classical period. In reward for their courtly and religious services, they received land grants—even entire villages—as gifts from Hindu monarchs. Their increasing prominence in all of these aspects of courtly life established a pattern for social change in those regions of the subcontinent where Hindus predominated. Today, to achieve higher status in the hierarchical caste structure, other communities emulate the patterns of behavior practiced by high-caste Brahmins. This process is called *Sanskritization,* a label that indicates how the pastoral religious traditions of the ancient Aryan cow herders in the central portion of the subcontinent have developed and gained authority over the many centuries since the Vedic age.

The Moghul Migration

The second migration to have a significant impact on the peoples of South Asia is more recent and reveals a different pattern of acceptance. This migration was of militant Turks from Persia, the Moghuls, who were forced to move into

(United Nations/WT/jr)

The greatest period of Muslim influence in South Asia began in the sixteenth century, when the Moghuls dominated the northern plains. The age was a period of grandeur and elegance; the Taj Mahal in Agra is one of the most famous monuments of this period.

South Asia by the Mongols' triumphant marches across Central Asia. Babur was the first, when he established a tenuous foothold by the capture of the city of Kabul, in what is now Afghanistan, in 1504. Competition for control of the north-central plains was fierce; and not until the reign of his grandson, Akbar (1556–1605), did Moghul rule begin to establish firm imperial control in that commanding region of the subcontinent. During Akbar's reign, he imposed an extremely effective administrative network to maintain his authority over the realms he conquered. He also maintained a luxurious court, which supported an extensive creativity in art, music, architecture, and literature. Akbar's rule was a magnificent time, driven by his desire to synthesize the best of the wealth of traditions—Persian, Indian, and even European—that he welcomed into his domain.

The fruits of Akbar's attempts to achieve cultural synthesis remain in the arts. The greatest is architectural: the Taj Mahal, the exquisitely beautiful mausoleum built in Agra by Akbar's grandson, Shah Jahan, in memory of his beloved wife, Mumtaz Mahal, who died in 1631. Miniature painting and Hindustani music continue to reveal the integration of art forms that were introduced under Akbar's imperial patronage. And remnants of his administrative structure, which was adopted by the British colonial government, also continue.

Moghul domination in the political realm and its inherent patronage did not, however, lead to mass conversions to Islam. Nor did they lead to the synthesis of their religious faith within a common South Asian culture. It did not even achieve a lasting accommodation among the different religious communities in the subcontinent. During the centuries of their political control, religious leaders like Kabir entertained

visions of religious unity. But distinct religious communities have retained their separate identities up to the present day.

The Moghuls were not the first Muslims to enter South Asia. Arab traders plying the coastal ports had introduced the new Islamic faith as early as the eighth century. They were followed by itinerant Sufi teachers, who settled in villages throughout the subcontinent. Their commitment to a religious life drew respect and veneration from a number of indigenous peoples receptive to spiritual insight and leadership. The more mystical quality of the faith of these masters converted large numbers of people to Islam, mostly in the northwest corner of the region, the Punjab, and the northeast, Bengal—areas in which Buddhists had previously been the most numerous. Further conversions took place during the militant rule of the sultans, who dominated portions of the Gangetic Plain for three centuries prior to the arrival of the Moghuls. The mosque, the daily calls to prayer, Muslim festivals, and Islamic law became an authentic part of the social fabric of South Asian life. They were accepted, even though Muslims were a small religious minority in most regions of the subcontinent.

The imperial stature, administrative acumen, and grandeur of Moghul rule did give immense institutional status to Islam as a distinct religious faith and political legitimacy to a significant, already extensive Muslim community. Even today, Pakistan's aspiration to identify itself as a modern Islamic republic builds upon the heritage of that Moghul imperial presence. But an immense issue remained during the time of the Moghul emperors: What was to be the status of the much larger Hindu population who resided in the central and southern portions of their empire?

Akbar tried to synthesize his refined, imperial Islamic faith within a common South Asian culture. His hope was that all his subjects might share in a single, universalist religion. But because of the diversity that existed even *within* these faiths, he was not successful. Their separate religious identities were emphasized during the nineteenth century, under British colonial rule. And they became the basis for the creation of Pakistan and, later, Bangladesh as independent countries, separate from India, with the departure of the British Raj in 1947. Religious identity has been at the heart of warfare between Pakistan and India since their independence. It is the source for communal riots throughout the subcontinent to this day. Muslims and Hindus remain two distinct, culturally diverse religious communities.

The Aryan and Moghul migrations reveal two very different experiences of incorporating foreign peoples into the social fabric of the subcontinent. But they also identify a single pattern of cultural integration. The early Aryan culture, through continuing interaction and adaptation over a long period of time, came to dominate the social realm—not by political force but, rather, by intellectual and religious authority, which set the norms that define the culture. One of those norms is to maintain the integrity of differing linguistic, religious, and ethnic groups who live in the subcontinent by isolating them as discrete cultural units within an abstract, hierarchical framework. The Moghul migration shows that even extensive political domination, both military and administrative, is not sufficient to create or coerce cultural assimilation in a social environment that accepts cultural pluralism as normal.

Both of these migrations contributed significantly to the development of South Asian civilization. They also demonstrate that the social diversity of language, religion, ethnic community, and social status is very deeply rooted in South Asia.

The British Raj

Another, more recent interaction of significant impact on the evolution of the distinct culture of South Asia was the arrival of the British Empire. It was not a migration; and, unlike the Moghul experience, it had little impact on the creative arts of the subcontinent. The so-called British Raj was primarily political, imposing colonial rule over the subcontinent from the mid-1800s until the 1940s. Its impact lies largely in the introduction of democracy, industrial development, and technology.

British presence on the subcontinent began in the early 1600s, when the East India Company, with head offices in London, England, started to establish trading centers, first in Indonesia, and then along the Indian coast. In this activity, the British entrepreneurs were following a pattern of maritime commerce in the region that goes back to the Harappan cities of the third millennium B.C., during the earliest days of South Asian civilization.

This British commercial interest, which became dominant in South Asia during the eighteenth century, had no intention of establishing any political authority in the subcontinent. The British were there primarily for economic advantage, and they spent much of their time and effort with local authorities, trying to curry favor and exclusive licenses for trade. But as they became more entangled with these authorities, especially as they struggled to diminish competing European interests in the region, they began to bring the peoples of the subcontinent increasingly under their own political control.

In the early 1800s, their greater political involvement stimulated a concern to bring social reform to the subcontinent as well. The character of their reform was most strikingly expressed in a famous "Minute on Education," written by an East India Company Supreme Council member, Thomas Macauly, in 1835. Macauly urged that the British administrators create a special class of South Asian people who would be "Indian in blood and color, but English in taste, in opinions, in morals, and in intellect." These clerks of the company would be groomed to bring the new ideas of individualism, technology, democracy, and nationalism, which were then evolving in Europe and America, to usher South Asia into the modern world.

This energizing—but ethnocentric—reform movement received a resounding jolt in British India in 1857, when an isolated British Indian Army unit rebelled because 85 soldiers were jailed for refusing to use ammunition greased with animal fat. Initially, it was a minor incident. But among other things, it revealed a British insensitivity to Hindu religious attitudes toward the use of beef fat (for Hindus, the cow is sacred) and Muslim religious attitudes toward pork (that it is polluting). This minor rebellion thus became the stimulus for a popular uprising throughout the north-central region of the subcontinent. People took it as an opportunity to express a shared and growing sense of dissatisfaction with the British domination of their land. It grew into the "Great Mutiny" of 1857.

The spontaneity of this revolt contributed to its lack of organization and direction, and it was soon subdued by British military might. But its widespread appeal revealed that for all of the enthusiasm and goodwill that the British rulers felt toward their South Asian subjects, their intentions—which appeared appropriate in a Western context—were not going to be readily accepted. The cultural context of South Asia was too substantial, too complex, and too different to be easily reformed.

The reform movement of the early nineteenth century gave way to a more blatant colonial domination of the subcontinent during the second half of the century. In 1858, the British Crown assumed direct control of British India. Queen Victoria became the first to bear the title "Empress of India."

The impact of the British Raj is still evident in the setting of the dividing lines that established the boundaries between the nations in the northern part of the subcontinent. It set the northern borders of Bhutan and Nepal with Tibet, by a line drawn along the peaks of the Himalayan Mountains—the

McMahon Line. British authorities also secured the other borders of these two countries, which had been determined before British rule by Gurkha and Tibetan conquests. In affirming these boundaries, the Raj used existing natural and political realities to assert its own political authority within them.

In contrast, the setting of the borders of Afghanistan do not appear to have recognized any indigenous factors. They were established by treaty between Czarist Russia and Great Britain in 1907 in response to competing colonial interests. The British objective was to contain any Russian aspirations to gain access to the Arabian Sea.

The border determination of greatest impact was the decision by the Raj in 1947 not only to grant independence to a large portion of British India as a new republic, but also to establish a separate Islamic country, called *Pakistan* ("Land of the Pure"). At that time, those administrative districts under direct British control that had a majority Muslim population were assigned to Pakistan, and those with a Hindu majority to India. The accession of the princely states that were not under direct British control—about 40 percent of the subcontinent—into either India or Pakistan, was to be based on the preference of the ruling *maharajas* of these states.

There were two major exceptions to this process of accession. The princely state of Hyderabad, in the Deccan, which had a Muslim leader and a Hindu majority population, was absorbed into India when Indian troops rushed into the state to quell riots that came in the wake of the partition of India and Pakistan in 1947. The princely state of Kashmir, on the other hand, with a majority Muslim population and a Hindu maharaja, was nominally acceded to India by the maharaja when Pakistani forces began to enter Kashmir at that time.

The result of this process of border determination was a Pakistan divided into two sections, East and West, on the shoulders of the subcontinent, separated by 1,000 miles of India; and a Kashmir still divided between the unresolved claims of both India and Pakistan and a United Nations (UN) resolution to encourage the people of Kashmir to have a choice.

Even with the setback experienced in the Great Mutiny of 1857, Western political ideas of democracy, social reform, and freedom of expression continued to spread through the subcontinent. The Indian National Congress was formed in 1887 to seek opportunities for South Asians to shape and to participate in a growing body politic. In 1919, Mohandas Gandhi emerged as the leader of this movement. Through the power of his example and his great organizational skills, he was able to build grassroots support for the Congress throughout British India. Enlivened by a spirit of democracy and of political freedom, this movement first paralleled, and then superseded, British colonial rule.

The British imperial presence also brought to South Asia the concept of a modern nation. An independent, democratically elected government was the goal—certainly for those who were under foreign colonial domination; but also for those who had been under traditional, autocratic rule of hereditary maharajas, tribal leaders, and vestigial imperial domains. Upon achieving independence, South Asian peoples awakened from a long era of unrepresentative leadership. Forceful ideas were beginning to take on relevance: of liberty achieved through democracy, prosperity through economic growth, and individual human rights sustained by law. These have become the standards by which the success of a nation's quest for modernization are being measured. Such is the case because the British colonial government set these standards as its expectation of the countries to which it granted independence in the middle of the twentieth century—to India and Pakistan in 1947, and Sri Lanka in 1948. The other, smaller nations—Afghanistan, Bhutan, Maldives, Nepal—which trace the origin of their governments to more autocratic traditions of long standing in the subcontinent, are challenged to hold these same standards to their performance for recognition as modern states. They are all seeking new opportunities for expression, for economic growth, and for taking control of their destiny as politically free peoples among the nations of the world.

The British colonial interaction with the subcontinent is now over. Yet it continues, like the Aryan and Moghul experiences, to have a discernible impact in the region. Significant changes are occurring in the political and economic life because of the British Raj, just as the artistic and Islamic influences of the Moghul era are also evident in contemporary South Asia. And the religious and intellectual heritage shaped by the evolution of Aryan culture continues to be profoundly present.

All of these threads—Aryan, Moghul, and British Raj—contribute to a unique culture. They are intricately interwoven among themselves, and with the many other influences both indigenous and brought by centuries of maritime commerce, to form the tapestry of the long, rich, and varied heritage of the peoples who belong to South Asia.

IMAGE 2: A DIVERSE SOCIAL ENVIRONMENT

It is the endurance of this civilization, despite its encounter with a host of other cultures and other political influences, that has led many observers to conclude that the Hindu style is absorptive, synthesizing, or tolerant. What they see is something quite different, namely, Indian civilization's ability to encapsulate other cultures and make it possible for many levels of civilization to live side by side. But encapsulation is neither toleration, absorption, nor synthesis.

—Ainslie T. Embree

The sheer multitude of the 1.3 billion people who live in South Asia is impressive. They already represent more than a fifth of the total population of the world—and they are growing in numbers at an alarming pace. According to projections prepared by the World Bank, at the current rate of growth, the population of the subcontinent will exceed 1.8 billion by the year 2025. Each of the countries of the subcontinent has developed policies to try to limit this rate, with varying degrees of success. The most effective effort has been in Sri Lanka. Analysts relate this achievement to the high level of literacy that the country has attained. Education, especially of women, appears to be the key to limiting the rate of population growth.

South Asia is not only crowded, but it is also a land of immense human contrasts. There are many different social groups from different parts of the subcontinent, each displaying a distinctive variety of belief and custom, language and culture. Sikhs and Buddhists and Jains; fishermen and pit weavers along the tropical shores of the coast lands; elegant, urban aristocrats and naked religious mendicants; tribal peoples and computer engineers; beggars, film stars, and Kathakali dancers; and many more—all are interwoven into the multistranded fabric of South Asian life. It is a rich panoply of activities and conditions of humanity.

The distinctiveness of most of these social groups, especially the caste communities called jatis, must be delineated by very small strokes to retain their diversity. To the unfamiliar eye, many may look the same. Their distinguishing characteristics can be more readily identified in broader sweeps that identify people in regional, religious, and linguistic categories. Each group retains discernible characteristics of the part of the subcontinent in which its members live, of the religious faith to which they belong, and the language that they speak.

Regional differences among South Asians are the most obvious. Those belonging to a common religious faith tend to concentrate in specific regions of the subcontinent. The same is true of those speaking the same language. But there are so many more languages than religions, and people of the same language group do not always share the same religion.

Differences of region, religion, and language are also important because they are the most general groupings into which the peoples of South Asia have long been separated into social enclaves. To belong to a religious community in a separate language area in a particular region of the subcontinent clearly sets one apart from others and establishes one's distinctive sense of identity as a person. As traditional sources of identity, firmly rooted in their heritage, they remain persistent and vital descriptors of who the people of South Asia are.

MANY RELIGIONS

South Asia is home to several of the world's major religions, some of which originated there. Hinduism and Islam—one indigenous, the other imported—are by far the largest, followed, respectively, by approximately two thirds and one fifth of the people of the region. Hinduism is the dominant religion in Nepal (90 percent of the population) and India (80 per-

cent). Islam is dominant in Maldives (100 percent), Pakistan (95 percent), Afghanistan (99 percent) and Bangladesh (83 percent). Buddhism, which began with the enlightenment of Siddharta Gautama in the lower Gangetic Plains of India, while not so large—constituting 1.8 percent of the total population of the subcontinent—is the predominant religion in Sri Lanka and Bhutan.

Jains are another, smaller, religious community that originated in the subcontinent. Jains, like the Buddhists, trace their faith to a religious leader who lived in northern India in the sixth century B.C. There are also Sikhs, whose religion was founded by Guru Nanak during the sixteenth century A.D., in the northwestern part of South Asia known as the Punjab. Other religious communities include Christians, Jews, and the Parsis, whose Zoroastrian faith had its origin in ancient Persia at the time of the Vedas, more than 3,500 years ago.

All of these faiths evolved in the South Asian context as distinct, structurally integrated expressions of different communities' religious experiences. Although aware of and interacting with peoples of other religious faiths, they have retained an essential sacred identity in their lives as a distinct community. Even when influencing one another, these many religious communities in South Asia continually reaffirm the structural integrity of their own faith as separate from the faiths of others. This recognition of the religious integrity of other groups became the basis of the wide and rapid spread of the influence of Islamic mystics, called Sufis, during the early years of Islamic influence in the subcontinent. Where Sufi teaching and practice were consistent with the values and experience of the religious communities already there, they were readily venerated and even co-opted. People of many different faiths participated in worship at shrines honoring Sufi saints. The Islamic faith of the sultans and the Moghuls who followed the Sufis into South Asia was recognized, but not so readily accepted.

This persistence of the structural integrity of many different religious communities' sacred identity also accounts for the immense variety of Hinduism. *Hinduism* is really a composite term that includes a multitude of quite diverse religious groups. Hindus do share some common teachings and perspectives. They all, for example, affirm the transmigration of the soul after death to some other form of life. This belief they share with Buddhists and Jains, which is why many Hindus consider Buddhists and Jains to be within the inclusive umbrella of Hinduism. These many different communities practice their separate religious traditions in an immense variety of forms, each the result of an evolution over a distinct path during many centuries.

The earliest record of the Hindu religious tradition is the *Rg Veda,* the set of 1,028 poems that were collected into their current form around the tenth century B.C. The poems themselves were composed earlier, and presuppose an even earlier history of religious belief and practice. Traditionally the sacred preserve of the Brahmin priesthood, the *Veda* is not widely known or understood among Hindus today. And the Vedic sacrifices around which the collection of sacred poems was initially created and remembered—and upon which the religious authority of the Brahmin priesthood was initially established—are rarely performed. More characteristic of Hindu life today are the rituals, traditions, and festivals celebrated at the innumerable temples and shrines that dot the countryside, daily worship (*puja*), and the sanctity of an epic fragment called *Bhagavad Gita* ("The Song of the Lord"). All of these have been added to the religious traditions of the Hindus since the Vedic period (1500–500 B.C.).

These accretions to Vedic religion reveal that Hinduism has changed over the centuries. Yet as we have seen, Hinduism evolved not as a single religious tradition but in many different ways. It incorporated and encompassed many diverse strands to become the intricate interweaving of schools and sects and disciplines that are encompassed by that religion today. Among these sects are the Vaishnavites, who worship God as first revealed in the *Rg Veda* as Vishnu. But they recognize His manifestation in a number of *avatars* (incarnations) drawn from other and later traditions. These incarnations include Krishna, the Buddha, and *Kalki* (the "One Who Is to Come"). Shaivites belong to a separate sect that traces the origin of its faith even further back, to representations of Shiva as *Pasupati* (the "Lord of Animals"), found in the artifacts of the Harappan civilization, and as *Nataraj* (the "Lord of the Cosmic Dance").

In addition, Hinduism includes worshipers of Krishna and Ram and of the Goddess in a variety of manifestations: in the Great Tradition as Kali, Durga, or Devi; but also among innumerable regional and local deities who benefit specific villages or protect against certain diseases. Their virtues and powers are enthusiastically celebrated throughout the country in an annual cycle of religious festivals unique to every village. And there is yoga, a spiritual discipline that does not affirm the existence of any deity. Any description of Hinduism must attempt to contain all this array of different forms and practices, each with its own history, tradition, and authority, for a vast number of religious communities who consider themselves Hindu.

Buddhism also originated in South Asia and has evolved as a separate religion since the sixth century B.C. Siddhartha Gautama, the founder of the faith, was born a prince in a remote north Indian kingdom not under the sway of a Brahmin priesthood. He renounced his royal inheritance to seek an ultimate meaning for his life. After many years of diligent search, he received the enlightenment of the "Four-fold Truth." His teaching to his disciples about the pervasive presence of misery (*dukha*), of its cause and its removal, was the basis on which this religion developed and expanded throughout the subcontinent.

Buddhism was originally the faith of a monastic community, the *sangha*. It was composed of those who, attracted by the Buddha's example and teaching, abandoned their worldly activities to commit themselves to following his path, or *Dhamma,* in communal and meditative isolation. The conversion of the Mauryon emperor Asoka to the Buddha's teaching in the third century B.C. brought about a significant change in the Buddhist tradition. His political authority gave greater currency to the Buddha's Dhamma throughout the society. He also endowed the community with royal patronage, which encouraged not only its growth but also spawned a creative outburst of Buddhist art, literature, and philosophy. Tributes to this heritage have survived in the exuberant carvings and frescoes in the caves at Ajanta, and in the majestic tranquillity of the sculpture of the Buddha teaching at Sarnath. It was this highly expressive and energetic Buddhism that, during the centuries following Asoka, burst forth into the far reaches of Asia—to Sri Lanka, to Southeast Asia, and to China, Japan, Mongolia, and Tibet.

As in the case of Islam under Moghul rule, Buddhism, though indigenous, remained among a dominant Hindu society an encapsulated religious community, even when favored by imperial patronage for several centuries after Asoka. During that time it did manage to introduce vegetarianism as a social virtue to be observed by Brahmins among the Hindus. Unlike Hinduism, it declined dramatically in the north-central region of the subcontinent toward the end of the first millennium, as many were drawn to the teachings of Sufi mystics. Beginning in the eleventh century A.D. , that region was subjected to the military attacks and religious zeal of Islamic potentates from Central Asia. Buddhism survives today in enclaves along the borders of South Asia: in Ladakh, the section of Kashmir closest to China; in Bhutan, along the Himalayan border, next to Tibet; and in Sri Lanka, off the southeastern coast of peninsular India. It has recently been revived in India as a separate religious faith by the Mahar community in Maharastra, under the leadership of Dr. Ambedkar, who converted to Buddhism in 1956 to protest the Hindu attitude of abhorrence and discrimination toward communities designated by Hindus as "untouchable."

Islam is another significant religious community in South Asia. This faith was brought initially by Arab traders plying the coastal shores of peninsular India, soon after the *hegira,* or the flight of Mohammed from Mecca in A.D. 622. It was then spread throughout the subcontinent by itinerant Sufi mystics. Muslims finally became established as a distinct religious community under the political ascendance of the sultans who began to rule portions of the northern plains during the eleventh century. The predominance of Muslims in the western and eastern ends of the north-central plains region led to the creation of the separate—western and eastern—arms of the original nation of Pakistan in 1947. Although several million Muslims migrated from India to Pakistan at the time of independence in 1947, some 120 million still reside in India today, forming a significant religious minority (12 percent). The population of all Muslims in the subcontinent—more than 345 million—is the

(United Nations/WT/ARA)

In South Asia, individuals often identify with societies and religions rather than with a specific country. Modern national boundaries imposed over historically diverse language and religious populations result in weak political identification. This pluralism complicates the establishment of a workable political base as minorities strive to find a legitimate place and voice in national life. This religious allegiance is exemplified by this Sikh teacher addressing some of his followers at the Golden Temple in Amritsar, India. What he tells people is likely to be more relevant to social and political change than what any politician may say.

second-largest Muslim population in the world, smaller only than in Southeast Asia.

Christianity in South Asia also reveals the persistence of the various strands of traditions that developed independently, interacting with but not being assimilated into other strands. According to legend, it was first introduced in the subcontinent by the Apostle Thomas during the first century A.D. It was certainly known to silk traders from Egypt passing through northwest Pakistan to China during the second century. Evidence of Syrian Christians having migrated and living along the southwest coast of the subcontinent dates from the fourth century. Christians continued as a small, separate religious community for many centuries, and they did not increase significantly in number until the arrival of Western colonial powers.

The Portuguese first brought Roman Catholicism to the western coast of India during the 1400s. Under the restraining eye of the English East India Company, Protestant missions began to work in the subcontinent only in 1813. Today, all of these Christian faiths comprise less than 3 percent of the total population of South Asia. They have become significant as a force in the political life of the subcontinent only in the state of Kerala, in southwest India, where they form nearly one third of the population.

The many different religious-minority communities have tended to concentrate in specific regions, where they have become significant political forces. Religious persecution against them in a variety of forms is evident throughout the subcontinent: of the Ahmadiyas in Pakistan; Hindus in Sri Lanka and Bhutan; and, of growing concern, of Christians in northern India, where the Hindu nationalist zeal of the conservative wing of the ruling Bharatiya Janata Party (BJP) has become more assertive. But different religious communities are evident and have been generally accepted where their presence has not become a political issue everywhere throughout the subcontinent.

MANY LANGUAGES

British visitors to the growing commercial city of Calcutta during the late 1700s would immediately be struck by the immense diversity of languages encountered there. The language of the Calcutta marketplace was Portuguese, a vestige of the early domination of East Indian trade by Portugal. The language of government was Persian, a vestige of the Moghul imperial past. By contrast, the languages of the courts were Sanskrit and Arabic (depending upon which tradition of law those who were pursuing legal redress belonged). Though each had a specific context in which it was considered appropriate, none of these languages belonged to that area. None was the common tongue, or vernacular, of the people who lived in Calcutta.

Had the visitors wandered into the streets or into homes, they would have discovered another variety of languages. Different tongues spoken by the common people reflected the diverse places of origin of those who moved to Calcutta to take part in the growing activity and prosperity there. The majority of these people came from the immediately surrounding area, so the most prevalent vernacular was Bengali.

Today, English has replaced the many languages used in the more formal aspects of contemporary urban life, and Bengali remains the most prevalent language of the people. But many other languages are spoken in the streets and homes of the city.

Hundreds of vernaculars are spoken throughout South Asia today. In India alone, 35 different languages are spoken by more than a million people each. These languages belong to four distinct language families, broadly distributed across specific regions of the subcontinent. The major dialects in the northernmost, Himalayan region are Tibeto-Burmese, related to the languages across the northern and eastern borders of the subcontinent. Their presence reveals that those living in the remote valleys of that region had more extensive cultural interaction with people in the rugged and forbidding mountains and jungles along those borders than with people in the more settled plains areas to the south.

The prevalent languages of the northern plains region, Sri Lanka, and Maldives belong to the Indo-European family of languages. They are distant cousins of Latin, Greek, and the Germanic tongues of the West. They were introduced in their earliest form by Aryans—migrating cattle herders from Central Asia who wandered into the subcontinent almost 3,500 years ago. A second, totally separate family of languages is spoken among the tribal peoples who still inhabit the remote hill regions of peninsular India. These are generally called Munda languages, which are related to those spoken by the Aboriginal peoples of Australia, far to the southeast. The Indo-European and tribal families of languages reveal far-reaching interconnections that existed thousands of years ago among peoples who are now widely separated.

Dravidian is yet another language family. Its roots can be traced only to the South Asian subcontinent. Today, the Dravidian languages are spoken mostly in the south of India and the northern part of Sri Lanka. But they are not confined to the subcontinent. They have been carried to East Africa, Singapore, the Fiji Islands, and the West Indies by immigrants who continue to affirm their South Asian heritage in these many parts of the world.

Each of the numerous languages that belong to these four language families has a specific area in the subcontinent in which it is spoken by the vast majority of the people. It is easy to see where these languages predominate in India and Pakistan, because state borders within these countries have been drawn to enclose specific dominant-language groups. Afghanistan and Sri Lanka are also divided into language-area sections.

The integrity of these languages is retained even beyond the region where they are predominant. They extend as minority linguistic pockets in other language areas. Thus, a variety of languages may be found anywhere, especially in cities, where migrants from many parts of the country tend to gather in

(United Nations/JL, 80478)

Because of changing circumstances, the Hindu majority of India are continually adjusting themselves to maintain the allegiance and participation of their members. These children are saying their Hindu prayers before the midday meal at their school.

sections of the city with others who share their native language.

Some of these languages have developed literary and classical forms of expression, but all are most widely familiar as colloquial dialects, which, like accents, reflect common usage among specific groups of people in particular places. Colloquial dialects would seem to be the form of language most subject to assimilation with other languages that are spoken around it. Because of the diverse social context in which they are spoken, these languages do interact and influence one another. But this interaction has not led to their becoming assimilated into a common tongue. That each continues distinct in its integrity as a separate language is a primary example of encapsulation as a way of describing the social dynamics of the peoples of South Asia.

The language that one learns first in childhood, of whichever of the families of languages to which it belongs, is called one's mother tongue. This way of describing one's native language reveals that, for the peoples of South Asia, one is born into a language community that is intrinsic to one's identity as a person, even when residing in countries far away from the subcontinent. The same is true for one's caste community and religion. One is born into them, and they remain inherently descriptive of who one is.

A map that delineates the predominant language areas throughout the entire subcontinent, like a map of the religious communities described earlier, looks like an intricate patchwork quilt. The pattern of the language quilt, however, is not the same as for religions. Generally speaking, people belonging to different religions in the same place speak the same language, but those belonging to the same religion speak many different languages. Only in the smaller countries of the subcontinent—Bhutan, Maldives, and Sri Lanka—do religious identities and language identities tend to correspond with each other. And only in Maldives, the smallest of the countries of the subcontinent, do these categories coincide with the national boundaries; only there does being a citizen of the country generally mean that one speaks the same language and worships in a common faith.

RELIGIOUS NATIONALISM

Differences in religious and language identities continue to play an important role in South Asian life. Because of their persistence as defining distinct social groups, they are easily invoked in conflicts that result from so many densely populated groups striving for limited resources. Social unrest, communal disputes, and outright rioting occur frequently. Even when disputes originate between individuals, they rapidly become characterized by the religious or linguistic identity of the participants.

The Sikh nationalist movement in the Punjab during the 1980s—even though it was pursued by an unrepresentative splinter group led by the headmaster of a rural Sikh school, a young religious zealot named Bhindranwale—was a war that engaged large segments of the Sikh community. Newspapers reported almost daily of what appeared as random, indiscriminate strafing of buses along the highways and shootings into wedding parties by snipers on passing motor scooters. These acts of violence were sanctioned by the Damdami Taksal militants and the All India Sikh Students Federation because they had Hindus—as well as Sikhs unsympathetic to their cause—as their targets. Bhindranwale's death in 1984 at the hand of Indian Army troops in the Golden Temple, the sacred center of Sikhism in Amritsar, led to the assassination of Indira Gandhi, then prime minister of India, by Sikh members of her bodyguard. Her death was followed by massive riots in the streets of Delhi and the murder of many Sikhs throughout the country. It was a "holy war."

In neighboring Kashmir, the quest for independence is also expressed in religious terms. It is a battle for the freedom of a predominantly Muslim population from what is experienced as an oppressive Hindu India. Heavily armed bands of militants ambush, burn, and kidnap throughout the mountain valleys and in the once placid Vale, all in the name of their religion. Thousands of Hindu families have fled their homes in fear of this violence.

The issue of whether India is, in fact, a Hindu or a secular nation was put to the test in 1992 in the northern city of Ayodhya. An old mosque, built there at the time of the first Moghul emperor, Babur, in the sixteenth century A.D., was identified by a Hindu-nationalist political party as the site of an earlier Hindu temple claimed to be the birthplace of Lord Rama. Destruction of the Babari Masjid mosque by a band of Hindu pilgrims on December 6, 1992, led to widespread communal rioting across India and retaliatory destruction of Hindu temples in Pakistan, Bangladesh, and even in Britain.

This event made it evident that the religious identity of the peoples of South Asia is a decisive, immediate, and intense component in the political life of the subcontinent. Religious nationalism, especially in India, with its large Hindu majority, severely challenges the quest for a unifying political identity to include all its people, who belong to many different religions. Yet the results of national elections reveal that although Hindu-nationalist sentiment is a formidable force, it does not command a majority. The ideal of a secular national identity, inclusive of all its religious minorities, is still a viable objective. By contrast, Bhutan and Pakistan are deliberately seeking to affirm modern religious national identities—Bhutan as a Buddhist nation, and Pakistan as an Islamic one.

Sri Lanka represents a different configuration. There, linguistic identity reinforces the separation between the regions of the country where different religions are predominant. Most Sri Lankans are Buddhists who speak the Sinhalese language. In the northeast region of the country, however, most of the people are Hindu, with significant Muslim enclaves, and are Tamil-speakers. The regional basis of this separation has allowed these communities to coexist for centuries.

(United Nations/A. Hollmann)

Educating children is something that cannot be delayed if a cohesive social structure and heritage are to be saved. These refugee children are striving for an education in a makeshift school in a land that is not their own.

But the quest to achieve a single national identity since the independence of the country in 1948 has resulted in intense warfare between nationalist groups. Because of the importance of their language differences, these militant groups see the conflict more as cultural—as tigers against lions—rather than as religious.

LINGUISTIC NATIONALISM

Political identity based on language plays a much more important role than religion in Pakistan, which has been intentionally Islamic since its independence. The common Muslim faith of the peoples of East and West Pakistan did not override the ethnic and linguistic differences between the Bengali-speaking peoples of the east and the Punjabi-dominated western wing of the country in the years leading up to the independence of Bangladesh as a separate country in 1971.

Even today, language identity is a vital factor in the distinction between the *muhajirs*—families who migrated from India at the time of Pakistan's independence in 1947—and the indigenous peoples of the country. The muhajirs retain and cultivate the use of Urdu, the mother tongue they brought with them. They are also primarily an urban community, living mostly in the city of Karachi. To maintain their identity as a distinct community in the independent Republic of Pakistan, about 20 million muhajirs formed a political party, the Mohajir Quami Movement (MQM), to represent their interests as a group in the affairs of state. Members in this party have been subjected to severe political harassment in Karachi,

which recorded 1,800 people killed on its streets in 1995. The imposition of federal rule and the creation of military courts in the city in November 1998 is understood by the MQM as an effort to destroy the movement as a political force. The leader of the party now resides in self-imposed exile in London.

Afghanistan, which, like Pakistan, is predominantly Islamic, also has many different language groups throughout the regions of the country. The distinct ethnic identities of these language groups did not prevent their leaders from joining together to fight against the Soviet invasion of their country in 1979. However, they have been unable to get together to form a single government since the Soviet withdrawal in 1989 and the downfall of the surviving Communist government in Kabul in 1992. The Taliban and the Northern Alliance remain in conflict even today.

The difference between urban and rural perspectives has also been significant in the political life of Afghanistan. It divided the People's Democratic (Communist) Party from its beginning in the early 1960s. This rift gave occasion for the Soviet forces to invade the country in 1979.

The distinction between the more cosmopolitan environment of Kabul and the conservative countryside is also evident in the impact of the reforming zeal of the Taliban movement, which emerged out of the provincial city of Kandahar in 1996 and has since enveloped most of the country. The devastation brought upon the city of Kabul by this movement is indicative of the disdain in which the Taliban holds those urbanites who do not share its reactionary religious agenda.

AN ENCAPSULATED SOCIETY

There are many significant bases of social distinction in the subcontinent: regional, religious, linguistic, and urban–rural. The latter distinction is important because the subcontinent has a much greater rural population than an urban one. The average urban population in South Asia is only 24 percent, as compared with 74 percent in the United States. India will soon have the second-largest urban population in the world, but urban dwellers still constitute less than a quarter of the total population of the country. Thus, rural ways and the rural voice still have a significant role in the priorities and direction of South Asian life.

There is also a vast disparity between the wealthiest and the poorest of the poor. Recognition of the inequities of this division has led to the development of the Self-Employed Women's Association (SEWA) in India and the Grameen Bank in Bangladesh. These institutions have created effective methods for providing capitalization of assets among the poor. Cooperatives devoted primarily to helping women develop self-supporting careers have been set up throughout the subcontinent, modeled on these programs.

All of these bases of social distinction reveal the immense diversity and variety in the social fabric of South Asia. The violence that often results from their interaction reveals the depth and the extent of these differences as establishing the unique identity of each of the many social groupings. Each, affirmed in the integrity of its own identity, has coexisted—sometimes in harmony, sometimes at odds—with other distinct groups for many centuries. Social pressures toward conformity within each group are so immense that these groups are not expected to assimilate or fit in with the distinguishing characteristics of other groups. This process functions among the smallest of social groupings, even on the level of the jati caste communities. Extended kinship groups, tribes, migrant peoples, and even highly mobile social classes are accepted as they are simply by placing them as a distinct community within a stratified social hierarchy. Every community, no matter how different its values and character, has a place. Each thus remains a distinct yet an integral part within the whole fabric of South Asian society.

This second image of South Asia is one of many people displaying an immense variety of cultural attributes. All of these socially distinct groups are encapsulated in enclaves in which they are expected to exist in the integrity of their own traditional identity among a large number of culturally different peoples. Even though there have been periods of great confrontation, discrimination, and violence, there is also the acceptance that such wide diversity among so many different peoples is both inevitable and normal. Like the four-fold layering of humanity set forth in the Vedic hymn celebrating the creation sacrifice of primordial man, social diversity is a cosmic reality.

IMAGE 3: THE WORLD AS SYMBOL

The first function [of a symbol] is the representative function. The symbol represents something which is not itself, for which it stands and in the power and meaning of which it participates . . . . And now we come to something which is perhaps the main function of the symbol—namely, the opening up of levels of reality which otherwise are hidden and cannot be grasped in any other way.

Every symbol opens up a level of reality for which non-symbolic speaking is inadequate. The more we try to enter into the meaning of symbols, the more we become aware that it is the function of art to open up levels of reality; in poetry, in visual art, and in music, levels of reality are opened up which can be opened up in no other way.

But in order to do this, something else must be opened up—namely, levels of the soul, levels of our interior reality. And they must correspond to the levels in exterior reality which are opened up by a symbol. So every symbol is two-edged. It opens up reality and it opens up the soul. There are, of course, those people who are not opened up by music or who are not opened up by poetry, or more of them who are not opened up at all by visual arts. The "opening up" is a two sided function—namely, reality in deeper levels and the human soul in special levels.

—Paul Tillich, *Theology of Culture*

During the long evolution of civilization in South Asia, creative patterns of thinking about the world gradually formed out of the earliest stages of Vedic musings into a classical tradition. From very early times, Vedic priests looked at the world as a cosmic sacrifice, as an experience of sacred celebration, rather than as a natural reality. Their intellectual pursuits to describe the world as sacrifice created opportunities to see and understand what is beyond the empirical world of objects. They sought to identify a deeper level of reality that gives the experiences and objects of this world the quality of being sacred. They expressed this level of reality in symbols, as what experiences and objects represent, rather than just the fact of their being. They saw the world as an arena for the refinement of human experience—to realize not just what *is* but also what is *beyond*—to deeper levels of their being.

We understand the world around us in many different ways. Some things, like our hereditary traits, we experience as natural. Others, like our languages and patterns of behavior, we experience as cultural. Because of the great diversity of cultures in the world, what we experience culturally is understood in very different ways, depending on the context in which it is experienced. One way to distinguish these differences in understanding is to describe them as experienced in different dimensions. For example, an object or experience can be perceived in the natural dimension. That perception tells us what it is, what we call the facts of its physical existence.

The pervasive authority of scientific thinking in Western culture encourages the perception of things primarily as experienced in the natural dimension. Objects are acknowledged to be as they are observed, and our understanding of the world is built around relationships revealed and confirmed by such perceptual data. These relationships are called models, whether they be of things observed directly, like gravity, or, of abstract patterns, like atomic structure or galaxies. All of these descriptions are based on, and authenticated by, what we perceive as an objective, natural world.

Human experience can also be understood in the historical dimension. Perceiving an object or experience in this dimension reveals something more than the facts of its existence. It represents something more by pointing to a special meaning or interpretation for a significant group of people. For example, a flag can be seen naturally, as a piece of colored cloth. If the pattern of the colors does not represent something to us, it remains a natural object. But if we recognize the pattern of the flag as belonging to a specific group of people, like a tribe or a country, it becomes more than a natural object. It stands for something. In understanding what it stands for, we look at it from the historical dimension to see what defines the people for whom it is their flag.

What defines a people historically is events, what actually happens to them of special, even exclusive significance to them as a distinct group. In this dimension, people are defined by their understanding of what happens to them, not by what

These young women of Pushkar, India, are part of the vast cultural mosaic of peoples in South Asia.

they are as natural beings. In American experience, such events include the landing of Pilgrims at Plymouth; the Battle of Yorktown, which ended the Revolutionary War and brought freedom from British control to the American colonies; and the assassination of President John F. Kennedy. They also include something as far away as the escape of a group of slaves from ancient Egypt, known as the Exodus experience. They are events because they affirm as real something more than just that they happened.

People identify the significance of what happens to them in innumerable ways to express their impact, their identity-defining meaning, and their authority. Thus, by expressing allegiance to their flag, in celebrating Thanksgiving or the Fourth of July, in parades and in elections, Americans experience the world in the historical dimension. These activities give meaning and direction to their lives as a people who have a shared identity and destiny. All of the things that Americans recognize or do to affirm this historical reality point beyond what they are as things to this level of their experience. In this power to point beyond, to represent events, they are more than facts; they are symbols.

A language is itself a symbol system. Particular sounds articulated in a distinct way represent a specific meaning to those who share in understanding that language. Its symbolic character is especially expressive in revealing levels of experience beyond the physical world. Words, sentences, stories, even myths not only express, but they also create the significance of what has happened to make real for us the historical dimension of our experience. Words allow us to enter into experiences that happen as events—as they happen, and also long after they have happened. Through language, we become part of and celebrate whole new worlds.

The development of the "Great Tradition" in South Asia pursued yet another dimension of human experience. In their concern to identify their experience as sacrifice, as having sacred significance, the ancient Vedic priests entered into a religious dimension of human experience. They sought to discover the world itself as symbol.

This religious dimension shares with the historical dimension in that it is expressed in symbols, in what exterior reality *represents* rather than what it *is*. It is different from the historical, in that its symbols point to and identify levels of reality that transcend the natural and cultural worlds in which people live. When religious rituals and myths express for a people what is ultimately real and absolutely true for them, then they function as symbols of transcendence. If rituals and myths are reduced to a natural description of what they are, such as dance patterns or interesting stories, they simply cease to be religious symbols.

The early pursuit of the religious dimension of human experience in South Asia appears in the *Rg Veda,* the anthology of religious poems collected some 3,000 years ago during the period of the settlement of the Aryan people in the subcontinent. The men of wisdom during those early times—the Brahmin priesthood—understood their experience of living in the world as participating in an act of cosmic sacrifice. They took upon themselves the exclusive task of developing and giving authenticity to this symbolic perception of the world, not only by asserting their social priority, as in the Vedic passage that describes them as the mouth of primordial man. They also developed an elaborate system of rituals that they performed as religious acts, to reenact, express, and celebrate the transcending reality of the natural world as a sacrificial event.

These scholar-priests then created a series of profoundly stimulating discourses called the *Upanishads* to portray the transcendent reality that their ritual activity, as symbols, represented. Their search for the sacred meaning of our lives also led to a number of impressive studies, *sastras*, on different aspects of human experience. These analyses, though based on careful observation, were not so much descriptions of the natural world around them as they were reflections on what this world might be as expressive of a deeper level or order of being.

One of the sastras, the *Laws of Manu*, is a remarkable treatise on social structure. It presents an elaborate set of rules of appropriate behavior for a society as though it were divided and ranked into the four *varna*, or classical caste, groups set forward in the *Rg Veda*: *Brahmin* (priests), *Kshatriya* (rulers), *Vaisya* (citizens), and *Sudra* (laborers). It also divides one's life into four stages, called *ashramas*, which are each to take one quarter of an entire lifetime: that of being a student, a householder, a mendicant, and an ascetic. The *Laws*, rather than assuming that a single behavioral norm can apply to all of life, prescribe a distinct set of rules appropriate for each stage. A clear structure thus places specific expectations of how people ought to act in a wide variety of conditions of class and age. It is a comprehensive and authoritative model for social behavior—not because it describes what actually happens, but because it expresses a vision of cosmic social order. It is something to live up to.

Other sastras, focus on such topics as statecraft, poetics, philosophy, music, ritual, and the arts. These works are remarkable for the depth and precision of analysis that their authors undertook. They reveal that the classical scholar-priests who composed them did not find order or ultimate meaning immediately in the natural world about them. They had too strong a sense of flux and uncertainty in their normal human experience. They sought consistency, rather, in more abstract intellectual patterns, in the refinement rather the description of what was about them. In art, for example, they suggested that aesthetic value was not in the experience of raw emotion (*bhava*), but in the refinement of that emotion into a pure sentiment (*rasa*) that generates a sense of awe and beauty. Their attention was thus on what their experience pointed to as symbol rather than what it was as fact. It was out of this refining analysis that the concept of the number zero emerged—it was in the classical South Asian way of looking at objects that the idea arose that there is something in the number system that is to be counted, even if it is not here.

Of all the works of analysis during the classical tradition, none is greater than the earliest: the description of the structure of language by Panini, the classical grammarian of the Sanskrit language. Panini probably lived during the fourth century B.C. He analyzed how sounds, as the basic structural units of a language (morphemes), fit together to form a word or a sentence. Only specific combinations of sounds form words, and specific combinations of words form sentences.

When we use them to communicate, words and sentences reveal patterns that are related to their meanings, to what we are trying to say. Panini's insight was that these patterns are not established by their meanings but, rather, by the structure of language itself.

Panini, in his analysis of Sanskrit, discovered patterns that are revealed by the way words and sentences are used—not in ordinary, colloquial language, but in the highly refined, classical form of the language of the priesthood. (The word *sanskrit* means "refined" or "perfected." It identifies the level of abstraction to which the formal use of that language had progressed among the intensively trained scholar-priests during the late Vedic period.) In his quest to discover the structure of this highly refined language, Panini identified its abstract form as a profound source of order in human life that is presupposed of any attempt to use words to describe it. He perceived language as an intricately developed symbol system capable of giving expression to a transcendent level of being, because of its own, self-generating power of expression. Its greatest potential as language was not to describe what is but, rather, to point to and affirm what is ultimately real in human experience.

Panini reduced his study of Sanskrit to eight concise chapters of grammatical rules, wherein each successive rule was an exception to all the rules that preceded it. This impressive intellectual achievement appears all the more remarkable in that he achieved this structure without the use of writing; he did it all in his head.

Panini's achievement was matched by other important intellectual quests during the classical period. Elaborations of the concept of cosmic time, or time that is ceaselessly revolving, are mind-boggling because of the vast span of the cycles proposed. They were described in the Puranic literature as extending through four eras, called *yugas*, ranging in length from 432,000 years to 1,728,000 years. One thousand of these four-era periods add up to a *kalpa*, or a day of Brahma. At the end of a 4,320,000,000-year day of Brahma, the created universe comes to an end, or is dormant during Brahma's night, of equal duration, before the cycle begins again.

Brahma is now in the first kalpa of his fifty-first year. Six Manus of that *kalpa* have passed away. We are living in the Kaliyuga of the twenty-eighth four-age period (*caturyuga*) of the seventh *manvantara* of Brahma's fifty-first year. The Kaliyuga began on February 18, 3102 B.C. This would seem to indicate that we have a little less than 426,933 years to go until the Kaliyuga with its twilight comes to an end, and we have to face dissolution!

—W. Norman Brown, *Man in the Universe*

This concept of time generated many imaginative images in Sanskrit literature, such as the account of an *apsara*, an angel, who lived in the realm of heaven within a different time frame. One heaven day, while at play with her friends in a garden, she fell off a swing and fainted. While unconscious, she went to Earth to be born as a child. She reached adulthood, married, gave birth to children, attended her eldest son's wedding, and saw her grandchildren before she died. She then returned to her apsara friends in the heaven garden. They had anxiously gathered around upon her fall from the swing, and were fanning her to help her recover. Upon reviving, she told her friends of her earthly experience. They were astounded that so much could have happened to her in so short a span of their time.

Imaginative and creative intellectual effort was also devoted to find an adequate understanding of self—an answer to the question "Who am I?" And again, the analysis pursued not the question "What am I?" but "Of what is my being a symbol?"

This philosophical tradition distinguished early on between the self who acts, the agent—"I am the one who does, thinks, feels things"—and the self who observes this agency—the witness. The active self was called *jiva* (the living thing), the aspect of self to which the acts of *karma* (acts having moral consequences) become attached. It is this karma that determines into what form of life the jiva transmigrates when reincarnated.

The classical scholar-priests devoted to the study of self affirmed another dimension of self standing apart from oneself as doing. Because this witness self is detached, observing rather than doing, it transcends the activity in which the jiva is involved. This aspect of self is called *atma*. The atma, because it transcends the natural self, is affirmed as more real, as the ultimate self, of which the natural, active self is a symbol.

The Vedanta philosopher Shankara, who lived during the eighth century A.D., ranks with Panini as an intellectual giant among the classical scholars of South Asia. Shankara identified the experience of consciousness as the primary designation of the atma. It is in witnessing ourselves as being conscious as a symbol that we gain some insight into who we really are, of our ultimately real self.

This way of thinking is not available to those who have become literalists, who think that what they see is all that there is to human experience. The classical thinkers of South Asia envisioned and opened up impressive avenues of awareness and expression, realized in creative works of art, music, dance, sculpture, and literature. They also discovered and affirmed a transcendent unity in human experience that can be realized through a multitude of symbols. This unity can even be discovered in experiencing the transcendence of our own, isolated, individual selves, if we can discover the "ultimate beyond" within.

This heritage helps to explain why encapsulation as a social process is such an integral part of the culture of South Asia. The classical scholars understood that languages and religions are cultural constructs. No language or religion is natural in the sense that each has to be what it is, or that it can be fully explained in natural terms. Different peoples express their experience of identical things, even the same event, in very different ways. They even experience them differently.

Thus, attempts to construct a universal language, religion, or nationality have failed because the cultural contexts in which the necessary claims to absolutism are expressed, be it truth or allegiance, are not shared by all peoples in common. We see things, experience them, and talk about them in different ways, based upon the cultural context in which we are raised.

This understanding of the cultural relativity of language and religion, which is so evident in the pluralistic social context in which the peoples of South Asia live, does not negate the absolute claims to meaning and truth of the many separate languages and religions around them. Each is recognized to have a functional integrity that distinguishes it from all other languages and religions. For example, a specific religion evolves as a structural abstraction among a group of people to reflect the uniqueness of their experience of transcendence as a group. In this structural integrity as a religious faith, the group's religious practices become symbols that point beyond what they are as activities to the identity and the integrity of those who acknowledge and worship what is ultimately real for them together as a community. This structural integrity is self-validating in the community in which it is affirmed.

Among the Brahmin community, for example, it is not the colloquial or even ritual use of Sanskrit that makes it sacred. It is, rather, the structure of that highly refined language that makes it symbolically expressive of the ultimate meaning of the universe.

A Brahmin teaching states that when God came to create the universe, He did not create objects and then allow Adam, a human being, to invent language by naming them. Instead, He went to the ultimate meaning of what is universally expressed symbolically in the language of the *Rg Veda* to find out what He was to create. That level of reality is for the classical tradition more real than the reality of the natural world. Nothing can be literally true in the *Veda* unless it be ultimately true.

Recognition of structural integrity as characteristic of differing languages and religions is the basis for understanding them, as symbols, not as absolutes in themselves but as pointing to a transcendent level of reality that is. One can accept the ultimate claim to universality of others for their religious faith to the degree that one understands the ultimacy of that universal reality to which one's own faith is a symbol. It is not a matter of accepting, or even tolerating, another's religion. It is, rather, the challenge of discovering that transcendent level of reality of which one's own faith is a symbol. To people of great faith, that ultimate reality affirmed by all religions is one.

As a social process in South Asia, encapsulation is based on this recognition of many different, structurally integrated, cultural abstractions as expressions of another level of being than that defined within the natural and historical dimensions of human experience. Each language and each religion, as a

(World Bank)

The crush of peoples and cultures poses significant challenges to democracy in South Asia. Here, afternoon traffic builds near the India Exchange in Calcutta, India.

symbol in its structural integrity, is expressive of what is ultimately true. They are isolated and preserved, then, not for what they are, but for what they represent to those for whom they are authentic symbols. The recognition of the structural integrity of languages and religions as symbols explains why the pluralistic social environment of South Asia can be so resilient and accepting of difference.

Recognition of the structural integrity of the many different languages and religions in South Asia also affirms a vital sense of community among those who speak the same mother tongue and join in common religious practices. Because sharing a language and a religious faith so clearly differentiates one group from all those who do not, language and religious identities are sources of strong social bonding as well. That is why languages and religions play such an important role in the unfolding of democracy as a way of affirming a political identity for the peoples of South Asia.

IMAGE 4: DEMOCRACY IN SOUTH ASIA

> The spirit of democracy is not a mechanical thing to be adjusted by the abolition of forms. It requires a change of the heart.
> —Mohandas K. Gandhi

The road to democracy in each of the countries in South Asia since the end of British colonial rule has been arduous. Many obstacles, both indigenous and imposed, have impeded the progress of all the nations of the subcontinent toward democratically elected representative governments.

The concept of a modern democratic state is a political abstraction developed in the West. A nation based on the sovereignty of the governed is a cultural construct, not a natural entity, that developed in the experience of particular groups of people within a European cultural context. Specifically, the formation of nations in Western Europe and America took place among dominant groups of culturally homogeneous people. Those of different cultural backgrounds, those who spoke different languages, and even women, were simply ignored in this process. Because this assumption of a dominant male ethnicity was unchallenged, it was taken for granted that their shared sense of identity as a nation would take precedence over any cultural differences among residual minority groups within the nation. All participants in the political process would blend into the culture of the politically dominant.

Such a concept of nationality did not transfer easily to South Asia. In particular, the assumption of dominant ethnicity as determining the distinctive character of a nation could not be easily transposed into the diverse cultural environment of the peoples of South Asia. They are so accustomed to living in what Sushi Tharoor calls "a singular land of the plural," in which no ethnic nor linguistic group is in a majority, that they do not understand common citizenship to be something that would demand greater allegiance than the community identities that separate them from all other linguistic, religious, and social groups among whom they live. They were thus not prepared to think of themselves as having a shared political identity as a nation.

The concept of modern nationality faced difficulties in being accepted in the subcontinent also because the democratic models of government introduced by British colonial rule did not enter a political vacuum. The Great Mutiny of 1857 in British India demonstrated widespread indigenous resistance to British colonial attempts to enlighten its South Asian subjects. It also demonstrated the resiliency of the established bastions of public power based on traditional patriarchal authority structures within the family and in the villages.

Efforts to encourage public participation in the political process, to make a government of the people, reveal the adaptability of village-level, caste-community, and language-area institutions as well. Established patterns of grassroots governance continue to be significant factors in both implementing and shaping the transition from traditional power structures into democratic forms. Even in those countries that have adopted policies that reserve public offices for women, those women elected to responsible positions still meet strong resistance to their authority by entrenched patriarchal power elites. The number of women who have served as prime ministers in India, Bangladesh, Pakistan, and Sri Lanka is remarkable. Yet each of them has gained prominence in national political life because of the dominant roles of their fathers or husbands. Traditional power structures do not relinquish their authority easily, if at all.

RELIGION AND NATIONAL IDENTITY
The most devastating consequence of the imposition of Western nationality into the South Asian political arena has been the use of religious allegiances to create a sense of national identity. Nationhood is a cultural construct that, like language and religion, needs to develop a sense of corporate identity among particular groups of people. It also has a structural integrity, expressed in institutions and symbols of public power or authority, that distinguishes it from the domain of other nations. Unlike religion, however, its institutions and symbols are identified almost entirely within the historical dimension of a community's experience. Nationalisms even create their own histories.

Because of the similarity of language, religion, and nationality as creating self-authenticating corporate identities, the leaders of the freedom movements during the twentieth century drew upon established language and religious community identities to generate a sense of participation in the public domain in order to create a national identity for their peoples. The traditional affiliations of dominant religious groups were especially convenient for this purpose. The partitioning of those districts of the British Raj in which the majority of the population was Muslim as belonging to the nation of Pakistan, and Hindu-majority districts to India, is the most explicit

example of this exploitation of religious identity to attempt to create political cohesion.

Religious identity is available for political bonding because religious communities must continually reaffirm their identity and relevance as worshiping communities. Even very traditional communities have developed mechanisms to adjust themselves in changing circumstances, to maintain the allegiance and participation of their members.

The danger in using the bonding dynamic of religious communities as a way of bringing people together as nations is that it essentially changes the nature of the relationship it affirms among the people. The effective working of the multicultural social environment in South Asia is based on the understanding that different religious communities are symbolic expressions of a transcendent, unified reality. Each community's life is an authentic, symbolic expression of this ultimate truth. The political use of a religious community's bonding dynamic reduces religious identity from a symbolic expression of ultimate truth to something historically concrete, literally true, and both socially and geographically exclusive. At its worst, the political use of religious symbols has led to absolutizing the nation-state itself.

The reduction of religious identity to national identity is pervasive throughout the world and has led to severe violence and suffering. It has left a trail of human misery in the Middle East, Africa, Northern Ireland, the former Yugoslavia, and in South Asia.

THE PARTITION OF BRITISH INDIA IN 1947
The ethnic, linguistic, religious groupings used in Western Europe to build the political identity of nations became especially divisive in South Asia's pluralistic social environment. The creation of the new nations of India and Pakistan out of the British Indian Empire isolated vast numbers of people not included in the dominant religious identity around which the national borders were drawn. Literally millions of Hindus and Sikhs living in areas of the subcontinent that became Pakistan, and Muslims finding themselves in an independent India, felt threatened as minorities in these newly established nations. Communal violence erupted across the subcontinent.

Children of many different faiths and backgrounds who had grown up together, had learned and played together in the same school for years, suddenly, on the day of the independence of their country, became enemies. They thought that they were going to be free. But what they experienced, inexplicably, was severe division and hatred. Dazed and mystified, those of minority faiths were whisked away during the night to seek asylum across the border. And many did not make it.

More than 12 million people fled, the largest refugee migration ever experienced in the world. Homeless and threatened in their own lands, they were forced to flee in haste, destitute of any possessions, to cross the new national borders in a quest for survival. As Hindus and Sikhs moved toward India and Muslims toward Pakistan, in opposite directions across the border drawn between the two countries, many hundreds of thousands were senselessly killed. Kushwant Singh writes movingly of the devastating impact of that violent confrontation on a Sikh village near the border, in his novel *Train to Pakistan:*

> Early in September the time schedule in Mano Majra started going wrong. . . . Goods trains had stopped running altogether, so there was no lullaby to lull them to sleep. . . . All trains [now crowded with refugees] coming from Delhi stopped and changed their drivers and guards before moving on to Pakistan. One morning, a train from Pakistan halted at Mano Majra railway station. At first glance it had the look of trains in the days of peace. No one sat on the roof. No one clung between the bogies. No one was balanced on the foot-boards. But somehow it was different. There was something uneasy about it. It had a ghostly quality. . . .
>
> [That evening] the northern horizon, which had turned a bluish grey, showed orange again. The orange turned into copper and then into luminous russet. Red tongues of flame leaped into the black sky. A soft breeze began to blow towards the village. It brought the smell of burning kerosene, then of wood. And then—a faint acrid smell of searing flesh.
>
> The village was stilled in deathly silence. No one asked anyone else what the odour was. They all knew. They had known it all the time. The answer was implicit in the fact that the train had come from Pakistan.
>
> That evening, for the first time in the memory of Mano Majra, Imam Baksh's sonorous cry did not rise to the heavens to proclaim the glory of God.

Those who survived this massive migration found themselves bewildered refugees rather than experiencing the exhilaration of political freedom. They were homeless in the lands of their birth, unwelcome in the lands to which they came.

THE INDEPENDENCE OF BANGLADESH IN 1971

Islamic religious identity was used to create a single, independent Pakistan in 1947 for Muslims in the two sections of the subcontinent where they were in the majority. Yet their shared Islamic faith did not prevent the uprising of the peoples of the eastern region of Pakistan in 1971, a quarter-century after the partition of British India, to seek their own independence from Pakistan. That movement revealed that the ethnic and linguistic identity of the Bengali people of East Pakistan was stronger than their religious identity as Muslims in a country dominated by the ethnically and linguistically different, and financially advantaged, Muslim population of West Pakistan.

(United Nations/BP)

With the partitioning of India and Pakistan, masses of people migrated because of their religious affiliations. More than 12 million people fled, including these refugees, making it the largest migration in history.

National identity based on ethnicity rather than religion proved to be no less of a human tragedy. The reign of fury brought on the Bengali people by the Pakistan government, as it tried to preserve the union of its eastern wing with West Pakistan by military repression, caused more than 200,000 deaths. According to a *New York Times* report at that time (June 7, 1971):

> People have killed each other because of race, politics, and religion; no community is entirely free of guilt. But the principal agent of death and hatred has been the Pakistani Army. And its killing has been selective. According to reliable reports from inside East Pakistan, the Army's particular targets have been intellectuals and leaders of opinion—doctors, professors, students, writers.

Eight million people fled across the East Pakistan border during the spring and summer of 1971, into the squalor of refugee camps in the neighboring states of India. That number included more than 1,500 physicians and 10,000 teachers. According to an International Rescue Committee report in 1971:

> With the closure of the borders by the Pakistani military, large numbers are continuing to infiltrate through the 1,300 mile border with India through forest and swamps. These groups, with numbers sometimes up to 50,000 in a 24 hour period, have for the most part settled along major routes in India. They are found wherever there is a combination of available ground and minimal water supply. . . . The refugee camps may vary in size from small groups to upwards of 50,000. There has been an extraordinary effort on the part of the West Bengal and Indian government to organize these camps and supply them with at least minimal amounts of food and water.
>
> The refugee diet . . . consists of rice boiled in open clay pots, some powdered milk which is occasionally available, and dall, which is a lentil type of bean used for a thin soup. . . . At this point the diet would be classified as barely adequate.

Because uncertain conditions, both political and natural, continue to plague the people of Bangladesh, the flow of refugees into India since the independence of Bangladesh in 1971 has continued. It is estimated that anywhere from 7 million to 12 million Bangladeshis now live in India. The continuing existence of such a large number of refugees illustrates what a heavy toll in human displacement and suffering has resulted from the imposition of religious nationality as a way of grouping the culturally diverse peoples of the subcontinent.

This pattern is not unique to the partition of British India into districts of Hindu and Muslim majorities. Large numbers of people have become refugees in both Sri Lanka and Bhutan, where the overwhelming majority of the populations are Buddhists. That those belonging to religious minorities in these countries also speak different languages adds to their separation from the dominant religious minorities.

THE SRI LANKAN EXPERIENCE

Sri Lanka began the practice of democracy earlier than the other nations of South Asia. Free and general elections for political office were first held there in 1935. The country also has the highest level of education and literacy, an accomplishment that accounts for its maintaining the lowest birth rate and rate of population growth in the subcontinent. Yet with all of these achievements, the country is entangled in devastating communal warfare. This intense violence and suffering rises out of the insecurity created among religious and linguistic minority groups by a national identity shaped around the religious and linguistic identity of a Sinhala-speaking, Buddhist majority.

Within this island-nation is a large minority of Tamil-speaking Hindus, who comprise about 17 percent of the total population. Though ethnically the same as the Buddhist majority, they are geographically separate. Living mostly in the northern part of the country, they constitute a plurality if not an outright majority in the political districts of that region. Still, the political repression they have experienced in other regions of the country and on the national level led in the early 1980s to outbursts of communal violence. These outbursts were followed by the growth of a militant and bloody separatist movement, which has refused to be quelled even to this day.

The example of the creation of India and Pakistan would have suggested the division of the island into two countries, based on the majority populations in each of the districts of the British Crown colony, then called Ceylon. But at the time of independence, it was hoped that the political identity of a unified island-nation would take precedence over the religious and linguistic identities of its constituent regions. It was also hoped that such a unifying political identity would prevail over any cultural and linguistic affinity of the minority Tamil population of Sri Lanka with the larger neighboring state of Tamil Nadu, across the Palk Strait in south India. In 1948, all districts were included under a single, democratically elected, parliamentary government. This government assured a commanding majority to the larger Buddhist, Sinhala-speaking population, without sufficient safeguards to guarantee the rights and safety of its minorities.

At the time of independence, 800,000 Indian Tamils worked on the coffee, rubber, and tea plantations in the southern hills of the colony. They were not part of the distinct, indigenous Tamil community of the north; they had been imported by the British from Tamil-speaking south India during the nineteenth century. The "solution" to their presence as an ethnically distinct minority with strong ties to the large Tamil population in south India was for the Ceylonese government to declare them stateless and to push for their repatriation to India. In 1964, and again in 1974, the government of India agreed to receive 600,000 "plantation Tamils" back into India. The north Ceylonese Tamils, for whom the island had been homeland for more than 2,000 years, saw these deportations as ominous.

Tensions between the Sinhalese majority and Tamil minority increased during a period of uneasy accommodation. Then, in 1983, anti-Tamil riots broke out throughout the country. The defense of the linguistic identity and political freedom of the Tamil people was then seized by a militant separatist group called the Liberation Tigers for Tamil Eelam (Nation), or LTTE. Guerrilla warfare broke out in the predominantly Tamil-speaking areas of the north and east. Thirty thousand Tamils fled to India that year, to be followed by almost 100,000 more refugees in 1984.

Since then, many thousands have been killed in the attacks and counterattacks of the LTTE and the Sri Lankan Army. In 1987, at the invitation of the Sri Lankan government, India sent a strong "Peace Keeping Force" to attempt to bring order to the troubled country. But the deployment of Indian Army units was not able to bring the two sides together, and the invitation was withdrawn in 1990.

Between 1990 and 1995, fighting between the LTTE and the Sri Lankan government increased in intensity and devastation. With the destruction of their homes and means of livelihood, even entire villages, more than 1 million people became refugees.

Because ocean waters and navy ships surround Sri Lanka, escape has been extremely difficult. Fewer than 20 percent have been able to afford the expense and risk of crossing the Palk Strait to India. Saraswathi Sevakam, a refugee in a camp in India, testified in 1991:

In July 1990, I left my village and got into a boat for India. There were 45 of us, all civilians. We were about to leave the cove when a navy gunboat came at us, shooting. We jumped into the shallow water. Some people were waving white flags to show we were not militants. We lay in the water for two hours before the navy boats came back and took us to shore. They threatened that if they found any LTTE in the area, we would be killed. We were taken to a navy camp. My husband was taken away. I have not seen him or heard from him since.

By May 1991, some 210,000 refugees were reported to have made it to south India. Another 200,000 have sought asylum in Europe. But most of those who have suffered the ravages of communal violence in Sri Lanka have remained there and been dependent upon relief efforts set up within the country itself. They are refugees in their own land.

Since the election of the Chandrika Kumaratunga government in 1995, there have been renewed efforts to find paths toward a political solution for the division among the opposed religious communities in Sri Lanka. In 1998, with lack of progress on this front, indicated by numerous suicide bombings in the capital city of Columbo, the government launched a major military offensive that wrested control of the Jaffna Peninsula, the Tamil militants' stronghold in the north, from the LTTE. In the spring of 2000, the LTTE mounted a counterattack that threatened to recapture the city of Jaffna. In December 2000, the LTTE changed its strategy by declaring a unilateral cease-fire, in hopes of promoting a Norwegian-government initiative to mediate the conflict. Still, the fighting, killing, and destruction continue. And those who survive remain desperate for food and shelter.

Sri Lanka's experience in seeking an inclusive national identity has taken a heavy toll among its people. Although they remain hopeful, those who have been ravaged by this warfare do not see an early end to their plight.

BHUTAN: A GROWING REFUGEE PROBLEM

Even the small country of Bhutan, tucked away in the high Himalayan Mountains on the northeast side of the subcontinent, has not been immune from a refugee crisis. And the shape of the issue appears discouragingly familiar: Can the identity of the nation include all those living within its borders who belong to distinct ethnic, religious, and linguistic minorities?

The gradual move toward modernization in this mountain kingdom has led to the migration of laborers, some from India, but in greater numbers from Nepal. The Nepali immigrants have settled almost entirely in the more productive, southern part of the country, where they live as a distinct minority. In recent years, their number has grown to more than a quarter of the population of Bhutan.

The trend toward modernization has also challenged the traditional way of life of the Bhutanese people. In the face of this challenge, made more intense by the awareness that other Buddhist kingdoms in that region—Tibet, Sikkim, and Ladakh—have not survived, the government of Bhutan has taken a number of actions to create a national identity based upon its Buddhist heritage. These actions include the adoption of Dzongkha as the national language and the mandating of a national dress for formal occasions. These actions were not specifically aimed at the Nepali population. However, they were taken with the clear recollection that it was the agitation of Nepalis living in the neighboring kingdom of Sikkim that led to its absorption into India in 1974.

In 1985, the government allowed citizenship to only those Nepalis who could claim residency before 1958. In 1988, this Citizenship Act was enforced by a census in southern Bhutan, to identify those immigrants who were not legal residents. The rigor of the census became a direct assault on the Nepalis, threatening both their heritage and their status as citizens in the country. The deportations, social unrest, and terrorist acts that followed the census led to the flight of many Nepalis from the country. By July 1993, some 85,000 had made their way into refugee camps set up by the United Nations in eastern Nepal. A number of protest marches to Bhutan have been staged from these camps, but with little noticeable impact. In 1996, 110,000

(UN/DPI Photo by Eskinder Debebe)

Palijor Dorji, minister of the environment of the Kingdom of Bhutan, addresses the 19th special session of the UN's General Assembly.

refugees were reported to be living in eight refugee camps in Nepal.

The governments of Bhutan and Nepal have been seeking to work out an agreement on this refugee problem for years. Yet the issue as to who is legitimately a citizen of Bhutan remains unresolved.

POLITICAL CRISIS IN AFGHANISTAN

Afghanistan had a head start in nation building over the other South Asian countries. Following a brief incursion of British forces into Afghan territory in 1878, the British withdrew to leave these lands under the authority of Abdur Rahman Khan, the emir of Kabul. During his reign, from 1880 to 1901, he managed to bring what he discribed as "hundreds of petty chiefs, plunderers, robbers, and cutthroats" under his domain, giving to that region the beginning of a national identity. In 1923, his grandson Amanullah Khan attempted to introduce modern reforms and democratically elected representative government into his domain. His quest to establish a modern state ran into many of the difficulties shared by all of the nations of the subcontinent.

Afghanistan is a country divided by a formidable natural barrier, by differing ethnic and linguistic groups, by a modernizing urban population and conservative rural petty states and tribes, fractured among themselves into militant factions. Amanullah Khan's attempts at reform were resisted from the beginning by the many autonomous warlords who held abso-

lute control over isolated regions of the country. He was forced into exile in 1928.

Two years later, a distant cousin of Amanulla Khan, Sardar Mohammad Nadir Khan, returned from exile in France to reclaim the country and was proclaimed king of Afghanistan by a national assembly of tribal leaders. Upon his assassination in 1933, he was succeeded by his son Mohammad Zahir. During Zahir Shah's long reign, the central authority of his government increased throughout the country. In 1953, a cousin, Sadar Mohammad Daoud Khan, seized the office of prime minister and introduced many reforms and institutions of modern government.

In 1964, Sadar Daoud's reforming efforts led to the adoption of a constitutional monarchy, with elections for public office. A succession of coups during the 1970s, however, created sufficient political instability to allow the Afghan People's Democratic (Communist) Party, with Soviet encouragement, to take over the reins of government in Kabul in 1977. Its hold was tenuous, and within a year it appealed for help from the Soviet Union. In order to assert its influence and protect its investment in the country, the Soviets sent an army of 85,000 troops to suppress all those who were opposed to Communist rule.

The arrival of the Soviet Army caused the immediate flight of some 400,000 Afghans refugees into Pakistan. Over the next decade, Soviet forces conducted such a devastating "scorched earth" policy that the number of refugees increased to 6 million, more than one third of the total population of the country. They fled across their borders to refugee camps in Pakistan and Iran.

Support for the Afghan refugees came from many sources. The U.S. government, eager to contain further Soviet expansion in this region, contributed supplies, medical assistance, terrorist training, and encouragement to those who fled the devastation of Soviet attacks on their lands. Pakistan, finding support for its own military government by assisting the United States in its objectives, took up the Afghan cause. As a result, the refugee camps became not just places of refuge for those displaced from Afghanistan, but also staging and rehabilitation areas for those returning to fight against Soviet forces in their country.

The gathered strength of these forces of resistance led to a military stalemate and, in 1989, the withdrawal of Soviet forces. Their departure left a wide swath of devastation and impoverishment. There were miles of land mines through wide, unmapped areas of the country, and a Communist government was still in control. These conditions, combined with intense internal fighting among the rival *mujahideen* (resistance) groups that opposed the Communist government, offered small inducement to the refugees to return to their former homes. When they had strong international support, the refugee camps had provided some opportunities for education, social reform, health care, and employment, which many feared would not be available in their homelands. In 1999, with diminishing international aid and growing hardship in the refugee camps, 100,000 refugees returned from Pakistan voluntarily. Another 100,000 were forced to return from Iran, while 60,000 others went home on their own. Still, 1¼ million Afghans remain in some 200 refugee villages in Pakistan, and an equal number remain in Iran.

Since 1992, with the fall of the Communist government in Kabul, efforts to restore some kind of order in these war-ravaged lands and among the diverse ethnic constituencies of the country have resulted in intense infighting among rival mujahideen groups, all competing for control of the country. This continuing warfare has caused hundreds of thousands to flee the city of Kabul, reducing to 500,000 its prewar population of close to 1 million. And countless others abandoned their villages.

In 1994, the Taliban, a militant Islamic revolutionary force arose amid this political chaos, with an urgent call for reform. With Pakistani support, the Taliban began to take control of Afghanistan. Its forces now dominate some 95 percent of the country, and have imposed upon the lands they control a sense of peace and an extreme fundamentalist religious order. Military conflict continues over the remaining lands under the authority of a remnant of Mujahideen leaders called the Northern Alliance. This remnant is still the officially recognized government of the country by those countries that reject the Taliban's claim to rule because of its human-rights abuses and its harboring of terrorist Osama Bin Laden. When peace

talks between the Taliban and the Northern Alliance failed in July 1999, a Taliban offensive into the northern provinces of the country caused another 100,000 Afghans, mostly of Hazara origin, to flee into Pakistan. There they have been joined by 30,000 refugees forced out of their homelands by a severe, three-year drought.

With the country so divided by fully armed, opposing religious and ethnic forces, the Afghan people continue to be adrift. They live in need, uncertainty, and unrelenting anxiety on both sides of the borders between Afghanistan, Pakistan, and Iran. In such circumstances, there is little opportunity to affirm a common political identity as a people, let alone exercise any instruments of a stable, democratic government.

OTHER REFUGEES

Refugees, by definition, are aliens in the lands in which they live. They remain outside the perimeters of the identity of those who form the nation. Unless they assimilate into that identity, they cannot participate in government. The presence of so many refugees in the South Asian subcontinent is indicative of a state of political upheaval in which democracy cannot function.

Not all of these refugees are South Asian. The Chinese takeover of Tibet in 1951 led to the flight of the Dalai Lama, the religious and temporal leader of the Tibetan people, into India in 1959. Hundreds of thousands of his followers also fled into India, and into neighboring Nepal and Bhutan, seeking refuge from the repression of Chinese domination in their homeland. In their adopted homes, the Tibetan refugees continue to search for ways to maintain their identity as a Buddhist people in exile.

And the military repression that followed upon the thwarting of elections in Myanmar (Burma) in May 1990 has caused many to flee across its border into Bangladesh and the states of eastern India. Some 280,000 refugees are now reported to be in camps along the border of eastern Bangladesh. They remain hopeful that the courageous Nobel laureate, Aung San Suu Kyi, and her National League for Democracy will succeed in their quest to achieve a stable, democratically elected government, accountable to all the people of that country and protective of their human rights.

These struggles for national identity and democracy are taking a heavy toll. As long as these struggles continue, refugees will search for shelter and survival throughout these lands.

The extensive presence of refugees throughout the subcontinent bears witness to the challenge in every country in South Asia to achieve a basis for its political identity as a nation that is both true to and expressive of the unique multicultural diversity within each of their borders. Still, the nations of South Asia are making strides toward democracy. With the exception of Bhutan and Afghanistan, and notwithstanding a military coup in Pakistan in 1999, six nations of South Asia have held more than one full and free national election since

1993, with high levels of voter participation. Except for Maldives, which forbids by law the existence of opposition political parties, all of these most recent elections have resulted in the civil transfer of power from one political party to another. Democracy is taking hold. In South Asia today, it is the basis of governance among more people than anywhere else in the world.

The nations of South Asia still face many challenges: Indicative of the diversity among the nations themselves, none of them has responded to these challenges in the same way. How each of these countries is progressing on its separate path toward democracy is discussed in each of the country reports that follow this essay.

A common thread among these varied responses has been the attempt to achieve a political solution to adversarial relationships among peoples that are based on more traditional and profound expressions of human identity than that of the nation-state. A political solution to human strife was the assumption and the promise in the formation of nations in Western Europe during the eighteenth and nineteenth centuries. But the experience of two world wars and the continuing presence of refugees throughout the world suggest the inadequacy of nationalism based on self-determination as a way to achieve lasting unity and peace.

The independence of nations and freedom of the individual are worthy political goals. But the South Asia experience reveals to us that they are not ends in themselves. Nor can they be imposed.

Alexis de Tocqueville observed in the early years of the nineteenth century that the long-term success of democracy in the United States depended not upon the structure and institutions of the government, but upon the habits of the heart of the American people. Mahatma Gandhi, on the threshold of political independence for the people of India, also realized that democracy was not just a matter of form. It is a matter of the heart and the soul of a people.

IMAGE 5: MAHATMA GANDHI

Generations to come, it may be, will scarce believe that such a one as this ever in flesh and blood walked upon this earth.
—Albert Einstein

The name of Mahatma Gandhi comes up in a number of contexts in looking at the uniqueness of South Asia. His role in shaping the freedom movement on the subcontinent was immense. He identified himself with the common people, adopted their dress and simplicity of life, and traveled from village to village to spread his message of reform. He encouraged everyone to use the spinning wheel and to wear clothes made of the hand-spun cloth called *khadi*. He called for national boycotts. And he fasted. In these many ways, he managed to get everyone involved in the political process of becoming a new nation.

In this way he was able to restructure the Indian National Congress as the instrument for India's freedom. The power base of the movement had resided among the elitist group of intellectuals at the top, who had shaped its policies for achieving independence since 1887. Gandhi, building on a large number of grassroots initiatives, brought the power base to the village level, to where the people are. Under his leadership, removing the oppression of colonial rule was something that was happening to everyone, in every corner of the land.

Of greater international significance is the method of nonviolent protest against social injustice that Gandhi developed during his years in South Africa. He applied this method with confounding consistency in leading the peoples of British India to freedom in 1947. Its effectiveness was partly the result of his ability to discipline people in the deployment of his method. He was also able to command accountability from those who were the oppressors. In this way, he established a viable alternative to power politics to achieve historic goals. Gandhi called this method *satyagraha,* or "Soul Force." And he encouraged its use to empower all who are oppressed and powerless to gain the courage, the discipline, and the vision to become free.

In the time since his death in 1948, a number of important events have changed the course of history. The rise of the Solidarity movement in Poland initiated the crumbling of the Soviet Union and its grasp on Central/Eastern Europe. The civil-rights movement in the United States, under the inspiring leadership of Dr. Martin Luther King, Jr., initiated a national policy on race relations to correct historic injustices to minority students and workers. And the election of Nelson Mandela and his African National Congress to political leadership in 1994 led to the end of apartheid in South Africa. These events released new energy and a vision of hope for positive change in the world. They also share a common source: They all trace their inspiration for how to disarm oppressive political power with nonviolent public protest to Mohandas Karamchand Gandhi, the man who came to be called the Mahatma.

EARLY YEARS

Gandhi was born in Porbandar, a small seaport town along the western coast of the Kathiawar Peninsula in western India, on October 2, 1869. His father was a *diwan,* or prime minister, in the employ of local maharajas in that region. Although Mohandas was the youngest, the fourth child of his father's fourth wife, it was expected that he would continue his father's—and grandfather's—political careers. He was groomed from an early age for leadership.

Yet Gandhi proved to be an indifferent student. He found mathematics particularly difficult. When he was 13, his parents arranged for his marriage to Kasturbai, a young woman his same age. In spite of her gentle and accepting nature, he accounted himself an immature, jealous, and domineering husband. He was later to credit her example as a patient and

(Photo credit UPI/Bettmann Archives-AGM 5/831)

Mohandas Gandhi spent more than 20 years in South Africa as a result of becoming so involved in battling the prejudice against Indians living in that country. Gandhi is pictured above (center) sitting in front of his office In South Africa. On the left is his friend H. S. L. Polak. On the right is his secretary, and standing behind him are two office clerks.

devoted wife in leading him to see the virtues of a life committed to nonviolence.

Gandhi's mother also had a deep influence on his life. She was a devout Hindu, who revealed to him by her life of devotion the power of religious faith and fasting. When, at age 18, Gandhi went to England to study law, he made a vow to her that he would abstain from meat and wine while he was away. His determination to honor this vow set a pattern of persistence and discipline in keeping commitments for the rest of his life.

Gandhi stayed in England for just three years. He proved an able enough student to pass the London Matriculation examinations in Latin, French, and chemistry, and, a year later, his law examinations. He was admitted to the bar on June 10, 1891, enrolled in the High Court on June 11, and sailed for India on June 12.

Shy and sensitive, Gandhi was not able to establish a law practice in Bombay, nor with his brother back in Porbandar. He therefore leapt at an opportunity with a local firm of Muslim merchants to work on a case in South Africa. The original assignment was for one year. But in the course of that year, he became so involved in the plight of Indians living in South Africa that he stayed there for more than 20 years—and changed the course of history in two continents.

IN SOUTH AFRICA

Gandhi's first intense encounter with discrimination against Indians in South Africa came when he was thrown out of a first-class compartment of the train he was taking to Pretoria in 1893. His enraged reaction to this and subsequent affronts convinced him that an appropriate response would be to encourage the diffuse group of Indians living there to work together to protest the many abuses they all experienced as nonwhites in that country. He became engrossed in organizing campaigns and demonstrations for Indian rights. Finding his work demanding and effective, he decided to stay in Africa. He established a law practice in Johannesburg to support his family, whom he brought from India in 1896, and his reform efforts. He also set up a weekly newspaper, *Indian Opinion,* and purchased a farm at Phoenix on which to set up a commune to maintain the paper's publication.

As the South African government imposed more and more restraints on the Indian people living in the country, Gandhi orchestrated a series of nonviolent protest demonstrations, which engaged increasing numbers of Indians. His last protest march recruited more than 2,000 men, women, and children, and was joined in sympathy by 50,000 miners and indentured laborers. Such wide participation led the government to reconsider its policy and enact a law in 1914 to prohibit offensive discriminatory practices against all Indians living in South Africa. This movement was so ordered and disciplined by his own commitment to effective nonviolent resistance, which he called *satyagraha,* or Soul Force, that Gandhi emerged from this experience a leader of immense stature. He was someone to be reckoned with in South Africa, an achievement that was noticed in England and India.

The direction of Gandhi's growth in South Africa was, in a significant way, thrust upon him. He could have been treated there with polite respect, done his job, and returned to India unnoticed. That he was physically thrown out of the railway car was not a deliberate act of his own doing. In responding to this immediate experience of social injustice, he gained a sense of something much greater than just what was happening to him. He was discovering a personal mission that he felt compelled to fulfill: to bring together an oppressed people in a quest for social justice.

Being by temperament introspective, deliberate, even fastidious, Gandhi searched for the resources to meet this challenge within himself. This quest brought him to affirm intuitively—for he had no formal training in its conceptual intricacies—two precepts drawn from the classical heritage of South Asia. First, and more consciously, Gandhi identified his mission with the ancient concept of *dharma,* of cosmic moral order. This concept was set forward in the early Sanskrit epics, the *Mahabharata* and the *Ramayana,* as the proper behavior for ruling princes—not only as the moral foundation of their authority to rule, but also as the source of the well-being and prosperity of their subjects.

Gandhi pursued the private aspect of dharma—the moral foundation for leadership—with determination. His autobiography, *The Story of My Experiments with Truth,* written mostly in 1926, is replete with descriptions of his attempts to discipline his personal life around issues of celibacy, vegetarianism, purification, and self-control. He continued this pattern of moral exploration and testing throughout his life, always seeking to be better prepared—by which he meant morally adequate—to undertake the public tasks that he felt compelled to perform. Even toward the end of the long struggle for national independence, Gandhi did not question whether the British would grant freedom to the people of the subcontinent. Rather, his greatest concern was whether he, personally, was morally pure enough to lead the people of India to this goal.

Equally important to Gandhi was the public aspect of dharma—that it was to be realized for everyone's benefit. The cosmic dimension of dharma is realized not in the abstract, nor just in one's personal life, but in the public affairs of humanity. This awareness made his personal experience of discrimination in South Africa a public offense. It would be righted only when discrimination would not be practiced against any Indian residing there. Gandhi's awareness of the epic precept of dharma made him sensitive not only to the stringent moral demands of his mission, but also to the magnitude of its objective. He ultimately sought to liberate a people not just from the injustice of colonial rule but from all oppression, to allow them to become truly free.

The second precept of the classical heritage that Gandhi affirmed by his experience in South Africa was an awareness of a truer, deeper reality of "self" than he normally experienced in the everyday world. He experienced glimpses of a more ultimate reality of being, what in the classical heritage of South Asia was called *atma.* In his quest for this higher being of self, Gandhi intuited that a vital quality that distinguishes it from the ordinary experience of self is that it is by nature nonviolent: "Non-violence is not a garment to be put on and off at will. Its seat is in the heart, and it must be an inseparable part of our very being." It was this deeper, more refined self that was to define the distinctive character of the mission to which he had been called—that only the means could justify the end. Above all else, it had to be nonviolent.

Gandhi's concern to reduce the level of violence in our everyday lives and in the world around us reinforced his moral image of dharma. Joined with an intimation of atma, nonviolence requires a discipline that identifies and refines our awareness of our true self.

> The acquisition of the spirit of non-violence is a matter of long training in self-denial and appreciation of the hidden forces within ourselves. It changes one's outlook on life; it is the greatest force because it is the highest expression of the soul.

Gandhi's experience of these important concepts of dharma and atma, drawn from his South Asian cultural heritage, identified him on a profound level with the people from India who were then living in South Africa. He spoke to them out of a context to which they were uniquely prepared to respond as a distinct group of people. It is also significant that his initial steps to leadership took place a great distance away from India. Author V. S. Naipaul, based upon his own upbringing as an Indian in Trinidad, describes an important social dimension to Indian life that Gandhi could only have experienced outside of India:

> These overseas Indian groups were mixed. They were miniature Indias, with Hindus and Muslims, and people of different castes. They were disadvantaged, without representation, and without a political tradition. They were isolated by language and culture from the people they found themselves among; they were isolated from India itself. In these special circumstances they developed something they never would have

known in India: a sense of belonging to an Indian community. This feeling of community could override religion and caste.

Naipaul goes on to write that it was essential for Gandhi to have begun his freedom movement among the Indian peoples in South Africa. "It is during his . . . years in South Africa that intimations came to Gandhi of an all-India religious-political mission."

Had he begun in India, he would not have known for whom he was seeking independence. In South Africa, Gandhi discovered a destiny for a people to become a free nation. As in the case of his own sense of mission, Gandhi returned to India with the conviction that it would not happen until the people of India had discovered their soul.

RETURN TO INDIA

Gandhi returned to India in 1915, at the age of 45. By then, he was recognized as a national hero to a people without a nation. Soon, he was widely acclaimed as the *Mahatma,* the "Great Souled One."

Gandhi worked toward the removal of British colonial domination in India much as he had worked to overcome discrimination in South Africa: by addressing particular instances of oppression. These did not initially involve the government. Gandhi first addressed the inequities between English plantation owners and peasants (in the eastern province of Bihar), and Indian mill owners and mill workers (in the western city of Ahmedabad). Feeling that Indian independence from British colonial rule should not replace one oppression with another, he attacked the subservient role placed upon women in Indian society. He also took up the plight of "untouchable" communities—what he called "the ulcer of untouchability" in Indian life. Between 1915 and 1948, Gandhi initiated hundreds of nonviolent protest actions against a wide range of social injustices and abuse throughout the country.

One of Gandhi's most important achievements during the independence movement of India was leading the diverse peoples of the subcontinent to a shared vision of what it meant to be free. Drawing upon the importance of symbolic thought as developed in the classical heritage of his people, he insisted that people of all stations and walks of life take on the daily discipline of spinning thread for their clothing on a spinning wheel. This action not only freed them from the economic tyranny of dependence upon cloth manufactured in England; but more important, as an expression of individual independence, spinning encouraged them to be self-reliant even while living under the burden of British colonial rule.

Gandhi's most dramatic act of satyagraha was in 1930, when he led his followers from Ahmedabad on a 200-mile walk to collect salt from the sea, in protest against the salt tax imposed by the British government. What began as a march of 78 men and boys specially trained to undertake the journey with him gathered more and more people as they made their way through the Gujarati countryside. By the time the column

of marchers reached Dandi on the shore, the company had grown to thousands. The Oscar-winning film *Gandhi* gives a vivid picture not only of the energetic figure of Gandhi himself leading the march, but also of the dramatic swelling of the crowds who joined behind him to make the salt march such a powerful expression of public support. Gandhi compared it to the Boston Tea Party, which anticipated the war for independence in America. The march was the culminating act of a series of nonviolent protests against British rule that led to the beginning of home rule in 1937, and the total withdrawal of British colonial government in 1947.

These examples reveal Gandhi's immense power to draw people into the modern political process by creating powerful symbolic actions. In performing them, people in all reaches of British India began to assert and discover the qualities of freedom among some of the simplest and most immediate elements of their lives: their clothing and their food. These simple acts were symbolic in the classical sense in pointing beyond themselves to express what it is to be truly free.

Fasting became another aspect of Gandhi's leadership role during his years in India. He conducted 17 fasts "to the death." The first happened as a part of his efforts to resolve the dispute over wages between the mill workers and the mill owners in Ahmedabad in 1918, soon after his return from South Africa. Like his earlier actions, it was not premeditated but, rather, grew out of the circumstances in which he found himself in that dispute. The strike that he was urging the workers to sustain was exhausting their resources and their resolve. To encourage them to continue, he decided to subject himself to the same threat of starvation that the prolonged strike was imposing upon them. He would not demand of the striking workers more than he would demand of himself. And so he began a fast on March 15, 1918, which would continue until the workers received the wages they were demanding of the mill owners.

Unlike later fasts, there was not wide public awareness or concern. Nor was Gandhi himself totally comfortable with the coercive elements of his action. But the mill owners were moved by this dramatic placing of himself on the line. After three days, they agreed to a compromise in which all parties could feel some gain. Of more lasting significance, Gandhi's action and resolution did not allow the workers to abandon their own commitment to improve their lot. He taught them by example to become empowered by their own inner strength.

In 1932, Gandhi began a series of fasts based on his concern for the plight of the "untouchables" in India. He first protested the attempt by the British to set up separate untouchable electorates in a provisional government in British India, a policy that was supported by Dr. Ambedkar and other leaders of the untouchable communities. Gandhi's objection was that giving the untouchables separate political status removed from the Indian community as a whole the need to reform itself by to eliminating the scourge of discrimination and oppression based on caste. Dr. Ambedkar, however, saw

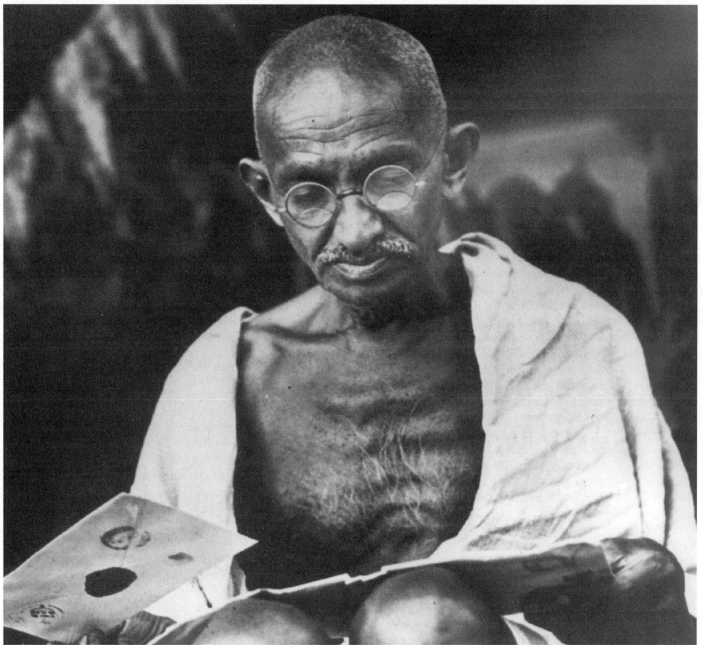

(Photo credit Bettmann Archives)

The protests against the British-imposed salt tax precipitated the India Round Table Conference in London in 1931. A controversy arose when Mahatma Gandhi appeared in his traditional garb, but it quickly settled when he emphatically declared that he would wear his customary attire even when being received by King George at Buckingham Palace. These talks, along with a number of nonviolent protests in India, led to the withdrawal of the British colonial government in 1947.

Gandhi's objection as an attempt to keep untouchables under Hindu oppression. But Gandhi was adamant, and on September 20, he began a fast to raise Hindu consciousness and alter the British proposal. Resolutions against discrimination and intense discussions with the untouchable leaders immediately ensued. Five days later, a compromise pact was achieved and sent to London, where it was accepted by the prime minister. By this fast, Gandhi made a significant impact, for the first time, on a specific British government policy in India. And, as fate would have it, it happened while he was imprisoned in Yeravda Prison, where he had been detained since January of that year under a century-old regulation that allowed the government to hold him for suspected sedition, without sentence or trial.

During the spring of 1933, Gandhi fasted again on behalf of the untouchable communities, this time not to achieve a specific political objective, but as an act of purification. He described it as "an uninterrupted twenty-one days' prayer."

Gandhi fasted twice during the final year of his life, in Calcutta from September 1 to 5, 1947, and in New Delhi, beginning on January 13, 1948. In both instances, he was responding to the communal rioting between Hindus and Muslims following the partition of British India and the independence of India and Pakistan on August 15, 1947. By this time, as Gandhi entered his 78th year, people throughout the subcontinent were caught up in daily reports on the state of his health during the fasts. And they were stirred to meet his expectations of amity between the two new countries and among the religious communities that resided in both. In January, Gandhi specifically demanded as a condition of ending his fast the reparation to Pakistan of its share of British India's assets retained by the Indian government. When that was done, the Pakistani foreign minister before the United Nations Security Council directly attributed to Gandhi's fast a "new and tremendous wave of feeling and desire for friendship between the two Dominions."

By his many and creative acts for freedom and by his fasting, Gandhi was able to command enormous authority among the people—all without the benefit of any political office. During his many years of leadership of the independence movement, he held only one elective office. He served as president of the Indian National Congress in 1925, but held the position for only one year. He stepped down to give a place to Sarojini Naidu, the first woman to be elected to that office.

Being out of political office seemed to increase the impact of his singular, moral basis for authority. It was even more commanding when he took moral positions in direct confrontation with the institutional authority structures of this time. He spent 2,049 of his politically most active days—in total, more than 5½ years—in jail. His self-affirming authority as a political figure and his commitment to nonviolence as the guiding principle for political action won for Gandhi universal recognition as the conscience of an empire and the "Father of the Republic of India."

Any sense of achievement that Gandhi might have felt because of India's independence in 1947 was negated by the scourge of communal rioting and bloodshed that swept across the subcontinent as the specter of partition of British India into two separate countries loomed. As the time of independence approached, Gandhi did not go to the capital to see the reins of power passed. Instead, he walked from village to village in the Noakhali district of East Bengal, seeking to quench the flames of violence that scorched that land. Gandhi himself was shaken, doubting his effectiveness in bringing the message of nonviolence to the people. Lord Mountbatten, who was in New Delhi as the governor-general of newly independent India, described Gandhi's effectiveness in a very different way: "In the Punjab we have 55,000 soldiers and large scale rioting is on our hands. In Bengal our forces consist of one man, and there is no rioting."

THE END

Gandhi remained convinced that Muslims and Hindus could live at peace together in a single, secular nation. For Gandhi, truth was not the exclusive possession of any religious community but, rather, what revealed the transcendent unity of all people. But this conviction was to cost him his life.

A young Hindu, passionately afraid that Gandhi was threatening Hinduism by being too accommodating to Muslims, assassinated him at his evening prayer meeting on January 30, 1948. That evening, Gandhi's long-time friend and protégé, the prime minister of the newly formed government of India, Jawaharlal Nehru, announced his death over the radio:

> Our beloved leader, Bapu, as we call him, the father of our nation is no more . . . . The light has gone out, I said, and yet I was wrong. For the light that shone in this country was no ordinary light. The light that has illumined this country for these many years will illumine this country for many more years . . .and the world will see it and it will give solace to innumerable hearts.

In leading the vastly diverse peoples of India to their independence through the early years of the twentieth century, Gandhi learned that political power is normally based on oppression and the use of force. Such power leads only to bondage, violence, and suffering. It became his conviction that political freedom cannot be achieved by force—he believed that it can be realized only in discovering within ourselves a more profound and demanding quality of human identity and relationship, a quality that is characterized by nonviolence. Only when we become genuinely nonviolent in ourselves and in our relationships with others can we become truly ourselves. Nations also must become genuinely nonviolent. Then they, too, will discover their identity as a people that is inclusive of all who live within their borders. Only then can we begin to think about achieving peace among nations.

Eric Ericson, in his perceptive biography of Mahatma Gandhi called *Gandhi's Truth,* describes this insight as a profound source of hope for the survival of the human race:

> To have faced mankind with nonviolence as the alternative to [such policing activities as the British massacre in Amritsar] marks the Mahatma's deed in 1919. In a period when proud statesmen could speak of a "war to end war"; when the superpolicemen of Versailles could bathe in the glory of a peace that would make "the world safe for democracy"; when the revolutionaries in Russia could entertain the belief that terror could initiate an eventual "withering away of the State"—during that same period, one man in India confronted the world with the strong suggestion that a new political instrument, endowed with a new kind of religious fervor, may yet provide mankind with a choice.

India Map

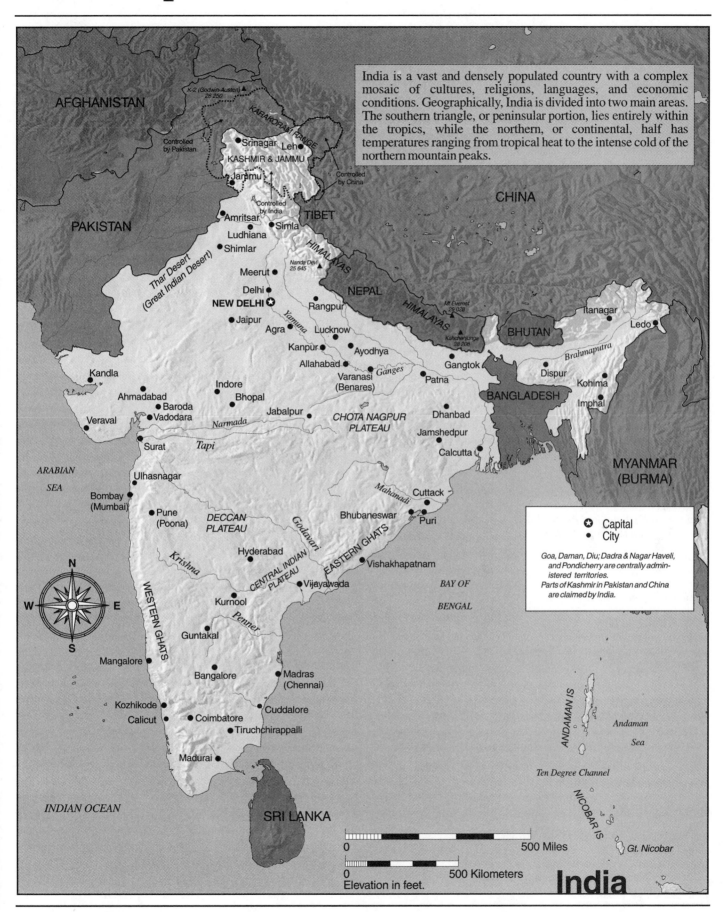

India is a vast and densely populated country with a complex mosaic of cultures, religions, languages, and economic conditions. Geographically, India is divided into two main areas. The southern triangle, or peninsular portion, lies entirely within the tropics, while the northern, or continental, half has temperatures ranging from tropical heat to the intense cold of the northern mountain peaks.

AFGHANISTAN

K-2 (Godwin-Austen) 28,250

KARAKORAM RANGE

Controlled by Pakistan

Srinagar
Leh
KASHMIR & JAMMU

Jammu

Controlled by China

CHINA

PAKISTAN

Controlled by India

Amritsar
Ludhiana
Shimlar
Simla
TIBET

HIMALAYAS

Nanda Devi 25,645

Meerut

Delhi
NEW DELHI

Jaipur

Agra

Yamuna

Rangpur

Lucknow

NEPAL

HIMALAYAS

Mt Everest 29,028

Kanchenjunga 28,208

Itanagar
Ledo

BHUTAN

Brahmaputra

Thar Desert (Great Indian Desert)

Kanpur
Ayodhya
Allahabad
Varanasi (Benares)
Ganges
Patna
Gangtok
Dispur
Kohima

Kandla
Ahmadabad
Baroda
Vadodara
Veraval
Indore
Bhopal
Jabalpur
Narmada
CHOTA NAGPUR PLATEAU
Dhanbad
Jamshedpur
BANGLADESH
Imphal

Surat
Tapi
Calcutta

MYANMAR (BURMA)

ARABIAN SEA

Ulhasnagar

Bombay (Mumbai)
Pune (Poona)
DECCAN PLATEAU
Godavari
Mahanadi
Cuttack
Bhubaneswar
Puri

Hyderabad
CENTRAL INDIAN PLATEAU
Vijayawada
EASTERN GHATS
Vishakhapatnam

⊗ Capital
• City

Goa, Daman, Diu; Dadra & Nagar Haveli, and Pondicherry are centrally administered territories.
Parts of Kashmir in Pakistan and China are claimed by India.

Krishna

Kurnool

Penner

BAY OF BENGAL

N
W E
S

WESTERN GHATS

Guntakal

Mangalore
Bangalore
Madras (Chennai)

ANDAMAN IS

Andaman Sea

Kozhikode
Calicut
Coimbatore
Cuddalore
Tiruchchirappalli

Madurai

Ten Degree Channel

NICOBAR IS

INDIAN OCEAN

SRI LANKA

Gt. Nicobar

0   500 Miles

0   500 Kilometers
Elevation in feet.

India

35

India (Republic of India)

GEOGRAPHY
Area in Square Miles (Kilometers):
1,269,010 (3,287,590) (about one third
the size of the United States)
Capital (Population): New Delhi (8,300,000)
Environmental Concerns: soil erosion;
deforestation; overgrazing;
desertification; air and water pollution;
lack of potable water; overpopulation
Geographical Features: upland plain
(Deccan Plateau) in south; flat to rolling
plain along the Ganges; deserts in the
west; Himalaya Mountains in the north
Climate: varies from tropical monsoon in
the south, to temperate in the north, to
arctic in the Himalayas

PEOPLE

Population
Total: 1,000,850,000
Annual Growth Rate: 1.68%
Rural/Urban Population Ratio: 72/28
Major Languages: Hindi; English; Bengali;
Telugu; Marathi; Tamil; Urdu; others; 24
languages each spoken by 1 million or
more persons; numerous other languages
and dialects
Ethnic Makeup: 72% Indo-Aryan groups;
25% Dravidian; 3% Mongoloid and others
Religions: 80% Hindu; 14% Muslim; 2%
Christian; 2% Sikh; 2% Buddhist, Jain,
and others

Health
Life Expectancy at Birth: 63 years (male);
64 years (female)
Infant Mortality Rate (Ratio): 60.8/1,000
Physicians Available (Ratio): 1/2,173

Education
Adult Literacy Rate: 52%
Compulsory (Ages): theoretically
compulsory in 23 states to age 14

COMMUNICATION
Telephones: 1 per 78 people
Daily Newspaper Circulation: 21 per 1,000
people
Televisions: 1 per 25 people

TRANSPORTATION
Highways in Miles (Kilometers): 1,991,786
(3,319,644)
Railroads in Miles (Kilometers): 37,477
(62,462)
Usable Airfields: 341
Motor Vehicles in Use: 6,550,000

GOVERNMENT
Type: federal republic
Independence Date: August 15, 1947 (from
the United Kingdom)
Head of State/Government: President
Kicheril Raman Narayanan; Prime
Minister Atal Behari Vajpayee

Political Parties: Congress Party; Bharatiya
Janata Party; Bahujan Samaj Party;
Communist Party of India/Marxist;
Janata Dal Party; Samajwadi Party;
All-India Forward Bloc; United Front;
many regional parties
Suffrage: universal at 18

MILITARY
Military Expenditures (% of GDP): 2.7%
Current Disputes: communal unrest;
militant nationalist movements; claims to
Kashmir with Pakistan; border disputes
with China; refugee repatriation,
territorial, and water-sharing disputes
with Bangladesh

ECONOMY
Currency ($ U.S. Equivalent): 46.58 rupees = $1
Per Capita Income/GDP: $1,720/$1.689
trillion
GDP Growth Rate: 6%
Inflation Rate: 8.2%
Natural Resources: coal; iron ore;
manganese; mica; bauxite; titanium ore;
chromite; natural gas; diamonds;
petroleum; limestone

Agriculture: rice; wheat; oilseed; cotton; jute;
tea; sugarcane; potatoes; livestock; fish
Industry: electronics; textiles; chemicals;
food processing; steel; machinery;
transportation equipment; cement;
mining; petroleum
Exports: $32.1 billion (primary partners
United States, Hong Kong, United Kingdom)
Imports: $41.3 billion (primary partners
United States, Belgium, United Kingdom)

http://www.wcmc.org.uk/igcmc/
main.html#APP
http://www.cia.gov/cia/publications/
factbook/geos/in.html
http://www.economictimes.com
http://www.economictimes.com/
today/pagepoli.htm
http://www.indiaserver.com/
thehindu/thehindu.html
http://www.newsindia-times.com/
http://www.gorp.com/gorp/location/
asia/india/np_into.htm
http://www.indnet.org
http://www.123india.com
http://southasia.net/India/

INDIA

India is by far the largest of the countries of South Asia. It is also the land of greatest contrasts. It is the only country to extend through all of the subcontinent's geographical regions, from the frigid, snowy peaks of the Himalayas, more than 25,000 feet high, down to the hot, tropical beaches of the Malabar Coast on the Laccadive Sea. And its population is incredibly diverse, divided by languages, religions, and cultures, by cities and villages, by extremes of poverty and wealth.

India's diverse population is also expanding, at a national annual growth rate of 1.68 percent. On May 11, 2000, the government of India officially recognized the birth of the child who extended its population to 1 billion people. This number represents about 16 percent of the entire population of the world, on only about 2.3 percent of its total land mass. That is about 3½ times more people than live in the United States, in one third the amount of space.

India reaches farthest to the north among the high peaks of the Karakuram Range in the western Himalayan Mountains, beyond the glacial plateau of Ladakh. There, west of Tibet, India shares a disputed border with China. This boundary extends east through the high ridges of the Himalayas, skirting the mountainous kingdoms of Nepal and Bhutan to the hill country of the northeast frontier. There it again encounters a contested border with China, before swinging south along the western edge of Myanmar (Burma) and back around Bangladesh to the Bay of Bengal.

Because of the high altitude and the unrelenting arctic cold of the barren glaciers coursing the steep, southern slopes of the Himalayas, much of the northern border area of India is uninhabitable. The average population density of this mountainous region is a sparse 70 people per square mile, who are interspersed among the high peaks and the foothills in protected gorges and fertile valleys that sustain isolated settlements. Most of the Himalayan peoples tend flocks of sheep, yak, and goats; or they work the tea plantations and orchards on the lower foothills. In some seasons they form small bands of traders and bearers, making arduous, heavy-laden treks through the snow-clad passes over the divide into Tibet. The extreme height, isolation, and breathtaking beauty of this region have found expression in a multitude of distinctive folk traditions of colorful art, music, and dance. Numerous Buddhist monasteries dot the rugged mountain landscape.

This remote Himalayan region is the source of a great river system: the Jumna-Ganges. These rivers provide an uneven but unbroken flow of life-sustaining water down the mountain valleys and into the great northern plains, the "breadbasket" of northern India. The cultivation of grains and rice is the main economic activity on these plains, by peoples who live closer and closer together as the region extends to the east toward the Bay of Bengal. The density of the rural population rises to more than 2,000 people per square mile in the delta area of the Ganges River.

The great central plain of northern India is the most arable part of the country. It is also the most populated, and historically the most influential, region. The great empires of India—the Mauryan (320–125 B.C.), Gupta (A.D. 250–500), and Moghul (A.D. 1508–1857) dynasties—rose to prominence in this region. New Delhi, the capital of India, is located at the upper end of the central plains region, on the Jumna River. Although it became the capital of colonial British India only in 1911, it is from this site that Islamic sultans in the thirteenth century and Moghul kings in the sixteenth century controlled the plains to the east and the Deccan Plateau to the south. Farther east on the Ganges are the even more ancient cities of Varanasi and Patna, known before the time of the Buddha in the sixth century B.C. as Kasi and Pataliputra, renowned for their commerce and learning. Much of India's wondrous classical tradition in art, literature, music, and philosophy evolved during the times of imperial dominance and patronage. Even today, the Gangetic plains retain their importance in the political and cultural life of India.

Rising to the south of the Gangetic plains, in peninsular India, is a wide plateau flanked by two mountain ranges. These ranges, though smaller and warmer than the Himalayas, are also sparsely populated. They have long provided refuge for renegade princes, slopes for coffee and tea plantations, shelters for wild game, and homes for most of India's tribal population.

As in the central plain, most of the people in the Deccan Plateau live in small villages and are dependent upon agriculture for their subsistence. Because the only sources of water for farming are the seasonal, but unpredictable, annual rains brought by the southwest monsoon, this region has not had the economic base for the political domination experienced in the Gangetic plains. Only when the great empires of the north have swept south has this region shared in a common history with the rest of the country. Otherwise, separated by geography and language, the Deccan has supported many local kingdoms and developed its own traditions and distinctive cultures.

Three of India's larger and most industrial cities—Hyderabad, Ahmadabad, and Bangalore—are in the Deccan region. Ahmadabad, long known for its textile mills, is today capital of India's fastest-growing industrial state. Bangalore has become the center of the nation's high-technology industries: telephones, jet engines, and computers. Hyderabad is also rapidly developing its own high-tech industries.

The fourth region of India is the coastal plain, a narrow strip of low-lying, tropical land around the edge of the Indian peninsula. During the rainy monsoon seasons, this plain is filled with luxuriant growth, especially along the southwest Malabar Coast. Its rich harvests of rice and fruits support the highest rural population density in the country—more than 4,000 people per square mile.

India's two largest urban centers, the port cities of Calcutta and Bombay (Mumbai), and its fourth-largest city, Madras

(United Nations)

The central plains are the most arable region of India and account for much of the country's grain production. This rice field produces a large quantity of grain, which is harvested by traditional labor-intensive methods.

(Chennai), are in this coastal region. These cities were built during the expansion of European commerce in the sixteenth and seventeenth centuries. They became thriving hubs of commerce under British colonial rule. Today, they are the most important centers for banking, investment capital, and international trade for all of India.

India's largest cities are spread throughout the different regions, except for the Himalayas. And they are expanding rapidly. The average increase in population of India's five largest cities from 1980 to 2000 was more than 103 percent per *year*. The population of Bombay is projected by the United Nations to almost double in a decade, from 15 million in 1995 to 27.4 million by 2005. That will make Bombay the second-largest city in the world. By then, India will have the largest urban population in the world.

This increase in population is due as much to in-migration from the villages, due to the lure of urban opportunity, as to the high birth rate and increasing life expectancy of urban dwellers. With this dramatic increase, the pressure on urban lands and services is staggering, the ability to cope near—many people would say past—its limit.

This limit was certainly passed by an outburst of urban rioting, resulting in widespread destruction and bloodshed, that erupted in Bombay for 10 days in January 1993. It began in a climate of communal tension between Hindus and Muslims throughout the nation following the destruction of a Muslim mosque in Ayodhya in north-central India on December 6, 1992. Roused to violence, mobs swept through the slum areas of the city, burning, stabbing, and looting. According to Humans Rights Watch, more than 1,000 people were killed and thousands wounded. Many more fled, homeless, to other parts of the country in the wake of this devastation. While revealing tensions of national scope, the Bombay riots also expressed the latent social unrest and uncontrollable violence that lurk amid the increasing economic hardship and oppression that accompany such a fast-growing urban population.

Even with this staggering urban growth, India's cities still hold only 28 percent of the total population of the country. Nearly three quarters of the population live in small, agricultural villages. For the foreseeable future India will be primarily a rural country, a nation of villages that are tied to traditional patterns of life in separate geographic environments that are strikingly diverse in terrain, temperatures, rainfall, food production, and population densities.

THE SOCIETY

The differences among the geographic regions of India and between urban and rural life within the regions are not the only sources of contrast in this diverse country. Even within a single region, people are divided in many other ways—by language, by religion, and by complex social groupings called *castes*. The differences in the geography from region to region contribute to, but do not wholly account for, the complex mingling of distinct languages and religions and communities that are found in such wide array throughout the country. India is a land of so many contrasts that one wonders how it holds together. From the day of its independence as a nation in 1947, India has been especially challenged to find its political identity as a multiethnic, multireligious, multilingual country.

Language

A recent comprehensive ethnographic study, "Peoples of India," identified 324 distinct languages used in the country. Among these are the major languages used in the northern plains region. Hindi is the most prevalent, but others spoken widely include Bengali, Punjabi, Bihari, and Urdu. All of these belong to the Indo-European family of languages. Other languages with Indo-European roots (Oriya, Marathi, and Gujarati) extend beyond the northern plains region into the northern parts of the Deccan and the coastal plain. The languages spoken in the southern part of peninsular India (Tamil, Telugu, Kanarese, and Malayalam) belong to a totally different family of languages, the Dravidian family.

The Constitution of the Republic of India recognizes 17 different Indo-European and Dravidian languages in the country. This list does not include English, which is still the "link language"—the language of higher education, the professions, and national business and government in most parts of the nation. Nor does it include the many tongues spoken by the mountain and tribal peoples who live in the remote regions of the north, east, and peninsular India. These languages belong to the very different families of languages that are spoken by Tibetans, Burmese (people of Myanmar), and even by the Aboriginal peoples of Australia.

The peoples of India have long been separated into distinct language groups; or, looking at it from their point of view, they share a unique identity with those who speak the same mother tongue. These language groups are predominant in particular parts of the country, a native place toward which those language speakers venerate a sense of social roots, even when they have traveled far afield. The government of India recognized the importance of this language identity when, soon after the country's independence from British colonial rule, it established the boundaries of new states. The old British colonial province of Bombay, for example, was divided in 1956 into the states of Maharashtra and Gujarat. A political boundary was then set between those who speak mainly the Marathi language and those for whom Gujurati is the mother tongue.

The political divisions in these instances were based on language, and not the other way around. In India, each individual's identification with a particular language comes about through the family into which one is born—by one's mother—not by one's location. Adjusting the boundaries of a new state to coincide with the predominance of a language group did not change the linguistic identity of those who speak other mother tongues in that state. These other-language speakers live as minority groups, many times in enclaves in order to preserve the distinctive ethos of their linguistic identities. These different linguistic groups are clearly identifiable in the cities—for example, as Bengalis and Tamils in Bombay (now called Mumbai), or as Malayalis and Telugus in Madras (Chennai).

India is a nation of linguistic minorities. No single language is spoken or understood by more than 40 percent of the people. There have been efforts since India became independent in 1947 to establish Hindi, the most prevalent language among the states in the north-central region of India, as the national language. The states of the other regions of the country have resisted this status for *any* language, particularly one that is not their own. People cannot easily accept having their political identity defined, nor their primary education taught, in any other language than their own.

Religion

India is divided also by religions, but in a different pattern, and in a slightly different way. Hindi is nationally a minority language in spite of its prevalence in several of the northern states. But people belonging to the Hindu religion comprise some 80 percent of the total population and command a majority in almost every region of the country. Islam is the largest of the minority religions—there are 140 million Muslims in India, close to the total populations of the neighboring Islamic countries, Pakistan and Bangladesh. Muslims are nevertheless only about 14 percent of the total population of India. All other religious minorities—Sikhs, Jains, Christians, Buddhists, and others—together add up to only 6 percent of the population.

The minority religious groups tend, however, to concentrate in specific regions of the country, in large enough numbers to be politically significant. Muslims are an overwhelming majority in Kashmir, and they are a sizable minority in the north-central state of Uttar Pradesh. Sikhs comprise approximately 62 percent of the population in the Punjab. And Jains are in sufficient numbers in Gujarat, and Christians along the southwest Malabar Coast, to have an impact on the cultural, educational, and political aspects of life in those areas.

Economic Disparity

A four-year-old girl with her legs crippled by polio drags herself to the nearest open drain in Bombay's shantytown Dharavi. She cups the foul-smelling water and pours it on her body. That is her daily morning bath, a ritual repeated by children in thousands of slums across the country.

Some 15 miles south of Dharavi in the expensive neighborhood of Altamount Road, the six-year-old son of a wealthy businessman has a massive birthday bash on the manicured lawns of his father's palatial villa as similar rich children from the neighborhood ride around on camels and ponies supplied for the occasion.

What bonds these two children are the extremes of life that India's 350 million children face every day. By all accounts, the children in the condition that the Dharavi girl finds herself grossly outnumber those who can afford the lifestyle of the boy on Altamount Road.

—Neelish Misra, *India Abroad* (November 1, 1996)

Another challenge in modern India is the extent and the visibility, especially in the urban areas, of poverty. It is estimated that about 20 percent of India's urban population live in slums. And in Calcutta it is estimated that, beyond the slum dwellers, some 700,000 people sleep on the streets each night.

The scope of India's urban poverty is hard to imagine. V. S. Naipaul gives this vivid description of his visit to the Bombay slum called Dharavi:

Back-to-back and side-to-side shacks and shelters, a general impression of blackness and grayness and mud, narrow ragged lanes curving out of view; then a side of the main road dug up; then black mud, with men and women and children defecating on the edge of a black lake, swamp and sewage, with hellish oily iridescence. . . . [It] was also an industrial area of sorts, with many unauthorized businesses, leather works and chemical works among them which wouldn't have been permitted in a better regulated city area. . . . Petrol and kerosene fumes added to the stench. In this stench, many bare-armed people were at work: gathering or unpacking cloth waste and cardboard waste, working in grey-white dust that banked up on the ground like snow and stifled the sounds of hands and feet, working beside the road itself or in small shanties: large scale rag-picking.

—From India, A Million Mutinies Now

In all of India, some 35 percent of the population live in poverty, half of those in extreme poverty. But because the village economy is based upon the production and distribution of food in exchange for craft services or labor—the *jajmani* system—low income does not necessarily mean starvation. As a result of the Green Revolution, which in the late 1950s resulted from the introduction of new, hybrid strains of rice and wheat, grain production has increased dramatically. Since 1970, India has imported grains only once, in 1987, when monsoon rain failure diminished the yields enough to create a shortage. Other times of famine have occurred in different parts of the country, especially after devastating earthquakes and typhoons. And many millions of people in both cities and villages live continually on the edge of subsistence. Without some reduction in India's birth rate and an increase in urban planning and control, it is hard to imagine how the nation's considerable economic progress will be able to reduce the anguish of poverty and environmental decay for

an increasing number of its population. All of the gains now have to be distributed among too many additional needy people.

Remarkable in this context has been the emergence during the past decade of a significant middle class, of households that are earning more than is necessary for mere survival— food, clothing, and housing. A report to the Millennium Conference, held in New Delhi in February 2000, estimated about 25 percent of India's total population as being affluent and upper middle class, with sufficient income to stimulate a market economy as consumers. These people are creating new markets, new opportunities, and new objectives for a population long characterized as impoverished, austere, and subject to very restrictive economic planning and import controls. Another 40 percent of the population is identified as lower middle class. This group has for the most part risen out of the throes of subsistence and is increasing the level of household incomes at impressive rates. National economic policy began to change in 1985, several years before the collapse of the socialist economy in the Soviet Union, so that today, India is well on its way to being a consumer-driven economy. Change is in the air.

A COUNTRY OF CHANGE
Change is expected in India. This attitude is revealed in the dramatic anticipation each year of the time and amount of the monsoon rains, which sometimes bring flood-producing torrents to end an intolerably hot, dry spring season, and sometimes produces very little rain at all. It also has to do with the unpredictable, terrifying specter of disease and sudden death;

(United Nations/Jongen)

Poverty is very pronounced in India's urban areas. An estimated 20 percent of India's urban population live in slums. These squatters are preparing a meal in the only home they have, the street.

(United Nations)

In 1950, India adopted its Constitution, thus formally establishing itself as a democratic, secular nation. The first prime minister of this new country was Jawarhalal Nehru (above left), the head of the Congress Party.

with the rise and fall of fortunes and of transient petty kingdoms and even mighty empires. The people have a conscious heritage of many thousands of years, during which countless profound changes have taken place.

The word for "life" in India is *samsara,* which literally means "flowing," like a river. Sometimes, like a river in flood, change is traumatic. Such was the partition of India and Pakistan at the time of their independence from British colonial rule in 1947. Millions of people suddenly were displaced from their homes, and close to a million lost their lives in senseless, random massacres. The horrendous earthquake in Gujarat in January 2001 was also a traumatic event, destroying entire villages and causing the death of 30,000 people. For the most part, however, life in India flows in a single direction, never at quite the same pace, but usually within its banks. Life's flow is never quite predictable, but there are enough patterns to give a sense that in India, even in times of great change, everything is essentially very much the same.

The rate of total population growth in India presents such a picture of uneven, but significant, change. Nine of the states and union territories, mostly in the south of India, which govern about 12 percent of the total population, have made remarkable progress in reducing their rate of population growth in recent years to less than 1.2 percent per year. These states have shown that family-planning policies can control the rate of growth. And they are conscientiously working

toward a goal of eliminating growth altogether—of achieving a "replacement level" of population. However, 12 Indian states with 55 percent of the population still have growth rates above 2 percent. It is their lack of progress toward limiting growth that places the national growth rate at 1.68 percent. In February 2000, in response to this imbalance, the national government adopted for the first time a 10-year "population policy" that would encourage all of the states to work toward replacement levels of growth. It also proposed not to change the number of representatives from each state in the national Legislature for the next 25 years, so that no state would be penalized politically for reducing its proportion of the nation's population.

INDIA SINCE INDEPENDENCE

The substantial economic development and efforts to control population growth in India have occurred within the context of an enormous change in the lives of the Indian people: that is, with the achievement of independence in 1947, India became a democratic republic.

As a new nation, India had first to establish an independent, sovereign government, free of colonial domination. This task was achieved by the transition of the Indian National Congress—which had, since 1885, led the movement for India's political freedom—to the majority political party in a Constituent Assembly that had been set up by the British Raj in 1935. At the time of independence, the Congress Party formed an interim government, with its leader, Jawarhalal Nehru, serving as prime minister.

The formal beginning of the Republic of India as a democratic, secular nation took place with the adoption of its Constitution in 1950. This Constitution incorporated many concepts from Western political theory. Its framers, under the leadership of Dr. B. R. Ambedkar, deliberately drew upon the U.S., French, and Irish Constitutions as viable models for a modern democratic republic. Its Preamble has a familiar sound: "It is the responsibility of the Republic to ensure that all citizens enjoy"

> JUSTICE, social, economic, and political; LIBERTY of thought, expression, belief, faith and worship; EQUALITY of status and opportunity; and . . . FRATERNITY assuring the dignity of the individual and the unity of the nation.

And it granted to every adult in the country, male and female, the right to vote.

The Constitution of India separates the powers of the government into three branches: legislative, executive, and judicial. This pattern is familiar to Americans, though the relationship between the legislative and executive branches follows the parliamentary model of Great Britain. The initiative and responsibility for executive leadership rest in India's Parliament, in the office of the prime minister, not with the executive-branch president. Neither of these offices, prime minister or president, is attained by direct popular vote.

The president is elected to a five-year term by a majority of all the elected and appointed representatives to the two houses of the national Legislature: the *Lok Sabha* (House of the People), with 545 members; and the *Rajya Sabha* (Council of States), with 12 members appointed by the president and 238 members elected proportionately by the legislative assemblies in each of India's states. The role of the president is so severely limited by the Constitution that he or she rarely has an opportunity to determine national policy. But the president can, upon the advice of the prime minister, declare a state of emergency and suspend both national and state governments—an executive tool that has been used far more frequently than the framers of the Indian Constitution envisioned. In general the president serves more as a symbolic head of state.

The prime minister, as the person primarily responsible to lead the country, is officially invited by the president to form a ministry and conduct the business of government. But he or she must enjoy the support of a majority of the Lok Sabha to remain in power. The president therefore looks first to the leadership of the majority party to nominate its candidate for this position. In most national elections since 1952, the Congress Party has either won a majority of the seats in the Lok Sabha or has been able to hold together a ruling coalition of parties. As a result, the selection of the prime minister has typically been made within the ranks of the Congress Party. Recently, with the Congress Party no longer winning a majority of seats in the Legislature, the process has become more complex, and more tenuous.

In elections in the spring of 1991, the Congress Party won the most number of legislative seats, but it fell 37 seats short of a majority. President Ramaswamy Iyer Venkataraman still felt that the leader of the Congress Party, P. V. Narasimha Rao, was the person best suited to serve as prime minister, even though he did not at that time hold a seat in the Lok Sabha. The president invited him to form the government. Narasimha Rao was able to win the support of the Lok Sabha and subsequently won a seat in a November 1991 by-election. In further by-elections in February 1992, the Congress Party won enough seats to command a majority in Parliament, which it held for five years. Narasimha Rao's effective leadership and growing support showed that President Venkataraman's confidence in him was well placed.

In the next national elections, held in the spring of 1996, the Bharatiya Janata Party (BJP) and its allies won 186 seats, mostly from the north-central plains states. Narasimha Rao's Congress Party came in a distant second, with 136 seats. President Shankar Dayal Sharma initially invited Atal Behari Vajpayee, leader of the BJP, to become prime minister. But the BJP leader was not able to garner the support of the 269-seat majority needed to gain the confidence of the Lok Sabha, and he resigned even before the newly elected Legislature convened. President Sharma then invited the chief minister of the state of Karnataka, Deve Gowda, to form a government. Gowda, the leader of one of six political parties that formed the National Left Front coalition, was able, with the support of the Congress Party, to win the votes of a majority of the House and became prime minister. Not until November did he become a sitting member of Parliament. At that time, he was elected to a seat in the Rajya Sabha, or Upper House, by the Karnataka State Legislature.

Deve Gowda's United Front coalition government was not expected to survive very long, due to the tenuous alliance among so many parties and the government's dependency upon the support of the Congress Party. Yet Gowda managed to steer a sufficiently inclusive and moderate course in Parliament to hold the reins of power for almost a year. Then, in April 1997, the Congress Party chose to withdraw its support, and Gowda was forced to resign. In order to avoid holding new national elections, frantic negotiations began among the United Front parties and the Congress Party to find an acceptable prime minister. They finally agreed upon I. K. Gujral, who had been very successful as external-affairs minister in the Gowda government, to be the new leader of the United Front. With renewed but still tenuous Congress Party support, the United Front was thus able to continue in power. But just seven months later, the Congress Party withdrew its support for Gujral's government. With no further compromises in the offing, President Sharma dissolved Parliament and called for new elections in March 1998.

In the elections of 1998, the BJP again won the most legislative seats, but its 182-seat victory still fell short of commanding a majority. This time, however, BJP leader Vajpayee was able to bring together a coalition of 19 parties to form a government. He was able to hold this coalition together to remain in office as prime minister for a little more than a year. Then Jayalalitha, leader of one of the coalition parties to join with the BJP, withdrew her party's support of Vajpayee's government in the Lok Sabha, because she was unsuccessful in getting the Vajpayee government to intervene on her behalf in lawsuits accusing her of mismanagement of state funds. Without her party's votes, Vajpayee lost the majority of the Legislature he needed to continue as prime minister, and he was forced to resign. With no alternative leadership able to achieve a majority, new elections were then held again in the fall of 1999. The BJP was returned to power in a newly formed coalition of 24 parties, called the National Democratic Alliance.

According to the Constitution, an election must be held at least every five years. If none is called before that time, Parliament is automatically dissolved. All 545 members of the Lok Sabha must then stand for reelection in an electoral district in each of the states of India. Five uninterrupted years in office was the rule during the early years of the republic, when the government was firmly under the control of Prime Minister Jawarhalal Nehru. Nehru's charismatic leadership and commitment to democracy brought together many disparate interests into the Congress Party. Since Nehru's death in 1964, many of the country's social and regional factions have become more politically savvy in gaining their own representation in the national Legislature. The Lok Sabha has thus become more representative of the diversity of the country. However, its institutional authority has diminished, with regional, ethnic, and special interests more dominant. Thus, only those parties with the ability to keep so many disparate groups to a common political agenda are able to form a stable majority.

Establishing such coalitions entails a great deal of political bargaining and compromise. They tend to have a moderating impact on what can be accomplished in the Legislature. The BJP's move early in its first term to test the country's nuclear capability was, among other things, a dramatic attempt to establish a national awareness and agenda for its parliamentary leadership role. An event of such international consequence reveals the extent to which the party felt it had to go to gain legislative initiative. At the same time, it was the only plank on its election platform to which all of its coalition partners could readily agree.

The moderating impact of the need to form coalitions in order to win the support of a majority of the members of the Lok Sabha was also revealed early in the BJP's second term. At its national meeting in Madras in December 1999, the BJP declared a moratorium on three of its most important campaign issues—to build a temple on the site of the Babri Masjid mosque in Ayodhya, to remove the special federal status given to the state of Kashmir, and to adopt a uniform civil code—in order to hold the allegiance of its 24-party coalition in the national Legislature.

Democracy in a parliamentary form of government, as implemented in 1950 by the Constitution of the Republic of India, has worked well. The creation of political parties and the ballot box have been effective in establishing the public will and determining the direction of policy in the Lok Sabha on the national level, even for some of the most secessionist-minded groups in the country. The ballot box has also worked to determine the membership and agendas of the similarly structured, though less orderly, legislative assemblies on the state level and the municipal governments in the cities. A further step toward democracy was implemented in 1993, when India adopted a constitutional amendment that requires one third of all elected members of the local village councils (*panchayat*) throughout the country be women. A portion of these seats are reserved for women from the lower castes.

CHALLENGES TO DEMOCRACY

A great challenge to the democratic system of government in India came in 1975, when Prime Minister Indira Gandhi, in order to protect herself from a legal challenge to her office, had an "Emergency" proclaimed by the president, under the "President's Rule Provision" in the Constitution. That act suspended for two years the normal function of government and the civil liberties protected by the Constitution. National elections were postponed, opposition leaders were put in prison, and press censorship was imposed.

When national elections were reinstated in 1977, the people of India, voted Gandhi and the Congress Party out of office. They were not going to have their political freedom eroded. And theirs was the final say.

A second great challenge, though of a different sort, came with the destruction of a Muslim mosque in the northern city of Ayodhya on December 6, 1992. Hindu nationalist forces—sanctioned, if not actually led, by the popularly elected state government—roused communal religious antagonism among Hindus and Muslims throughout India and in surrounding countries. The riots that followed led to great misgivings about the ability of the government to maintain order and protect its people from uncontrolled violence. This Babri Masjid episode also raised questions, because of the communal tensions that were unleashed, about India's viability as a secular nation.

Both of these crises reveal the depth of the challenge that democracy in India still faces, after half a century of independence. Its future is not assured for many different reasons. One basic problem is that democracy in India has been implemented in political structures—a constitution and a parliament—that are not indigenous to India, but were instead imposed from the West. The effectiveness of these structures presupposes the existence of a nation as a unified sovereign entity, recognized and respected by the people. Indians' political awareness of themselves as a nation did not exist before these structures were put into place; the people have had to create for themselves a national identity. That challenge has not been easy.

In India, in contrast to the United States, there is no awareness of a total, inclusive community defined by a political event. In one sense, there are simply too many events, too much history in India to be affirmed. So many kingdoms and empires have been experienced so differently by so many different groups of people that they are not understood as shared. In addition, there are so many more immediate and compelling bases of their identity as communities. Thus, their existence as a nation, even since 1950, is more of an abstraction than an immediate reality.

During his travels across India, the writer V. S. Naipaul rediscovered this obstacle to national identity among the peoples of this disparate land. His awareness of being an Indian, which existed among those of many different languages and religions who had migrated from India to the Caribbean island of Trinidad, where he grew up, was not shared at all by the people who lived in India itself:

> When I got there I found [that the idea of an Indian community] had no meaning in India. In the torrent of India, with its hundreds of millions, that continental idea was no comfort at all. People needed to hold on to smaller ideas of who and what they were; they found stability in the smaller groupings of region, clan, caste, family.
>
> —From *India: A Million Mutinies Now*

(United Nations)

In India, religious identity often takes precedence over the idea of belonging to a nation. Many religious sects demand political recognition. In 1984, the Indian Army stormed the Golden Temple in Amritsar (pictured above), the sacred shrine of the Sikh community. This action was in response to Sikhs' demand for the establishment of an independent state in Punjab. In retaliation, a group of Sikhs assassinated Prime Minister Indira Gandhi.

The most pervasive of these smaller ideas of identity are not based on political groupings. They are, rather, linguistic, religious, and, as Naipaul suggests, social—such as caste, into which the people of India are grouped not by events, but by birth.

Language, because it was used to define the borders of states in India, has become the basis for regional political identity. It has also contributed to an awakening of political awareness. Being grouped together by language has identi- fied other causes that people share and can seek to achieve for their common good. Yet because there are so many languages, each predominant in a separate region of the country, but none commanding a majority in the country as a whole, language identity has not contributed to a sense of national identity. As in Canada and in some European countires, differing lan- guages have generated forces of disintegration rather than of unification.

Religious identity has also been a major factor in India's political experience since independence. The partition of In- dia and Pakistan in 1947 was done on the basis of the majority religion on the district (county) level in those regions of the subcontinent administered by the British Raj. Those districts that were predominantly Muslim went to Pakistan; those predominantly Hindu were apportioned to India.

Even though 80 percent of the people of India are identified as Hindus, they do not consider themselves as a political bloc. Their overwhelming number is still a source of great concern to those who find themselves a religious minority: Muslims, Sikhs, Parsis, Buddhists, Jains, Christians, and Jews. The call for the separate nation of Pakistan was due in large part to just this anxiety among the Muslim community in British India. How could such a predominantly Hindu society, determined to meet its own objectives in a democracy, not discriminate against, if not actually oppress, people of other religions?

The response of the leaders of the Indian National Con- gress—which for more than 50 years worked constructively and diligently for India's independence from British rule— was to define the Republic of India as a secular state. They argued that the government must recognize the presence and the integrity of the many different religious communities in the nation. It must not promote and interfere with them. In the words of India's Constitution, "all persons are equally enti- tled to freedom of conscience and the right freely to profess, practice, and propagate religion." The separation between the secular objectives of the nation-state and the religious identity of its peoples has not always been clear, revealing again that religious identity has taken precedence over the more abstract idea of "belonging" to a nation.

Two specific movements are challenging the commitment to political secularism in India today. First is the outright demand by a militant wing of the Sikh community for an independent state, called Khalistan, to be established in the current state of Punjab, in northwest India. A number of events have contributed to the vehemence and intensity of this nationalist demand, which was expressed for a time in almost daily, random terrorist attacks and kidnappings. These acts of violence led to the suspension in Punjab of the elections that took place in most of the rest of India during the spring of 1991. Most provocative was the storming of the Golden Temple in Amritsar, the sacred shrine of the entire Sikh community, by the Indian Army in 1984. This attack, called Operation Blue Star, was meant to rout out of the temple's protective walls a militant Sikh separatist leader who had sought sanctuary there. The outrage felt by the Sikh commu- nity over this assault was expressed by the assassination later that same year of Prime Minister Indira Gandhi by two members of her bodyguard who were Sikhs. Her death in turn stirred reprisals against the Sikh community, leading to the killing of some 3,000 in riots across the north of India. Political order was restored in Punjab under the leadership of a more moderate Sikh, Prakash Singh Badal, who became chief minister of the state after the delayed elections were held in February 1992. His assassination in August 1995 revealed that tension still exists among Sikhs and surrounding Hindu communities. Yet stable government continues, and both the 1996 and 1998 elections were conducted with a remarkable reduction of violence in the region.

Indira Gandhi's response to Sikh militancy was secular in intent: to hold India, with all of its religious differences, together as one nation. But the participants in this confrontation were defined by their religious rather than their political identities. The drastic consequences were the result of the Sikhs' and Hindus' greater allegiance to their religious communities than to the political state.

A second recent challenge to political secularism in India has been the revival of Hindu nationalist sentiment. The man who assassinated Mahatma Gandhi in 1948 did so in the name of Hindu nationalism—he felt that Gandhi's attempts to accommodate the Muslim communities into an independent India were compromising his Hindu faith too much. By this action, he affirmed the greatest fears of those advocating an independent Pakistan: that they would not receive equal status as a religious minority in the new nation of India. As a consequence of Mahatma Gandhi's example and his death, the quest to achieve a truly secular nation took on great urgency during the early years of India's independence.

As political awareness and participation have increased among India's peoples, their religious identities have also been stimulated. One impetus was a television extravaganza. Its impact, which was a direct result of the emergence of a middle class in India, revealed just how subtle and complex the manifestations of change in the modern world are. In 1987, at the invitation of the national government, a film producer created a television series based on the *Ramayana,* a classical Indian epic. The original Sanskrit account of the ideal Indian prince, Rama, recognized by Hindus as an incarnation of the Supreme God Vishnu, was composed around 2,000 years ago. The story is more popularly known and celebrated among the Hindi-speaking population in a translation of this epic done by a religious poet, Tulsidas, in the sixteenth century. The modern television serial, described as "a mixture of soap opera and national mythology," was broadcast in 104 half-hour episodes by Doordarshan, the national television channel, on Sunday mornings. During its broadcast times, almost all of India came to a halt. A viewership of more than 100 million people were glued to whatever television sets (some 25 million of them) they could find. The serial was an immense success, both in telling the story and in spreading the virtues of television among millions of new viewers.

The intent of the government and the serial's producer had been to extol India's ancient, albeit Hindu, heritage as a way of encouraging a greater sense of national pride. The result was to stir up religious sentiments of both Hindus and the minorities who had reason to fear the arousal of such passion. Broadcast of the television serial coincided with the rise of a new political organization committed to Hindu nationalism, the Bharatiya Janata Party. In a country where many have risen to political prominence through the film industry, it is not difficult to ascribe increasing popularity of this new party

directly to the broadcast of *Ramayana.* The BJP gained even more from a sequel, the broadcast of India's other, older, and longer epic, the *Mahabharata,* as a television serial in 93 hour-long episodes from October 1988 to July 1990. This epic also extols the virtues of an ancient Hindu past. And it includes the original recitation of the most revered text of contemporary Hinduism, *Bhagavad Gita* ("The Song of the Lord").

The Bharatiya Janata Party won only two seats in Parliament in the elections of 1984. In 1989, its holdings jumped to 89. In the 1991 elections, the BJP gathered 118 seats, second only to the Congress Party, which won 225 seats, briefly diminishing that party's hopes for a majority in the national Legislature, the Lok Sabha. The BJP won a slim majority that year in the legislative assembly of India's largest state, Uttar Pradesh, long a Congress Party stronghold.

In this rise to political prominence, the Bharatiya Janata Party tied its fortunes directly to another incident that is also related to Rama, the hero of the *Ramayana,* and that also received extensive television-viewing attention—but this time as national news. The BJP leadership became actively involved in a campaign to build a temple to Rama on the site of his legendary birthplace, in the city of Ayodhya, in eastern Uttar Pradesh. Through a number of public demonstrations, including a chariot procession across northern India, the party was able to rouse a large amount of public support for the building project and for the leadership itself as a political force. Such a mingling of religion and politics was effective, but potentially dangerous.

What made the building campaign particularly volatile was that the specific location for the proposed temple to Rama was on the site of the Babri Masjid—a mosque, a Muslim house of prayer. This mosque was built in 1528, purportedly on the site of a temple that had been destroyed, for Babur, the first of the Islamic Moghul emperors who ruled in India from the early 1500s until 1857. Because the Muslim community is equally eager to preserve the vestiges of its own glorious past in India, the project placed the BJP and its followers in direct conflict with the Indian Muslim minority. In hopes of working out a political compromise that would not stimulate further religious antagonism between Hindus and Muslims, Prime Minister Narasimha Rao placed the dispute over the ownership of this land in the hands of the Supreme Court of India.

The BJP, in control of the Uttar Pradesh government on the state level, became impatient with the maneuvering by the prime minister on the national level. The party thus supported a rally on December 6, 1992, at the Babri mosque/proposed Rama temple site in Ayodhya. The BJP's aim was to keep national attention on its objective to promote the interests of the Hindus, and to urge approval to build the temple. A crowd of more than 700,000 people from across the country gathered for the rally in that city of some 70,000 residents. Even though the national government had assigned 15,000 troops there to maintain order, the situation got out of control, and a small group of enthusiasts scaled the Babri mosque and demolished it.

The response was immediate and devastating. Dormant feelings of anger, fear, frustration, and hatred erupted into communal riots across the country. Hundreds of people were killed; vast numbers of shops and homes were destroyed, from Assam to Kashmir to Kerala. The violence quickly spread into neighboring Pakistan and Bangladesh, where Hindu temples and homes were destroyed in reprisal. A tinderbox of communal resentment based on religion had exploded.

Realizing its complicity in the far-reaching violence caused by the mosque's demolition, the BJP government of Uttar Pradesh resigned. Narasimha Rao, prime minister of India, imprisoned the national leaders of the BJP, and he urged India's president to dismiss the governments in the three other states where the BJP held power: Madhya Pradesh, Rajasthan, and Himachal Pradesh. And, recognizing the challenge to his own government that this unrest and destruction created, he called for the resignation of his entire cabinet.

The Babri Masjid episode severely challenged the commitment to a secular, democratic Republic of India. The outburst of rioting that followed upon the demolition of the mosque, and the increasing strength and impact of the BJP as a political party, both suggest that the Hindu religious identity of the majority of the Indian people was continuing to define their national character more powerfully than the political institutions that were established by the Constitution in 1950. The dawn of "Ram Raj," an idyllic age of government led by the power of God, was being proclaimed, and the specter of Hindu religious fundamentalism was on the rise.

In the 1996 elections, the BJP continued to gain popular support. It won 160 seats, 42 more than in the 1991 elections, to outstrip all the other parties. But the victories did not achieve a majority. In 1998, the BJP fared slightly better, with 182 seats—and, with allied parties, a potential total of 264. In these elections, the appeal of the BJP appears to have reached its peak. The vote-of-confidence for the A. B. Vajpayee government, held in March 1998, was a narrow victory of 274 to 261. This was achieved only by the last-minute support of a regional party from the state of Andhra Pradesh that, during the previous term of the Legislature, had been a major player in the United Front. In the 1999 elections, the number of seats won by the BJP remained at 182.

In order to assuage the fears of opposition groups and to gain majority support in the Lok Sabha, the leaders of the BJP claim to have tempered their extremist Hindu positions. *Hindutva* (Hindu-ness), they assert, is a cultural, not a religious term. And, for them, its defining characteristics are significantly selective, to sound more like patriotism than symbols of transcendence. They are striving to build a national political party, not to establish a new religious cult.

The BJP's continuing rise to national prominence indicates its success in engaging people in the historical process of becoming "a people" with the political image of India as being exclusively a Hindu nation. Its success has been particularly strong among an emerging rural middle class throughout north India. This constituency will have a significant voice in determining India's political future. Its support suggests, however, that the real power of the BJP may not be religious but, rather, the conservative forces of the privileged who dominate India's agrarian society.

Other factions in the political spectrum are also having a growing impact. The interests of minorities and the underprivileged received greater voice through the by-elections of 1993, and in the 1996, 1998, and 1999 general elections. Coalitions were formed among parties representing Muslims (14 percent of the nation's population) and Dalits (traditional "untouchable" communities; 16 percent of the people), especially in Uttar Pradesh, the country's largest state, where these two groups are most numerous. Two Dalit leaders—Mayawati, leader of the Bahujan Samaj Party (BSP), and Mulayam Singh Yadav, of the Samajwadi Party (SP)—have become particularly prominent, although they aligned themselves in opposition for the 1996 national elections. After those elections, Mayawati entered into a coalition agreement with the BJP leadership in Uttar Pradesh and became the first woman Dalit to hold the office of chief minister of an Indian state.

The Samajwadi Party gained enough seats in the 1998 elections to become the second-largest delegation from Uttar Pradesh, limiting the BJP's dominance of the elections in that state and preventing it from winning a majority in the national Legislature. Analysis of the election results suggests that if the BSP and the SP had joined forces, they might even have routed the BJP in its greatest stronghold in India. The success of these parties in representing the "underclasses" reveals a growing awareness on the part of the disadvantaged communities of the political process of democracy—and of how it can be used for their advantage.

There are other, more long-term grounds for optimism that Hindu nationalist sentiment will not undermine democracy in India. The thrust of the BJP's assertion of quasi-religious symbols has been to increase its power within the constitutional structure of government—to receive more popular support for its political agenda, not to undermine the government itself. And where its religious agenda has created animosity and even violence against minorities, particularly Muslims and Christians, public apprehension and concern have generated government response. When the government has not responded with reviews and inquiries, the courts have exposed the opportunistic use of communal politics. The institutions of government are funcioning to perpetuate themselves as secular.

The electorate in general, by not electing a majority of BJP candidates, has restrained the religious nationalist elements in the party. Even the political capital that the BJP hoped to garner by testing India's nuclear arms in May 1998 did not translate into votes for BJP candidates in the by-elections that

(United Nations/J. P. Laffont)

The hierarchical ranking of the cast system in India is very complex and has no Western equivalent. These young women harvesting grain in the Gujurat State are generally accepted as being higher on the social ladder than potters, herders, and washermen.

followed. And the BJP's coalition partners, who are essential to its leadership because the party has not been able to win a national mandate on its own, have also tempered the party's nationalist agenda. Both of these constituencies affirm religious pluralism as a reality of their life together as an Indian people.

India's history is replete with religious strife. The communal outburst in Bombay in 1993 and the continuing terrorist acts of Sikh, Assamese, and Kashmiri militants and repressive counter-measures by the government form another gruesome chapter. But the more normal pattern is one of acceptance of a wide variety of forms of religious practice and expression, even within Hinduism itself. Overwhelming to the outsider are the myriads of gods and goddesses who populate Hindu mythology. Hinduism can also be described as a collection of many different religious communities who all worship one God (or, as Mahatma Gandhi would say, one Truth) in very different ways. Writes Indian author Shashi Taroor:

It pains me to read in the American newspapers of "Hindu fundamentalism," when Hinduism is a religion without compulsory fundamentals. That devotees of this essentially tolerant faith are desecrating a place of worship and assaulting Muslims in its name is a source of both sorrow and shame. India has survived the Aryans, the Mughuls, the British; it has taken from each—language, art, food, learning—and outlasted them all. The Hinduism that I know understands that faith is a matter of hearts and minds, not bricks and stone.

—From *Indian Express* (January 20, 1993)

An example of India's religious acceptance is the Jewish community in Cochin. Jews have lived in that city on the Malabar coast for many centuries, maintaining the distinctive

practices of their faith without any experience of abuse or persecution. Their survival in India is in striking contrast to the experience of the Jewish people who have lived in China, where they have been forced to assimilate into Chinese society in order to survive.

Another basis for optimism regarding democracy in India is the amazing capacity for adaptation that Indian social institutions display. Many factors have contributed to the success that democracy has enjoyed in India since the country's independence. Some people will point to the example and the many years of preparation promoted by British colonial rule. Others look to the inspiration of Mahatma Gandhi and his leadership of the Indian National Congress, which brought the independence movement to the people of the subcontinent. Also important have been the Constitution and the vital leadership and vision of Jawarhalal Nehru and the Congress Party in implementing its guarantees. Other factors include the remarkable restraint of the Indian Army, the dedicated service of the Indian Administrative Service, and an enlightened press.

THE CASTE SYSTEM

All of these factors have contributed significantly to the continued strength of democracy in India. Even more important has been the accommodation of the principles of democracy in the traditional pattern of social organization in India: the caste system.

Many have the impression that the caste system in India is a rigid structure that divides people into distinct social groups, ranked in a fixed hierarchy. We are used to hearing that it is a social evil that has no place in a democracy and ought to be abolished. The reality is that the caste system has provided the indigenous social context that has made it possible for democracy to be introduced into India and to work.

As with so much about India, the caste system is much more complex and more flexible than it appears on the surface.

Because of its hierarchical structure, the caste system is by definition inequitable, and thus a contradiction to democracy, which assumes everyone to be equal. Yet to many Indians, the system is seen not as separating basically common people but, rather, as what holds very diverse groups of people together. And its hierarchical structure, rather than fixing people into permanent levels, provides them with some opportunity for social mobility. Nevertheless, it is true that those who find themselves of lower rank feel the tremendous weight of its oppression, whereas those whose rank level is higher or improving are not so troubled by its inherent inequality. One's attitude toward the caste system thus depends a great deal on one's place in the system.

The Indian caste system is based upon a social group for which Westerners do not have a counterpart. In the north of India, the caste community is generally called a *jati* (the word is based on a verbal root meaning "to be born"). It is an extended kinship group whose perimeters extend beyond the natural family. The jati is also endogamous, which means that it includes those relations whom one is expected to marry. Natural family members are excluded from this group by generally accepted rules against incest. A jati thus extends the idea of a family to a larger social group of cousins and potential in-laws.

The jati is further defined by a traditional occupation, which has been passed on from generation to generation, and which gives each jati its name. There are several thousand separate jatis, or caste communities, throughout India, most of them confined to a single linguistic region. There may be as few as two or three jatis in the remote mountain valleys of the Himalayas. Generally, in the more densely populated areas of India, a villager will interact with about 20 different such caste groups in his or her normal daily life.

Jati has an important role in an Indian's self-identity. Whereas Westerners tend to think of themselves in society primarily as individuals, in India, one is more apt to think of oneself primarily in society as a member of one's jati. It provides a context for all of one's interactions with other people, with respect to working, socializing, eating, and especially as regards marriage. In India, where marriages are mostly arranged by one's parents, the expectation to marry someone of one's own jati is generally the rule.

The jati is the social unit that is placed in the hierarchical ranking called the caste system. Here is where the possibility of flexibility, or mobility, arises. That one belongs to a certain jati is fixed by birth. But where that jati is ranked in the hierarchical caste order is not. Its rank is based on some general rules that are accepted by almost everyone. For example, those belonging to Brahmin, or traditional priestly, jatis are placed at the top of the caste hierarchy. It is a significant feature of this system that those who are traditionally given highest rank are expected to abjure wealth, practice asceti-

cism, and revere learning. It does not give as high esteem for those who hold political power or pursue money and become conspicuous spenders.

The hierarchical ranking of this system demeans in rank those jatis that perform menial tasks such as cleaning latrines, sweeping streets, and removing the carcasses of dead animals. People belonging to these jatis are called "untouchables," a designation that reveals the ancient priestly caste's understanding of its own supremacy in rank. Brahmins as a community had to remain ritually pure in order to retain the efficacy and respect for their priestly functions. People who performed "polluting" functions in the society—those involving dealing with human waste and animals—had to be avoided for fear of their diminishing the priests' sacred power. They were thus placed the lowest on the hierarchical scale and declared "outcastes." Mahatma Gandhi, in his crusade to remove the scourge of the demeaning term "untouchable," called them *Harijans,* "children of God," and encouraged members of his religious community to perform the "polluting" functions for themselves. In many parts of India today, people in these jatis prefer to be called Dalits (meaning the "oppressed"), and they are seeking recognition as equal members of Indian society. Their quest, however, still meets with a great deal of resistance throughout the country.

For those jatis that fall in between the high-ranked Brahmins and the low-ranked Dalits, the basis of ranking is not so clear or consistent. Some occupations, such as land cultivators or carpenters, are generally accepted as higher than potters, herders, and washermen. Land or industrial ownership, and thus control over production in a village, known as *dominance,* is a very important determinant in caste rank. Social practices, such as ritual observance, dress, vegetarian diet, and with whom one eats, may also determine rank. Different rules apply in different situations. As norms and conditions change, so is the rank of one's jati open to change.

Many examples illustrate this fluidity of ranking. The jati names of several ancient emperors betray an absence of royal blood, or, at least, of earlier royal rank for their caste. Such did not prevent them from becoming kings. A striking, more contemporary example is the Nadar community in south India. It was considered an untouchable community in the nineteenth century, but is now accepted as a merchant caste. Even Mahatma Gandhi's family was not fixed in jati rank. The family name (*gandhi* means "grocer") identifies a *bania,* or merchant, background. But both Gandhi's grandfather and father served as chief ministers for maharajas of small Indian states, a role traditionally reserved for Brahmins. Gandhi was himself thrown out of his jati by the elders of his community when he went to England to study law. He stepped out of the caste system altogether when he was accepted as a person committed to a religious life, when he became the Mahatma.

Although rules of ranking in the caste hierarchy apply generally, the position of any specific jati is based primarily on the acceptance of its claim to rank by members of the other jatis with which it interacts. Because mobility is open only to the entire jati, not to individuals within it, and members of other jatis need to agree, change in rank does not happen quickly. Nevertheless a social dynamic extends through the system that asserts a claim to higher rank and encourages others to accept that claim.

The Caste System and Political Change

The cohesion and flexibility in the caste structure provides the dynamic within the traditional social context for democracy to work. The role of democracy is to establish and distribute public power by vote of the majority of adults in a society. This right of individuals to vote to determine their government was new to India. In a system in which rules of ascendancy are continually being worked out, the role of the vote to grant public power emerged as an acceptable way to establish rank within the village hierarchy. The system does not have to change; it simply has to adapt itself to an additional way to determine ascendancy.

The most obvious way in which the traditional caste structure adapts to democratic elections is by creating voting blocs out of the local authority structures already in place in the villages. A decisive factor in determining who has the most power and higher cast rank within a village is the control of the production and distribution of the food that is harvested from village lands. Those who dominate the village resources and have higher caste status are quick to convert into votes for their chosen candidates the allegiances created by the dependency of those of lower jati rank in the village who serve and get food from them. Individual jatis, because they extend as distinct social groups through many villages within a linguistic region, also serve to implement democracy beyond the village level. They provide cohesive units for region-wide associations formed to promote political causes important to their jati members. Jati associations function both as voting blocs in elections and as lobbies in the halls of government. In these ways, democracy is co-opted to *support* traditional patterns of social life, rather than to *reform* them.

Clear evidence of this adaptation has been the slow pace of land reform in India, in contrast to the rapid acceptance of new methods of agriculture that produced abundant supplies of grain in the Green Revolution. New laws have broken up large land estates and reduced absentee landlordism. But politically active regional landholder jati associations have been able to block legislative action on some of the most difficult village problems: landlessness and underemployment, the inequities of wealth and privilege, and landowner–laborer relations. Disputes between landowners and their laborers are still mostly resolved by force, with little interference from the police or protection from the courts.

Because of the inherent flexibility and adaptability evident in the jati caste structure, democracy has not caused as much social change in India as initially was expected. Such is true also for economic development. While Americans have tended to view economic improvement and prosperity as direct consequences of political democracy, the developing world in general and India in particular have shown that the two are not necessarily connected—that prosperity is the result of many other factors than just political structure. Population density and population growth, for example, have had greater impact on economic growth than form of governance. Cultural factors, geo-commercial considerations, international economic forces, and specific economic policies of the government of India have also contributed to its continuing struggle to provide economic well-being for all of its people.

To the extent that democracy has not lived up to economic promise nor contributed to radical social change, those most oppressed and disadvantaged in India today are becoming more disenchanted. Ironically, as they have come to experience the benefts of national affirmative-action policies and become more politically aware, they have become less hopeful about the effectiveness for them of ordered, democratic institutions. The continued burden of poverty has become itself another real threat to democracy in India. Yet hope for more effective government for the disadvantaged is suggested by the results of the 1993 midterm elections in four Indian states and the 1996, 1998, and 1999 general elections, where the voice of the Dalits began to be heard at the polls.

And so there are new levels of violence: violence caused by the very struggle to become a democracy and at the same time to negate it. In the general elections in 1991, voter turnout was only 54 percent. That is high by North American standards, but it was the lowest participation in a national election in 40 years of democracy in India. Most attribute this decline to the increase in violence and terrorism that has surrounded the election process itself. By mid-June 1991, more than 800 deaths had been recorded as a result of people going to the polls. In the state of Punjab, elections were postponed because 23 of the more than 1,000 candidates who were running for public office had been killed while campaigning. It was not until February 1992 that enough confidence was restored to hold the elections there. Even then, they were boycotted by five Sikh political parties, and the turnout was less than 22 percent of the entire voting-age population.

The 1996 national elections showed a significant turn away from the violence that surrounded the 1991 elections. The large turnout of 530 million voters was a record high. The elections in Punjab recorded the highest level of voter turnout in the country. The number of election-related deaths fell dramatically, from more than 800 in 1991 to 50 in 1996—and those were mostly due to electoral feuds in the state of Bihar. State elections were held for the first time in six years in Jammu/Kashmir, with some foreboding because of the activity of militant separatist movements in that state. Yet more than 53 percent of the electorate took part, and that war-torn part of the country is now being ruled by a democratically elected state government.

National elections have become an important part of Indian life. Among the many villages in the country, they have even taken on the character of a festival, as reported under the headline "Joy and Order as India's Voting Starts":

> What seemed important was not so much which of the dozens of political parties was up or down, or which local candidate from among the 15,000 running across India was likely to win. What permeated the mood was something as old as independent India itself—the sheer pleasure of taking part in a basic democratic rite, the business of appointing and dismissing governments, that has survived all of the disappointments that Indians have endured in the past half-century. In a troubled land, democracy means there is hope.
>
> —*The New York Times* (April 18, 1996)

REGIONAL POLITICAL CONCERNS

Dominance, a primary factor in village life, also characterizes India's relationship with its closest, South Asian neighbors. By far the largest country of the subcontinent, in both size and population, India is an overbearing presence to those that surround it.

The nations of Nepal and Bhutan, and the tiny kingdom of Sikkim, before it was absorbed into India in 1974, are isolated by India against the Himalayan Mountains to the north. They are particularly aware of India's dominance. Bhutan's economic development is almost totally dependent upon Indian investment. And its foreign relations are, by long-standing treaty, handled by the government of India. Nepal maintains a fragile neutrality, circumscribed by its economic ties and a "Treaty of Peace and Friendship" with India signed in 1950.

Sri Lanka is geographically separate from India and, except for infrequent discussions about some small islands that lie between them, has had generally peaceful relations with it. In 1964 and 1974, the government of India agreed to help Sri Lanka by repatriating half of the 1 million Indian Tamils whose forebears were taken to Sri Lanka by the British during the nineteenth century to work on the rubber, coffee, and tea plantations. This agreement helped to ease the unemployment created by the breakup of plantations at that time. An increase in discrimination during the 1980s felt by the remaining Indian Tamils and Sri Lanka Tamils (about 17 percent of the total population of the country) strengthened their language and cultural ties with the nearby Indian state of Tamil Nadu. The subsequent rise of militant Tamil separatist and Sinhalese nationalist movements led to outright warfare in Sri Lanka. About 70,000 refugees fled to south India in 1983. That number increased to more than 200,000 in 1991.

In 1987, Rajiv Gandhi, then prime minister of India, made an agreement with the Sri Lankan government to send a peacekeeping force of 70,000 Indian Army troops to contain the Tamil violence. When this force proved ineffective in putting down what was a guerrilla war in a foreign country, the Sri Lankan government asked India to withdraw. Rajiv Gandhi's international initiative became to Sri Lankans an overbearing display of military power imposed upon them. Yet the forces were there long enough to win sufficient enmity of the Tamil militants in Sri Lanka for them to plot Gandhi's death. The consequences proved dire for all involved, most particularly for Rajiv Gandhi himself, when he became the victim of a "suicide bomber" attack in south India during the 1991 general elections. India remains supportive of the Sri Lankan government in its protracted war against the Tamil separatist group LTTE, but it is now wary of giving any military support to this effort.

Pakistan and Bangladesh have their own access to the sea, to the west and east of India, and thus to the world. Yet they are both aware that they are much smaller than India; and that their large neighbor, by attacking Pakistan in 1971, determined that they are two nations instead of one. Even more important, rivers, which are the major source of water for irrigation in both Pakistan and Bangladesh, originate in and are controlled by their powerful neighbor.

Negotiations between India and Bangladesh over the distribution of the waters of the Ganges River through the Farakka Barrage near the border between the two countries began in 1977. A dramatic resolution was achieved in December 1996, assuring Bangladesh of at least half of the available flow. This agreement came partially as an act of goodwill toward the new government of Bangladesh with the electoral victory of Sheikh Hasina Wazed, daughter of Mujibur Rahman. (India had helped Rahman win independence for Bangladesh in 1971.) But it also reflected a growing understanding among India's leaders that India's status as a modern industrial nation depends upon constructive economic relationships with its neighbors.

Another major issue of contention between Bangladesh and India has been the repatriation of undocumented refugees. Millions came into India during the military repression leading up to the independence of Bangladesh in 1971; many have remained because of a lack of agreement between the two countries on a process for their transfer. Some progress on this issue was realized in a recent settlement with insurgent tribal groups in eastern Bangladesh. The settlement included repatriation of more than 60,000 Chakmas from refugee camps in the Indian state of Tripura.

Efforts toward greater cooperation among the nations of South Asia began with the creation of the South Asian Association for Regional Cooperation (SAARC) in 1985. Although progress has been slow, the member nations did initiate a South Asian Preferential Trade Agreement (SAPTA) in December 1996, which established some modest, mutual tariff concessions. Impatient with the pace of SAARC, India also set up two subregional cooperation groups: one with Nepal, Bhutan, and Bangladesh; and another with Sri Lanka and Maldives. A further step is a free-trade agreement signed between Sri Lanka and India in December 1998. These agreements isolate Pakistan, the seventh member of SAARC, and identify a history of altercation and restrictive trade between India and Pakistan.

| Harappan city culture **3000–1500** B.C. | Aryan Vedic culture **1500–500** B.C. | Buddhist civilization **500** B.C.–A.D. **300** | Classical Hindu civilization A.D. **200–1000** | Medieval Islamic civilization **1200–1857** | British East India Company **1602–1857** | The British Raj era **1857–1947** | The founding of the Indian National Congress; start of the independence movement **1885** | Mohandas Gandhi returns to India from South Africa **1915** |

The long-standing dispute between India and Pakistan over Kashmir, which led to outright warfare between the two countries in 1948, 1965, and 1971, has sustained a high level of tension between the two countries since the time of independence. It has placed a constant drain on the resources that both countries need for social services and economic development. High-level bilateral discussions to resolve this intractable issue followed a meeting of Prime Ministers Sharif of Pakistan and Vajpayee of India at the United Nations in October 1998. Attempts were made to declare a cease-fire on the Siachen Glacier, along the line of control between India and Pakistan-occupied Kashmir; to increase the flow of Jhelam River waters through the Pulkal Barrage; and to increase trade and people-to-people contacts. But all attempts at resolution were dashed when Pakistan staged an incursion of its troops across the long-established line of control into the Kargil region of Kashmir during the summer of 1999. India continues to assert that Kashmir has been an integral part of its country since the maharajah of Kashmir acceded it to India in 1947, in accordance with the terms of the partition of India and Pakistan. India argues that to detach Kashmir would be to dismember itself as a nation. With the new military government in Pakistan since October 1999, resolution of the issue of Kashmir appears more intractable than ever.

Nuclear proliferation is another major issue in Pakistan–Indian relations. The world was shocked when both India and Pakistan tested nuclear devices in May 1998. In spite of extensive election rhetoric about such testing in India during the months leading up to the national elections in February–March, it came as an unexpected surprise to all but a very few in the newly elected Bharatiya Janata Party–controlled government.

The United States was especially outraged by these tests, because they represented an unqualified failure of U.S. policy to contain nuclear-weapons capability throughout the world. India, and subsequently Pakistan, had unleashed expanding nuclear armaments, threatening the stability of the South Asian region and giving precedence for the development of nuclear arms in other volatile areas of the world. The U.S. government responded by imposing sanctions on India, which have turned out to be small in terms of foreign-aid support for India, and largely ineffective. Their greatest impact appears to have been on American investors and farmers, who brought pressure to bear on the U.S. Congress to have them removed.

Ironically, this horrified response to the nuclear testings did not acknowledge that U.S. policy itself contributed to India's growing need to acquire what its strategic planners called "credible minimum nuclear deterrence." In the absence of binding international disarmament or control over nuclear-weapons development, India's security depends upon its developing sufficient second-strike capability to have a credible response to a nuclear attack. Such deterrence, and India's unilateral commitment not to make a first strike using nuclear arms, are the two pillars of the country's nuclear policy.

The government of India has long been concerned that U.S. nuclear policy is not committed to a workable timetable to eliminate nuclear weapons, as part of its compliance with the Nuclear Non-Proliferation Treaty, which the United States signed in 1968. Nor does the United States appear effective in enforcing the compliance of other signers of that treaty to not provide nuclear know-how and fissionable materials to other nations. Specifically, India does not have any confidence that U.S. policy can restrain China's ability to destabilize South Asia by providing nuclear materials to Pakistan. In the absence of such assurance, India's own security needs have required it to retain its nuclear-testing option. Therefore, in spite of immense diplomatic pressure, India has refused to sign the U.S.–sponsored Comprehensive Test Ban Treaty.

Because of its history of stable, civilian government, India does not see developing its nuclear-arms capability, which began in 1974, as threatening to its South Asian neighbors. Pakistan, on the other hand, recognizes that some factions in India see its very existence as an Islamic nation as a judgment on India's credibility as a secular state; Pakistan thus does not feel secure with India having an overwhelming nuclear advantage. The rise to power of the BJP as a Hindu nationalist party has added to Pakistan's apprehensions. It therefore felt compelled to answer India's test with tests of its own two weeks later. India did not react to these tests in any dramatic way, as its own need for nuclear deterrence, even since 1974, has been not to defend itself from Pakistan, but from China.

India's one attempt to confront its large Asian neighbor, China, with conventional arms was to settle a border dispute in 1962. This confrontation led to a humiliating rout of India's border forces. Since then, relations with China have been formal, and largely inconsequential, due mainly to a lack of interest on China's part. India cannot help feeling that its nuclear capability has been an important protection, and it is reluctant to participate in any regional nuclear agreement from which China is excluded. Its preference would be to have all the major powers, including the United States, join in an enforceable nuclear-disarmament treaty.

Gandhi conducts the Salt March
1930

The Government of India Act provides limited self-government
1935

Independence
1947

The Jawarhalal Nehru era
1947–1964

The Constitution establishes India as a democratic, secular, sovereign nation
1950

The Indira Gandhi era
1965–1984

National emergency was declared and led to the suspension of civil liberties
1975

Operation Blue-star: attack on the Golden Temple, Amritsar; the assassination of Indira Gandhi
1984

The Rajiv Gandhi era
1984–1991

Rajiv Gandhi is assassinated; the Babri Masjid is destroyed and leads to riots nationwide; nuclear tests startle the world
1990s

2000s

The Kashmir dispute remains intractable and dangerous

India expands its role in regional and global political and economic organizations

A monster earthquake in Gujarat kills more than 30,000 and leaves hundreds of thousands homeless

India continues to pursue avenues of wider economic and diplomatic cooperation. It maintains an active role in the 113-nation Non-Aligned Movement, which met in South Africa in September 1998. It also became a full dialogue partner in the Association of Southeast Asian Nations (ASEAN) in January 1997. This status in ASEAN is shared with the United States, the European Union, Australia, Japan, and South Korea. India's admission overcame the concerns of Southeast Asian leaders that they not be drawn into such South Asian issues as the Kashmir dispute. And India remains hopeful, even after its recent nuclear tests, of becoming a permanent member of an expanded United Nations Security Council.

During the Cold War, India sought to remain nonaligned by negotiating with the United States and Europe for economic aid, and with the Soviet Union for military aid to match the military assistance offered by the U.S. government to Pakistan. With the collapse of the Soviet Union, the government of India has sought to open its economy to greater Japanese and American industrial investment. Because of its earlier, restrictive import policies, which forced IBM and Coca-Cola to withdraw during the 1970s, the country established a good industrial base of its own. Its growth since independence has been significant. A rapidly developing middle-class market, decreasing restrictions on foreign investment, and government divestment of its public-sector industries have created opportunities for even faster growth. This promise was affirmed by the commitment of more than $6 billion in assistance to India in recent years by the Aid India Consortium, international aid agencies, and industrialized countries.

Several factors support such optimism for India's economic growth. The U.S. sanctions imposed on India following its nuclear tests in 1998 reduced foreign-aid assistance by a little less than $1 billion. The government of India made up for this loss through increases in foreign direct investments, which have grown dramatically with the liberalizing of India's econ-

omy since 1991. These investments reached $3.5 billion in 1997 but subsequently slowed to $2.2 billion in 1999 with the uncertainties created by the Asian economic crises in 1997–1998. India received increased investments of $4.2 billion by nonresident Indians and other investors from more economically prosperous regions of the world to assist it in sustaining an encouraging rate of growth during these troubled times. The World Bank reported a 6 percent increase in India's gross domestic product in 1999, and it anticipates even greater increases as consumer buying and domestic investments continue to rise.

Promises for the economic future of India are tempered by the overwhelming demands of contemporary life in India: a teeming population, extensive poverty, profound environmental degradation, and civil strife. "Excess," V. S. Naipaul calls them, recognizing that so much of the conflict and violence is the result of an awakening of a new political consciousness. "A million mutinies supported by twenty kinds of group excess, sectarian excess, religious excess, regional excess." Yet he finds even in this awakening a vision of hope: "the beginnings of self-awareness . . . the beginning of a new way for the millions, part of India's growth, part of its restoration."

DEVELOPMENT

India has the most diversified industrial economy in South Asia and ranks among the world's top 10 industrial powers. Industry now equals agriculture in its share of GDP. Agriculture still employs two thirds of the labor force. The government has recently moved to sell state-run industries and limit restrictions to encourage more private growth and foreign investment.

FREEDOM

The largest democracy in the world, India has maintained stable parliamentary and local government through elections and rule of law since the adoption of its Constitution in 1950. Frontier territories have been brought into full statehood, and separatist movements have been held in check. Amnesty International has cited some human-rights abuses by security forces and militant separatist groups in Kashmir, Punjab, and Assam.

HEALTH/WELFARE

India's commitment to village development and universal education has improved diet, hygiene, medical services, and literacy. Birth-control policies remain difficult to implement, and urban slums need continuing attention. The awarding of the Nobel Peace Prize to Mother Teresa indicates the magnitude of both the challenge and the vision of health care in India.

ACHIEVEMENTS

Through its Green Revolution, India has been self-sufficient in grain production since 1970. Its high-tech industrial capability and growing middle class have attracted increasing direct investment in the economy. Its leadership among nonaligned and developing countries and the world popularity of artists like musician Ravi Shankar reveal the vitality of India's ancient tradition of creativity in language, art, and human relations.

Afghanistan (Islamic State of Afghanistan)

GEOGRAPHY

Area in Square Miles (Kilometers):
249,935 (647,500) (about the size of Texas)

Capital (Population): Kabul (500,000) (est.)

Environmental Concerns: soil degradation; overgrazing; deforestation; desertification

Geographical Features: mostly rugged mountains; valleys in the north and southwest

Climate: arid to semiarid; cold winters and hot summers

PEOPLE

Population

Total: 25,839,000 (including refugees in Pakistan and Iran)

Annual Growth Rate: 3.54% (reflects the return of refugees)

Rural/Urban Population Ratio: 80/20

Major Languages: Pashto; Dari; Turkic; 30 minor languages; much bilingualism

Ethnic Makeup: 38% Pashtun; 25% Tajik; 19% Hazara; 6% Uzbek; 12% others

Religions: 84% Sunni Muslim; 15% Shia Muslim; 1% others

Health

Life Expectancy at Birth: 47 years (male); 47 years (female)

Infant Mortality Rate (Ratio): 149.3/1,000

Physicians Available (Ratio): 1/6,690

Education

Adult Literacy Rate: 31.5% overall; 15% for females

Compulsory (Ages): 7–13

COMMUNICATION

Telephones: 29,000 main lines

Daily Newspaper Circulation: 11 per 1,000 people

Televisions: 10 per 1,000 people

Internet Service Providers: na

TRANSPORTATION

Highways in Miles (Kilometers): 13,640 (22,000)

Railroads in Miles (Kilometers): 15.4 (24.6)

Usable Airfields: 46

Motor Vehicles in Use: 67,000

GOVERNMENT

Type: no functioning central government

Independence Date: August 19, 1919 (from United Kingdom control over Afghan foreign affairs)

Head of State/Government: no functioning government at this time

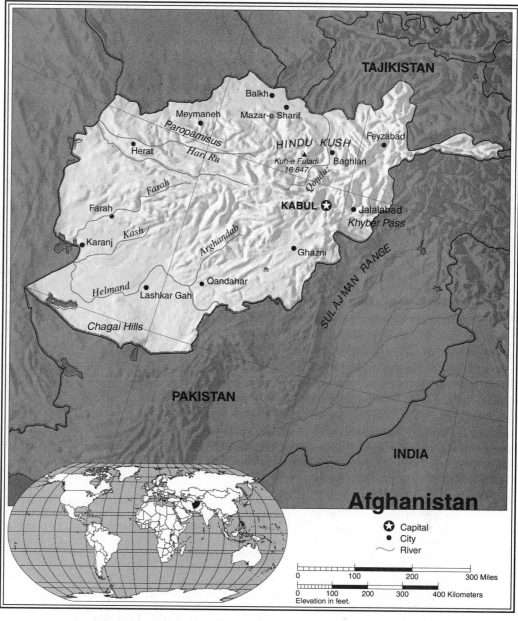

Political Parties: Taliban; others

Suffrage: currently undetermined

MILITARY

Military Expenditures (% of GDP): no national military

Current Disputes: severe internal conflicts; border disputes with Pakistan and Iran

ECONOMY

Currency ($ U.S. Equivalent): 4,750 afghani = $1 (bazaar rate)

Per Capita Income/GDP: $800/$21 billion (1996 est.)

Unemployment Rate: 8%

Labor Force: 8,000,000

Natural Resources: natural gas; petroleum; coal; copper; talc; barite; sulphur; lead; zinc; iron ore; salt; precious and semiprecious stones

Agriculture: opium poppies; wheat; fruits; nuts; karakul pelts; wool; mutton

Industry: small-scale production of textiles, soap, furniture, shoes, fertilizer, and cement; handwoven carpets; natural gas; oil; coal; copper

Exports: $80 million (does not include opium poppies) (primary partners former Soviet Union, Pakistan, Iran)

Imports: $150 million (primary partners former Soviet Union, Pakistan, Iran)

 http://www.afghan-web.com
http://cia.gov/cia/publications/factbook/geos/af.html

AFGHANISTAN

Afghanistan is a rugged, mountainous country nearly the size of Texas, divided by a high mountain ridge that extendes right through its center. It is also divided by ethnic conflicts, competing political and religious ideologies, old superpower strategies, and war.

The natural terrain of Afghanistan has never supported an easy or affluent life for its people. The western extension of the high Himalayan mountain range known as the Hindu Kush is an imposing, 600-mile-long barrier through the middle of the country. The land slopes away from this range in three different directions, into jagged foothills and stark river valleys. Only 12 percent of this land is arable; even more challenging to agricultural subsistence, the area receives an average rainfall of less than 12 inches a year. Severe drought conditions throughout the country since 1996 have drastically reduced even that rainfall for agricultural production and decimated the animals of the Kuchi people, Afghanistan's nomadic herders. Toward the south, the land is normally inhospitable desert, wracked by seasonal sandstorms that have been known to bury entire villages. The mountainous terrain in the north has unexploited (but hard-to-obtain) mineral resources, primarily iron ore and natural gas. This land experienced a severe earthquake in February 1998 that destroyed more than 20 villages, killing several thousand people. Nowhere in the country can life be characterized as naturally comfortable or abundant.

The three-way slope of the landscape down from the high, forbidding ridge of the Hindu Kush divides the country into three distinct ethnic and linguistic regions. Northern Afghans are predominantly Uzbeks and Turkmen, who share a strong sense of identity, as well as the Turkic language, with the peoples who live across their northern border in Turkmenistan, Uzbekistan, and Tajikistan—all former republics of the Soviet Union.

The Tajik and Hazara peoples live on the western slope of the Hindu Kush. They belong to different Islamic traditions—the Tajik primarily Sunni Muslim, the Hazara Shias—but they share a common language, Dari, which is a dialect of Farsi, the language of Iran (where Shia Muslims are predominant).

The Pathans, or Pushtuns, the largest ethnic group, live on the southeastern slope of the country. They are, like the Tajik and northern Afghans, mainly Sunni Muslims, but they speak a different language, Pashto. They share both this language and their ethnic identity with the people across their southeastern boundary, in the Northwest Province of Pakistan.

Such a geographically separated and diverse population has not provided an easy basis for a shared identity as a nation. Emperors briefly united these lands in the twelfth and eighteenth centuries A.D., but neither empire lasted more than a generation. Historically, local chieftains and warlords held fragmented political control, each dominant over their own estates.

Afghanistan's traditional importance and wealth was not based on its political power but, rather, on its position along the ancient silk trade route between China and Europe. It extracted from those traveling through their lands a significant bounty of customs fees, commissions for protection, or loot. The prominent role of drug trafficking and arms dealing in Afghan life today reflects the marauding and opportunistic character of this heritage, preserved by the independent tribal warlords scattered across the rugged landscape. According to United Nations reports, Afghanistan in 1999, produced three quarters of the world's supply of heroin.

In the modern era, global competition among European colonial powers for influence in this region—called the "Great Game"—consolidated the power of the emir of Kabul over the country. With the approval of Czarist forces to the north and the British Raj to the south, Abdur Rahman Khan ruled as emir from 1880 to 1901. He was committed, in his own words, to "breaking down the feudal and tribal system and substituting one grand community under one law and one rule." Czarist Russia and Great Britain again asserted their imperial presence to establish the borders of modern Afghanistan by treaty in 1907, with the intent to contain each other's colonial ambitions. Abdur Rahman's efforts to rule over "all those hundreds of petty chiefs, plunderers, robbers and cutthroats" throughout the country did not last long. His grandson, Amanulla Khan, was forced to flee in 1928.

More recently, during the Cold War, Afghanistan became a base for contention between the United States and the former Soviet Union, which transformed the country into an international battlefield. The victim of those superpowers' quest for political advantage, Afghanistan was ravaged, with much of its population displaced by war.

Since 1996, the Taliban, an extreme Islamic fundamentalist group, with Pakistani support, has extended its military control and religious fervor over most of the country. Yet a vestige of the anti-Soviet resistance forces called the Northern Alliance continues to hold out in the northern corner of the country. Its support from the bordering former Soviet republics and from Iran threatens to expand this

conflict into further international warfare. With such tensions and political instability, a sense of national unity in which democracy and social welfare can develop continues to elude the ethnically diverse and war-ravaged people of Afghanistan.

MODERN HISTORY

In 1953, Sadar (Prince) Mohammed Daoud Khan, then commander of the Afghan Army, seized the authority of prime minister. He managed to institute many economic and social reforms, leading up to the adoption of a constitutional monarchy in 1964. As an indication of Daoud's reforming zeal, in 1959 women were officially allowed to remove the *chadri* (the traditional heavy veil worn in public), and they participated for the first time in the elections that took place in 1964. Also participating in those elections was a newly formed, but already fractious, Communist Party, led by Nur Mohammed Taraki, son of a nomadic Pushtun family, and Babrak Karmal, an upper-class intellectual from Kabul.

Elections were held again in 1969, but by then, local tribal leaders, who were both religiously and socially conservative, better understood the electoral process. They gained control of the Assembly, in order to preserve their traditional authority, and effectively limited further reform.

Impatient with this resistance, Sadar Daoud, with the help of the army, overthrew the government in 1973. He sent Emir Zahir Shah into exile and set himself up as the military dictator of the country. To secure his rule, he strengthened the army and the bureaucracy. With Soviet-government aid, he strove to build an industrial sector to replace agriculture and handicrafts as the primary sources of the country's wealth. By encouraging the growth and loyalty of these sectors, Daoud hoped to have their support to establish a more independent nation and to usher in even broader reforms. To assert this independence, he promulgated a new Constitution in 1977 that outlawed all political parties other than his own, including the largely urban and intellectual Communist Party. A new Assembly then elected Daoud president of the Republic of Afghanistan.

The Soviet Invasion

Resistance to Daoud's nationalist reform program came from both sides of the political spectrum—from the leftist, modernizing groups in the city of Kabul, and from the more conservative elements in the countryside. A zealous group of militant tribal leaders called the *mujahideen* emerged at this time. Armed and trained by Pakistan, the mujahideen sporadically

(Photo: United Nations/A. Hollmann)

Millions of refugees who fled to Pakistan and Iran during the Soviet occupation of Afghanistan have been reluctant to return to Afghanistan. This is due, in no small part, to the constant fighting among the mujahideen and today's problems with the Taliban. Women and children are particularly vulnerable groups of refugees.

attacked various targets to harass Daoud's government. But Daoud was more concerned about the growing influence (encouraged by the Soviets) of the urban forces of the left, and he began to purge suspected Communist Party members from the military and the bureaucracy.

Within a year of the formation of his new government, Daoud was overthrown by army officers who felt threatened by his purge. Nur Mohammed Taraki, leader of the People's Democratic (Communist) Party, then took over the reins of government. Infighting among the Communist Party leadership led to President Taraki's assassination in 1979 and the subsequent rise to power of his former associate and arch rival, Hafizullah Amin.

Both leaders were encouraged by the Soviet Union to reform Afghanistan into a socialist industrial state. They adopted a vigorous campaign to break up the landholdings of the local chieftains and to teach literacy among the people. Mujahideen resistance to these reforms intensified to a point where President Amin sought Soviet military force to protect his government in Kabul. The Soviets feared that continuing civil strife caused by Amin in Afghanistan would diminish their influence and investment there, as well as threaten the security of the adjoining Soviet states to the north. The Soviet Union sent 85,000 troops to Kabul in December 1979—not to protect Amin, but to depose him and his radical faction of the Communist Party. The Soviet forces installed in Amin's place an early factional leader in the Communist Party, Babrak Karmal, to undertake a more moderate approach to socialist reform.

When the Soviet military forces entered Afghanistan, hordes of refugees fled across those borders of the country that placed them among neighboring peoples with whom they felt a strong sense of kinship. More than 3 million Afghans crossed the border into the Northwest Province of Pakistan, where they lived in refugee camps; two decades later, 1.25 million are still awaiting a time of sufficient peace and political stability for them to return home. Another 2 million people fled across the border into Iran, where they have been largely assimilated. Although the Iranian government speaks occasionally of deportation, fewer than half of those refugees have returned from Iran since the departure of the Soviet Army in 1989. At their peak, these two groups of refugees comprised more than one third of the total population of Afghanistan.

Equally impressive was the large influx of the rural population into Kabul during the time of Soviet occupation, to seek protection there. The city's population grew from about 500,000 in 1970 to more than 1 million in 1989. With the overthrow of Communist rule in Kabul in April 1993, this trend was totally reversed. The periodic assaults and bombings due to the infighting among rival political parties seeking control of the city, as the seat of power over the entire country, reduced Kabul's population to its pre-1970 level.

During the years of Soviet occupation, the number of military forces continued to increase, climbing to 120,000 troops by 1986. Forces of resistance in the countryside—now being called upon to oppose the foreign, Soviet intervention as well as the movements within Afghanistan toward centralization, industrialization, and social modernization—also intensified. The mujahideen, a disparate collection of warlords, were strengthened by a rising Islamic fundamentalist zeal and encouraged by Paki-

stani, Iranian, Arabic, and U.S. support. Many of them gathered their families into the safety of Pakistan and prepared to fight back. Wrote one observer:

Most came across in groups of fifty or one hundred, villages or nomad clans led by maliks, the local tribal chieftains. They brought more than 2 million animals with them—goats, sheep, buffalos and camels. It was a timeless sight. The men in turbans or woolen or embroidered caps, baggy pants and vests or robes like academic gowns, bandoliers of cartridges across their chests, old rifles or new machine guns on one shoulder. Their sons were dressed the same way, miniatures of their fathers. The animals and the women walked behind. When they stopped, they sometimes took the tents offered by the United Nations or, sometimes, just re-created their katchi villages on the other side of the mountains. Then the men, many of them, went back to kill Russians.

—Richard Reeves, *Passage to Peshawar*

This conflict took a heavy toll, destroying 12,000 of the 22,000 villages in the country and more than 2,000 schools. It left more than 1 million Afghans and 13,000 Soviet troops dead.

The Soviet Withdrawal

In 1986, Babrak Karmal resigned as president. The following year, he was replaced by an associate, Dr. Muhammed Najibullah, to rule the country from Kabul. In 1988, the leaders of nine Sunni Muslim rebel groups joined in Pakistan to form an interim government in exile. Faced with this more

| Loose tribal federation A.D. 1747–1973 | The British and Russians establish the boundaries of modern Afghanistan 1907 | Military dictatorship 1973–1978 | Communist Party rule 1978–1992 | Soviet military occupation 1979–1989 | A mujahideen resistance is formed in Pakistan; the new Constitution is adopted 1980s | Taliban forces capture Kabul and control nearly all of the country 1990s |

2000s

The Taliban remain in control

Deeming them "Un-Islamic," the Taliban destroys ancient Buddhist statues

united resistance, the Soviet Union became unwilling to sustain the losses of the intensifying military stalemate. It entered into an accord with the United States to withdraw all of its forces by February 15, 1989. In September 1991, the United States and the Soviet Union further agreed to stop providing arms to the warring factions in Afghanistan effective on January 1, 1992, and to urge a cease-fire in that troubled land.

Warfare between President Najibullah's government and the mujahideen continued unabated for more than three years after the Soviet troop departure. The mujahideen had tried to adopt a common strategy and combine their military forces. Lack of cohesion—religious, ethnic, and military—thwarted their attempts to overthrow the Kabul government. President Najibullah offered to form a joint government with the leaders of the resistance, but these leaders could agree only that they did not want the Communists to share in any part of a new government.

In March 1992, Najibullah was overthrown by his army, and mujahideen forces under the command of Ahmad Shah Masood, a Tajik Afghan, overtook the city of Kabul. In June, a "national council" of mujahideen leaders elected Burhanuddin Rabbani as interim president. But rival mujahideen groups, particularly the forces led by Gulbuddin Hekmatyar, a Pushtun, continued to contend for recognition and power in Kabul and the surrounding countryside.

In December, a "Council for Resolution and Settlement," consisting of 1,400 delegates, met in Kabul to elect Rabbani to another 18 months as president. It also set up a 250-member Parliament to draw up a new Constitution in anticipation of nationwide elections in 1994. But not all of the rival mujahideen groups supported the Council. The competing political forces of President

Burhanuddin Rabbani and Prime Minister Gulbuddin Hekmatyar, leaders of the two strongest factions, continued to ravage the country.

In 1994, as President Rabbani began to gain the upper hand in the mujahideen infighting, a new force arrived to intensify the conflict. The Taliban ("seekers of religious knowledge") started as a group of Pushtun religious students from the southern Afghan city of Kandahar. They rose up in indignation to oppose the corruption of local warlords in that area of the country. Their reforming fervor spread rapidly among a people weary of the militancy and corruption of the mujahideen. By the fall of 1996, Taliban forces, supplied by arms from Pakistan, won a following and were in control of the southern two thirds of the country. In September, they drove the mujahideen government out of Kabul, and established a reign of reactionary religious terror in a city that had aspired to become modern. The Taliban's reforming zeal has countenanced many human-rights abuses. Most severely oppressed are the women of Afghanistan, particularly widows, who are deprived of jobs, humanitarian aid, and education under the Taliban regime. By 1999, the Taliban controlled 90 percent of the country.

AN UNCERTAIN FUTURE
Since the Soviet withdrawal from the country, with all of the fighting among the mujahideen and the rise of the Taliban, the Afghan people throughout the land continue to suffer the ravages of war. Many of the millions of refugees who fled to Pakistan and Iran during the time of Soviet occupation are hesitant to return. The destruction of their villages, the soil depletion and the mining of their fields, and severe drought also make the prospect of return far less secure than the stark but adequate support they receive in refugee

camps. And some refugees, especially women, express fear of repression in their homeland because of the Islamic fundamentalist fervor of both the mujahideen and Taliban leaders who are competing for control of their country.

Afghanistan's neighbors, and most recently the UN secretary general's special envoy to Afghanistan, are attempting to resolve the conflict between the warring parties. UN negotiations have defused tensions between Afghanistan and Iran. However, they have not resolved the more intractable internal disputes nor the human-rights abuses that repress and unsettle the Afghan people. The country has been torn by too many levels of conflict: between modernization and traditional ways of life; between democratic and socialist ideals; between fundamentalist and reform Islam; between ethnic and linguistic groups; between tribes and factions within parties and religious sects; between the interests of Iran and Pakistan. Because of the level of destruction, arms trading, and terrorist training that it introduced into the country, perhaps the most devastating conflict of all was that between the global agendas of the United States and the Soviet Union. It is no wonder that many people in Afghanistan find comfort even in the severe control of the Taliban, which has extended to encompass almost all of the country: The Taliban's religious zeal and military domination has at least stopped the fighting in most of the land.

DEVELOPMENT

In the 1980s, the Soviet government made a concerted effort to establish an industrial base, particularly in mining and processing Afghanistan's natural resources. With the increasing intensity of the warfare between the Afghan rebels and the Soviet occupying forces, these efforts collapsed. It is estimated that agricultural production declined by more than half, complicated by severe drought.

FREEDOM

Afghanistan is in a time of political recovery following the Soviet military occupation. Millions who fled into Pakistan and Iran are slowly making their way back to their devastated lands. Rival groups among the resistance forces, the mujahideen, and the Taliban continue to fight for power. The world community has been increasingly alarmed by the Taliban's zealous repression of women and other human-rights abuses.

HEALTH/WELFARE

The family and tribe have been the traditional sources of welfare in Afghanistan. Because of continuing warfare and limited access to safe water supplies, disease is prevalent. The overall life expectancy and the literacy rate are among the lowest in South Asia. The ban on woman's activities by the Taliban is severely limiting health and social services in the country.

ACHIEVEMENTS

Given the warfare and devastation to their country that the Afghan people have been through during the past 2½ decades, their greatest achievement may simply be their survival.

Bangladesh (People's Republic of Bangladesh)

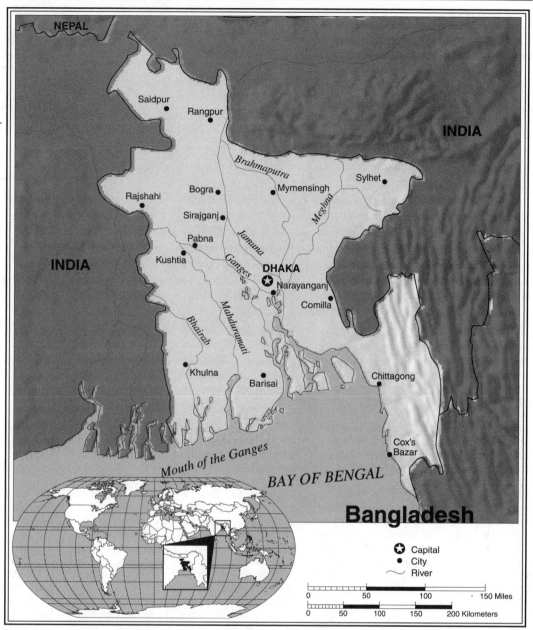

GEOGRAPHY

Area in Square Miles (Kilometers):
55,584 (144,000) (about the size of Wisconsin)
Capital (Population): Dhaka (8,545,000)
Environmental Concerns: water pollution; soil degradation; deforestation; severe overpopulation
Geographical Features: mostly flat alluvial plain; hilly in the southeast
Climate: tropical; monsoon; cool, dry winter; hot, humid summer

PEOPLE

Population
Total: 129,195,000
Annual Growth Rate: 1.59%
Rural/Urban Population Ratio: 81/19
Major Languages: Bangla; English
Ethnic Makeup: 98% Bengali; 2% Biharis and various tribes
Religions: 83% Muslim; 16% Hindu; 1% others

Health
Life Expectancy at Birth: 60 years (male); 60 years (female)
Infant Mortality Rate (Ratio): 71.6/1,000
Physicians Available (Ratio): 1/4,759

Education
Adult Literacy Rate: 38%
Compulsory (Ages): 6–11; free

COMMUNICATION

Telephones: 316,000 main lines
Daily Newspaper Circulation: 0.4 per 1,000 people
Televisions: 5 per 1,000 people
Internet Service Providers: 6 (1999)

TRANSPORTATION

Highways in Miles (Kilometers): 124,733 (201,182)
Railroads in Miles (Kilometers): 1,702 (2,745)
Usable Airfields: 16
Motor Vehicles in Use: 227,000

GOVERNMENT

Type: republic
Independence Date: December 16, 1971 (from Pakistan)
Head of State/Government: President Shahabuddin Ahmed; Prime Minister Sheikh Hasina Wajed

Political Parties: Bangladesh Nationalist Party; Awami League; Jatiyo Party; Jamaat-e-Islami; Bangladesh Communist Party
Suffrage: universal at 18

MILITARY

Military Expenditures (% of GDP): 1.8%
Current Disputes: boundary and territorial disputes with India

ECONOMY

Currency ($ U.S. Equivalent): 54.35 taka = $1
Per Capita Income/GDP: $1,470/$187 billion
GDP Growth Rate: 5.2%
Inflation Rate: 9%
Unemployment Rate: 35%

Labor Force: 56,000,000
Natural Resources: natural gas; arable land; timber
Agriculture: rice; jute; tea; wheat; sugarcane; potatoes; beef; milk; poultry
Industry: jute; garments; textiles; food processing; newsprint; cement; light engineering; fertilizer
Exports: $5.1 billion (primary partners United States, Germany, United Kingdom)
Imports: $8.01 billion (primary partners India, China, Japan)

http://www.virtualbangladesh.com
http://southasia.net/Bangladesh

BANGLADESH

Having won its independence from Pakistan in 1971, Bandladesh is the youngest nation of South Asia. Although it is one of the smaller countries of the subcontinent, it is also the most densely populated. More than 129 million people—almost half the population of the entire United States—live in an area smaller than the state of Wisconsin, at an average density of more than 2,000 per square mile. Only 19 percent of these people live in cities, but even in rural areas, the land is very crowded.

Bangladesh has the most cohesive population in South Asia. Almost all citizens share a common Bengali ethnic and language identity, and the majority are Sunni Muslims. However, with so much going for it upon which to build a democratic nation—language, religion, culture, and a successful fight for its independence—the country has had extensive struggles to achieve political stability. Because of its large and rapidly growing population, its limited resources, and a continuous succession of floods and cyclones, it has also had to struggle to achieve economic well-being for its people. It remains one of the poorest countries in the world; 61 percent of the urban population, according to a recent Asian Development Bank survey, and 80 percent of the total population, according to some estimates, live below the poverty line.

CULTURAL DIVERSITY ENDURES

Isolated among the hills and jungles in the eastern regions of Bangladesh, approximately 300,000 tribal peoples continue to live in much the same way as they have for thousands of years. Their cultures show little impact from the more dominant Muslim and Hindu populations, which make up the vast majority of the country. The languages spoken by the tribal peoples are obscure in origin; some have never been studied. Some of these groups, such as the Lushai, Murung, and Kuki, still practice slash-and-burn agriculture and the rite of bride capture.

COLONIAL HISTORY

The origin of Bangladesh as a separate political entity goes back to 1905, when Lord Curzon, the British viceroy in India, attempted to divide the Colonial Province of Bengal into a predominantly Muslim East Bengal (which then included Assam) and a Hindu West Bengal. In the 1947 partition of the subcontinent, when India and Pakistan received their independence of the British Raj, a truncated yet predominantly Muslim province of East Bengal became the eastern wing of Pakistan.

(United Nations/Wolff)

Bangladesh is often challenged by devastating cyclones that wreak havoc with rice production, not to mention the loss of life. This farmer planting rice in the paddies near Dhaka has no guarantee that the crop will survive the violent weather that will, in all likelihood, arrive in the months ahead.

East Pakistan had the larger population of the two wings of the new country, but economic and political power resided in the western wing. Attempts to impose the Urdu language as the national language of Pakistan, and favoritism toward the western wing in economic development, led during those early years to a sense of isolation and discrimination among the East Pakistanis. In 1970, when the first popular national elections were held, the Awami League Party, led by Sheikh Mujibur Rahman, won a majority of seats in the Pakistan national Legislature. Because this result was not acceptable to the political leaders in West Pakistan, President Yahya Khan suspended the Assembly. The people of East Bengal immediately began to riot in protest. The president tried to suppress this public outcry by military force. During eight months of military repression, the Pakistan Army killed many hundreds of thousands of people. Ten million fled as refugees into India.

INDEPENDENCE

In December 1971, India attacked Pakistan in support of the Bengali resistance fighters *(Mukti Bahini)*. Within two weeks, the people of East Bengal were free of Pakistan military rule. A government of the nation of Bangladesh was then established, with Mujibur Rahman as prime minister.

Although he was a popular, charismatic leader, Mujibur Rahman did not prove an effective administrator of a new nation facing severe overpopulation, poverty, and frequent natural disasters. In 1974, flooding left millions of people homeless and more than 400,000 dead. The prime minister's increasingly authoritarian rule in the face of such crises led in 1975 to a military coup, in which he and most of his family were killed.

General Ziaur Rahman, army chief of staff, became martial-law administrator in the political turmoil that followed. As he had been an officer in the Pakistan Army in East Pakistan in 1971, Zia faced opposition from younger officers who were part of the revolution that led to Bangladesh's independence. But he was equally committed to the establishment of Bangladesh as a separate, independent state; and he used his office to return the country to the path toward democracy.

During this martial-rule period, General Zia created his own political party, the Bangladesh Nationalist Party (BNP). He encouraged others to participate in national elections to elect 300 members to the national Legislature. (An additional 30 members were to be women subsequently elected by vote of the Legislature.) He also developed an economic policy to increase agricultural production, education, and health care. To assure administrative

After the Persian Gulf War in 1991, many Bangladeshis who were working in the region were forced to move back to their homeland. As these unemployed workers flooded back into urban areas, the cities rapidly became overcrowded. This teeming city street in Dhaka illustrates the crush of people.

control of the government, Zia retained the independent executive presidency that had been established by Mujibur Rahman, to which office he acceded in the presidential election held in 1978. In the legislative elections of 1979, his BNP won two thirds of the seats in the national Legislature.

Zia was well on the way to establishing popular, democratic government when, in 1981, he was assassinated by some dissident military officers. The power vacuum created by his death led to a dispute over the role of the army in the government. This dispute was resolved in 1982, when General Hussain Muhammed Ershad, chief of staff of the army, seized the reins of government.

Ershad wanted to further General Zia's policies of economic development and social reform. At the same time, he reduced the role of the Legislature by instituting direct military participation in public affairs in an influential "National Security Advisory Council." This favoritism toward the military caused political unrest among the people and eventually led to his downfall. Although Ershad won the presidential election in 1986, his party won only a very slim—and questioned—majority in the parliamentary elections that followed.

Two new leaders, each related to Ershad's more charismatic predecessors, came onto the national scene during the 1986 election campaigns. Begum Khaleda Zia was the widow of General Zia. She became head of the Bangladesh Nationalist Party after her husband's death. Sheikh Hasina Wajed was the sole surviving daughter of Mujibar Rahman, leading the Awami League.

The BNP and the Awami League jointly initiated a public protest soon after Ershad's election as president in 1986, calling for his resignation and new elections. The rivalry between these two leaders has set the political agenda ever since.

President Ershad first attempted to suppress their protest. Then, in December 1987, he dissolved the Legislature and called for new elections. The BNP and the Awami League called upon the electorate to boycott these elections. Even though Ershad's party won, voter turnout was very small, and public opinion began to rise against him. In 1990, in response to the public outcry, Ershad resigned. Justice Shahabuddin Ahmed of the Supreme Court was appointed acting president.

National elections were held in February 1991, and Begum Zia's BNP, polling 31 percent of the votes, won 140 seats in the 300-member Legislature. The Awami League, although gaining almost the same percentage of the votes, came in a distant second in the Legislature, with 84 seats.

A national referendum in September 1991, supported by both the BNP and the Awami League, voted to reduce the power of the president by placing the executive power in the hands of the prime minister of the national Legislature. Begum Zia then stepped down as president to become the prime minister of the new government.

Because Begum Zia's government did not command a majority of Assembly seats, she depended upon the help of the Jamaat-e-Islami, a conservative Islamic party that won 18 seats, to retain the prime minister's office. Even though that party represented a small minority, its vital role in supporting the prime minister emboldened it to condemn and seek the execution of a young doctor-turned-author, Dr. Taslima Nasreen, for alleged "blasphemy" in her novel *Lajja*. The government responded by arresting Nasreen—as much for her own protection, one suspects, as for her prosecution for "outrag[ing] the religious feelings" of the people of Bangladesh. Having posted bail, Nasreen escaped to live in exile in Sweden, Germany, and the United States.

The episode raised international concern, not only on behalf of the right of freedom of expression but also as an indicator of the strength of religious fundamentalism in the political life of Bangladesh. In subsequent elections, the Jamaat-e-Islami's legislative strength was reduced to three seats.

The closeness of the split of the popular vote between Begum Zia and Sheikh Hasina Wajed in the 1991 elections led Sheikh Hasina's Awami League to continue protests and, in 1994, a total boycott of the Legislature, with a call for new elections. The resultant political turmoil created a breakdown in government. New elections were held in June 1996, in which the BNP's standing was reduced from 140 to 116 seats. With the support of the 18 seats won by General Ershad's Jatiya Party, Sheikh Hasina garnered the votes needed to become prime minister. This time the BNP boycotted the Legislature.

| British control over Bengal A.D. 1757–1947 | East Pakistan 1947–1971 | The birth of Bangladesh 1971 | Mujibur Rahman's presidential rule 1972–1975 | Severe flooding causes 400,000 deaths 1974 | Martial law 1975–1989 | In 1991, a cyclone causes 130,000 deaths; flooding in 1998 kills 800 and leaves 30 million homeless; Bangladesh returns to parliamentary government 1990s | 2000s |

Women seek more reserved seats in the national Legislature

Bangladeshis continue to seek grassroots solutions to their country's severe economic and social problems

Because of the fierce rivalry between the Awami League and the BNP, the affairs of state appear to be conducted more on the streets, through the promotion of national strikes to protest legislation, rather than in the halls of the Legislature. Because of the intensity of this wrangling, political stability is still not assured for the government of Bangladesh.

Even without the participation of the BNP, the Legislature enacted an important initiative for women in government in September 1997. This law reserves for women three of the 10 directly elected seats in the 4,298 local councils that form the lowest tier of government in Bangladesh. Elections started in December 1997, with immense excitement and participation among the women of the country. More than 45,000 women were elected to council seats. This local initiative is an important step toward increasing the place of women in a country where traditional religious teachings and social customs have advocated their repression. Women leaders are now calling for direct elections of women to the national Legislature, and urging that the number of reserved seats be increased from 30 to 110 in that 330-member body.

Outside of government channels, the Bangladeshi people have shown outstanding initiative in meeting the many challenges caused by population growth and rural poverty, through grassroots, voluntary organizations such as the Bangladesh Rural Advancement Committee. Such efforts have built local schools, improved farming practices, and reduced the average number of births per Bangladeshi woman from more than seven in 1975 to less than four today.

The Grameen Bank is another important initiative to improve the plight of the poor from the ground up. It was founded in the 1970s by economics professor Mohammed Yunus to provide small loans without collateral to help the landless poor, in this country where more than half of the population live in poverty. It has been successful in creating credit for more than 1.4 million borrowers, 90 percent of whom are women. The bank also trains its borrowers in management skills, public health, and family planning. Its effectiveness among the impoverished in Bangladesh has established it as a model for economic empowerment in many other countries.

CHALLENGES

Economic problems have also continued to grow during the recent years of political unrest, presenting immense challenges to Sheikh Hasina's government. Among these problems are a diminishing world market for jute (the country's largest export product) and the lack of sufficient natural resources and energy sources to broaden its industrial base and create new employment.

High unemployment increased due to the loss of jobs for many Bangladeshis who worked in the Persian Gulf prior to the Gulf War in 1991. Skilled workers, who had earlier returned more than $500 million in remittances to Bangladesh each year, flooded the country's already overcrowded job market.

A devastating cycle of cyclones and floods has severely reduced domestic rice production—which is barely sufficient to feed Bangladesh's large and growing population even in good times. A cyclone in May 1991 killed 130,000 people. And the worst flood of the century, during the summer of 1998, paralyzed the central part of the country, killing 800 people and leaving almost 30 million homeless. Natural disasters remain a constant threat to all aspects of life in Bangladesh. Yet the population continues to grow, though at a decreasing rate (currently about 1.59 percent per year).

Another challenge has been the need to receive from India a more favorable distribution of Ganges River waters through the Farakka Barrage into Bangladesh. Through its control of this major source of vital water for irrigation and commerce in northwestern Bangladesh, India has a stranglehold on the smaller country. Indicative of a new spirit of cooperation among India and its neighbors, a major agreement was signed by the prime ministers of Bangladesh and India on December 12, 1996, to assure Bangladesh of at least half the water flow through the Barrage.

Bangladesh has also been fortunate in the support it has received from many government and independent agencies in response to its great needs. In 1992, such donors provided $1.9 billion, of which the United States (the fourth-largest bilateral donor) provided $99 million targeted to reduce population growth and increase food availability. With continued grants of humanitarian and economic aid, and with stable, democratically elected leadership, a resilient and responsive people remain hopeful for their health and well-being as a nation.

DEVELOPMENT

Bangladesh is an agricultural country with a very small industrial sector, few natural resources, and 35% unemployment plus substantial underemployment. Bangladesh's per capita income has grown an average of only 0.4% per year since 1960. The country continues to rely heavily on relief aid from the international community.

FREEDOM

Bangladesh has reverted to martial law in order to maintain social order several times since its independence in 1971. With reports of an estimated 3 million children in the workforce, their abuse is also a source of concern. In 1994, novelist Taslima Nasreen was prosecuted on charges of blasphemy, raising an international outcry.

HEALTH/WELFARE

In spite of many obstacles, overall life expectancy has increased from 27 to 60 years over the past two decades. Forty-five percent of the population have access to health care, and the number of hospital beds per population has doubled. Literacy has also increased, from 20% to 38%. The country has made significant strides in reducing the rate of population growth, from 3.3% to 1.59% per year.

ACHIEVEMENTS

Surviving extensive flooding in 1975 and a horrific cyclone in 1991, the resilient people of Bangladesh continue to develop their wealth of human resources, mostly through volunteer and nongovernment agencies such as the Grameen Bank. In 1991, a national referendum to restrain the military and restrict the power of the executive branch of government made a strong commitment to parliamentary democracy.

Bhutan (Kingdom of Bhutan)

GEOGRAPHY

Area in Square Miles (Kilometers): 18,142 (47,000) (about the size of Vermont and New Hampshire combined)

Capital (Population): Thimphu (30,300)

Environmental Concerns: soil erosion; limited access to potable water

Geographical Features: mostly mountainous; some fertile valleys and savanna

Climate: tropical in southern plains; cool winters and hot summers in central valleys; severe winters and cool summers in the Himalayas

PEOPLE

Population

Total: 2,005,000; some estimates as low as 600,000

Annual Growth Rate: 2.2%

Rural/Urban Population Ratio: 94/6

Major Languages: Dzongkha; various Tibetan dialects; Nepalese dialects

Ethnic Makeup: 50% Bhote; 35% ethnic Nepalese; 15% indigenous or migrant tribes (estimates vary widely)

Religions: 75% Lamaistic Buddhism; 25% Indian- and Nepalese-influenced Hinduism

Health

Life Expectancy at Birth: 53 years (male); 52 years (female)

Infant Mortality Rate (Ratio): 109/1,000

Physicians Available (Ratio): 1/8,000

Education

Adult Literacy Rate: 42%

Compulsory (Ages): none

COMMUNICATION

Telephones: 6,400 main lines

Internet Service Providers: na

TRANSPORTATION

Highways in Miles (Kilometers): 1,971 (3,285)

Railroads in Miles (Kilometers): none

Usable Airfields: 2

GOVERNMENT

Type: monarchy; special treaty relationship with India

Independence Date: August 8, 1949 (from India)

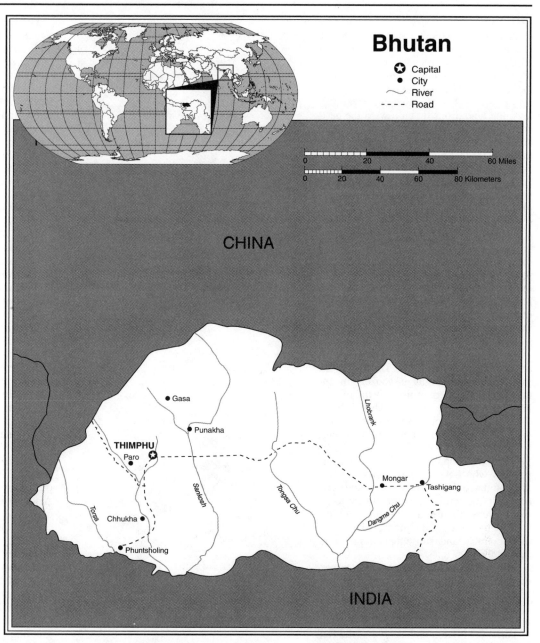

Head of State/Government: King Jigme Singye Wangchuk; Foreign Minister Jigme Yoeser Thinley

Political Parties: none legal

Suffrage: each family has one vote in village-level elections

MILITARY

Current Disputes: internal unrest; refugee issues

ECONOMY

Currency ($ U.S. Equivalent): 46.54 ngultrum = $1

Per Capita Income/GDP: $1,060/$2.1 billion

GDP Growth Rate: 7%

Inflation Rate: 9%

Natural Resources: timber; hydropower; gypsum; calcium carbide

Agriculture: rice; corn; root crops; citrus fruit; food grains; dairy products; eggs

Industry: cement; wood products; distilling; food processing; calcium carbide; tourism

Exports: $111 million (primary partners India, Bangladesh)

Imports: $136 million (primary partners India, Japan, United Kingdom)

http://www.cia.gov/cia/publications/factbook/geos.bt.html
http://southasia.net/Bhutan/

BHUTAN

Bhutan is the smallest nation on the South Asian subcontinent, about the size of Vermont and New Hampshire combined. Its highest point reaches 24,783 feet, along the Himalayan ridge border with Tibet. Through a series of cascading river valleys, the land drops down toward the eastern side of the subcontinent. Its southern border—barely 100 miles away, yet more than 24,000 feet below the country's highest point—touches the edge of the Brahmaputra River plain, through narrow, humid, gorgelike valleys of bamboo jungle. Most of the people in the country (population estimates vary widely, from 600,000 to nearly 2 million) live in the broader, fertile, pine-filled valleys of the central region, which lie from 5,000 to 9,000 feet above sea level. Isolated by its terrain and intent on preserving its Mahayana Buddhist heritage, the country has moved very cautiously into the modern world.

Culturally, religiously, and linguistically, 75 percent of the people of Bhutan are closely related to Tibet. Dzongkha, the most common language spoken in the nothern and western regions, is the official language of the country. Other Tibetan dialects are spoken in the easter regions, where the people are more closely related by custom to Assam. The remaining 25 percent are Nepali- and Hindi-speaking peoples who have recently migrated into the country, mostly as laborers, and have settled in the southern region closest to India. Several thousand Tibetans fled into Bhutan following the Chinese takeover of their country and subsequent repressions during the 1950s.

The Mahayana Buddhist religion predominant in Bhutan—as distinct from the Hirayana or Theravada Buddhism of Sri Lanka and Southeast Asia—also traces its origin to the earliest tradition of Buddhism in Tibet: the Nyingmapa school of the Red Hat sect. Important monasteries, such as at Takshang, celebrate the advance of the learned Indian monk Padma Sambhava, who introduced Buddhism into Tibet in the eighth century, as the heroic *Guru Rimpoche* ("Precious Teacher"). He is described as coming on a flying tiger to drive the forces of evil out of *Druk Yul,* "Land of the Thunder Dragon."

The oldest-recorded consolidation of the remote valley peoples under a single authority occurred in the 1600s by a Tibetan lama, Shabdrung Ngawang Namgyal. He established a tradition of autonomous religious leadership over the entire country that was sustained by the identification of the embodiment of his mind reincarnation (*Dharma Raja*) through

(Reuters/Bettmann)

Jigme Singye Wangchuk became the king of Bhutan in 1972, at the age of 17.

successive generations. The religious authority of his Dharma Raja was finally subsumed during the 1930s under the temporal authority of a dynastic monarchy that was established in 1907 under British colonial rule.

COLONIAL RULE

British military forces advanced into Bhutan in 1864 to repel Tibetan and Chinese claims of control over the Himalayan Mountains. In gratitude for his help in their successful attack of Tibet in 1903, the British rewarded Ugyen Wangchuk, then feudal lord (*Penlop*) of the north-central district of Tongsa, by assisting him to become *Druk Gyalpo,* the hereditary "Dragon King" of Bhutan, in 1907.

The British continued to oversee the external affairs of the country but allowed the new king to rule independently in domestic matters. In 1949, with the end of the British Raj, Bhutan extended this agreement "to be guided in regard to its foreign relations" with the government of India. India has allowed Bhutan latitude in establishing international agreements, including support of Bhutan's admission to the United Nations in 1971, but it remains the largest investor in the development of Bhutan's economy.

THE MONARCHY

Jigme Dorji Wangchuk, grandson of Ugyen Wangchuk and successor to his throne, instituted a number of reforms to bring his country cautiously into the modern era. However, Jigme Dorji, as king, remained the religious head and chief executive of the nation.

To encourage more public participation in government, Jigme Dorji Wangchuk established a National Assembly, the Tshoghdu, in 1952. The Assembly had 151 members, 31 of whom were appointed by the king. The remainder were elected by hereditary village headmen in the districts, who also served as local judges in a judicial system in which the king remained the chief justice.

In 1968, the Assembly was granted powers to limit the absolute authority of the king. No longer can he veto legislation passed by majority vote of the Assembly. Also, by a two-thirds vote, the Assembly can force the king to abdicate. But in that case, he can be succeeded only by the next claimant in his hereditary line. This provision reproduces on the national level the traditional family expectation that a landholder will pass on his lands to his eldest son as soon as the heir comes of age.

Jigme Dorji Wangchuk's reforms included the elimination of serfdom by granting public lands to landless servants. But he did not break up large private landholdings, so as not to disrupt traditional social patterns and create unemployment. In the face of Chinese threats of invasion during the 1950s, the king also opened the country to the outside world by allowing the Indian government to build a road from Bhutan's southern border with India to the capital, Thimphu. It took 112 miles of winding roadway to cover this straight-line distance of 45 miles. In 1996, the government of India undertook a project to extend this roadway into eastern Bhutan.

THE CHALLENGE
OF MODERNIZATION

Jigme Dorji Wangchuk died in 1972 and was succeeded by his 17-year-old son,

Dharma Raja of
Tibetan lamas
A.D. **1616–1950**

Tongsa Penlop
becomes
hereditary king
1907

British control
over Bhutan's
external affairs
1910–1947

Indian control
over Bhutan's
external affairs
begins
1949

A constitutional
monarchy is
established; the
national
Assembly has
power to limit
authority of king
1953

King Jigme
Singe Wangchuk
becomes king
1972

Cautious
modernization
efforts begin; the
Citizenship Act
aims at limiting
citizenship
1980s

Many Nepali
immigrants are
denied citizenship;
demonstrators
protest government
policies toward
Nepalis
1990s

2000s

Tens of
thousands of
Nepali residents
of Bhutan remain
in refugee camps
in eastern Nepal

Cautious
modernization
remains a priority
of the government

Jigme Singye Wangchuk. He has continued his father's policies of cautious change. He proposed during the summer of 1998 to expand and make more representative the powers of the National Assembly by replacing his royal Council of Ministers with a cabinet elected by the Assembly and "vested with full executive powers to provide efficient and effective governance of our country." The Assembly, with some reluctance to adopt the change, carried out his wishes by electing a cabinet from a list of candidates that he provided. In a further step toward modernization, the Assembly voted in November 1998 to impose an income tax on all citizens who earned more than an equivalent of $100 per month to supplement its industrial tax revenues.

With India's help, Bhutan has increased the country's energy potential. The largest of six new hydroelectric generators, the 336-megawatt Chuka Hydroelectric Project, was financed by the Indian government. It was completed in 1987 and now exports $25 million worth of electricity to India annually.

Bhutan's forestry reserves are extensive but remain virtually unexploited. Even tourism is being developed on a very modest scale.

The policy of the government is to develop the country's economy so as not to undermine the traditional Buddhist life of the majority of its people. It is also concerned about maintaining Bhutan's dramatically beautiful environment. Twenty percent of the country has been set aside for preservation. The Royal Manas National Park, a 165-square-mile sanctuary established along the southern border of Bhutan, is designed to protect the natural wildlife of South Asia. Many of the creatures that find refuge there are among the world's endangered species.

The emphasis on preserving Bhutan's heritage and protecting its environment has slowed the impact of modern advances on the lives of the people of Bhutan. A Canadian Jesuit priest, William Mackey, has led the development of the nation's educational system, to provide 180 schools and a national college. Still, only 21 percent of children attend school (attendance is not compulsory), and the literacy rate today is only about 42 percent. Health services are also meager, and the expectation is that the family unit will remain the primary source of social welfare. The annual birth rate is a significant 2 percent, but the level of infant mortality is also high. The average life expectancy among the Bhutanese people is only about 52 years.

Bhutan is facing many severe challenges as it seeks to adopt the positive aspects of a modern industrial society while maintaining the values of its rich natural and religious heritage. Part of the problem is that greater industrialization requires more labor. Ninety-five percent of the workforce of Bhutan are employed in subsistence farming on the 16 percent of the land that is available for cultivation and pasture. To provide the labor needed to develop industry, the country has had to import workers from neighboring Nepal and India. Their very presence challenges the indigenous peoples' attempt to create a Bhutanese national identity out of the exclusive cultural characteristics of the dominant Buddhist community. Rather than fostering the integrity and richness of the cultural diversity of the many peoples who live within the nation's borders, the government began in 1985 to promote distinctively northern traditions of language and custom as being nationally correct.

This nationalistic policy has been particularly hard on the Nepali population,

who have settled mostly in the southern part of the country. Although the government's intent is to promote political unity, its efforts have led to political unrest, terrorist attacks on schools and other public buildings, and deportations. Tens of thousands of people have fled Bhutan and are now living in refugee camps in the eastern part of Nepal. The governments of Nepal and Bhutan are working together to find a solution to this difficult situation. Significantly, in this age of democracy, the role of the enlightened monarch, King Jigme Singye Wangchuk, appears to be the most promising in leading to a resolution of the cultural and political tensions created by modernization.

DEVELOPMENT

Bhutan's economy is based on agricultural self-sufficiency and barter. More than 95% of the workforce are in the agricultural sector. Bhutan is among the poorest countries in the world. The government is cautiously developing the country's vast hydropower potential and a modest tourist industry.

FREEDOM

In this traditional society, thinly dispersed across rugged mountain slopes, the king instituted political reform in 1952 by creating an advisory National Assembly, the Tshoghdu. The Assembly has enacted various laws that repress Nepali and Indian residents.

HEALTH/WELFARE

The family and the village have the primary responsibility for the welfare of the people. In the 1950s, the king instituted a program of social work for monks living in the country's numerous state-supported monasteries. The government has recently undertaken an education program, but the literacy rate in Bhutan remains one of the lowest in South Asia.

ACHIEVEMENTS

Twenty percent of the country has been set aside for the preservation of its vast forest and for wildlife reserves. Efforts at reform are done in the context of maintaining Bhutan's unique and distinctive Buddhist cultural heritage.

Maldives (Republic of Maldives)

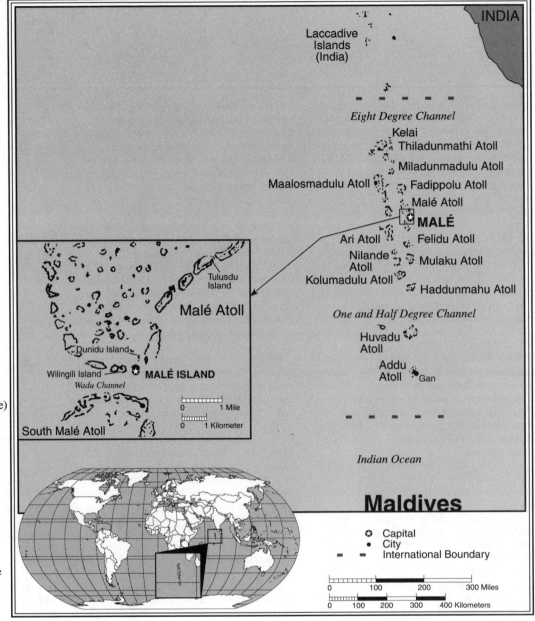

GEOGRAPHY

Area in Square Miles (Kilometers):
186 (300) (about 1½ times
the size of Washington, D.C.)

Capital (Population): Malé
(63,000)

Environmental Concerns:
depletion of freshwater
aquifers; global warming
and sea-level rise; coral-reef
bleaching

Geographical Features: flat,
with white sandy beaches

Climate: tropical; monsoon

PEOPLE

Population

Total: 301,500

Annual Growth Rate: 3.06%

Rural/Urban Population Ratio:
73/27

Major Languages: Maldivian
Divehi; English is spoken by
most government officials

Ethnic Makeup: Sinhalese;
Dravidian; Arab; Black

Religion: 100% Sunni Muslim

Health

Life Expectancy at Birth: 61
years (male); 63 years (female)

Infant Mortality Rate (Ratio):
65.5/1,000

Physicians Available (Ratio):
1/2,587

Education

Adult Literacy Rate: 93%

COMMUNICATION

Telephones: 18,000 main lines

Daily Newspaper Circulation:
12 per 1,000 people

Televisions: 19 per 1,000 people

Internet Service Providers: na

TRANSPORTATION

Highways in Miles (Kilometers):
6 (9.6) in Malé

Railroads in Miles (Kilometers): none

Usable Airfields: 5

GOVERNMENT

Type: republic

Independence Date: July 26, 1965 (from
the United Kingdom)

Head of State/Government: President
Maumoon Abdul Gayoom is both head
of state and head of government

Political Parties: none; the country has
been governed by the Didi clan for 8
centuries

Suffrage: universal at 21

MILITARY

Current Disputes: none

ECONOMY

Currency ($ U.S. Equivalent):
11.77 rufiyaa = $1

Per Capita Income/GDP: $1,800/$540
million

GDP Growth Rate: 7%

Inflation Rate: 3%

Unemployment Rate: negligible

Labor Force: 67,000

Natural Resource: fish

Agriculture: fish; corn; coconuts; sweet
potatoes

Industry: tourism; fish processing;
shipping; boat building;
coconut processing; garments; woven
mats; rope; handicrafts; coral and sand
mining

Exports: $98 million (primary partners
United States, United Kingdom, Sri
Lanka)

Imports: $312 million (primary partners
Singapore, India, Sri Lanka)

http://www.maldive.com/hist/
mhisto.html
http://www.cia.gov/cia/publications/
factbook/geos/mv.html
http://www.undp.org/missions/
maldives
http://southasia.net/Maldives/

MALDIVES

Maldives is a string of 1,190 tiny tropical islands grouped into 26 atolls in the Indian Ocean. Located about 400 miles southwest of India and west of Sri Lanka, the island chain stretches for some 510 miles north to south across the equator. The largest of the islands is less than five square miles in area, and the highest elevation is only 80 feet above sea level. Most of the islands are much smaller, rising barely six feet above sea level. They are easily submerged by tidal waves and storm swells. These are very fragile, remote, but enticingly beautiful.

Most of the islands are covered with lush scrub growth. Some have coconut-palm groves, and all are surrounded by coral reefs and clear waters laden with fish. The mean daily temperature remains at 80°F year-round. The climate is humid, especially during the rainy monsoon season, from June to August. Yet because of a shortage of fresh water and arable land on most of the islands, only 200 of them are inhabited.

About one fifth of the total population of 301,500 people live in the capital city on the island of Malé, which is only seven tenths of a square mile in area. An increasing population, due to longer life expectancy and a high birth rate, is rapidly draining the island's limited resources. The daily use of fresh water is drawing upon the island's aquifer faster than the annual rainfall replenishes the supply. And increasing contamination threatens what water is available.

The inhabitants of Maldives appear to have come originally from south India and Sri Lanka. Remains of shrines indicate the migration of Buddhists from the mainland of the subcontinent around the second century B.C. The prevailing language of the islands is further evidence of early Buddhist settlement. Maldivian Divehi is derived from Pali, the classical language of Buddhism in India, from which the Sinhalese language of Sri Lanka also comes. The arrival of an Islamic Sufi saint in A.D. 1153 led to the conversion of the peoples of the islands to Islam. Because of this mass conversion, the Divehi language is now written in the Arabic script, with the addition of many Arabic and Urdu words.

Because the Maldive islands lie across the maritime trade route between Africa and eastern Asia, Arab traders often stopped there. The Moroccan explorer Ibn Battuta visited Malé in the fourteenth century, during his extensive travels through North Africa and Asia. Because of his Islamic scholarship, he was invited to stay on Malé as a judge. During his eight-month stay, he married and divorced six times. The accounts of his time in Maldives give a colorful description of island life at that time.

The people of Maldives continue to affirm their Islamic faith. Citizenship is restricted to Sunni Muslims, and the country's legal system is based on Shari'a, the Islamic law.

A HISTORY OF INDEPENDENCE

Strongly united under the authority of a sultan (an Islamic monarch), the Maldivians remained fiercely independent through the centuries. A local leader, Bodu Muhammad Takurufanu, repulsed a brief Portuguese colonial intrusion in 1573. Maldives became a protectorate under the British Crown in 1887. Even then, however, the Maldivian leaders did not permit British interference in their governance. The southern island of Gan became a British military base during World War II and, in 1956, the site of an air base. But strong antiforeign sentiment forced the closing of the base in 1976, some 14 years before the end of a 30-year lease with the British. The following year, Maldives rejected a Soviet offer to lease the base for $1 million per year.

In 1953, the sultan, Muhammad Amin Didi, declared Maldives a democratic republic, with himself as the president. But

(Reuters/Bettmann)

The fragile character of Maldives' environment and the economic reliance of its inhabitants on the environment make international cooperation an important element in future development. Regional associations and international organizations are important forums for communication. One such organization is the South Asian Association for Regional Cooperation. Pictured above are representatives of the member governments who met on November 21, 1990, in Malé. From left to right were Prime Minister Krishna Prasad Bhattaria of Nepal, India's Prime Minister Chandra Shekhar, Bangladesh's President Hussain Muhammed Ershad, Pakistan's Prime Minister Nawaz Sharif, Bhutan's King Jigme Singye Wangchuk, Maldives' President Maumoon Abdul Gayoom, and Sri Lanka's President Dingiri Banda Wijetunge.

| The earliest evidence of Indian Buddhist civilization **300 B.C.** | Maldives' conversion to Islam **A.D. 1153** | Maldives is an Islamic sultanate; Bodu Muhammed Takurufanu repulses brief Portuguese intrusion to the islands in 1573 **1153–1968** | Maldives is a British protectorate **1887–1968** | Maldives becomes an independent democratic republic without political parties **1968** | An attempted coup is put down by the Indian Army **1988** | The government seeks to improve social services, incurring substantial debt in the process; Maldives agitates for global environmental responsibility **1990s** | **2000s** |

At the Coral Reef Symposium in October 2000, Maldives' marine environment is cited as heavily damaged by global warming

the power of governance remained with an appointed Regency Committee. In 1968, Amin Ibrahim Nasir, who had served since 1957 as prime minister in the Committee, successfully instituted a new Constitution with an elected legislative Parliament (*Majlis*). This body selected him as nominee to run for president of the country. The new Constitution also did not allow for political parties.

During his tenure as president, Ibrahim Nasir abolished the post of prime minister and increased the power of the presidency to quasi-sultan status. He won a second five-year term in 1973. Nasir decided not to run for a third term and was succeeded in 1978 by Maumoon Abdul Gayoom.

President Gayoom was reelected by large majorities in the elections of 1983, 1988, 1993, and 1998. In 1993, he received 93 percent of the popular vote as the single candidate in a referendum to approve his nomination by a majority vote of the 48-seat Citizen's Majlis. An opposition candidate who won 18 votes in the parliamentary election was subsequently charged, according to an Amnesty International report, with violating the Constitution, and was sentenced to banishment from the country for 15 years.

In November 1998, the Majlis amended the Constitution with a view to assuring citizens' guarantees of civil rights and decentralizing government administration among the many islands of the country. But it did not change the electoral process for the presidency. On October 16, 1998, 90.9 percent of the voters approved President Gayoom's nomination by the Majlis to a fifth five-year term.

An attempted coup, thought to have been instigated by Sri Lankan Tamil militants, was put down in 1988 by an Indian military unit called in by President Gayoom. Ties with the Indian government have become increasingly strong since that time.

QUALITY OF LIFE
The major industries of Maldives are fishing and tourism, both of which are heavily supported by the government. Almost half of the country's workers are employed in fishing, mostly using traditional offshore craft called *dhonis*. In the 1980s, government funds helped to construct canning and cold-storage facilities, as well as more than 200 modern fishing boats, in order to expand the catch—and the markets—for this valuable resource. In 1981, an international airport was constructed on the island of Malé to serve an increasing number of tourists. Together with the airports on the islands of Hulule and Gan, it received 395,000 visitors in 1998 to vacation in the more than 60 new hotels spread over the various atolls.

These industries, even with a reviving coconut crop and a modest shipping fleet, do not balance out the import needs of the country, especially for food. The country receives more than 20 percent of its revenue as foreign aid, and it continues to accumulate debt. Like most regions of the world that are strongly dependent upon the tourist industry for their economic health, Maldives' fortunes are based upon the prosperity of the wealthier nations. In recent years the country has sustained an impressive economic growth rate, rising to 7 percent in 1999, leading to the highest per capita income in South Asia. Still, because of its fragile environment and economy, the government of Maldives objected very strongly to its removal from the United Nations list of the world's poorest nations to the developing-countries category, during the meeting of the UN General Assembly in 1998.

In spite of setbacks, the Maldivian government has extended education and health services throughout the inhabited islands in the archipelago. The number of primary schools has increased. Adult literacy has also increased, from 82 percent to 93 percent, a result of the outreach of the educational programs to the outer islands.

Maldives has no institutions of higher learning. Medical facilities are also limited. There are only four hospitals in the entire country, plus an emergency medical rescue service among the outlying islands. The government, however, continues to work to improve water supplies and to eliminate water-borne diseases through water-purification and other public-health measures.

Although the country does not function as a totally free, modern democracy, the government has retained the confidence of its independent, peace-loving people, through its policies to encourage economic growth and expand social services. Because of the fragile character of its environment, upon which so much of the economy depends, Maldives is eager to stimulate increasing international concern for the preservation of the global environment. The country also appears to be making progress in its appeal to its neighbors to establish the Indian Ocean as a nuclear-free zone.

DEVELOPMENT

The major economic activity of this nation of islands is fishing, which provides about 20% of its gross domestic product and employs half of its workforce. Tourism has also gained tremendously in importance and is attracting foreign investment. Maldives' gross domestic product per capita, though still very low, has increased dramatically since 1960.

FREEDOM

Maldives became a democratic republic in 1968. It adopted a popularly elected unicameral Legislature and made provisions for an independently elected president; but it prohibited the formation of political parties. Rights of citizenship in Maldives, an Islamic nation, are restricted to Sunni Muslims.

HEALTH/WELFARE

Health and educational services are hard to provide to a population widely dispersed among the habitable islands of the country. Still, the government has developed an emergency rescue service that is able to reach 97% of the population. The average overall life expectancy is 62 years.

ACHIEVEMENTS

Maldives has resisted superpower attempts to place a naval base on its territory. To preserve its fragile environment and its peace-loving character, the country has become a strong advocate to make the Indian Ocean an arms-free, and particularly a nuclear-free, zone.

Nepal (Kingdom of Nepal)

GEOGRAPHY
Area in Square Miles (Kilometers):
54,349 (140,800) (about the
size of Arkansas)
Capital (Population):
Kathmandu (535,000)
Environmental Concerns:
widespread deforestation;
soil erosion; water and air
pollution
Geographical Features: flat river
plain in the south; central
hills; rugged Himalayas in
the north
Climate: cool summers and
severe winters in the north;
subtropical in the south

PEOPLE

Population
Total: 24,703,000
Annual Growth Rate: 2.34%
Rural/Urban Population Ratio:
89/11
Major Languages: Nepali;
numerous dialects
Ethnic Makeup: Newar; Indian;
Tibetan; Gurung; Magar;
Tamang; Bhotia' Rais; Limbu;
Sherpa; many smaller groups
Religions: 90% Hindu; 5%
Buddhist; 3% Muslim; 2% others

Health
Life Expectancy at Birth: 58
years (male); 57 years (female)
Infant Mortality Rate (Ratio):
76/1,000
Physicians Available (Ratio):
1/13,777

Education
Adult Literacy Rate: 27.5%
Compulsory (Ages): 6–11; free

COMMUNICATION
Telephones: 194,000 main lines
Daily Newspaper Circulation: 8
per 1,000 people
Televisions: 12 per 1,000 people
Internet Service Providers: na

TRANSPORTATION
Highways in Miles (Kilometers): 8,198
(13,223)
Railroads in Miles (Kilometers): 63 (101)
Usable Airfields: 45

GOVERNMENT
Type: parliamentary democracy
Independence Date: 1768 (unified)
Head of State/Government: King Birendra
Bir Bikram Shah Dev; Prime Minister
Girija Prasad Koirala

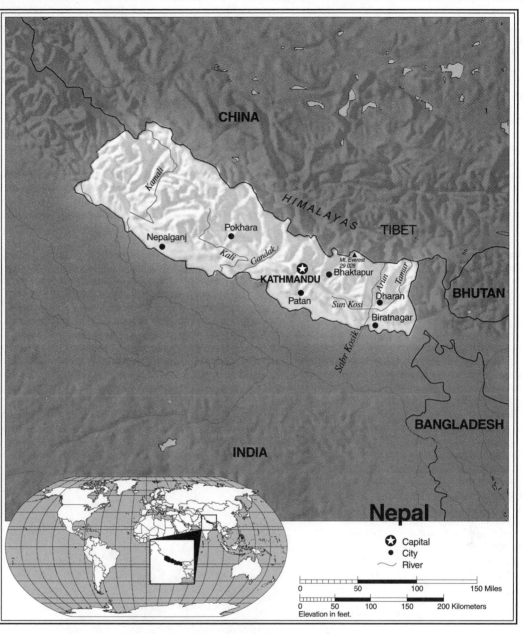

Political Parties: Communist Party of
Nepal/Unified Marxist-Leninist Party;
Nepali Congress Party; National
Democratic Party; Nepal Sadbhavana
(Goodwill) Party; Nepal Workers and
Peasants Party; others
Suffrage: universal at 18

MILITARY
Military Expenditures (% of GDP): 0.9%
Current Disputes: dispute over Bhutanese
refugees in Nepal

ECONOMY
Currency ($ U.S. Equivalent): 74.56
Nepalese rupees = $1
Per Capita Income/GDP: $1,100/$27.4 billion
GDP Growth Rate: 3.4%

Inflation Rate: 11.8%
Labor Force: 10,000,000
Natural Resources: quartz; timber;
hydropower; lignite; copper; cobalt;
iron ore
Agriculture: rice; corn; wheat; sugarcane;
root crops; milk; water buffalo meat
Industry: carpets; textiles; rice, jute, sugar,
and oilseed mills; cigarettes; tourism;
cement and brick production
Exports: $485 million (primary partners
India, United States, Germany)
Imports: $1.2 billion (primary partners
India, China/Hong Kong, Singapore)

http://rip.physics.unk.edu/Nepal/
NPD.html
http://www.catmando.com/nepal.htm

NEPAL

Nepal is like a Tantric mandala: colorful, dramatic, intense, intricate, mystifying. The country is breathtaking, like the magnificent Mount Everest—awesome to behold, confounding to ponder. Everest's peak, the highest in the world, dominates a majestic row of 10 Himalayan mountains over 26,000 feet high, a row that marks the imposing, formidably high boundary between Nepal and Tibet. The land falls steeply, dramatically, from this arctic height into the lush Kathmandu Valley, some 20,000 feet below. It then rises again over the smaller, barren Mahabharat range, up to 11,000 feet, and drops down once more through the foothills into a marshy plain along the Ganges River, about 900 feet above sea level. Nepal is a land of immense natural contrast, covering a descent from the highest point on Mount Everest down more than 28,000 feet in less than 100 miles. Habitat for a wide variety of species, from the elusive snow leopards to elephants, monkeys, tigers, and crocodiles, the land fills one with a sense of wonder.

Nepal is also home to an immense variety of people. In the broadest of terms, they can be divided by region, religion, and language into three distinct groups. The high mountainous regions to the north are sparsely inhabited, mostly by people of Tibetan descent and language who follow the Lamaist, or Tibetan Buddhist tradition. Their dress and many customs are from Tibet. Some, for example, practice polyandrous marriage, wherein the wife of the eldest son is also married to his younger brothers. In such families, their lands are not usually subdivided. The brothers also share in the few seasonal occupations that the frigid terrain allows: cultivating in spring, herding in summer, and trading in winter. Because of these practices, even though arable land is scarce and trade has been drastically reduced by the Chinese takeover of Tibet, the people of the northern mountain region are more prosperous than those living in the more fertile valleys to the south. The alternative to family life presented by the Buddhist monastic tradition also restrains their growth in population. Although they occupy almost half of the total land area, they constitute only about 3 percent of the total population of Nepal.

About 31 percent of the population live in the Terai, the low-lying, southernmost region of the country that is in the Gangetic plain. These people are mostly Hindu, although some are Muslim. They speak dialects of Hindi and are ethnically and culturally very close to their Indian neighbors. Because the land is flat, fertile, and nurtured by the snow-fed rivers flowing out of the mountains, agriculture is the primary activity. Although it is a narrow strip of land, only about 20 miles wide and occupying only 17 percent of the country, it produces more than 60 percent of Nepal's gross national product.

Two thirds of the population of Nepal live in the interlying hill region, which is also predominantly agricultural, although most of the country's urban population live in this region. Arable lands are scarcer than in the Terai and are terraced for farming. Because of the altitude, the growing season is shorter and the yields are lower.

At the center of this region is the Kathmandu Valley, a lush alluvial plain 15 miles long and 12 miles wide. Nepal's three largest cities—Kathmandu, Patan, and Bhaktapur—lie in the valley. These cities threaten to absorb most of the valley as they continue to expand. Dominant among the peoples of the valley are Newars, who have lived there as a distinct community for many centuries. They were known in ancient times for their skill as artisans and merchants, interacting with the many surrounding cultures to create a distinctive artistic style and to fuse an overwhelming multiplicity of religious expression. The Nepali language, spoken by about 60 percent of the total population, is itself a combination, based on the Indo-European languages of India infused with extensive Tibeto–Burman borrowings.

(UN photo/Ray Witlin)

The festive costume on this child shows the continuation of distinct religious traditions in Nepal.

There is a wide array of ethnic and cultural identities as well as urban/rural and rich/poor contrasts in this central valley region of Nepal.

SOCIAL DIVERSITY

Nepali social diversity is partly due to the rugged terrain, which has kept many small groups isolated east to west in the several river valleys that descend down the steep southern slopes of the mountains. Also important, Nepal has been since ancient times on the main trade routes from India north up the river valleys, through the high mountain passes into Tibet, and on into China. Nepali traders along these routes have maintained distinct ethnic identities, whether their primary interaction has been with the Tibetan culture to the north or with the Hindu culture to the south. The success of their mercantile activity with such very different partners has reinforced the cultural contrasts between Tibet and India within the central region of Nepal itself.

The influence of the hierarchical social structure known in India as the caste system has also contributed to Nepal's social diversity. This system, in ranking rather than assimilating differing social and vocational groups, affirms the unique customs of each group. The Nepalese criteria for ranking appear more flexible than in India. Ethnic identity and adaptive behavior to form distinct social groupings appear to change readily and to add to the diversity of their configuration. The Gurkhas, for example, famous for their military prowess and courage, have been recruited from three different Tibeto–Burman language communities, from different parts of Nepal. They join together because of the opportunity for military employment that a shared identity as Gurkhas affords. Similarly, several distinct tribal groups in the Terai have claimed a single ethnic identity as Tharus in order to gain strength as a political force not available to them as separate minority groups. In contrast, Thaksatae villagers have distanced themselves from other Thakalis—with whom they share ethnic, linguistic, and religious identities—in order to maintain the trading privileges that they have achieved as a distinct community within that group.

POLITICS

The immense and confusing diversity of Nepal's population has contributed to the country's struggle with democracy. For many years it was felt that only a strong, absolute monarchy would be able to hold it together.

The unity of present-day Nepal was forged in the eighteenth century A.D. by Prithvi Narayan Shah, king of the western province of Gorkha, who conquered the surrounding kingdoms and established his dynasty in Kathmandu, the capital of the defeated Newar ruler. His family's reign was circumscribed first by the British East India Company, in 1815; and later, in 1845, by the Kathmandu Rana family, which established a powerful and hereditary prime ministry to rule the Shah domain.

(UN photo/Ray Witlin)

The geographic contrast in Nepal is dramatic. The Himalayas are the highest mountains in the world and act as an impressive backdrop for many of the populated areas.

In 1950, with the departure of British support from the subcontinent, a national movement, led by the Nepali Congress Party, overthrew the Rana family. Because of his support for the anti-Rana movement, King Tribhuvan Vir Vikram Shah became a national hero. Upon his reinstitution as full monarch in February 1951, he worked to bring constitutional democracy to Nepal. In 1959, under a new Constitution that set up a national Parliament and limited the powers of the king, elections were held. The Congress Party won 74 of the 109 seats in the Legislature.

King Tribhuvan died in 1955 and was succeeded by his son, Mahendra. In 1960, in a surprise move to assert his power as absolute monarch, King Mahendra dismissed the Nepali Congress Party government and banned all political parties. In 1962, he established a pyramidal process for electing representatives to the national legislative Assembly—not based on nationwide elections. General elections were held on the local level to choose the village council (*panchayat*). Members of the local panchayat then elected representatives to an 11-member district panchayat, which in turn elected members to the National Panchayat. The National Panchayat elected its own prime minister. However, the king reserved the power to appoint all the members of the Council of Ministers, whose job it is to oversee the operation of the different departments of government. In this way, he was able to reinforce the traditional seats of political power held by the local landlords throughout the diverse regions of the country. They, in turn, reaffirmed the authority of the king.

| The Shah dynasty's expansion of the Kingdom of Gorkha A.D. 1742–1814 | The British East India Company reduces the Gorkha domain to the Kingdom of Nepal 1815 | Rana family domination of the Shah dynasty 1845–1950 | The founding of the Nepali Congress Party 1949 | Constitutional monarchy 1959–1960 | Absolute monarchy; constitutional monarchy established with a multiparty, democratically elected Parliament 1960–1991 | The first national democratic elections in 32 years are held 1990s |

2000s

Nepal continues to struggle with widespread and severe poverty

Continued upheavals in the top Nepali leadership

Upon the death of King Mahendra, in 1972, his son Birendra became king. In 1980, in response to growing public concern for greater democracy, he held a referendum to see whether the people would prefer a multiparty electoral process or a continuation of the party-banned, tiered elections to determine membership in the National Panchayat. The tiered panchayat system won by a 54.7 percent vote. In response, King Birendra retained the ban on political parties, but the electoral process was amended to have the National Panchayat representatives elected by direct vote of the people.

Elections were held in 1986, and a majority who favored limiting the power of the king were elected. Encouraged by these results, the combined leadership of the banned Nepali Congress Party (NCP) and Communist Party of Nepal (CPN) organized public demonstrations for greater democracy. Their agitation found support among a growing middle class, disaffected by economic hardship and a bungling, opportunistic panchayat leadership. In response to this popular outcry, King Birendra removed the ban on political parties in 1990. In November of that year, he proclaimed a new Constitution, which he had worked out with the party leaders, that limited his absolute sovereign power and marked the beginning of a multiparty, democratically elected, parliamentary government.

National democratic elections—the first in 32 years—were held on May 12, 1991. The Nepali Congress won 114 seats in the new 205-seat Parliament. But the Nepali Congress Party continued to struggle with its diversity. In July 1994, some 36 dissident members of the Congress refused to attend the prime minister's annual address. Their absence led to a no-confidence vote

in Parliament, its dissolution, and new elections, set for November 1994.

In the 1994 elections, the Unified Marxist-Leninist Party (UMLP), which had been the major opposition party in the previous Legislature, won the most parliamentary seats. However, its 88-member plurality was not enough for a majority. The UMLP managed to put together a fragile coalition, which lasted for less than a year before the party was forced to step down. The Nepali Congress Party, which held 86 seats, then formed a coalition with two other parties to gain the majority needed to lead the government. Two years later, this fragile coalition also fell apart. Still not wishing to face a new general election, the UMLP gathered yet another coalition to achieve a majority. It gave its support to the party of Lokendra Bahadur Chand, a monarchist whose leadership harked back to the days of King Mahendra, even though his party held only 10 seats in Parliament. Prime Minister Chand was ousted six months later by Surya Bahadur Thapa, a member of his own party who managed to form a new coalition with the Nepali Congress Party. After a stormy six months, during which the UMLP split and the NCP demanded that it lead the coalition, Thapa first sought to have King Birendra dissolve the Parliament and call for new elections. Unsuccessful in this strategy, he resigned, and on April 12, Girija Prasad Koirala, long-time leader of the NCP, became the fifth prime minister of Nepal to serve since the national elections in November 1994.

In the elections that had to be held five years later, in 1999, the Nepali Congress Party won a decisive victory of 104 seats, sufficient to form a government on its own. A revolt within the party in 2000 forced the resignation of Krishna Prasad Bhattarai as prime minister. Girija Prasad

Koirala, the strongest leader in the NCP, became the prime minister again.

CHALLENGES
Each new Nepalese government has been faced with demanding parliamentary struggles to maintain its leadership. Yet beyond the walls of government, the ruling party is more substantively challenged by the country's staggering problems of poverty, high population growth, and illiteracy. More than 90 percent of the workforce barely survive by subsistence farming. According to a recent World Bank report, 40 percent of the people live in absolute poverty. The incidences of malnutrition-related retardation and blindness are also high. And HIV, the virus that causes AIDS, is beginning to take its toll on the population. In education and in medical and social services, the country struggles with limited resources, geographic isolation, and ethnosocial diversity.

The country needs a consistent, stable, and purposeful government to confront and solve these difficult problems. Nepal's industrial potential has long been restrained by trade agreements tying the country to India's development policies, and its commerce has been severely limited by the difficulty in traversing the trade routes to Tibet. There is immense potential for improvement in Nepal's economic and social conditions, but among such an incredibly awesome array of peoples, even contemplating the challenge leaves one with a sense of wonder.

DEVELOPMENT

Most of Nepal's economy relies on subsistence agriculture, which involves more than 90% of the labor force. The successful ascent of Mount Everest has introduced a thriving tourist industry. Tourism is up by 20% in recent years. Yet per capita income has increased at an annual rate of only 0.1%, placing Nepal among the poorest nations in South Asia and the world.

FREEDOM

The Kingdom of Nepal became a constitutional monarchy in 1959 but reserved executive power with the king and preserved the traditional powers of local chieftans in tiered elections to the Legislature. In 1991 popular elections were held for the first time in 32 years. Limits on royal authority were also established.

HEALTH/WELFARE

In education and social services, the country struggles with limited resources, isolation, and diversity. Malnutrition, caused by a limited growing season and urban crowding, has led to high levels of retardation and blindness. Adult literacy is only 27.5%, while overall life expectancy is but 57 years.

ACHIEVEMENTS

Democracy is beginning to take root in this mountain kingdom long ruled by an entrenched establishment. Tourism has introduced environmental degradation, but it has also brought the stimulus to develop industry based on its large hydropower potential and to undertake social-service and educational reforms.

Pakistan (Islamic Republic of Pakistan)

GEOGRAPHY
Area in Square Miles (Kilometers):
310,320 (803,940) (about
twice the size of California)
Capital (Population): Islamabad (na)
Environmental Concerns: water
pollution; deforestation; soil
erosion; desertification;
limited freshwater supplies
Geographical Features: flat
plain in the east; mountains in
the north and northwest
Climate: mostly hot, dry desert;
temperate in the northwest;
arctic in the north

PEOPLE

Population
Total: 141,554,000
Annual Growth Rate: 2.17%
Rural/Urban Population Ratio:
65/35
Major Languages: Punjabi;
Sindhi; Siraiki; Pashto; Urdu;
Balochi; Hindko; English; others
Ethnic Makeup: 63% Punjabi;
12% Sindhi; 10% Pushtun
(Pathan); 8% Urdu;
10% others
Religions: 95% Muslim; 5%
others

Health
Life Expectancy at Birth: 58
years (male); 60 years (female)
Infant Mortality Rate (Ratio):
82.5/1,000
Physicians Available (Ratio):
1/1,863

Education
Adult Literacy Rate: 38%

COMMUNICATION
Telephones: 2,560,000 main lines
Daily Newspaper Circulation:
22 per 1,000 people
Televisions: 16 per 1,000 people
Internet Service Providers: 26 (1999)

TRANSPORTATION
Highways in Miles (Kilometers): 153,643
(247,811)
Railroads in Miles (Kilometers): 4,898
(8,163)
Usable Airfields: 118
Motor Vehicles in Use: 1,100,000

GOVERNMENT
Type: federal republic
Independence Date: August 14, 1947
(from the United Kingdom)
Head of State/Government: President
Mohammad Rafiq Tarar; Chief
Executive (General) Pervez Musharraf

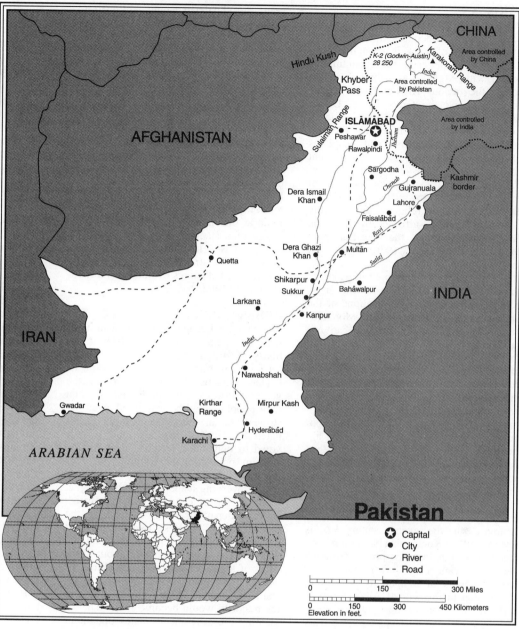

Political Parties: various government and
opposition parties
Suffrage: universal at 21; separate electorates
and reserved parliamentary seats for
non-Muslims

MILITARY
Military Expenditures (% of GDP): 3.9%
Current Disputes: support of the Taliban
in Afghanistan; border disputes with
Afghanistan; disputes over Kashmir and
water-sharing problems with India

ECONOMY
Currency ($ U.S. Equivalent): 58.90
rupees = $1
Per Capita Income/GDP: $2,000/$282 billion
GDP Growth Rate: 3.1%

Inflation Rate: 6%
Unemployment Rate: 7%
Labor Force: 38,600,000
Natural Resources: natural gas; petroleum;
coal; iron ore; copper; salt; limestone
Agriculture: cotton; grains; sugarcane;
fruits; vegetables; livestock
Industry: textiles; food processing;
construction materials; consumer goods
Exports: $8.4 billion (primary partners
United States, United Kingdom, Hong
Kong)
Imports: $9.8 billion (primary partners
Japan, United States, Malaysia)

 http://www.clas.ufl.edu/users/
gthursby/pak/

PAKISTAN

Pakistan is the second-largest nation of the South Asian subcontinent, about one fourth the size of India. It lies in the Indus River Valley, between the mountainous border with Afghanistan—through which comes the famous Khyber Pass—on the northwest, and the Great Indian Desert and the Rann of Ktch on the southeast. Long a land of transition between the rugged steppes of Inner Asia and the plains of India, it is today a young nation caught between the heritage of a glorious imperial past and the poetic image of an ideal theocratic future. Its goal to become an exemplary modern religious state, a truly Islamic republic, is affirmed by the name *Pakistan,* given by the Muslim poet Muhammed Iqbal in 1930. The word means "Land of the Pure."

The heritage of the people of Pakistan traces back to the earliest-known urban culture in South Asia. Excavations of the ancient cities of Harappa and Mohenjo-daro, discovered in 1922, reveal an impressive civilization that dates from 3000 to 1500 B.C. Distinctive for its knowledge of hydrologics and its use of irrigation to cultivate the valley with the rich waters of the Indus River, the Harappan city culture developed an extensive commerce with the emerging civilizations in the Mesopotamian Valley to the west. Patterns of agriculture, craft, and commerce that began during that early urban era persist in the social and economic life of the country to this day.

Islam, a religious faith based upon the teachings of the prophet Muhammad in Arabia during the seventh century A.D., as revealed in the Koran, also has a long heritage in Pakistan. Invading princes from the west and wandering Sufi mystics drew large numbers of indigenous peoples to submission to the will of Allah (God) as early as the eighth century, by their spiritual discipline and religious teaching. This vibrant faith, now so firmly woven into the fabric of the people's lives, was the basis for the creation of Pakistan as an Islamic republic in 1947. Today, 95 percent of the 141.5 million people in the country are Muslim. Of these, 77 percent belong to the Sunni tradition.

The invasion of Moghul princes, who marched their conquering forces across the northern plains of South Asia to the Bay of Bengal in the sixteenth century, marked the period of greatest glory in the heritage of the Pakistani people. The Moghuls were militant Turks refined by the elegance of Persia and energized by their Islamic faith. Akbar (1556–1605), the greatest of these emperors, is remembered for the opulence and splendor of his court, for the far-reaching administrative control of his empire, and for his elaborate building projects, which still stand as massive tribute to his commanding wealth and intellect. The Taj Mahal, built by his grandson, Shah Jahan, is the crowning architectural achievement of this magnificent imperial past. Although the Moghul dynasty declined in its later years, it continued to dominate northern South Asia until the middle of the nineteenth century, when it fell to British colonial rule. Pakistan became an independent nation with the departure of the British Raj in 1947. It was created then, especially by the 7.2 million people who migrated from central India at the time of independence, in the image of a staunch Islamic and glorious imperial past. This heritage has been both a tremendous strength and a challenging obstacle to Pakistan's evolution as a modern nation state.

INDEPENDENCE MOVEMENT

The Muslim League was formed in 1906 to represent the interests of the Islamic minority in British India, in the movement for freedom from colonial domination. Its leaders became convinced through the years of struggle with the British Raj that their people would be oppressed, even destroyed, in an independent India dominated by Hindus. In 1940, the League voted to demand a separate state for the Muslim population of South Asia. Muhammad Ali Jinnah, through his persistent, unswerving leadership of the League, realized this objective when the British Raj, in departing in 1947, set up the mechanism to establish two independent nations instead of one. Those districts that were under British control (about three fifths of the subcontinent) where Muslims were predominant would become Pakistan; the districts where Hindus were in the majority would become India. The remaining areas—princely states not under direct British administrative control—would accede to either country by their own determination.

This plan to partition a separate Islamic state out of British India created two wings: a smaller but more populous East Pakistan; and a larger, dominant West Pakistan. These two wings were separated by nearly 1,000 miles of India. This partition scheme had disastrous consequences in purely human terms. The Muslims in British India who most feared Hindu oppression were not those who had the local security of living in Muslim-majority districts; rather, they were those who lived in the Hindu-majority districts in north-central India. They felt endangered in their own lands, and forced to move. Similarly,

Hindu minorities in districts where the Muslims were in a majority also feared for their lives. This mutual fear caused the migration of more than 14 million people—Hindus and Muslims moving in opposite directions. The clashes of these two groups in the border areas, especially in the Punjab, which was split in half between Muslim and Hindu districts, led to the killing of hundreds of thousands of bewildered, anxious people. It was a huge human catastrophe that has left an abiding scar.

The process for the accession of the princely states of British India into either India or Pakistan led to a strenuous dispute that also had severe consequences. The former princely state of Kashmir, on the border between India and Pakistan, had a large Muslim majority, but was headed by a Hindu maharaja. The dispute over whether the maharaja could, or in fact did, accede the state to India led to three wars between India and Pakistan, an unresolved UN resolution for a plebiscite, continuing tension, and violent atrocities committed both by and against militant separatist groups.

In 1999, Pakistani forces infiltrated across the line of control between Pakistani- and India-occupied Kashmir into the Kargil District on the Indian side. Indian Army units eventually pushed the infiltrators back to sustain the earlier stalemate. Even today, military units of the two countries fire artillery rounds at each other on the Siachen Glacier, a small, uninhabited Himalayan plateau, 20,000 feet high. This confrontation costs more than $1 million per day and over $6,000 per soldier per year, with 80 percent of the casualties "environment-induced," just to assert the mutual claim of Pakistan and India to control a divided Kashmir.

Pakistan commits a quarter of its annual budget to the military, in large part to defend its claim to Kashmir. The high expenditure also reflects the dominant role the military establishment has in Pakistan's national life—a role that feeds upon the pervasive fear of an attack from India. This fear contributed to the government's decision to test its nuclear capability immediately following India's nuclear tests on May 11 and 13, 1998, even at the high cost of international disapproval and U.S. economic sanctions.

The bloodshed of the migrations, and the homelessness, caused by the partition of British India in 1947 taxed to the limit the meager human resources of the new nation of Pakistan. Because its lands were on the outer fringes of the British Raj, the country lacked adequate administrative services to pull itself together. Muhammad

Ali Jinnah took upon himself the chief-executive duties as governor-general in the interim government. Unfortunately, he became seriously ill and died 13 months later. Liaquat Ali Khan, who succeeded him as prime minister, was assassinated three years later, in 1951. The Muslim League, which had been imported from British India, lost control of a unifying national agenda to the indigenous, traditional sources of provincial power: wealthy land-owners and tribal leaders. Even though a Constitution was adopted in 1956 that affirmed the common sovereign identity of the two wings of Pakistan as an Islamic republic, the country was in political disarray.

STRIVING FOR POLITICAL STABILITY

In a move to develop political stability in the young nation, General Mohammad Ayub Khan, the commander-in-chief of the Pakistan Army, became martial-law administrator in 1958. In hopes of stimulating economic growth among a people "not yet ready for democracy," Ayub Khan instituted a new Constitution that delegated extensive executive power to a president elected by those elected to local political offices. This Constitution also established a tiered representative structure, built on local elections, to elect a National Assembly.

In 1965, Ayub Khan was elected president by a limited electorate of "Basic Democrats"—80,000 locally elected council members whom Ayub Khan accepted as prepared to exercise a presidential vote. War broke out between India and Pakistan over the Kashmir issue in that same year, resulting in a military stalemate and a renewed UN cease-fire. The peace settlement with India in the Tashkent Agreement of 1966 was a tremendous political setback for Ayub Khan.

Growing discontent spawned two new political leaders, one in each of the wings of Pakistan, who developed followings in their respective regions sufficient to bring down Ayub Khan's government and divide the one nation into two. Mujibur Rahman, leader of the Awami League in East Pakistan, capitalized on the perception among the people of that region that they were second-class citizens of the country. His charismatic leadership won immense popular support for greater regional autonomy. At the same time, Zulfikar Ali Bhutto, a Western-educated diplomat from a large land-holding family in the province of Sindh in West Pakistan, formed the Pakistan People's Party (PPP). Adopting the campaign slogan *Roti, Kapra aur Makon* ("Bread, clothes and shelter"), he mobilized a wide popular following in the western region toward a policy of democratic socialism. Committed to creating a political base in the west, he did not attempt to generate a following in East Pakistan. Nor did he anticipate the rise of the Awami League.

President Ayub Khan was not able to contain either the Bhutto or the Rahman initiatives; in 1969, he was forced to resign. In a quest to bring order, his successor, General Yahya Khan, declared the first popular national elections in Pakistan since its independence, to be held on December 7, 1970. In these elections, the Awami League won 160 of the 162 seats in the National Assembly assigned to the more populous East Pakistan. Bhutto's Pakistan People's Party won 81 seats of the 132 assigned to West Pakistan.

Bhutto felt that, by winning a majority of the seats (58.7 percent) from West Pakistan, he was the rightful leader of the country. He therefore refused to join the newly elected national Legislature until he was assured a position in the government. In response to Bhutto's boycott, President Yahya Khan suspended the Legislature. This suspension led to a vehement cry for independence in East Pakistan. President Yahya Khan sought to suppress the freedom movement by severe military repression. Resistance of the people in East Pakistan mounted, and millions fled across the border to find refuge in India. After several months of unrelenting bloodshed, the Indian government launched a military attack in support of the Bengali rebels. They won independence for their own country on December 17, 1971.

The separation of East Pakistan to become the independent nation of Bangladesh left the Pakistan People's Party with a majority in the National Assembly, and Bhutto became the president of Pakistan. He set out immediately to bring what was left of the country together by nationalizing banking and such major industries as steel, chemicals, and cement. Bhutto thereby expanded an already cumbersome civil-service bureaucracy. His policy created employment opportunities in the central government, but it discouraged investment and led to a decline in industrial production.

Bhutto was more successful in restoring parliamentary government. He created a new Constitution—the nation's third in 26 years—which was adopted in 1973. It established a National Assembly of 207 members and four provincial assemblies of proportionate size. (Baluchistan was assigned 40 members; North-West Frontier, 80; Punjab, 240; and Sindh, 100.) All representatives were to be elected directly for five-year terms. Under its provisions, Bhutto became prime minister, the chief executive of the government, elected by a majority of the National Assembly.

National elections were again to become the nation's undoing. Bhutto called for elections in 1977, in hopes of getting endorsement for his leadership and his socialist economic policies. This call spurred an unexpected and virulent opposition of nine parties, which united to form the Pakistan National Alliance (PNA). Although Bhutto's Pakistan People's Party won the election, the PNA, which won only 36 of 207 seats in the National Assembly, charged that the elections had been fixed. The PNA took to the streets in protest.

In the political turmoil that followed, Bhutto called in the army to restore order and sought to negotiate with the PNA to hold new elections. Before agreement could be reached, Mohammad Zia-ul-Haq, chief of staff of the army, seized control of the government. He promised to hold elections within 90 days but cancelled them 2 weeks before they were to be held. He continued to hold out the promise of elections for the following 11 years, during which time he maintained firm military control. Part of that control was to bring charges against Bhutto of complicity in a political murder, which led to Bhutto's trial and execution on April 4, 1979.

In the fall of 1979, Zia took the country further away from democracy by banning all political parties and imposing censorship on the press. The following year, he removed from judicial review the actions of his government and the decisions of the military courts that he had set up to enforce his martial rule. Many of these measures were cloaked in a policy of "Islamization," through which his military regime sought to improve the religious quality of the people's public life by an appeal to the traditional laws and teachings of Sunni Islam. Once again, Pakistan's measured steps toward a stable, popularly elected government were thwarted by entrenched divisions, political turmoil, and strong repression more reminiscent of Moghul imperialism than expressive of modern representative democracy.

Zia's consolidation of power in Pakistan coincided with the collapse of the shah of Iran, the rise of Saudi Arabia as a huge power in the Middle East, and the Soviet invasion of Afghanistan. All of these developments gave Pakistan a place in the U.S. government's policies to contain Soviet expansion and protect Western sources of oil. These vital interests placed a higher priority on the stability of the Zia government in Pakistan than on the erosion of democracy that was taking place under his rule. Increasing U.S. support for his repressive military rule had a negative impact not only on the quest for democracy among the people of Pakistan, but also on the strength of the Zia government. In the words of Mubashir Hasan, finance minister in the Bhutto government:

A government without a popular base can't really take a stand against anyone else. Dictatorships have the power to impose the policies demanded by outsiders in the short term. What they don't have is the power to say "No" to the U.S. or the [international] banks. The "strong" are actually weak because they are not being pushed by local interests and constituencies.

—Quoted by Richard Reeves in
Passage to Peshawar (p. 184)

A spirit of democracy did survive, if only partially, in a hasty referendum called in 1985 by General Zia to affirm his policy of Islamization by electing him an executive president for a five-year term. The Constitution of 1973 also survived, in an amended form. This set the stage for new elections, unexpectedly announced by Zia to be held in November 1988. These elections did take place, in spite of his death in a plane crash in August of that year. A ruling of the Supreme Court removed the ban on political parties, and Bhutto's Pakistan People's Party, led by his daughter, Benazir Bhutto, won 93 seats in the 217-member National Assembly. Although not commanding a majority of the Legislature, Benazir Bhutto was invited to become prime minister. Then just 35 years old, she was both the youngest person and the first woman to lead an Islamic nation.

Benazir Bhutto's government was formed by a very uneasy balance within the Legislature itself. In order to keep the support of a majority of the Legislature, necessary to continue as prime minister, she had to keep her opposition at bay by cultivating supporters from other political parties to her cause. Her tenure was fragile at best. It was further complicated by competing claims to her authority outside the Legislature by the nation's other large power brokers—the army leadership and the president. Even though General Beg, appointed army chief of staff in 1985, advocated restraint form involvement, the army remained a presence to contend with during her tenure as prime minister.

The leaders of the army had by this time a long tradition of standing in judgment on the conduct of the government—and intervening if they found it lacking. Such

had been done by General Ayub Khan in 1958, by General Yahya Khan in 1970, and by General Zia-ul-Haq in 1977. It occurred again by General Pervez Musharraf in 1999. Pakistan has thus been under military rule for half of its existence as a state.

All of these military leaders, when they intervened in the government, established their political role as independent administrators, not as prime ministers answerable to the Legislature. Thus, even though the Constitution of 1973 established a parliamentary form of government, General Zia modified it in 1985, by the Eighth Amendment, to give the president (in parliamentary government normally a formal position,) more power.

Benazir Bhutto tried in 1989 to get the full authority of the prime minister's office restored by having the Eighth Amendment repealed. Her failure to receive the necessary two-thirds vote of the Legislature led to the end of her first term as prime minister. Since the opposition in the National Assembly was not able to muster a no-confidence vote against her, President Ghulam Ishaq Khan issued a decree in August 1990, under the Eighth Amendment, to have her government dismissed. He then appointed a caretaker government, which brought charges of corruption and nepotism against the former prime minister in a bid to remove her as a candidate for reelection to the Legislature, by court decree. New elections were then set for October 1990.

ELECTORAL SHIFTS
In the 1990 elections, a coalition of eight parties, led by Mian Nawaz Sharif, chief minister of Punjab and head of the Islami Jamhorri Ittehad (IJI), or Islamic Democratic Alliance, won a decisive margin of 105 seats in the 217-member National Assembly. (This was an impressive jump from 55 seats in the 1988 elections.) In the provincial elections in Punjab, the IJI fared even better, winning 208 of the 240 seats. And in the North-West Province, it won a commanding 33 of 80 seats. His party achieved this legislative domination by winning 36.86 percent of the popular vote. Benazir Bhutto's People's Democratic Alliance (PDA), on the other hand, was severely reduced, in the National Assembly, down from 93 to 45 seats, even though it won 36.84 percent of the popular vote. Supported by the second-largest number of members, Bhutto joined the National Assembly as the leader of the opposition, a position her father had refused to accept in 1970.

Mian Nawaz Sharif is a member of a successful industrial family who migrated

from Amritsar in East Punjab to Pakistan in 1947. In the 1970s, Zulfikar Ali Bhutto nationalized the family's large foundry business. Its return to his family following the takeover of the government by General Zia in 1977 established both Sharif's stature and his leanings as a political figure. Based on the results of the national elections of 1990, he was invited by President Ghulam Ishaq Khan to head the new government.

The 1990 elections revealed the fragile nature of political parties and the necessity of their coalition on the national level. The financially conservative IJI was able to bring together the Communist-leaning Awami National Party, dominant in the North-West Frontier Province, and the fundamentalist Jamiat-Ulema-i-Islam party, in its bid to win the elections. Without their support, Sharif's party would not have succeeded.

Islamization is still a politically potent issue in Pakistan, enhanced by the recent successes of the Taliban in neighboring Afghanistan. The fundamentalist convictions of the Jamiat-Ulema-i-Islam, although a small minority, remain a significant force in Pakistani politics. In order to fulfill a promise made during the campaign to bring the fundamentalist Islamic groups into his coalition, Prime Minister Sharif introduced a law to make the Islamic code of Shari'a the supreme law of Pakistan. At the same time, he asserted that he would not present a Shari'a bill that would stand in the path of modernization in the country. The Jamiat-Ulema-i-Islam Party later objected to the Shari'a bill passed by the National Assembly, arguing that it was too vaguely worded and not being implemented. The party withdrew from the ruling coalition.

Variously interpreted, Islam still serves as a unifying force in holding the country together and in harmony with its neighboring countries to the west. The public has come to expect renewed political emphasis on Islamization during times of crisis. Blasphemy laws and efforts to amend the Constitution to make the Koran "the supreme law of the land" were implemented to divert attention from increasing economic instability in the country.

Mian Nawaz Sharif was not so successful in his attempt to limit the martial-law powers of the president granted by the Eighth Amendment to the Constitution. In response to Sharif's attempt to repeal the amendment, President Ghulam Ishaq Khan invoked it, for a second time, to dismiss the Sharif government on charges of corruption and nepotism, in April 1993. This time, the Supreme Court overruled

(UN Photo)

These farmers are from a village in West Pakistan. They are among the many who benefit from the Gudu Barrage, which provides water for irrigation into the dry desert areas of Pakistan.

the president and reinstated the Sharif government. The army chief of staff, General Abdul Waheed, then stepped into this political deadlock and brokered the resignation of both the prime minister and the president. The National Assembly and state legislatures were then dissolved, and new elections were set for October.

In the fall 1993 elections, Benazir Bhutto and her Pakistan People's Party were returned to power by a very slim margin. The PPP won 86 seats in the 217-member Legislature, as compared to 72 for Sharif's party. Her position was further strengthened by the election a month later of Farooq Leghari, deputy leader of the PPP, to the office of president. Equally important, her party's nominees for chief minister of the states of Punjab and Sindh were also elected to office.

Benazir Bhutto did not do well in her second term as prime minister. She pursued policies that destabilized the nation's economy, compromised foreign invest-ment, and produced 20 percent inflation. She imposed a sales tax that proved very unpopular among the people. An image of rampant corruption in government, together with an attempt to appoint sympathetic judges to the high courts, added to the erosion of her popular support. Her political stature was further compromised by accusations of complicity in the death of her brother, Murtaza Ali Bhutto, her most aggressive political rival, in a shootout with the police in Karachi in September 1996. All of these factors led to her dismissal by President Leghari in November, on charges of corruption and nepotism under the Eighth Amendment, and a call for new elections on February 3, 1997.

Even though voter turnout was low, Mian Nawaz Sharif and his Pakistan Muslim League Party won a strong mandate in this election. They garnered a two-thirds majority in the National Assembly and 215 of the 240 seats in the Punjab assembly. Benazir Bhutto's opposition party joined his government to repeal the Eighth Amendment to the Constitution.

Reducing the power of the president did not place any restraint on the military. In response to Prime Minister Sharif's repudiation of the military instigation of the infiltration into the Kargil District of Kashmir in the summer of 1999, the Army chief of staff, General Pervez Musharraf, staged a coup on October 12. He then brought charges against Sharif for treason and attempted murder. The courts found Sharif guilty, and he was sentenced to life in prison.

PAKISTAN IN THE MODERN AGE

The topsy-turvy period since the end of General Zia-ul-Haq's martial rule raises questions about the future of modern democracy in Pakistan. There are many obstacles even beyond the smooth working of the structure of government itself.

Foremost among these obstacles is an inherent regional division of the country

| Harappan city culture 3000–1500 B.C. | The Moghul empire A.D. 1526–1857 | The founding of the Muslim League 1907 | The Muslim League adopts the demand for the separate state of Pakistan 1940 | The partition of British India; the creation of Pakistan 1947 | War with India over Kashmir 1948 |

into four provinces. Because the regional identities of these provinces have been the primary basis for the formation of the political parties that have brought the people into the political process, the differences among these regions have been strengthened on the national level.

Each of the four provinces is defined not only by a distinct geography and ethnic group; each also has a distinct language that takes precedence in the regions over Urdu as the declared national language of Pakistan. Urdu is spoken by only about 8 percent of the Pakistani population—mostly the families of *mohajirs,* who brought the language when they came from India in 1947, and who live today primarily in Pakistan's major cities.

These regional identities further challenge the political future of Pakistan because Punjab is so clearly dominant. Punjabi-speakers comprise about two thirds of the total population of the country. Their lands, considered Pakistan's "breadbasket," are the most heavily irrigated and agriculturally the most productive. The greatest industrial development and most of the wealth is also concentrated there. And because Lahore, the capital city of Punjab, was the administrative center for the entire region under the British Raj, Punjabis have dominated the ranks of the army and the civil services.

Sindh is the next-most-important province, sharing with Punjab about 90 percent of the industrial production of the country. Karachi, Pakistan's largest city, with a population of 9 million, is the country's only port and a center of commerce. Yet only 12 percent of the country are Sindhi-speakers.

Even smaller in population are Baluchistan and the North-West Frontier Province, which lie to the west and north along the arid desert and mountainous borders with Iran and Afghanistan. The Baluchi language is spoken by less than 5 percent of the population. Pashto is the language of the Pushtuns (Pathans), who live in the rugged mountains of the North-West Province. The Pushtuns are only 10 percent of the total population, though their number was increased by the influx of more than 3 million Afghan Pushtuns forced across the border as refugees by the Soviet invasion of Afghanistan.

The recent rise of the Taliban movement across the border in Afghanistan is stirring new concerns—and opportunities. The shared Pushtun identity of the people of the North-West Province with the Taliban challenges the quest for their allegiance to Pakistan. And the extremely radical Islamic fervor of the new Afghan leadership also challenges the quest in Pakistan for a more moderate, modern expression of the Muslim faith. At the same time, Taliban control of Afghanistan presents the opportunity to extend a natural-gas pipeline into the former Soviet republics bordering Afghanistan to the north and to increase not only trade but also other alliances with those Islamic countries.

Together with language and ethnic differences among the regions of Pakistan, religious minorities are a source of significant division within the country. Because their faith is considered heretical by the orthodox, members of the Ahmadiya sect of Islam are being imprisoned and committed to death sentences under newly imposed blasphemy laws, enacted in response to political pressure for continued Islamization. Hindu and Christian communities also are not secure as minorities among such a highly dominant Sunni Muslim population.

There is also a striking contrast between the needs and expectations of the urban (35 percent) and rural (65 percent) populations, extenuated by the large influx of mohajirs from India into the cities of Pakistan in 1947. In the early years of independence, these immigrants comprised 46 percent of the urban population of the country. Today, the Muttahida Quami movement (until recently named the Mohajir Quami movement, but now divided into two hostile camps), is the third-largest political party in the country, although limited to Karachi for its political base.

Another challenge to a stable, democratically elected government in Pakistan is the wide division between the rich and the poor: between the traditionally entrenched, wealthy landholders and tribal leaders versus the landless peasants and herders in the countryside; and between the industrialists versus the slum-dwellers in the cities. The extraordinary extent of the urban disparity is revealed in a 1970 study that found that 80 percent of the capital wealth in Pakistan was owned by just 22 *families.*

New wealth and a new class were created in Pakistan during the 1980s by jobs in the Persian Gulf oil fields. At the peak, more than 2 million young people from all parts of the country were sending home more than $4 billion a year, or about 10 percent of the country's gross domestic product. The loss of jobs during the Persian Gulf War had a double impact on Pakistan's economy, as it both cut in half the remittances from overseas Pakistanis and increased the number of unemployed people within the country.

Even with the Soviet withdrawal from Afghanistan and loss of Western support, international forces continue to affect Pakistan. Both the Sharif government and the Musharraf military rule struggled to develop the nation's economy by encouraging private industrialization, through tax benefits and foreign investment. Still, the weakening of Asian economies beginning in 1997 and the imposition of sanctions by the United States following Pakistan's nuclear tests on May 28, 1998, have contributed to a decline in the country's economic growth.

Foreign investments are reported to have decreased by more than 50 percent and Pakistan's foreign reserves by 67 percent during the months immediately following the nuclear tests, as compared to the same months a year earlier. The U.S. government has since removed many of the sanctions imposed on Pakistan, and the International Monetary Fund has restored $575 million of a $1.5 billion loan to finance Pakistan's international debts, in efforts to stave off a financial crisis.

The terms of the IMF loan required the government to impose drastic austerity measures, which coincided with increasing political unrest and violence. Attacks among opposing factions in Karachi have led to many murders and to a general breakdown of law and order in that city. In response, Prime Minister Sharif imposed martial law in the city in November 1998. General Musharraf extended that rule to the entire country in October 1999.

Although Pakistan's plight has been extenuated by international forces and events, most of these crises have their origin within the country itself. Observers of Pakistan's plight point to several areas of internal concern: a disproportionately high defense budget (more than $4 billion per year), a high rate of population growth

The first Constitution establishing Pakistan as an Islamic republic
1956

Military rule of Ayub Khan
1958–1969

War with India over Kashmir
1965

Military rule of Yahya Khan
1969–1971

First national popular elections; Mujibar Rahman's Awami League wins majority of National Assembly; Zulfikar Ali Bhutto's Pakistan People's party wins West Pakistan majority
1970

War with India; the breakaway of East Pakistan to become Bangladesh; Zulfikar Ali Bhutto becomes president of Pakistan
1971

A Constitution establishing parliamentary democracy is adopted; Bhutto becomes prime minister
1973

Military rule of Zia-ul-Haq; national elections set; helicopter accident kills Zia; Benazir Bhutto becomes prime minister
1977–1988

Parliamentary democracy is restored; Pakistan tests its nuclear capability in the wake of Indian tests in May 1998
1990s

2000s

Military rule of General Musharraf

Growing financial problems threaten the nation's economy

(2.17 percent), the loss of human rights through the imposition of religiously sanctioned blasphemy laws, and the need for human-resources development. In the 1996 World Bank report on Pakistan, economist Hugo Diaz found that "Pakistan's performance in important human development indicators has been the Achilles heel of the country's development effort. Without sustained gains in health status and accumulation of skills, continuing growth in labor productivity and incomes will not be possible." The report further identified the fertility rate among women to be 65 percent higher, infant mortality to be 30 percent higher, and literacy 25 percent lower than the average among the world's poorer nations. A more recent report, entitled "Improving Women's Health in Pakistan," identified an extremely high rate of women dying from pregnancy-related causes—one in every thirty-eight.

The limited—and elitist—opportunity for education in Pakistan is a significant indicator of the need for human-resources development. The 1998 Census placed the level of literacy in the country at 36 percent—a small improvement over the level, according to UNICEF officials, when Pakistan received its independence in 1947. The Educational Grants Commission estimated in 1983 that fewer than 8 percent of the nation's children went to school. Only a quarter of this number went on to secondary school. And half of the secondary students were educated in private schools, the only place where they could get instruction in English, still the language of opportunity in the professions, technology, and trade.

Women are excluded even more from education: their level of literacy is around 16 percent—less than half that of the men. Girls comprise just a third of the total student population. This lack of education reflects the traditional expectation of their subservience and seclusion in Islamic society. General Zia-ul-Haq affirmed this attitude as national policy when making his commitment to Islamization in 1983.

In conflict with this traditional attitude is the assertion made at the same time by the economic planners in General Zia-ul-Haq's government in the formulation of the Sixth Five-Year Plan. They found that:

> In Pakistan today, the profile of women is simply shocking. The following cold statistics are a sad commentary on the legacy of neglect. . . . The participation of women in the compensated labour force is only 5 percent . . . less than 3 percent of civil service jobs . . . crippling handicaps of illiteracy, constant motherhood, poor health.

"In all societies," the document declared, "women's development is a prerequisite for overall national development; indeed no society can ever develop half-liberated and half-shackled."

Zulfikar Ali Bhutto encouraged opportunity for women to share in the national life of Pakistan when he became prime minister in 1973. The Constitution of 1973 reserved 27 seats for women in the 217-member National Assembly. That Bhutto's daughter Benazir was able to hold the office of prime minister gives encouragement that new roles and responsibilities are available to women as the country moves toward more stable democracy.

Benazir Bhutto's example is on an elite level of Pakistani society. Even so, her brother, Murtaza, challenged her leadership. As Zulfikar Ali Bhutto's son, as opposed to daughter, he claimed to be the more legitimate heir to their father's mantle. The need to "unshackle" and develop the vital resources of the country's entire female population remains an immense challenge to Pakistan in its quest for modernization.

Pakistan remains in a period of transition. The nation is still apprehensive about its survival as a unified, sovereign state. It is threatened by divisive political, social, and religious forces, and by economic challenges both within and outside the country. Pakistan is concerned about its integrity as an Islamic republic as it seeks ways to become less traditional while remaining faithful to the teachings of Islam. The military rule of General Musharraf is welcomed by many Pakistanis as stemming the excessive opportunism and corruption among the country's elected leaders. But his perceived buckling to Islamic fundamentalist pressures and his postponement of national elections add to the many challenges Pakistan faces in struggling to become a stable, prospering modern democracy.

DEVELOPMENT

Pakistan's per capita income has grown substantially since 1960. Industry, primarily cotton textiles and food processing, has grown at an impressive rate since 1980. This sector now produces more of the GDP than the agricultural sector, although agriculture still employs more than 50 percent of the labor force. However, there are vast inequities in income distribution among the people of Pakistan.

FREEDOM

Pakistan has experienced long years of martial law since independence in 1947. The first popular elections were not held until 1971, and not again until 1988. With the increasing political power of religious conservatives, women are held to their traditional, subservient role in Islamic society. Human-rights abuses are charged against the government, particularly against Hindus in the province of Sindh.

HEALTH/WELFARE

Emphasis on the military budget has slighted government attention to education and social services. Because of increasing agricultural production through the Green Revolution, life expectancy has doubled since 1960. The literacy rate among women is half that of the adult male population.

ACHIEVEMENTS

Pakistan has experienced political instability, warfare with India, the loss of East Pakistan, and the incursion of 3 million refugees from Afghanistan. Yet there has still been substantial industrial growth, and the Constitution, adopted in 1973, is working. The country continues to seek a government that is adequate to the needs of its peoples in the modern world and that is consistent with its Islamic faith and tradition.

Sri Lanka (Democratic Socialist Republic of Sri Lanka)

GEOGRAPHY

Area in Square Miles (Kilometers):
25,325 (65,610) (about the size of West Virginia)

Capital (Population): Colombo (1,300,000)

Environmental Concerns: deforestation; soil erosion; poaching; coastal degradation; water and air pollution; waste disposal

Geographical Features: mostly plain; mountains in the interior

Climate: tropical monsoon

PEOPLE

Population

Total: 19,239,000

Annual Growth Rate: 0.89%

Rural/Urban Population Ratio: 78/22

Major Languages: Sinhala; Tamil; English

Ethnic Makeup: 74% Sinhalese; 17% Tamil; 7% Moor; 2% others

Religions: 70% Buddhist; 15% Hindu; 8% Christian; 7% Muslim

Health

Life Expectancy at Birth: 69 years (male); 74 years (female)

Infant Mortality Rate (Ratio): 16.5/1,000

Physicians Available (Ratio): 1/4,750

Education

Adult Literacy Rate: 90.2%

Compulsory (Ages): 5–12; free

COMMUNICATION

Telephones: 524,000 main lines

Daily Newspaper Circulation: 25 per 1,000 people

Televisions: 39 per 1,000 people

Internet Service Providers: 4 (1999)

TRANSPORTATION

Highways in Miles (Kilometers): 6,997 (11,285)

Railroads in Miles (Kilometers): 890 (1,484)

Usable Airfields: 14

Motor Vehicles in Use: 469,000

GOVERNMENT

Type: republic

Independence Date: February 4, 1948 (from the United Kingdom)

Head of State/Government: President Chandrika Bandaranaike Kumaratunga is both head of state and head of government

Political Parties: All Ceylon Tamil Congress; United National Party; People's Alliance; Sri Lanka Freedom Party; Sri Lanka Progressive Front; People's United Front; Eelam People's Democratic Party; Tamil United Liberation Front; others

Suffrage: universal at 18

MILITARY

Military Expenditures (% of GDP): 4.2%

Current Disputes: civil war

ECONOMY

Currency ($ U.S. Equivalent): 85.10 Sri Lankan rupees = $1

Per Capita Income/GDP: $2,600/$50.5 billion

GDP Growth Rate: 3.7%

Inflation Rate: 6%

Unemployment Rate: 9.5%

Labor Force: 6,600,000

Natural Resources: limestone; graphite; mineral sands; gems; phosphates; clay; hydropower

Agriculture: tea; rubber; coconuts; rice; sugarcane; grains; pulses; oilseeds; spices; milk; eggs; hides; beef

Industry: processing of rubber, tea, coconuts, and other agricultural commodities; clothing; cement; petroleum refining; textiles; tobacco

Exports: $4.7 billion (primary partners United States, United Kingdom, Middle East)

Imports: $5.3 billion (primary partners India, Japan, South Korea)

http://www.lanka.net/home/
http://www.cia.gov/cia/publications/factbook/geos/ce.html

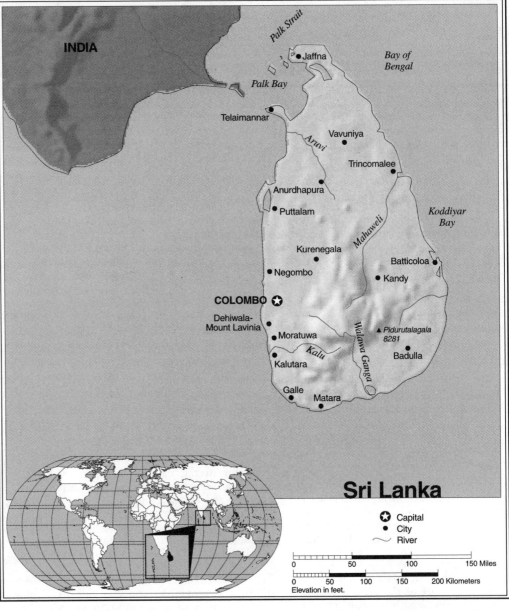

Sri Lanka

⊛ Capital
● City
〜 River

| 0 | 50 | 100 | 150 Miles |

| 0 | 50 | 100 | 150 | 200 Kilometers |
Elevation in feet.

SRI LANKA

Sri Lanka, previously named Ceylon, is a small island nation that hangs like a pendant off the southeast coast of India. Stretching 270 miles from north to south, it expands to 140 miles in width toward its southern end. In total area, it occupies just 1.5 percent of the total landmass of the South Asian subcontinent.

The island of Sri Lanka has two distinct regions: a northern, low-lying dry zone, and a mountainous wet zone to the south. At the center of the southern zone are the lush Kandyan Highlands, site of extensive tea and rubber plantations, watered by abundant rainfall, especially during the southwest monsoon season. Tea grown in the Highlands is considered to be among the finest in the world. Rubber and coconuts grown there account for most of the country's exports.

The northern plains are devoted mostly to rice cultivation for domestic consumption. This agriculture is sustained by extensive irrigation systems from artificial lakes to provide water during the long dry spells between the annual northeast monsoon rains. Construction of these irrigation systems dates back to the earliest record of settlers arriving in Ceylon from India, in the fifth century. B.C.

Because of its pleasant tropical climate and natural beauty, Sri Lanka once was known as the "Pearl of the Orient." In recent years, due to the ravages of social unrest, which has rocked its idyllic image of tranquillity, the country has come to be called the "Lebanon of South Asia."

Sri Lanka's population, now 19.2 million, is divided between two distinct language and religious identities. Speakers of the Sinhalese language are a dominant majority—74 percent of the total population of the country, of whom 93 percent are Theravada Buddhist. Seventeen percent of the total population are Tamil-speakers, a significant minority. Of them, two thirds are Hindu, mostly belonging to the Shaivite tradition.

Contemporary Sinhalese trace their origin to fifth-century B.C. settlers from India. Legend describes their leader, Prince Vijaya, as of the race of the lion, a Sinhal, a symbol of royalty adopted from ancient Persian culture. He was sent away from north India by his father and, according to tradition, arrived on Sri Lanka on the very day of the Buddha's death, in 483 B.C. He established a kingdom around the city of Anuradhapura in the north-central region of the country.

Theravada Buddhism, as distinct from the Mahayana Buddhist traditions of Tibet, China, and Japan, was brought to Sri Lanka in the third century B.C. by Mahinda, the son and emissary of the Indian emperor Asoka. This tradition of Buddhism reveres the teachings of the disciples of the Buddha—the elders (*thera*)—as contained in the *Pali Canon*. These sacred writings were produced in north India in the years immediately following the death (entering *nirvana*) of the Buddha. They were carried throughout South and Southeast Asia by missionary monks during the early years of expansion of the Buddhist faith.

Marauding forces from south India came to the island of Sri Lanka after the early period of Buddhist expansion. Most devastating was the Chola invasion, which destroyed Anuradhapura in the tenth century A.D. These attacks, together with the infestation of malaria, borne by mosquitoes bred in the still waters of the artificial irrigation lakes, drove the population of the north-central region to the coastlands.

The Portuguese arrived on the south coasts of Sri Lanka in the early 1500s and forced many of the Sinhalese people of the south into the mountains. There the Sinhalese established a kingdom around the city of Kandy. This dominant Sinhalese Buddhist group is divided today between the Kandyans, who live in the Highlands, and the "Low Country" people on the coastlands. The latter are more numerous (60 percent) and more prosperous, living in the more urban, coastal rim of the south.

Tamil-speakers are also divided into two groups: the Sri Lankan Tamils (70 percent) and the Indian Tamils (30 percent). The Sri Lankan Tamils are found mostly on the north and east coastlands, the dominant group belonging to a Sri Lankan *Vellalar,* or land-holding caste. Almost half of this Tamil community live in the northernmost district of Jaffna, where they make up 95 percent of the population. They have lived on the island since ancient times and share its long history with the Kandyan Sinhalese, with whom they have the most in common culturally and ethnically.

The Indian Tamils were brought to Sri Lanka in the 1800s by the British colonial government, to work as field laborers on the plantations that the British fostered in the Kandyan Highlands. The number of Indian Tamils has been reduced by half since Sri Lankan independence in 1948, primarily by their repatriation to India. Only during the 1960s did those Indian Tamils who remained, about 5 percent of the total population of Sri Lanka, receive status as citizens of Sri Lanka.

There are also significant Christian and Muslim communities, belonging to both language groups. The Tamil-speaking Muslims live mostly along the east coast. They are a distinct minority caught between the northern Tamil and the Kandyan Sinhalese communities.

The British were the first to unify these diverse peoples under a single government administration, in 1815. They introduced the rudiments of a national government in the port city of Colombo, on the southwest coast, and democratic institutions throughout the country. The first general elections were held in 1931, to select representatives for a National Assembly under strict colonial control.

INDEPENDENCE

On February 4, 1948, Sri Lanka, then called *Ceylon,* achieved its independence as a dominion in the British Commonwealth. In 1972, the government adopted a new Constitution as an independent republic, with a single national Legislature of 168 members. A further constitutional change, in 1978, endowed the presidency with extensive, independent executive authority. Junius Jayewardene, who had been appointed prime minister in 1978 following a sweeping victory of his United National Party (UNP) in 1977, was elected president in 1982.

The development of new lands for rice cultivation in the earlier malarial-infested and abandoned north-central region had started during the British colonial period. President Jayewardene pursued the development and resettlement of the region, not only to increase rice production, but also to provide homes and jobs for an increasing homeless population of Kandyan Sinhalese who were victims of land reform in the Highlands. He sought also in this way to defuse the impact and the appeal of a militant, Marxist youth group called the People's Liberation Front (JVP), which had been launching devastating attacks on villages throughout the south since 1971.

President Jayewardene's primary development effort was the Mahaweli River Project, an ambitious proposal for dams and irrigation works along the 207-mile course of the Mahaweli River from the central Highlands to Koddiyar Bay on the east coast. The project had first been proposed in 1968 as a 30-year development scheme to clear, resettle, and irrigate 900,000 acres of land in the north-central region of the country. In 1977, the Jayewardene government sought to complete the project in six years. Since then, four of the five major dams in the initial proposal have been built, largely with foreign aid, and 390,000 acres of "new" land have been prepared for settlement and cultivation. The results in terms of new production, employment, and electrical power have been impressive.

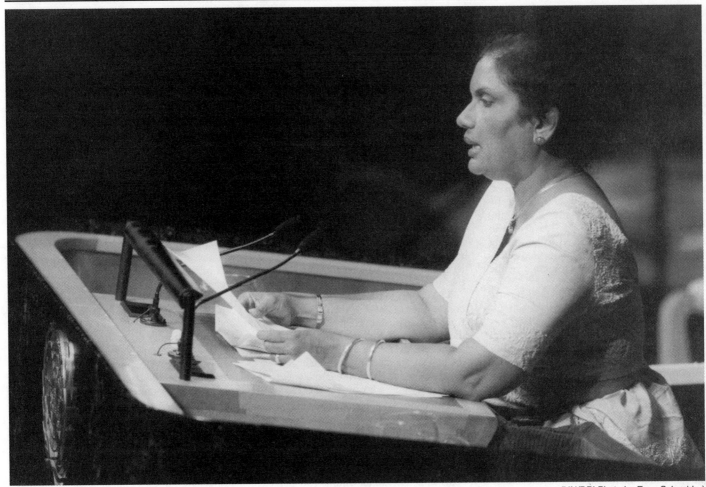

Despite widespread poverty, a severe refugee problem, and intense internal conflicts among different religious and linguistic groups, Sri Lanka's democratic political system endures. Here, President Chandrika Bandaranaike Kumaratunga addresses the UN General Assembly in September 1998.

As great as the economic benefits have been, such government resettlement projects such as the Mahaweli Programme have also had severe political consequences.

CIVIL WAR

In the years following the full independence of Sri Lanka, Tamil leaders sought in two ways to protect their people from the tyranny of an overwhelming Sinhalese majority. On the national level, Tamil legislators formed a solid political caucus known as the Federal Party, to hold a balance of votes between rival Sinhalese political parties. With that leverage, they were able to maintain a hearing for their concerns as a minority community. They also advocated for greater autonomy at the district level, which gave themselves greater freedom and voice in those northern districts where they were in the majority.

With the landslide victory of the United National Party in the 1977 elections, the Federal Party lost its leverage as a critical voting block on the national level. And when the UNP enacted resettlement and redistricting policies that placed more Sinhalese voters in redefined regional districts in the northern part of the country, Tamil voters found themselves in danger of losing what political power they had at the district level.

Tamil despair of attaining political accommodation at the national level and retaining control at the local level, combined with the increasing economic potential of the development projects in the north, fanned the fires of a militant secessionist group, the Liberation Tigers of Tamil Eelam (LTTE). Youthful, and eager for social as well as political change, the LTTE organized and carried out a sustained reign of terror throughout the northern regions of the country.

Unable to control such violence, President Jayewardene entered into an agreement with the government of India to send an Indian Peace Keeping Force (IPKF) to neutralize the conflict between militant Tamils and Sinhalese. But the IPKF failed to rout the LTTE, and as the battles continued, the IPKF began to take on the appearance of an occupation force. Faced with the IPKF's unpopularity and growing violence by the Sinhalese youth group JVP, Jayewardene did not seek reelection in 1988. The United National Party did remain in power in the Legislature, and its candidate, Ranasinghe Premadasa, was elected to succeed Jayewardene as president. As soon as Premadasa took office, he asked the Indian Army units to withdraw.

The Indian Peace Keeping Force left the LTTE weakened but no less resolved to seek independence for a separate Tamil state at any cost—including through the drug trade and political violence. This militant group was implicated in the assassination of President Premadasa on May 1, 1993, by a "human time bomb," in the same way that Prime Minister Ranjiv Gandhi, head of India's Congress Party, was killed by a Tamil separatist terrorist while he was campaigning in India in 1991.

Migration of Sinhalese Indians **500** B.C.	Mahinda introduces Buddhism **247** B.C.	British colonial rule A.D. **1815–1948**	The independence of Ceylon, as a British Commonwealth dominion **1948**	A new Constitution establishes Sri Lanka as a democratic republic **1972**	The United National Party wins elections by wide margin **1977**	The Constitution is modified to establish an independent president **1978**	Junius Jayewardene serves as president; anti-Tamil riots break out; Indian Peace Keeping Force **1982–1988**	Efforts to achieve a cease-fire between LTTE and Sri Lankan military forces and to negotiate a settlement in the dispute between the Tamil minority and Sinhalese majority fail **1990s**

2000s

Chandrika Kumaratunga remains president; continuing efforts to restore order in Sinhalese and Tamil communities

The Sri Lankan economy continues to grow

In 1994, the LTTE asserted its control in the northern Jaffna District by calling for a boycott there of national elections. Less than 10 percent of the electorate in that district voted. In other parts of Sri Lanka, the voters looked for new opportunities for a political rather than military solution to the conflict between the Tamil separatists and the Sinhalese majority. Thus, the United Front Party suffered its first defeat in 17 years.

The People's Alliance, a fragile coalition of leftist parties, won 105 seats in that election, and Chandrika Kumaratunga, leader of the Alliance, was elected president of Sri Lanka. Though her peace initiatives toward the LTTE have not been effective, she was elected to a second term in 1999. With the help of other parties, her Alliance has retained majority support in the 225-member Parliament.

President Kumaratunga is another illustration of the pattern for women leaders in South Asian national life. She received her introduction into national politics as the daughter of S. W. R. D. Bandaranaike, leader of the Sri Lanka Freedom Party (SLFP). This coalition of leftist, pro-Sinhala groups won control of the national Legislature in 1956. Even though he was a popular prime minister, he was assassinated by an extremist Buddhist monk in 1959. His wife, Sirimavo Bandaranaike, then became leader of his SLFP. She served as the nation's first woman prime minister from 1960 to 1965, from 1970 to 1977, and again since 1996 until her retirement in 2000, at age 84 (she died later that year). President Kumaratunga's husband, a popular film actor, had also entered national politics, until his assassination while a presidential candidate in 1988.

President Kumaratunga initiated a number of proposals for talks with the LTTE for a cease-fire and negotiations toward peace. When negotiations did not materialize, the Sri Lankan Army undertook a major offensive, which removed the LTTE from the ravaged city of Jaffna in October 1995. Although weakened and further isolated from any political base, the LTTE has continued to carry out guerrilla attacks in the northeastern coastal region of the country. It launched a substantial counterattack to recapture the town of Killinochchi on the vital highway to Jaffna in September 1998, to defeat the Sri Lankan forces in the Elephant Pass in April 2000, and to be on the verge of recapturing Jaffna. The LTTE also took responsibility for the bombing deaths in 1998 of the first two Tamil mayors of Jaffna—Sarojini Yogeswaran, in May, and P. Sivapalan in September—to protest the attempt of a more moderate Tamil United Liberation Front to reestablish civil order in the northern city.

The future of the Tamil population living within the nation, let alone the rehabilitation of the more than 400,000 refugees who have sought asylum in south India and other parts of the world, is unsure. In February 2000, the Norwegian government offered to help initiate direct talks between two warring forces. In the meantime, the Tamil population is caught between the fighting of a desperate LTTE and a demoralized Sri Lankan Army. The Tamils have experienced such extensive destruction throughout their northern homelands over such a long period of time that the opportunity for mediation and the prospect of a return to normal life seem very far away.

STILL A MODEL
Although the Tamil separatist movement has dominated the political agenda for many years and terrorist bombings remain a threat to everyday life in both the north and in the southern cities, the Sri Lankan economy has continued to prosper. The International Monetary Fund reported that Sri Lanka showed significant growth at a time when Asian economies in general were declining. Its economy grew in the mid- to late 1990s in all sectors, particularly in services and manufacturing. And in spite of all the political turmoil, Sri Lanka remains a model in South Asia for literacy, population growth, and human services, and a productive place for foreign investment.

DEVELOPMENT

Sri Lanka's economy is primarily agricultural, based on extensive plantation farming. Land reclamation for the production of rice has been its most ambitious development project. Stints of bad weather, a decline in the world tea market, and civil war have all hurt the economy in recent years, yet the country has still managed to prosper.

FREEDOM

Since 1983, Sri Lanka, the oldest democracy in South Asia, has been torn asunder by militant Sinhalese and Tamil rebels. Wanton destruction of peoples and lands, mostly in the more heavily Tamil- and Muslim-populated areas, has forced more than 1 million people to become refugees.

HEALTH/WELFARE

Sri Lanka has the most extensive social services in South Asia. Socialized medicine provides health care throughout the country. Literacy and average life expectancy are the highest in the subcontinent, while the rate of population growth is one of the lowest.

ACHIEVEMENTS

Though severe ethnic and linguistic violence is threatening the political stability of this island nation, the fruits of Buddhism and democracy in Sri Lanka have had exemplary results in economic development and social services.

Annotated Table of Contents for Articles

South Asia Articles

Topic Guide to Articles

TOPIC AREA	TREATED IN	TOPIC AREA	TREATED IN
Human Rights	9. India's Socioeconomic Makeover 13. India: Globalized Economy, Victimized Workers? 17. Enduring Stereotypes About Asia 26. Inspiring Devotion—and Fear 32. Rebels Without a Childhood in Sri Lanka War	**Religion and Spirituality**	5. Partition: The Human Cost 18. Ancient Jewel 21. Oldest Prophetic Religion Struggles for Survival 26. Inspiring Devotion—and Fear 27. Holy Men of Heroin
Industrial Development	8. Green Growth 22. Celluloid Hall of Mirrors 23. Wiring of India	**Science**	23. Wiring of India 24. Making Something Out of Nothing
Leaders	3. Lawless Frontier 4. Gandhi and Nehru: Frustrated Visionaries? 5. Partition: The Human Cost 6. What Does India Want? 14. Lower-Caste Women Turn Village Rule Upside Down	**Secession**	1. Competing Nationalisms
		Sex Roles	15. Dowry Deaths in India 16. Selling Birth Control to India's Poor 17. Enduring Stereotypes About Asia 20. In India, Men Challenge a Matrilineal Society
Minorities	20. In India, Men Challenge a Matrilineal Society 21. Oldest Prophetic Religion Struggles for Survival	**Social Reform**	2. India Rising 9. India's Socioeconomic Makeover 13. India: Globalized Economy, Victimized Workers?
National Resources	9. India's Socioeconomic Makeover 27. Holy Men of Heroin 30. Not Sinking but Drowning	**Social Unrest**	3. Lawless Frontier 4. Gandhi and Nehru: Frustrated Visionaries? 5. Partition: The Human Cost 11. Trouble With Wealth 31. Front Line, Fault Line 33. War the World Is Missing
Nationalism	1. Competing Nationalisms 3. Lawless Frontier 7. India and the Bomb 32. Rebels Without a Childhood in Sri Lanka War	**Women**	13. India: Globalized Economy, Victimized Workers? 14. Lower-Caste Women turn Village Rule Upside Down 15. Dowry Deaths in India 16. Selling Birth Control to India's Poor 17. Enduring Stereotypes About Asia 20. In India, Men Challenge a Matrilineal Society
Partition	5. Partition: The Human Cost		
Peasants	9. India's Socioeconomic Makeover 28. Grameen Bank		
Political Reform	14. Lower-Caste Women Turn Village Rule Upside Down 29. Bhutan: The Dilemmas of a Small State		

Article 1   *Harvard International Review,* Summer 1996

Identity and Politics in South Asia

Competing Nationalisms

Secessionist Movements and the State

Raju G.C. Thomas

Raju G.C. Thomas is Professor of Political Science at Marquette University.

South Asia is home to several world religions, over 30 major languages, a thousand dialects, and innumerable castes and subcastes. During the colonial era, princes held nominal rule over more than 580 separate states in India, while a number of other provinces were directly governed by the British. Although only two movements for national independence have succeeded since the departure of the British in 1947—those of Pakistan and Bangladesh—South Asia has experienced countless separatist movements based on religious, linguistic, or ethnic lines, including campaigns for Dravidastan, Assam, Nagaland, Gurkhaland, Kashmir, Khalistan, Pashtunistan, Baluchistan, Sind-hudesh, and Tamil Eelam.

With such diverse national movements continuing to challenge state lines, South Asia faces the question: should the territorial integrity and sovereignty of existing states be maintained, regardless of the history and legitimacy of their origins, or should the state's various ethnic groups or "nationalities" be allowed the right of self-determination and secession?

The recognition of new states in South Asia may lead to consequences even more disastrous than the status quo, just as the recognition of new states in Europe led to the complete disintegration of the Soviet Union and Yugoslavia. First, recognition would generate new problems arising from new boundaries and new minorities. Second, the recognition of some states could cause a chain reaction elsewhere, leading to the disintegration of India and Pakistan, and to a lesser extent, Sri Lanka. Third, the level of interethnic bloodshed and refugee flows would generate a humanitarian nightmare in South Asia surpassing that of Europe in the early 1990s.

Nation-states based on ethnic lines have rarely existed in South Asia. Instead, great multi-ethnic empires, like those of the Mauryans, Guptas, and Mughals, have arisen and disintegrated. The lesser empires and minor kingdoms that replaced them either comprised multiple ethnic groups or were ethnically pure, but rarely included all the members of the ethnic group within their boundaries. South Asia has no equivalent to Germany, Italy, or Japan, states formed by a group of people largely sharing the same race, language, culture, religion, and

historical experience. Even Bangladesh, united by the Bengali language, is divided by religion. Bhutan, too, comes close to an ethnic nation but retains a significant Nepali minority.

> With so many complex lines of religion, culture, and language in South Asia, allowing communities to secede would lead to a number of grave consequences. Regardless of the legitimacy or illegitimacy of the separatist demands, granting them could exacerbate existing tensions and unravel regional security.

Since the partition of British India in 1947, the nations that have formed in South Asia have not been ethnic nations but civic nations. The civic nation is based on a community of people who believe they compose a nation and who are willing to commit themselves to common political institutions and processes, regardless of cultural differences. India is the prime example of a civic nation, with Muslims, Sikhs, Bengalis, and other minorities owing allegiance to the country despite the fact that they may not speak Hindi or practice Hinduism. Pakistan, to a lesser extent, fits this broader conception of a nation because of the belief that all Muslims of the Indian subcontinent belonged in the Muslim state regardless of differences in race or language.

Although both India and Pakistan were formed as multi-ethnic nations, their founders espoused competing visions of nationhood. The state of Pakistan grew out of the vision of Muslim nationalist Mohammed Ali Jinnah, head of the All-India Muslim League between 1930 and 1947 and the first president of Pakistan. Jinnah argued that there were two separate nations in the Indian subcontinent, a nation of Hindus and a nation of Muslims, and that the Muslims should have their own state, Pakistan. He argued that Muslims shared religious practices and were expected to obey common laws based on the Quran and the Shariat, the body of Islamic law. Hindus and Muslims could be distinguished often by dress or lifestyle, if not by race or language, and they often lived separately within India.

Jawaharlal Nehru, leader of the Indian National Congress, argued that there was only one nation in India that encompassed all the peoples of the Indian subcontinent whatever their religion, race, language, or culture. Geography, history, and political experience—not religion—defined Nehru's Indian nation. The historical experience of the peoples of the subcontinent, from the coming of the Aryan invaders in 1700 B.C. through the end of British rule in 1947, set apart the people within the subcontinent from those outside it. History and geography had produced a broader Indian world-view and destined the peoples of the subcontinent to live together. Nehru argued that if religion formed the basis of nationhood, then India could easily be divided into many nations instead of two. Jinnah's "two nation" theory also did not explain why only "Indian" Muslims constituted part of this Islamic nation and not those beyond the subcontinent. Indeed, while Islam was the basis for the creation of Pakistan, the real link among all the Muslims of theoretical Pakistan was that they were all Indians. By focusing on the Islamic link between West and East Pakistan and ignoring the Indian link between the two wings, Pakistan may have undermined its unity.

As the partition-era clash continued between the exclusive concept of a Muslim (but multi-linguistic) Pakistan and an inclusive concept of a united, multi-religious, and multi-linguistic India, there were weaker claims for other nations and states. In Bengal, a region in the far east of the Indian subcontinent, nationalists argued that the Bengali language and culture constituted the basis of a single nation in spite of religious differences. Today, Bengalis are divided between Bangladesh and the Indian state of West Bengal, but these Bengali nationalists argued that while Jinnah could have his Pakistan and Gandhi and Nehru their Hindustan, there ought to be a separate independent state of Bengal consisting of Muslims and Hindus. Likewise, briefly in the 1920s, and then again briefly after Indian independence, the Tamils of the extreme southeast argued that they should have a state separate from the linguistically distinct Indo-Aryans of the north.

These original concepts of nation in South Asia all incorporated multiple identities of some kind, whether religious, cultural, or linguistic. The only one of these independence movements to succeed after 1947 was the Bengali secessionist movement, which triumphed in the creation of Bangladesh from East Pakistan in 1971. Bengali nationalists led by Sheikh Mujibur Rahman argued that Bengali language and culture justified separate statehood for both the majority Muslims and the minority Hindus in East Pakistan. But most post–independence ideas of nationhood have tended to be much more narrow. Nationalists among the Kashmiris, Sikhs, Assamese, Pashtuns, and to a lesser extent, Sindhis, have all pushed for nations based on one language and one religion.

Changing Identities

The paradox behind these and other nationalist movements is that perceptions of nationhood often change or overlap, or result in the creation of states quite different from those envisioned by the ideology that inspired the original movement. National identifications are not constant, but created and shaped through time. The Muslim nationalist movement that led to the establishment of Pakistan, for example, emerged only at the turn of the century, accelerating in the decades immediately preceding the British withdrawal from India. While Muslims ruled Hindus in India for several centuries before British rule, a great deal of political interaction and communal intermingling (through intermarriage or Hindu conversions to the Islamic faith) occurred so that the two religious groups became racially and culturally similar. Cultural and linguistic differences across India became more regional rather than religious, although religion may have dictated some differences in social practices within the same region. For example, while religion differentiated Muslim, Sikh, and Hindu Punjabis, or Muslim and Hindu Bengalis, race, language, and culture also united them.

It was not until the end of the nineteenth century that Indian Muslim political elites began to perceive the Muslims of India as a distinct nation that could find salvation only in the creation of an Islamic Pakistan. The founding of the Anglo-Mohammedan College (later Aligarh Muslim University) in 1877, and then the establishment of the All-India Muslim League in 1906, gave impetus to the development of a separate Muslim identity. Muslim elites, primarily from the Hindi-speaking Hindu heartland of the United and Central Province of British India, then began to emphasize Islamic symbols and identity in order to mobilize support in the 1930s for Jinnah's two nation theory.

Similarly, variations of twentieth century Bengali nationalism point to the shifting nature of national identity, sometimes influenced chiefly by culture and language and other times predominantly by religion. During the Pakistan movement of the late 1940s, some Bengali leaders had toyed with the idea of a united Hindu-Muslim Bengali state, separate from the proposed independent states of India and Pakistan. Underlying this outlook for a greater Bengal state was the belief that language and culture superseded religious differences. Instead, the partition arrangement split Bengalis between East Pakistan and the Indian state of West Bengal. At some point between the creation of Pakistan and the 1971 war that led to the creation of Bangladesh, Muslim Bengalis who had identified with Pakistan shifted emphasis to their Bengali culture and decided that they could accept nothing less than an independent Bangladesh.

A united Bengal concept may have occurred to some Bengali nationalists on either side in East Pakistan and West Bengal during the 1971 struggle for Bangladesh. Although Indian military intervention helped create Bangladesh, the possibility that Hindu Bengali nationalists in West Bengal would also want to join this "Bengal Nation" must have worried Indian policymakers as well. The total Bengali-speaking population of both Bangladesh and West Bengal in India today number almost 180 million, and would have constituted a powerful state if a united independent Bengal had been forged in 1947 or 1971. But reunification schemes for a "Greater Bengal" have not been heard since the creation of Bangladesh in December 1971. This may be because Bengali Hindus prefer to remain in a Hindu-dominated India rather than a Muslim-majority Greater Bengal. Similarly, while Bengali Muslims may want a united Greater Bengal where they form the majority, they do not wish to be part of the Muslim minority in India.

Self-perceptions among Kashmiri Muslims, many of whom are currently calling for independence for Kashmir, or incorporation with Pakistan, have also fluctuated over the last half century. The first of these identities drew from the ideology of the "Kashmiriyat," which perceived Muslims, Hindus, and Ladakhi Buddhists of Kashmir as sharing an identity that justified separate nationhood for the province. At one time or another, Hindus and Muslims alike have sought an independent multi-religious state of Kashmir. A second outlook, articulated by Nehru, himself a Kashmiri Hindu Pandit, and shared by some Muslim leaders at the time of partition, held that Kashmir was an integral part of a secular Indian heritage. A third outlook among Kashmiri Muslims saw Kashmir as a part of Pakistan because of the shared religious heritage, following the reasoning of Jinnah's two nation theory. A fourth Kashmiri identity is emerging from the spread of transnational Islamist values into the state, which makes Kashmiris feel part of the broader Islamic world of Central Asia and the Middle East.

Another important separatist movement in recent years, that of the Sikhs in the Indian state of Punjab, also drew from a history of shifting identities. The Sikh religion was originally classified as a subdivision of Hinduism, a classification that Sikhs only mildly resisted. Later, they categorically rejected Hindu absorption, and eventually they insisted on a separate state. The turnaround was dramatic; before the mid-1980s, Sikhs viewed themselves as staunch Indian nationalists, and Hindus saw the Sikhs as the "sword arm" of Hinduism. The Hindu-Sikh conflict that emerged in Punjab in the 1980s reveals the transforming nature of ethnicity and conflict in South Asia.

It is important to recall that the relations among Punjabi Muslims, Sikhs, and Hindus were cooperative and cordial under the British Raj. Indeed, Punjabis of all three religious persuasions constituted the bulk and the backbone of the British Indian Army. They fought shoulder-to-shoulder in two world wars. Even during the mass slaughter and migration of Hindus, Muslims, and Sikhs in Punjab that accompanied the partition of the province in 1947, members of these three religious communities in the British Indian Army remained disciplined. Since partition, however, Indo-Pakistani wars have resembled a civil war among the Punjabis: the Indian armed forces are 30 percent Hindu and Sikh Punjabi while Pakistan's forces are 80 percent Muslim Punjabi. From one racial, linguistic, and cultural ethnic group, Punjabis have become three separate communities.

> Even where separatist movements do not of themselves imperil regional stability, the domino effect they may create would have implications for the entire region.

These examples suggest that religion is more divisive than racial, cultural, and linguistic ties in South Asia. But past cooperation and goodwill among Hindus, Muslims, and Sikhs in Bengal, Kashmir, and Punjab show that such positive ties may be restored given the right attitudes and political conditions.

Territorial Secession?

All of the states of South Asia constitute political conglomerations of several ethnic nations, many of which are demanding separate independent states. India faces the independence movements of Muslim Kashmiris, Sikh Punjabis, and Hindu Assamese; Sri Lanka faces an insurgency from Hindu Tamils; and Pakistan has had demands for greater autonomy by groups including Sindhis and Muhajirs (immigrants). With so many complex lines of religion, culture, and language in South Asia, allowing communities to secede would lead to a number of grave consequences. Regardless of the legitimacy or illegitimacy of the separatist demands, granting them could exacerbate existing tensions and unravel regional security.

First, the detachment of Kashmir from India could easily lead to a communal bloodbath and national disintegration. Hard core insurgents seem determined to continue with their campaign whatever the outcome, but if Kashmir is dislodged from India, it could lead to the marginalization of the 115 million Muslims left in India. The Hindu nationalist Bharatiya Janata Party has declared on many occasions that a Kashmiri Muslim decision to leave India would reflect adversely on the loyalty of all Indian Muslims. Even some leaders of the secular Janata Dal and Congress party have hinted at such an interpretation. In response, the Imam Sayyid Bukhari of Jamma Masjid in Delhi stated that Indian Muslims can do no more than support the Indian position on Kashmir, and Indian Muslims publicly do not support the secession of Kashmir. However, if Kashmir were to secede, the Hindu-Muslim communal violence that could very likely arise would be beyond the control of any party or leader.

India considers the Kashmir issue integral to the ability of the Indian state to preserve its multi-religious, multi-ethnic, and secular status, and is thus determined to resist indefinitely the Kashmiri independence struggle. On the other hand, any international decision to maintain the status quo in Kashmir will not be acceptable to Pakistan. Pakistan feels that it was cheated at the time of partition when it failed to acquire Muslim-majority Kashmir. Although Pakistan would be willing to maintain the territorial status quo on all other cases of secessionist demands, it will insist on making Kashmir an exception since it believes that Kashmir should have joined Muslim Pakistan in 1947. The more important question today, however, is not what Pakistan considers its moral or legal right to Kashmir, but the probable consequences for the rest of the subcontinent in tampering with existing state boundaries.

The creation of an independent Khalistan out of the existing Indian Punjab, as demanded by many Sikhs, may prove to be as complicated for the region as the separation of Kashmir or the 1947 partition of India. Thousands of Sikhs, especially the business and professional classes, are scattered throughout India outside Punjab. About 45 percent of the population of Punjab—60 percent of most of its major cities—remains Hindu in spite of a 1966 partition which created two new states out of the formerly Hindu-majority areas of Punjab. Since Punjabi Hindus do not want to be part of an independent Sikh state, there would have to be yet another division of Punjab and the inevitable mass migration of millions of Sikhs and Hindus across new borders. These population transfers would lead to extensive communal bloodshed, as in the 1947 division of Punjab between India and Pakistan. In that partition, about 10 million Muslims, Sikhs, and Hindus were caught on the wrong side of the new frontier and forced to migrate within a month, and about half a million civilians lost their lives in the partition of Punjab.

Even where separatist movements do not of themselves imperil regional stability, the domino effect they may create would have implications for the entire region. In India, the northeastern tea-growing state of Assam has pushed for independence, but its loss would hurt the Indian economy and may eventually lead to the separation of the entire northeast sector of India. Assam would also be the first Hindu-majority state to gain independence, and

its secession could trigger similar movements in the Hindu-majority states of South India, like Tamil Nadu, Karnataka, and Telengana. Similarly, the partition of Sri Lanka could create a domino effect through South Asia, especially stimulating the Tamil separatist movement in Tamil Nadu. In addition, the highly contested east-central sector which contains both Tamils and Tamil-speaking Muslims will not be easily separated, since the Muslims prefer to remain in Sri Lanka.

In Pakistan, which has experienced a separation movement in Sindh, democratization and decentralization may not resolve the problem of power sharing among the Sindhis, Muhajirs, Pashtuns, and Punjabis, four of the largest ethnic communities in the province. Democratization and greater regional control may instead lead to greater economic and political power for the Muhajirs and Punjabis resident in Sindh. On the other hand, an independent Sindhi state may exacerbate the problem of Urdu-speaking Muslims from India, as in the case of the Bihari Muslims from East Pakistan. Following the independence of Bangladesh in 1971, over four million Muslims from the Indian state of Bihar who had earlier migrated to East Pakistan were accused of having fought with West Pakistan's military against Bangladeshi independence. Bangladeshis considered them to be Pakistanis and asked that they be repatriated. By the mid-1980s, the Pakistan government had repatriated about 1.8 million Biharis to Pakistan, most of whom joined other Indian immigrant communities in Sindh. But Sindhis resisted these new immigrants since this implied a further addition to the Urdu-speaking Muhajirs in Sindh. According to unofficial estimates, there are still some 2.5 million Biharis left behind in Bangladesh who wish to be repatriated. Thus, the existing 10 million Muhajirs are not likely to be absorbed in an independent Sindhi state, nor are they likely to be accepted back into India. Despite a temporary improvement in the situation of Sindh with the coming to power of Benazir Bhutto, the struggle between the Muhajirs and Sindhis has worsened in the mid-1990s.

Prospects for Confederation

To counter the trend of nationalist and secessionist movements in the region, the South Asian Association for Regional Cooperation (SAARC) has since 1984 attempted to build confidence in the region and encourage the growth of economic, social, and eventually political cooperation. The more optimistic, perhaps utopian, supporters of SAARC would like to see the organization grow into a larger confederation or "superstate" like the European Union. Such a development may serve to prevent the spread of nationalist movements and territorial fragmentation in South Asia. It may soften or even resolve issues such as the Kashmir dispute, Muhajir-Sindhi ethnic and territorial questions, the status of Bengali Muslims in Assam, and the Tamil secessionist struggle in Sri Lanka.

However, Pakistan prefers confederal arrangements with the Muslim countries of the Economic Cooperation Organization

(ECO) bloc rather than with the multi-religious countries of SAARC. One Pakistani analyst projects the eventual formation of a large Muslim confederation that would stretch from Pakistan to Turkey and encompass the newly independent Muslim states that emerged from the former Soviet Union. In a sense, this would be the logical extension of the concept of Pakistan as a Muslim homeland in the Indian subcontinent. But Pakistan's strategy of linking itself with the states of Central Asia and the Middle East also has some weaknesses. Afghanistan needs to be stabilized in order to establish road and rail communications with the Central Asian states, and the stability of Tajikistan is equally uncertain. There are also other socio-economic and demographic problems that stand in the way of fostering a strong Islamic confederation.

With the ECO fading away and SAARC making little progress, both India and Pakistan are seeking to join the Association for South East Asian Nations (ASEAN). India has already been accepted as a "dialogue partner" of ASEAN. A potentially larger South and Southeast Asian confederation may offset India's natural and overwhelming economic dominance of South Asia. Muslims and Buddhists in South Asia would also have less to fear from Hindu domination in a confederation which includes 300 million Muslim Indonesians and Malays, Buddhist Thais, Vietnamese, Laotians and Cambodians, and Christian Filipinos. However, ASEAN has been unwilling to admit India and Pakistan as full members partly because they are less economically developed than the ASEAN nations and partly because ASEAN does not want to drag Indo-Pakistani confrontations over Kashmir into its regional political arrangements.

If it is premature to establish a confederation in South Asia, perhaps the countries of South Asia should at least agree on two fundamental principles: that the existing international borders, whether good or bad, legal or illegal, are inviolable; and that none of the states in the region will aid and abet each other's separatist movements. India may find these proposals for maintaining the territorial status quo in South Asia to its liking. Pakistan will surely insist on making an exception for Kashmir, but the reality is that India can enforce the status quo in Kashmir by the sheer weight of its military power. It did so in the past and continues to do so during the present crisis. In any case, Pakistan would also have something to lose if Kashmiris had their way, since most of them would like to incorporate the areas of Kashmir currently under Pakistani control into an independent Kashmir. The most feasible solution short of greater confederation is to preserve the status quo—a conclusion that may not satisfy all the underlying national feelings, but one that addresses the reality of South Asian political life today. The alternative, a readjustment of the complex ethnic distribution of South Asia through territorial change, could fragment all the countries in the region into smaller states only at a very high cost in human life and regional stability.

Article 2

The Wilson Quarterly, Summer 2000

India Rising

by Stephen P. Cohen

In the wake of dramatic nuclear tests, quickening economic growth, and a highly publicized American presidential visit, India seems ready to take its place among the world's leading nations. But for that to happen, India will need to act like a major power, and the United States will need to recognize how much India has changed.

Since its birth as a nation more than 50 years ago, India has seemed poised on the edge of two very different futures. On one side lay greatness; on the other, collapse. That drama has now ended and a new one has begun. The specter of collapse has passed and India is emerging as a major Asian power, joining China and Japan. The 1998 nuclear tests in the Rajasthan desert that announced India's entry into the nuclear club only served to underscore the nation's new stature. India has begun economic reforms that promise at last to realize its vast economic potential. It possesses the world's third largest army. It occupies a strategic position at the crossroads of the Persian Gulf, Central Asia, and Southeast Asia. Its population, which crossed the one billion mark this year, may surpass China's within two decades. It is the site of one of the world's oldest civilizations, a powerful influence throughout Asia for thousands of years, and for the last 53 years, against all odds, it has maintained a functioning demo cracy.

For most of those 53 years, the United States and India have maintained a strained relationship—a relationship that has not been helped by years of American neglect and misunderstanding. Now there are signs of change. Despite the administration's anger over India's nuclear tests, Bill Clinton in March became the first American president to visit the subcontinent in more than two decades. Addressing the Indian Parliament, he acknowledged the richness of Indian civilization, noted the country's economic and scientific progress, and praised its adherence to democratic norms. "India is a leader," Clinton said, "a great nation, which by virtue of its size, its achievements, and its example, has the ability to shape the character of our time." Yet he tactfully noted areas of American concern and expressed alarm about Kashmir, India's relations with Pakistan, and nuclear proliferation. Speaking less guardedly before his visit, he had called the Indian subcontinent "perhaps the most dangerous place in the world."

Before winning independence in 1947, India was the jewel in the crown of the British Empire, an important military resource in a location of great geostrategic significance. But the Cold War diminished India's importance. Because it did not play a significant role in the balance of power between the Soviet Union and the Western alliance, the superpowers often took India for granted. At most, the two sides saw India as a potential counter to the People's Republic of China on the international chessboard—but only one of several.

American and Indian interests in China did briefly run along parallel lines. In the late 1950s, when the United States tried to weaken the Chinese hold on Tibet, the Indians provided a refuge for the Dalai Lama. When the short India-China war broke

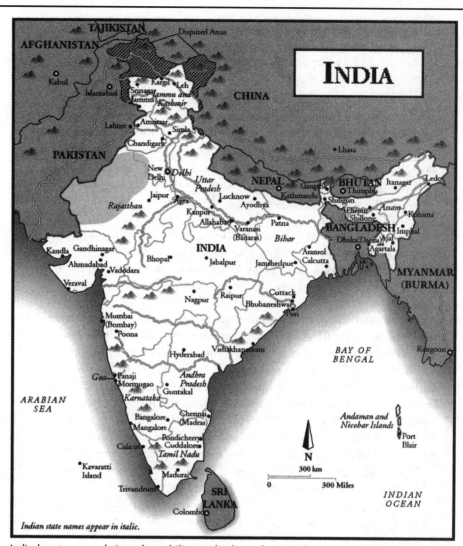

India boasts a population of one bilion and a host of outsized cities (Mumbai's population exceeds 15 million), but more than 70 percent of its people still live in rural areas.

out in 1962 over what remains one of the world's longest contested borders, Washington sent a military mission to India and supplied the country with small arms and a defensive radar system. This was a period of intense cooperation, with joint military exercises, U.S. military assistance, and U.S. help in setting up India's foreign intelligence service. President John F. Kennedy saw the competition between India and China as a struggle between the world's largest democracy and communism for the future of all of Asia; he continued the shift toward India that had begun in the last years of the Eisenhower administration. Kennedy praised the "soaring idealism" of Jawaharlal Nehru, prime minister from 1947 to 1964 (although

his contacts with Nehru were to prove disillu sioning). Some in Washington even argued that India should be encouraged to develop its own nuclear weapons program.

But India's long-simmering dispute with Pakistan (an American ally) over Kashmir kept the relationship from developing further, especially after the Sino-Indian clash ended. As the United States became increasingly entangled in Vietnam during the 1960s, interest in South Asia faded. The final break occurred after President Richard M. Nixon's historic visit to China in 1972. With China enlisted against the Soviets, India seemed irrelevant. This U.S. "tilt" toward China remains a major source of Indian anti-Americanism.

On the American side, India increasingly came to be seen as a de facto ally of Moscow. After 1971, the Soviet Union stepped in to forge an alliance with India, but it too sought to use Delhi against the Chinese. Over the years, the Soviets gave India billions of dollars worth of modern warplanes, tanks, and ships, and even loaned a nuclear submarine. At the United Nations, the Soviet Union and India were close partners; in 1970, the two powers signed a 25-year treaty of peace and friendship.

The Soviet invasion of Afghanistan in late 1979 reawakened American interest in South Asia. but in reviving its alliance with Pakistan, the United States only further alienated India. More recently, the Clinton administration pressured India to sign the NonProliferation Treaty and the Comprehensive Test Ban Treaty-which had the unintended consequence of strengthening the bomb lobby in Delhi.

In May 1998, India tested five nuclear devices. Pakistan promptly responded with its own nuclear tests. The United States reacted by imposing economic and political sanctions on Delhi. As if that weren't enough turmoil, India has had three national elections in three years, with the current government, led by Prime Minister Atal Bihari Vajpayee's Hindu Nationalist Bharatiya Janata Party (BJP), being the country's third coalition government. Events took an alarming turn in the summer of 1999, when India clashed with Pakistan in the Kargil district of Kashmir, raising fears that the war would escalate into a nuclear conflict. A few months later Pakistan's civilian government fell to a military coup, and in December 1999 Indians were unnerved by the hijacking of an Indian Airlines flight by Islamic extremists.

In the United States, India's nuclear tests and the events that followed have led to a certain amount of finger pointing in foreign policy circles, but the failure of American policy goes deeper than yesterday's decisions. For most of the last 50 years, America has had a hard time "getting India right." Americans have consistently failed to understand the

reasons for Indian behavior—and more often failed even to try. Whether or not India joins the ranks of major powers, and whether or not it pursues policies that are hostile to American interests, the United States will need to gain a deeper understanding of the subcontinent. That will require relinquishing a number of stereotypes that have long governed the American view of India.

India is virtually synonymous with poverty in the Western mind, and poverty will remain both a moral and a practical problem and a political embarrassment to any Indian government. More than half of the world's poorest people live in India, mostly in the rural north and east. Calcutta, the epicenter of this ocean of grief, has long been a universal metaphor for absolute poverty. The poorest 10 percent of the Indian population (more than 100 million people) earn slightly less than $1 a day, and 35 percent of all Indians—approximately 300 million people—fall below the government's own poverty line.

In the south and the west, however, many Indians are enjoying unprecedented economic growth. These are the regions, with a population much larger than that of either Indonesia or the United States, that have seen more thoroughgoing land reform. Along the coast, there is a long tradition of trade and contact with other countries. Major cities such as Hyderabad, Chennai, and Bangalore appear to be on their way to becoming world-class high-technology centers, attracting investment from dozens of American, Japanese, and Southeast Asian firms. India's 1998 gross national product of $420 billion was the world's 11th largest, and its annual growth rate exceeds five percent. (Gauged in terms of purchasing power parity, an alternative measure, India has the world's fifth largest economy, behind those of the United States, China, Japan, and Germany.)

India had a late start on economic reform. The Congress Party, which ruled India from 1947 to 1978 under Nehru and his daughter, Indira Gandhi, was deeply influenced by British Fabian so-

cialism. The country's "top-down" approach to economic planning paralleled a political system dominated by the upper castes. The castes and classes involved in business and commerce were held in low esteem in much of the country. Such traditions are now fading fast. In 1991, Congress Party Prime Minister Narasimha Rao began a program of economic liberalization, including industry deregulation, privatization of state monopolies, and easing of foreign investment rules. There is still a danger that unbalanced growth will exacerbate economic tensions within Indian society, but the old Fabian shibboleths about the need for slow, state-led growth have been shed.

The transition to a more market-oriented economy accelerated after the BJP came to power last year. Even though elements of the party are opposed to the internationalization of the Indian economy (the BJP has the reputation of drawing key support from the small shopkeepers of India), the more liberal leadership at its top has systematically moved ahead with reform. The notorious system of quotas and import licenses for machinery and consumer goods has been dismantled. Foreign ownership of Indian firms is now possible, and international brands including Pepsi, Coca-Cola, IBM, Sony, and Phillips have entered the Indian marketplace, giving consumers a much wider range of choice. India offers overseas firms a unique asset: the talents of an educated, highly trained, English-speaking elite. (Most of the 100 million members of the middle class speak at least some English.)

Foreign trade is growing smartly, more in services than in the traditional manufacturing sector. The nascent Indian software industry is spreading from its Bangalore and Hyderabad base and finding new customers abroad, especially in the United States. Software exports have been growing at an annual rate of 50 percent. Foreign firms trying to do business in India still complain about red tape and protectionism, but they see the country as a $100 billion market, especially in infrastructure sectors such as electrical power generation and roads. The foreigners are learning the ropes; India's much-maligned bureaucracy has even earned praise from business leaders for providing stability and balance during a decade of political turmoil.

During the past 15 years, American perceptions have also been clouded by the revival of the old image of India as a violent, unstable country. Two prime ministers have been assassinated—Indira Gandhi in 1984 by her two Sikh bodyguards, and her son, Rajiv Gandhi, in 1991 by a suicide bomber sent by the insurgent Sri Lankan Tamil Tigers. Graphic television coverage has thrown a spotlight on caste and religious riots, which reached a peak with the destruction in December 1992 of the Babri Masjid at Ayodhya, in eastern Uttar Pradesh, by saffron-clad Hindu fanatics. The incident sparked Hindu-Muslim riots throughout India that left some 2,000 dead. Limited but highly publicized subsequent attacks on Indian Christians and foreign missionaries by radical (and unrepentant) Hindu extremists have received wide publicity. Crime is up sharply in Delhi and other Indian cities, especially in the north, and officials admit that more than 200 of India's 534 districts (the basic administrative units of India's 25 states) are affected by insurgency, ethnic conflict, political extremism, or caste conflicts. Increasing population pressures, along with the conflicting demands of 20 different linguistic groups, 50,000 castes, and 500,000 villages all point to the prospect of disintegration.

This turmoil, however, is at least partly an unavoidable manifestation of healthy new forces at work in India. If India used to be easy to govern but hard to change, now it is quick to change and difficult to govern. The old bureaucratic systems have collapsed, and political parties have mushroomed in number and strength by voicing the demands of newly empowered castes and ethnic groups. The results are often messy. And because India has become a major center for Asian television services, images

of Indian violence are far more visible to Indians and the rest of the world.

India has endured bloody social violence before, and, if the past is any guide, today's strife does not presage the unraveling of the state. During the 1950s and 1960s, rioters clashed in several states, especially in the south, over language and caste politics. A few states had to be placed under "President's Rule" and were governed directly from Delhi. Many pundits predicted the breakup of India or the paralysis of the state, if not a movement to an authoritarian system. None of these things happened (although Indira Gandhi did impose a 15-month "emergency" rule in the 1970s). Instead, southern states such as Andhra Pradesh, Tamil Nadu, and Karnataka became among the most orderly (and prosperous) in the country, in large part because the great caste and language disputes were eventually resolved or negotiated away by new political parties that developed in each of the states. Today these southern states are in the forefront of a transformation of India's federal system, as the central government yields power and influence, especially on economic matters.

The turmoil and transformation owe a great deal to the decline of the long-ruling Indian National Congress Party. By the 1980s, Congress had become a highly centralized party that relied on a strong central leader to manage party affairs from Delhi. The "old" Congress Party had grassroots support, and Nehru tolerated strong state leaders. This system was swept away by Indira Gandhi and her son (and successor) Rajiv after she came to power in 1966. Today, the states are reasserting themselves. While Congress remains one of India's most popular parties, it has lost the support of key regional leaders, many of whom have formed their own state parties, appealing to regional pride and local economic and political interests. Indians have drifted away from the idea of government as *maa-baap*—mother and father.

The decline of the Congress Party has also led to a series of fragile coali-

tion governments in the center since 1989. The BJP, which won only two parliamentary seats in the 1984 election, thereafter embarked on a mass mobilization of voters, built around the themes of Hindu pride, Indian nationalism, and economic reform. Yet the BJP's popular vote barely matches that of Congress, and it is dependent on its coalition partners (mostly state-based parties) to continue in office. The present government, elected last year, is likely to remain in power a few more years, but it could fall quickly if its partners were to work out a power-sharing arrangement with the Congress Party. Yet neither Congress nor the BJP will be able to restore the old system of one-party predominance.

Today, the social turmoil that plagued the south 30 years ago afflicts some important northern states, especially the vast farm state of Uttar Pradesh (which would be the world's sixth most populous country if it were independent) and its neighbor, Bihar, once a superbly administered state but now the butt of jokes. (In responding to an offer by the Japanese prime minister to turn Bihar into a Japan in three years, a former chief minister of Bihar is said to have responded that, given three months, he could turn Japan into a Bihar.) These conflicts stem from a vast Indian social revolution, comparable to the civil rights movement in the United States or the antiapartheid campaigns in South Africa, that is the practical working out of the logic of democratic politics embedded in the Indian Constitution.

It has taken several generations, but many of India's lowest and poorest castes, including the Dalits (formerly labeled "untouchables"), are turning to the ballot and the street to gain political power. These castes—and poorer Muslims and other non-Hindu groups, including India's large heavily Christian and animist tribal population—have discovered that their one great political advantage in India's democracy is their numbers. They have learned to develop "vote banks" and negotiate with the political parties for their support, election by election, candidate by candidate. But in caste-ridden areas such as Uttar Pradesh, Bihar, and parts of other states, the democratic revolution meets stiff resistance from middle and high castes that are reluctant to share power. Violence is one result.

The social revolutions in the north parallel and sometimes intersect with the nationwide struggle between Hindu nationalists and a variety of other forces, including India's 120 million Muslims, its Christian population, most of the Congress Party, and the vast majority of intellectuals, who are staunch secularists. This battle for the ideological soul of India has been the cause of several major religious riots, turning Hindus against Muslims and, on occasion, Christians.

Yet there are practical limits to these conflicts. India is, overall, a highly accommodating society, and its politicians are skilled at the art of compromise. Historically, Hinduism has absorbed and incorporated outside ideologies and cultures, even as it has helped spawn other faiths, including Jainism, Sikhism, and Buddhism. There is no Hindu church, nor is there agreement on a "standard" Hinduism.

India's caste and class warfare will likely be confined to a few northern states. As for the struggle for a new Indian identity, the BJP does not want to push Muslims (who make up 12 percent of the population) into the arms of the Congress Party or alienate its coalition partners. Moderate elements of the BJP are aware that the extremism of the National Service Society (RSS), and other members of the family of Hindu organizations that provide the party's intellectual and political support could damage India's reputation abroad and hurt the party at the polls. Despite India's difficulties the BJP has been able to conduct a vigorous foreign policy and it has used foreign policy issues to rally the nation. Most recently, it turned the Kargil war into a demonstration of "Indian unity" by celebrating the valor of the Christians, Muslims, Hindus, and Sikhs who fought under the Indian flag.

India's political system is a complex machine that requires an enormous amount of maintenance, but it functions well enough to satisfy most of its members most of the time. Its national elites—managers of major corporations, leaders of the larger political parties, commanders of the armed forces, and the intellectuals, scientists, and academics of the "chattering classes"—have demonstrated a flexibility that has been absent in other complex, multiethnic, multinational states such as Pakistan, Yugoslavia, and the former Soviet Union. Like a ship with many watertight compartments, it is relatively immune to the kinds of large-scale, extremist, or totalitarian movements that have afflicted more homogeneous states such as China and Cambodia.

India's growing strength has been amplified by the end of the Cold War. Today the country sits in the middle of a vast band of economic and military power unregulated by any Cold War framework. The Indian and Pakistani nuclear weapons tests completed a chain of nuclear-capable states (most of which have strategic missiles) that stretches from Israel to North Korea and includes Iraq, China, Pakistan, and potentially Iran, Taiwan, and South Korea. Many of the states to India's east are economic "tigers" (Malaysia, Singapore, Thailand, and Taiwan); to the north and west are the Central Asian and Persian Gulf states with their vast reserves of oil and gas.

With its highly professional million-man army, significant naval forces, and a modern air force, India could be a strategic force in the region. In 1990, on the eve of the Persian Gulf War, it demonstrated some of these capabilities with one of the largest airlifts in history, quickly evacuating more than 100,000 Indian nationals from Iraq and Kuwait. India also plays an important role in UN peacekeeping operations. It recently sent to Sierra Leone a contingent of battle-hardened troops authorized to use deadly force.

India's expected prosperity would allow it to add teeth to a foreign policy that has been long on rhetoric about India's global greatness but short on achievement. Delhi has long maintained a number of small aid programs (in Bangladesh, Bhutan, Nepal, Sri Lanka, Vietnam, and several African states), and these can be expected to grow. The economy can also support a considerably larger defense budget, even after increases of 10 percent in 1997 and '98, and a 28 percent rise in 1999.

India will, for the first time, have the material means to be a major arms supplier, and to build sea-projection and airlift capabilities that could extend its military power across Asia. India could also forge alliances with other important states, providing personnel, some high-technology expertise, and an important location in exchange for political and military assistance. Delhi had expected such an arrangement to emerge from its ties to the Soviet Union. Now it is working closely with Israel; it has ties to Vietnam and other Asian middle powers, and its foreign policy experts even talk of a strategic relationship with the United States.

What will India do with its new power? Since the heady days of Nehru, all Indian leaders have proclaimed a special destiny or mission for India in Asia and the world, based on the greatness of its civilization, its strategic location, and its distinctive view of the world. The BJP's leaders are no exception, and the 1998 nuclear tests were one way of stating India's ambition to be taken seriously as a major power. But outsiders, contrasting the grand schemes of India's foreign policy establishment with the *jhuggis* (urban slums) of Delhi and Mumbai, not to mention those of Calcutta, wonder if it is serious. How can India, with a national literacy rate of only 55 percent, much lower than that in the poorest and most backward states, stake a claim to greatness?

The answer is that unlike the people of other middle powers such as Indonesia, Brazil, and Nigeria, Indians believe that their country has both a destiny and an obligation to play a large role on the international stage. India and China, after all, are the world's only major states that embody grand civilizations. India also claims to speak for the vast majority of the world, especially its poorest and most underrepresented people. Hence its demands for a seat on the UN Security Council.

India also has practical economic and strategic reasons for staking a claim to great-power status. Two years ago it joined the World Trade Organization, and with this opening to the world's markets, both as an importer and an exporter, it wants a larger voice in setting the rules and norms of the international economy.

Since the Nehru era, Indians have seen the world as unjust and dangerous. Nehru pursued a wide-ranging foreign policy with two major aims. The first was to speed up decolonization in Asia and Africa, the second to reduce the threat of nuclear war. In 1954, India became the first state to propose a comprehensive test ban treaty, and it has long been a major force in global disarmament discussions. Ironically, one of the Indian bomb lobby's arguments during the 1990s was that India had to go nuclear itself in order to put pressure on the existing nuclear powers to fulfill their obligation under the Non-Proliferation Treaty to discuss nuclear disarmament. (India, however, has refused to sign the treaty.)

Nehru's successors continue to challenge the world order, proposing schemes for nuclear disarmament and the radical restructuring of the UN Security Council. India emerged from World War II as the world's fourth largest industrial power and second most populous state, but it was not considered for a Security Council seat, nor did the Indian leadership, swamped with the politics of partition and independence, press for one. (Nehru rejected an American proposal that India take China's seat on the Security Council, believing that China would eventually, be grateful for this gesture.) Now India seeks a seat both for the status it would confer and the voice (and veto) it would provide on major global issues. Not incidentally, a veto would also allow Delhi to keep the United Nations out of the Kashmir conflict.

In the past, India was a less-than-great power attempting to act like a great one, which sometimes made it look foolish. When it challenged the Comprehensive Test Ban Treaty in a UN vote, only two countries—renegade Libya and India's vassal, Bhutan—supported it. But the gap between Indian ambitions and capabilities is slowly narrowing. Under the more assertive leadership of the BJP, despite the constraints of a coalition government, India has demonstrated a surprising ability to undertake bold initiatives: It has tested nuclear weapons, restructured its relationship with the United States, further liberalized the economy, established close relations with once-scorned Israel, and attempted a dramatic rapprochement with Pakistan. That effort, culminating in Prime Minister Vajpayee's trip last year to the city of Lahore in eastern Pakistan, ended in failure.

A new generation of Indian strategists, politicians, and officials is increasingly aware that the hectoring style of Krishna Menon, Nehru's defense minister, is counterproductive. Slowly, a new realism is creeping into the Indian foreign ministry, hitherto famed as one of the world's most skilled bureaucracies at "getting to no." Foreign Minister Jaswant Singh, for example, has held 13 meetings with U.S. Deputy Secretary of State Strobe Talbott, the longest sustained dialogue ever between senior Indian and American policymakers. Yet there are important areas where American and Indian policies are at cross-purposes, none more so than India's nuclear program.

No issue has contributed more to the failure of U.S. policy in South Asia than India's nuclear weapons program. But American policymakers who failed to prevent the Indian tests can plead extenuating circumstances, since the Indians themselves had long been of two minds about the pursuit of the bomb. Delhi's spokesmen traditionally had cast their opposition to all nuclear weapons in highly moralistic terms, leading many Americans to conclude that India was an ally in preventing their spread.

This was a miscalculation. While India strongly opposed "vertical" proliferation (the nuclear arms race between the Soviet Union and the United States, for example), it was more tolerant of "horizontal" proliferation (the spread of nuclear weapons from state to state) and fought bitterly to retain the option of becoming a nuclear weapons state, albeit choosing not to exercise it for several decades. After 1991, however, the world looked very different to Delhi. With the collapse of the Soviet Union, it had lost its major supporter in the world arena. The United States still seemed indifferent, even as Pakistan issued ambiguous nuclear threats, and China gained economic strength. Nuclear weapons suddenly had stronger appeal.

After the Cold War, Washington treated India (and Pakistan) simply like two more states that were part of the global proliferation problem. India, it was thought, could be induced—or coerced—into signing the nonproliferation and test ban treaties. Washington showed no understanding of India's acute sense of isolation, or of its feeling that the United States ranked it with Pakistan and accorded greater importance to China. The United States yielded to China during negotiations for the Comprehensive Test Ban Treaty, yet after the Indian nuclear tests, President Clinton stood next to Chinese President Jiang Zemin as they jointly condemned Delhi.

The appearance of a Pakistan-China-U.S. axis played into the hands of Indian hawks. India's most eminent nuclear theoretician, K. Subrahmanyam, argued that the country was compelled to go nuclear because of threats to its national security from its two traditional rivals and (implicitly) the United States. The United States, he argued, wished to strip India of its nuclear option. Once India joined the nuclear club, he continued, it could force the other members, especially the United States, to take serious steps toward global disarmament.

This argument may seem hypocritical, but it was widely believed and deeply felt in India. The Clinton administration never developed an effective response. President Clinton said on one occasion that the United States and India shared the ultimate goal of nuclear abolition, but senior administration officials privately contradicted him, even as others publicly reiterated earlier presidential commitments.

India's relationship with its neighbors, especially Pakistan, will be the most important factor in determining whether it emerges as a great Asian power.

The dispute with Pakistan has many layers, beginning with the botched partition of British India more than 50 years ago. Among the questions it left unanswered was the disposition of the princely state of Jammu and Kashmir. Because Kashmir was primarily Muslim, Pakistan argued that it should be part of Islamic Pakistan. India claimed that since British India was not divided strictly along religious lines (India still had a vast Muslim population), Kashmir should join secular India. The land is mostly mountainous and barren, but it has military value. Both nations agreed on one thing: Self-determination (which is what most Kashmiris wanted) could be ruled out.

After India's nuclear tests in 1998, the overt nuclearization of South Asia emboldened Islamabad to launch a brilliantly conceived (but strategically disastrous) attack across the line of control that temporarily separates Indian and Pakistani forces in Kashmir. The pressure on India was further increased after Pakistan's military coup last October. Pakistan's army chief, General Pervaiz Musharraf, who assumed the title of "chief executive," promised continued support for the separatist "freedom fighters" inside Kashmir.

Indian decisionmakers cannot bring themselves to negotiate with the new military regime, fearing that this would grant legitimacy to the idea of rule by the armed forces in South Asia, perhaps giving their own generals ideas. There are also powerful groups in both countries that oppose normalization or dialogue on almost every issue, including even people-to-people exchanges. Among them are smugglers and parts of the intelligence services, both of which stand to lose a great deal. Some diplomats and strategists in both countries fear that concessions would be the first step on a slippery slope.

As the larger power, India will have to figure out a way to initiate a credible dialogue with Pakistan, either directly or through intermediaries. The difficulty of doing this is especially evident in the case of Kashmir, where the two countries had to resort to secret diplomacy—which failed—for even the most preliminary talks. While the Indian government has issued strong statements about countering terrorism and isolating Pakistan, it is often in the position of merely reacting to Islamabad's increasingly risky measures. Instead, it needs to sort out those areas where cooperation and accommodation (by both countries) are possible from those areas where the two states have incompatible interests. And it needs to recognize that a failed Pakistan, with its potential to spread nuclear weapons and Islamic terrorism (as well as millions of refugees), would harm Indian interests.

Despite its own ambitions, India still finds itself linked with Pakistan, a country one-fifth its size. In international affairs, states are known by the enemies they keep, so India is doomed to be paired with Pakistan until it can either defeat or accommodate Islamabad.

India's other major neighbor, China, presents obstacles of a different sort to its aspirations for a larger world role. Delhi remains deeply ambivalent about Beijing. Nehru had envisioned a cooperative relationship between the two states, and some in Delhi still believe that India and China have a common interest in moderating American dominance. China, however, was responsible for India's humiliation in the 1962 war. So bad was the Indian military performance, and so incompetent India's political leadership, that this defeat ended any notion of a rivalry between the two states. If any doubt remained, it was laid to rest by China's speedier economic growth and the seat it eventually obtained on the UN Security Council.

Indians are also wary of becoming surrogates for the West as part of an anti-China alliance. If the Chinese conclude that India is actively opposing them (perhaps through increased support for Tibetan exiles, or support for ethnic minorities in western China), Beijing could easily increase its support of Islamabad and separatist movements in India itself.

Delhi is plagued by unresolved policy disagreements. After the 1998 nuclear tests, the BJP government labeled China the chief strategic threat to India. A few months later, it retreated from this confrontational line and completed another round of (fruitless) talks with Beijing on the border dispute. At the same moment, India was making a serious effort to begin a dialogue with Pakistan. That policy, too, was soon reversed. Indecision and ambiguity might have had certain advantages in the bipolar Cold War world, but they are liabilities today.

If India is slowly moving toward greatness, how should the United States respond? Traditionally, the great states of the world have resisted the entry of new members into the "club." Japan and the Soviet Union, for example, found their way blocked after World War I—which helped bring on the next world war.

The failure of the United States to reconsider how aspiring middle powers such as India might shape the emerging global order in the wake of the Cold War was a costly error. An India that did not seem to count for very much (in Washington, at least) became embroiled in crises and made itself (and thus Pakistan) a new member of the nuclear club. The time has come for the United States to reconsider its relationship with India. If it reforms its economy and comes to terms with Pakistan, India could be a force for stability in Asia and for the containment of China, as well as a strong support for humanitarian intervention in Africa and other war-torn regions. If it does not, it still will continue to have great influence in the non-Western world.

There are also negative reasons for the United States to re-examine its approach. Within the Indian military, some experts now argue that Delhi should abandon its historic restraint about exporting sensitive technologies. India, they say, can earn much-needed foreign exchange and tweak the nose of the West (and China) by selling nuclear knowledge and missile technology to Middle Eastern, Asian, and even lesser European states. And while India is unlikely ever to become an ally of China, it could side with Beijing (and Moscow) to challenge the American-dominated alliance system in East and Southeast Asia. Left to its own devices, it might also pursue a riskier strategy for dealing with Pakistan. Indian strategists have already increased tensions by embracing the idea that "limited" war between nuclear powers is possible.

The United States ought to recognize that India is not just another South Asian state but a player in the larger Asian sphere with an interest in—and influence on—the worldwide community of ex-colonial states. This does not mean abandoning important U.S. interests in Pakistan, a nuclear power that will soon be the world's fifth largest state. It means the expansion of American engagement with Delhi, including discussion of shared policy concerns (terrorism; narcotics; humanitarian intervention; political stability in fragmented, ethnically complex countries; and China). The Clinton visit produced a "vision statement" embracing such ideas, but it remains to be seen whether this commitment will extend beyond the Clinton administration, or even to its conclusion.

Treating India as a rising power means Delhi should be one of the capitals—along with London, Berlin, Beijing, Moscow, and Tokyo—that senior American officials visit and telephone about global developments. Like the French, Indians have a different and not necessarily hostile view of how the world should be organized. Regular consultation should help temper the sometimes abrasive Indian style.

The United States can also do more than merely point out the virtues of regional accommodation. It should encourage a greater sense of realism in Pakistan about possible solutions to the Kashmir conflict, while also urging the Indians to accommodate Pakistan's concerns about the treatment of Muslim Kashmiris. A more active yet low-key diplomacy is in order. It will not lead to an easy or rapid resolution of the Kashmir dispute, but it will enable the United States to retain influence in both countries should its services again be required to avert a war, or even a future nuclear crisis.

Finally, the United States must put nuclear proliferation in proper perspective. Many American officials remain embittered by what they believe to be Indian duplicity over the Comprehensive Test Ban Treaty and the 1998 nuclear tests. Yet both countries are essentially status quo powers when it comes to the proliferation of nuclear (and other) weapons and to crises that could escalate to a nuclear conflict. The next U.S. administration may be able to strike a bargain with Delhi, obtaining Indian cooperation on nuclear proliferation in exchange for dual-use technologies such as advanced computers, aerospace technology, and even civilian nuclear assistance.

A sound prescription for the U.S.-India relationship calls for neither opposition nor alliance but for something in between. There is no need to contain or oppose an India that is still struggling to reshape its economic and political order, especially since it is in America's interest that such reforms proceed. But the United States cannot expect, nor should it seek, a strategic alliance that Delhi would view as part of an anti-Pakistan or anti-China campaign. An "in-between" relationship would require developing new understandings in several areas: The conditions under which India and the United States might jointly engage in humanitarian intervention in various parts of the world, the means of deploying new defensive military technologies (such as theater missile defenses) without triggering regional arms races in Taiwan and South Asia, and the joint steps the two might take to strengthen fragile democratic regimes in Asia and elsewhere. A relationship with India offers an opportunity to influence directly the Indian worldview on issues that are of importance to the United States. India would also provide early warning of potentially harmful policies.

But even the best-intentioned American policy will have little impact if India cannot bring itself to think and behave strategically. The most important choice it must make concerns its relationship with Pakistan, but it must also show a greater willingness to engage with the United States. It must avail itself of its own cultural, economic, and ideological resources and not assume that great-power status will accrue because it can lay claim to a marginal nuclear weapons program or a history of accomplishments as a great civilization.

India is not a great power in the classic sense; it cannot challenge American military or economic strength. But in a transformed international order, its assets and resources are more relevant to a wide range of American interests than they have been for 50 years. They cannot be safely ignored in the future, as they have been in the past.

STEPHEN P. COHEN is a Senior Fellow in the Foreign Policy Studies Program and director of the India/South Asia Project at the Brookings Institution. His new book, India: An Emerging Power, will be published next year.

Berlin Wall obscured for a time the dissolution that had already begun in Yugoslavia, the current consternation over the extremist government in Afghanistan, Osama bin Laden, and the fighting in Kashmir obscures the core issue of South Asia: the institutional meltdown of Pakistan. And as was true of Yugoslavia, it is the bewildering complexity of ethnic and religious divisions that makes Pakistan so fragile. My comparison to 1980s Yugoslavia, a place that I also saw firsthand, is not casual. In both cases it was the very accumulation of disorder and irrationality that was so striking and that must be described in detail—not merely stated—to be understood.

PAKISTAN covers the desert frontier of the Subcontinent. British civil administration extended only to Lahore, in the fertile Punjab, near Pakistan's eastern border with India; its Mogul architecture, gardens, and rich bazaars give Lahore a closer resemblance to the Indian cities of New Delhi and Calcutta than to any other place in Pakistan. But the rest of Pakistan—the rugged Afghan-border regions of Baluchistan and the North-West Frontier Province, the alkaline wasteland of Sind, and the Hindu Kush and Karakoram Mountains embracing Kashmir—has never been subdued by the British or anyone else. This area was grossly underdeveloped compared with British India; the few entrepreneurs were Hindus, who fled after Partition, in 1947. Even Karachi, now Pakistan's business center and a city of 14 million riddled by sectarian violence, was only an isolated settlement on the Arabian Sea when the British departed. Karachi's lack of the prideful identity and civilizing urbanity found in Lahore and the great cities of India helps to explain its current unrest. Islamabad, Pakistan's sterile capital, with its vast, empty avenues lined with Mogul-cum-Stalinist structures, was not built until the 1960s.

When seven million Muslim refugees, fleeing India, created Pakistan, the role of the military became paramount, by necessity. The refugees were consumed by the need to manage enormous and unruly borderlands and by fear of their much larger, Hindu-dominated neighbor. Furthermore, with local tribal and ethnic identities so strong, civilian politics became a bureaucratic forum for revenge and unsavory tradeoffs. In the ancient tribal and feudal cultures of the region leaders bartered water wells and tracts of desert; in the new state they bartered flour mills, electricity grids, and transport systems.

Thinking purely in terms of blood and territory comes naturally in Quetta, a cinder-block jumble of shops whose outskirts are composed of walled tribal compounds and Afghan refugee camps. Since Afghanistan erupted into war, in the late 1970s, and refugees poured across the border, Quetta has increasingly become an Afghan city inside Pakistan. Cheap, Western-style polyesters have taken over much of the Third World, but in Quetta nearly everyone still wears traditional *shalwar kameez*: baggy cotton pants and a long, flowing shirt, with a blanket over the shoulder for praying and sleeping. The Baluch are identified by their grandiose white turbans, the Pashtoons from southern Afghanistan by smaller, darker ones, and the Pashtoons from northern Afghanistan by flat woolen caps called *pakols*. In addition there are Asian-looking Uzbeks and Shia Hazaras—descendants of Genghis Khan's Mongols who settled in central Afghanistan before becoming refugees here.

I had last visited Quetta in 1988, when it was a clean, relatively quiet place of fewer than 500,000 people. Now it was noisy and dirty, crowded with beggars and drug addicts, and its population was unofficially estimated at 1.2 million. A three-year drought afflicting southern Asia from Afghanistan to India had provoked an exodus from the surrounding desert into the city. The delightful water channels I remembered from the 1980s are now dry and filled with crud. Traveling outside Quetta, I saw empty riverbeds and dam catchments. Desperate men equipped with nothing but shovels dug ninety-foot-

deep wells in the 110 heat, searching for water near Hanna Lake, which was once beautiful and full, and is now brown and diminished. With irrigation canals dry, aquifers are being depleted by overuse. Agriculture is in decline because of the water shortage, with cultivation reduced in many areas by 70 percent. Political disorder and mismanagement have blocked new industry and investment.

Pakistan's Afghan-border region—1,000 miles long and 100 miles wide—is a deathly volcanic landscape of crags and winding canyons where the tropical floor of the Subcontinent pushes upward into the high, shaved wastes of Central Asia, and where desert and mountain tribesmen replace the darker-skinned people in the cities. From Baluchistan north through the "tribal agencies" of Waziristan, Kurram, Orakzai, Khyber, Mohmand, and Bajaur—near Peshawar, the destitute capital of the North-West Frontier Province—one finds an anarchic realm of highwaymen, religious and tribal violence, heroin laboratories, and weapons smuggling.

Here the religious extremism and disorder begot by two decades of war in Afghanistan merge with the troubles in Pakistan. With 148 million people, Pakistan is the world's seventh largest nation, and its annual population-growth rate of 2.6 percent will make it the third most populous nation by 2050, behind India and China—if it still exists.

Afghanistan and Pakistan should be seen as one political unit. This is a result of Pakistan's heavy involvement in the Afghan guerrilla struggle against Soviet occupation forces in the 1980s and in the rise of Afghanistan's Taliban extremists afterward. But geography and British colonial history are factors too.

No border here could be natural. The transition from the steamy lowlands of the Subcontinent to the high moonscapes of Central Asia is gradual. The Pashtoons controlling the frontier zone of eastern and southern Afghanistan have never accepted the arbitrary boundary between Afghanistan and colonial India drawn in 1893 by the British envoy, Sir Mortimer Durand. Moreover, the British bequeathed to the Pakistanis the belt of anarchic territories they called tribal agencies, which lie to the east of the Durand Line. This had the effect of further confusing the boundary between settled land and the chaos of Afghanistan. Pakistani governments have always felt besieged—not only by India but also by Afghan tribesmen. In order to fight India, in the Pakistani view, it is necessary to dominate Afghanistan.

But this Pakistan has never been able to accomplish. The story of the lawless frontier, and of its emerging importance as a crisis point, is the story of failure: the failure of a sophisticated people from the industrial and agricultural plain of Punjab—the Pakistani military and political elite—to dominate an unreconstructed tribal people of the high desert.

The Taliban

WHEN the explosions and gunfire awakened me in Quetta, I was staying at the home of a friend, Hamed Karzai, who from 1992 to 1994 had been Afghanistan's first deputy foreign minister. At that time Afghanistan was governed by the *mujahideen,* the "holy warriors" who had defeated the Soviets. That was before the emergence of the radical Taliban ("Knowledge Seekers"), of whom Karzai is now an outspoken opponent. Not only was the iron gate outside his home bolted at night, with an armed Afghan on duty, but Karzai insisted that a former *mujahideen* commander guard the door of my room. I forgave Karzai his anxiety on my behalf. In July of last year his father was assassinated while walking home from evening prayers at a nearby mosque; the gunman escaped on a waiting motorbike. The murder, together with many others in Pakistan's borderland, was attributed to the Taliban.

Karzai, forty-two, is Afghan royalty. He is tall and olive-complexioned, with a clipped salt-and-pepper beard and a starched *shalwar kameez.* The slope of his bald head and nose gives him the look of an eagle. After the murder of his father Karzai inher-

ited the title khan ("head") of the 500,000-strong Popolzai—the Pashtoon clan of Ahmad Shah Durrani, the Persian army commander who conquered the southern Afghan city of Kandahar and in 1747 became the first king of Afghanistan. Because tribal position is of great importance in Afghan society, the *mujahideen* always trusted the Westernized and moderate Karzai. The same went for the Taliban, who sought him out long before they seized power and later offered him the post of United Nations ambassador.

"The Taliban were good, honest people," Karzai told me over green Afghan tea and almonds. "They were connected to the *madrassas* [Islamic academies] in Quetta and Peshawar, and were my friends from the *jihad* [holy war] against the Soviets. They came to me in May, 1994, saying, 'Hamed, we must do something about the situation in Kandahar. It is unbearable.' I had no reservations about helping them. I had a lot of money and weapons left over from the *jihad.* I also helped them with political legitimacy. It was only in September of 1994 that others began to appear at the meetings—silent ones I did not recognize, people who took over the Taliban movement. That was the hidden hand of Pakistani intelligence."

I heard versions of this story from several former commanders of the *jihad,* who told me how they had supported the Taliban only to be deceived by the Pakistani intelligence agents who were behind the movement.

These incomplete and somewhat self-serving accounts encapsulated much complicated history. By early 1994 Afghanistan was in disarray. The *mujahideen* who warred against the Soviets had been a motley collection of seven Pakistan-based resistance groups, divided by region, clan, politics, and religious ideology. Worse, the resistance commanders inside Afghanistan had only the loosest of links to the seven groups. For them, party affiliation was merely a matter of access to weaponry—the groups were awash in guns and money, provided by the CIA

through Pakistan's Inter-Services Intelligence. Thus when the Soviet-backed Afghan regime collapsed in Kabul, the capital, in 1992, Afghanistan became a writhing nest of petty warlords who fought and negotiated with one another for small chunks of territory. Girls and young boys were raped and traded between commanders. The situation was especially bad in Kandahar. The road leading to it from Quetta was shared by at least twenty factions, each of which put a chain across the road and demanded tolls.

But there were also honest commanders, backwoodsmen who lived by a primitive creed called Pashtoonwali—"the way of the Pashtoons," a code more severe even than Koranic law. While emphasizing hospitality and chivalry, Pashtoonwali demands blood vengeance on fellow Muslims for killing and punishes adultery based on hearsay alone. In addition to these commanders there were hordes of young boys who had grown up in crowded refugee camps in Quetta and Peshawar, where they were educated in *madrassas* supported by Saudi Arabia. The schools taught a more ideological and austere brand of Islam than the ones practiced in the mountains of Afghanistan, where before the Soviet occupation religion had been a natural outgrowth of rural life. (In the mountains women need not always wear veils, for example, because in the course of a day the only males they encounter are their relatives.) In the urban anonymity of Pakistani cities and adjacent refugee camps religion was reinvented in harsher form, to preserve values suddenly under attack.

The communist ideology brought to Afghanistan by the Soviet occupation had required an equally harsh response, and throughout the 1980s and early 1990s the *madrassas* for Afghan refugees in Pakistan provided it. The fierce brand of Islam they taught was not just a reaction to urban conditions but also a result of evolving and intertwining Saudi and Pakistani philosophies. In the Afghan refugee academies Saudi Wahabism merged (as it did nowhere else) with the Deobandism of the Subcontinent. Wahabism arose in the Arabian peninsula in the eighteenth century with the teachings of Muhammad ibn Abdul Wahab, who led a puritanical reaction against what he considered lax observance. Deobandism takes its name from the village of Deoband, outside New Delhi, where in the nineteenth century an Islamic academy developed an orthodox pan-Islam in reaction against British rule. When the Muslim state of Pakistan was created, Deobandism was further radicalized by an Islamic theorist named Abdul A'la Maududi, who propagated a form of Islam with striking resemblances to totalitarianism. Maududi believed that the Koran had to be accepted in full and that many Muslims had corrupted Islam by letting themselves be influenced by the liberal West. Islam is perfect, Maududi asserted, and requires no judgment on the part of the believer. It should override all other laws of the state.

There is no contradiction between the radical Islamists' hatred for the Russians in Chechnya and their hatred for the Americans everywhere else: both are reactions to a challenge from an impure West that is more proximate than ever before, because of technology.

As Afghanistan fell apart in an orgy of banditry, *madrassa* students in Pakistan came into contact with uncorrupted backwoodsmen inside Afghanistan; together they filled the vacuum in authority. One of the backwoodsmen was Mullah Mohammed Omar, a *mujahideen* commander who is said to have ignited the Taliban revolt, in early 1994, by leading a small force in Kandahar that captured and hanged from the barrel of a tank a fellow commander guilty of raping two girls.

The Taliban rose and swept across late-twentieth-century Afghanistan much as Islam itself had swept across seventh-century Arabia and North Africa, filling the void left by the anarchy and decadence of waning Byzantine rule. In the process of overrunning 80 percent of the country, the Taliban captured Kabul, in 1996. There they carried out amputations and stonings and seized the Soviet puppet ruler of Af-

ghanistan, Najibullah, from a United Nations compound, castrating and jeep-dragging him before hanging him from a traffic post.

The Taliban embody a lethal combination: a primitive tribal creed, a fierce religious ideology, and the sheer incompetence, naivet, and cruelty that are begot by isolation.

The atrocities demonstrated the Taliban obsession with the notion that the city, with its foreign influences, is the root of all evil. In the recently published *Taliban* the journalist Ahmed Rashid writes that because many of the Taliban are orphans of war, who have never known the company of women, they have retreated into a male brotherhood reminiscent of the Crusaders. Indeed, the most dangerous movements are often composed of war orphans, who, being unsocialized, are exceptionally brutal (the Khmer Rouge, in Cambodia, and the Revolutionary United Front, in Sierra Leone, are two examples). Of course, the longer wars go on, the more orphans are created.

The Taliban embody a lethal combination: a primitive tribal creed, a fierce religious ideology, and the sheer incompetence, naivet, and cruelty that are begot by isolation from the outside world and growing up amid war without parents. They are also an example of globalization, influenced by imported pan-Islamic ideologies and supported economically by both Osama bin

Laden's worldwide terrorist network (for whom they provide a base) and a multibillion-dollar smuggling industry in which ships and trucks bring consumer goods from the wealthy Arabian Gulf emirate of Dubai (less a state than the world's largest shopping mall) through Iran and Afghanistan and on to Quetta and Karachi.

The Taliban takeover of Afghanistan also relied on crucial help from Pakistan. By 1994 Pakistan was tiring of its Afghan *mujahideen* puppet, Gulbuddin Hekmatyar. Throughout the 1980s and early 1990s its Inter-Services Intelligence had channeled more arms and money from the CIA to Hekmatyar's radical-fundamentalist faction than to any of the more moderate *mujahideen* groups. Hekmatyar was young, charismatic, highly educated, and power-hungry. Yet his attraction for the ISI lay in the fact that he had little grassroots support inside Afghanistan itself and was thus beholden to the Pakistanis. The continuing anarchy in Afghanistan after the departure of the Soviets showed the fundamental flaw in the ISI's policy. Hekmatyar could never consolidate power to the extent Pakistan required in order to safeguard its land routes to the new oil states of Central Asia—routes that would create a bulwark of Muslim states that could confront India.

It was a democratically elected Prime Minister, Benazir Bhutto, along with her Interior Minister, the retired general Naseerullah Babar, who conceived of the Taliban as a solution to Pakistan's problem. Through the ISI the Bhutto government began to provide the Taliban with money, fuel, subsidized wheat, vehicles, weapons, and volunteers from Pakistan's *madrassas*. It also linked Afghanistan to Pakistan's telephone grid.

But the Taliban won't play the role of puppet. And Afghanistan's religious extremism is accelerating Pakistan's, through the network of *madrassas*. Furthermore, the future of the Taliban themselves is uncertain. They have restored security in Afghanistan by disarming much of the countryside, but they have built no institutions to sustain their rule—and 70 percent of working-age Afghans are jobless. Just as the Taliban rose and spread like Islam itself, they could also descend into disorderly power struggles, much like the medieval Muslim rulers who followed the prophet Mohammed.

Ultimately, the Taliban are tribal Pashtoons from the southern and eastern Afghan borderlands—an anarchic mountain people who have ground up one foreign invader after another, defying attempts by the Moguls, the Sikhs, the British, the Soviets, and the Pakistanis to control them. As Mahauddin, a white-robed Pashtoon cleric from southwestern Afghanistan, told me in Karzai's home, "We are thirsty for a pure Afghan government, a *loya jirga* [grand council of tribal chiefs] without Russia or the ISI to influence us."

In fact, with *mujahideen* field commanders no longer getting CIA money and weapons through the ISI, power in Afghanistan is inexorably gravitating back to the tribal heads. For example, commanders of Popolzai descent who were loyal to Hekmatyar and the other *mujahideen* party leaders have returned to Karzai's fold, which is why he is so troublesome to the Taliban and their Pakistani backers—and why Quetta is dangerous for Karzai.

THE NORTH-WEST FRONTIER

SEVERAL hundred miles north of Quetta lies Peshawar, at the eastern end of the Khyber Pass—the fabled gateway connecting Central Asia to the Subcontinent, which in our day means connecting Afghanistan to Pakistan. Here the religious disputes that run parallel to tribal divides come more clearly into focus. In the late 1970s Peshawar went from being a quaint backwater whose bazaars were interspersed with stately lawns and red-brick mansions in Anglo-Indian Gothic style to becoming a geopolitical fault line. Afghan refugees poured through the Khyber Pass by the millions, escaping the Soviet invasion. At the same time, the Iranian revolution

closed off an important route for drug smugglers, who began transporting locally produced heroin eastward through the Khyber Pass and down to the port of Karachi. Peshawar's population doubled to a million. Throughout the 1980s war, crime, and urbanization generated an intolerant religiosity.

Returning to Peshawar for the first time in more than a decade, I found an even more crowded, poor, and polluted city than the one I remembered. It was also more Afghan. In the 1980s Peshawar's Afghan population consisted of refugees from the rural hinterlands. But from 1992 to 1994, when a civil war among the *mujahideen* destroyed Kabul with mortar fire and rocket-propelled grenades, the sophisticated urbanites of the Afghan capital migrated to Peshawar. Unlike the rural refugees, these people had an exportable cosmopolitan culture, and this added another layer of change to Peshawar. Now there are many more Afghan restaurants and carpet shops and nightclubs for Afghan music—especially owing to the Taliban ban on music in Kabul. There are also many Afghan prostitutes, fairer-skinned and reputed to be more compliant than their Pakistani counterparts. The presence of educated Afghans made me realize that the very element of the population most averse to Taliban rule was now absent from Afghanistan, reducing the likelihood of an uprising.

In the 1980s traveling outside Peshawar into the tribal agencies of the North-West Frontier Province was easy for journalists, because the Pakistani regime encouraged news coverage of the *mujahideen* struggle against the Soviets in Afghanistan. This time it took me several days to get a permit to travel from Peshawar into the Orakzai and Kurram tribal agencies, which in recent years have been plagued by communal violence between members of the Sunni and Shia sects of Islam. The permit was valid only provided that I was accompanied by an armed escort of local tribal militia.

The road south and west of Peshawar runs past squalid mud-brick and wattle

stalls crowded with bearded and turbaned Pashtoon men; the women, concealed under burkas, resemble moving tents. The sky is polluted by a greasy haze of black smoke from tire-fed fires, used to bake mud bricks. The odor in each town is a rich mixture of dung, hashish, grilled meat, and diesel oil—and also cordite in Darra Adam Khel, where Pashtoons work at foot-powered lathes producing local copies of Kalashnikovs and other assault rifles.

In one shop, whose glass cases were filled with rifles, pistols, and bullet magazines, I met Haji Mohammed Zaman Khan, a local tribal leader. Haji Zaman wore a bulbous red cloth hat with an ostentatious bow around it—the signature of the Afridi, a branch of the Pashtoons thought to be descended from Greek soldiers of Alexander the Great's army, which came down the Khyber Pass. Here, as in Quetta, all the stores had been closed in protest against the military government's plan to tax the smuggling trade. Haji Zaman explained, "The government tries to stop production of opium poppies, our only cash crop. It wants to ban the transport of guns, which will make thousands jobless. Smuggling is the only means of survival we have left. Why doesn't the government raise money from the corrupt? When we see that the corrupt are being punished, then maybe we will trust the government."

By "the corrupt," Zaman meant officials of previous democratic governments who are under investigation for taking billions of dollars in bribes and depositing them in foreign bank accounts. Throughout Baluchistan and the North-West Frontier, I heard calls for revenge against those officials. No one with whom I spoke voiced any interest in national elections, which are very tentatively scheduled to take place in three years; political analysts in Islamabad call them a dead issue among the masses, though only for now.

Beyond Darra Adam Khel the landscape consisted of naked rock, heat, and haze. High temperatures had come a month early, with 110° common by early May, and there had been no seasonal rains to cool the ground. I saw women in burkas searching for water trickling through otherwise dry gravel beds. Low-walled fortresses of red brick were scarred with graffiti that read, in English and Urdu, LONG LIVE OSAMA BIN LADEN AND WE WANT ISLAMIC LAW. Throughout the tribal lands of Pakistan people are naming their newborns Osama. To these people, Bin Laden represents an Islamic David against a global American Goliath. It is the American government's promotion of Bin Laden as a formidable enemy that helps to give him credibility here. To the poor, he embodies the idea that only strict Islam has the power to vanquish the advancing materialism of the West. In the nearby tribal agency of Waziristan, Pakistani members of the Taliban have been destroying television sets, videos, and other reminders of the West. Bin Laden's terrorist organization, with operatives on several continents, is both a symptom of and a reaction against globalization.

Parachinar, the largest town in the Kurram tribal agency, was a small market center twelve years ago. Now it is a crowded city of 300,000, characterized by brutal concrete, electricity outages, water shortages, battles over property rights, and terrorism powered by guns that are filtering back into Pakistan from Afghanistan. When I asked the assistant political agent for Kurram, Massoud Ur-rahma, if military rule had made a difference, he replied dismissively, "Whether the government in Islamabad is military or democratic doesn't matter. We have no civil law here—only Pashtoon tribal law."

The Pashtoon population of Kurram is split between Sunnis and Shias. In September of 1996 a gun battle among teenage members of the two rival Muslim sects escalated into a communal war in which more than 200 people were killed and women and children were kidnapped. A paramilitary official said that the atrocities were out of "the Stone Age"; militants even executed out-of-towners who were staying at a local hotel.

Now the situation in Parachinar is peaceful but extremely tense. Paramilitaries guard the streets around the Sunni and Shia mosques, which stand nearly side by side, their minarets scarred by bullet holes. Only a few weeks before my visit seventeen people had been killed in violence between Sunnis and Shias in another tribal region of the North-West Frontier.

"The Shias are eighty percent of the Kurram agency,"the Shia leader in Parachinar, Mohammed Anwar, told me. "The problems have all been caused by Afghan refugees who support the Sunnis."Yet the Sunni leader, Haji Asghar Din, claims that 75 percent of the local population is Sunni. He told me that Sunnis cannot buy land from Shias—"so how can we consider them our brothers?" The only certainty is that Parachinar, hemmed in by the Safed Koh Mountains on the Afghan border, has little more room to expand. A high birth rate and a flood of Afghan refugees have intensified the property conflicts. Population growth has also weakened the power of tribal elders and created extremist youth factions. The lack of water and electricity has increased anger. Meanwhile, the government schools are abysmal—often without teachers, books, and roofs. The poor, who form the overwhelming majority, cannot afford the private academies, so they send their children to Sunni and Shia *madrassas,* where students are well cared for and indoctrinated with sectarian beliefs.

Every person I interviewed was sullen and reticent. One day a crowd of men surrounded me and led me to the back of a pharmacy, where they took turns denouncing America and telling me that the Taliban were good because they had restored security to Afghanistan, ending *mujahideen* lawlessness. The "external hand of India" was to blame for the local troubles between Sunnis and Shias here, I was told. Conspiracy theories, I have noticed, are inflamed by illiteracy: people who can't read rely on hearsay. In Pakistan the adult literacy rate is below 33 percent. In the tribal areas it is below that. As

for the percentage of women in Parachinar who can read, I heard figures as low as two percent; nobody really knows.

KARACHI

TRIBAL and religious unrest in Pakistan is aggravated by terrible living conditions and divisive nationalisms. These are most clearly seen in Karachi, far to the south, on the Arabian Sea. Traditionless, dysfunctional, and unstable, Karachi is an unfortunately apt metaphor for Pakistan's general condition. Only a quarter of the 14 million residents are native to Sind, the region around Karachi, and are themselves migrants from the drought-stricken interior. The rest are immigrants from elsewhere on the Subcontinent. At least a quarter of the populace lives in *katchiabaadis,* "temporary houses" built haphazardly of corrugated iron, cinder blocks, wattle, burlap, and cardboard, with stones and tires anchoring their rattling roofs. Vistas of these houses go on for miles. Some *katchiabaadi* neighborhoods have existed for decades; they have shops, teahouses, and makeshift playgrounds. Goats wander everywhere. Children and adults sift through mounds of garbage in search of items to recycle. "The water situation is getting worse; electricity and other infrastructure are hopeless," a foreign expert told me. "The entire foundation of life here is imploding—except, of course, in the neighborhoods where people have lots of money."

Most Third World cities manifest dramatic contrasts between rich and poor. But in no other place have I seen rich and poor live in such close and hostile proximity as in Karachi. On one street a grimy warren of *katchiabaadis* lay to my right, and a high wall guarding luxury villas and a Kentucky Fried Chicken outlet lay to my left. Karachi's villas look like embassies, with guards, barbed wire, iron grilles, and beautiful bougainvillaea and jacaranda trees adorning stucco ramparts. The villas, with their satellite dishes for watching CNN, MTV, and other international channels, symbolize a high-end kind of globalization; the *katchiabaadis*—so much like the slums I have seen throughout the developing world—a low-end kind.

During the week that I was in Karachi in May, seven vehicles, including a bus, were set afire by rampaging youths, who also broke windows at a McDonald's and a Kentucky Fried Chicken. Seven other vehicles were carjacked. Bombs exploded near a police station and in the central business district, killing one person and injuring six others. Three people were murdered by unidentified assailants. As in Baluchistan and the North-West Frontier Province, political, ethnic, and religious reasons are given for the violence. But the evidence is often murky. Seeing how people lived in Karachi, I wondered if sheer rage might have much to do with it. I consider it a triumph of the human spirit, in fact, that there is not more violence here: the day that the youths went rampaging was the tenth in succession without water for part of the city. The wealthy have their own private water tanks, water-distribution network, and generators.

More than 4,000 people have been killed and more than 10,000 wounded in Karachi since the mid-1980s, when the city began to overflow with weapons from the Afghan war and communal fighting broke out between Pashtoons and two generations of *mohajirs,* Muslim refugees from India. In the late 1980s and the 1990s *mohajirs* and Sindhis fought each other here and elsewhere in Sind. In the first ten months of 1998 there were 629 murders in Karachi committed by what a local magazine called "unaffiliated contract killers"; none was solved by the police. Mobile phones were banned in the 1990s, because urban guerrillas were using them. Wire services dutifully report all the violence in Karachi, and in Baluchistan and the North-West Frontier, too. The reports are rarely picked up by the American media.

Just as the yearning for an independent Pashtoonistan is ever present in the Afghan borderlands, in southern Pakistan some Sindhis long for an independent Sind. Sind has been inhabited

for 6,000 years, and although the Sindhis are a mixture of Arabs, Persians, and other passing conquerors, they retain a strong cultural identity. But the idea of a stable, independent Sind is ludicrous, given the enmity between Sunnis and Shias that I saw in Karachi.

I waited as he knelt on the floor and prayed. Then he turned on the televison screens and observed two classes in progress, giving orders over the speakerphone.

I drove through a mishmash of gleaming high-rises, *katchiabaadis,* and sloppily constructed overpasses to arrive at a guarded house where a man introduced himself as a "retired school principal" and a "moderate Shia." Surrounded by his friends, he told me, "They'll kill us if you identify us by name."

General Musharraf, Pakistan's new ruler, "is a serious, humane man, but he has arrived too late to save Pakistan," the Shia leader explained. "With life getting worse materially, religion is more enticing, and tensions between us and the Sunni extremists are on the rise." The man spoke at length about universal love, honor, and tolerance in a very soft and patient tone, while offering me tea and dainty sweets. He gave me several books that laid out the Shia view of Muslim history—doctrines, he told me, that had gotten his friends murdered. Nothing he said seemed offensive or narrow-minded. Rather, it was the obsession

with Shi'ism itself that was the problem. His orthodoxy conflicted with others in a land where poverty is stark, ignorance and conspiracy-mongering are widespread, and the state itself is weak.

Next I visited the Sunnis. I drove through another succession of *katchiabaadis* to a bleak industrial zone, where I left the car and banged at an iron gate. Inside was a complex of school buildings with armed security guards. One of the guards led me to a room with a wall-to-wall carpet that had just been vacuumed. People sat on the floor with cushions behind them, in the traditional Oriental fashion. All had beards, skullcaps, and spotless white robes. The low glass coffee tables had just been polished. After the filth of so much of Karachi, I couldn't help being impressed.

I noticed security cameras mounted over all the doors. After removing my shoes, I was brought an ice-cold Pepsi. Then I was ushered into another spotless room, also with a vacuumed rug. Behind a low glass desk in a corner I saw three closed-circuit television screens, a speakerphone, headphones, a VCR, and a computer. A tiny, pudgy man with a gray beard and fashionable glasses, wearing a skullcap and a white *shalwar kameez,* entered the room.

"Will you excuse me while I say my prayers?" he asked. I waited as he knelt on the floor and prayed. Then he sat down behind the desk, turned on the television screens, put on the headphones, and proceeded to observe two classes in progress, giving orders to the teachers over the speakerphone while monitoring the entrance on a third screen. Speaking in a finely enunciated blend of Urdu and Arabic, he seemed both meticulous and relentless.

Mufti Mohammed Naeem is the rector of the Jamia Binoria, a "society" of Islamic *madrassas* linked to the extreme Wahabi and Deobandi traditions. (Masood Azhar, a militant whom India jailed for fanning Islamic separatism in Kashmir and was forced to release after an airline hijacking last December, studied in one of these academies.) Mufti

Naeem rattled off statistics for me: the Jamia Binoria has 2,300 students, ages eight through twenty, from thirty countries, including the United States. The twelve-acre campus includes a hotel and a supermarket. Separate accommodations and cafeterias are provided for boys and girls. "The girls arrive from abroad with skirts, but now they are fully covered," he said breezily. "We have changed their minds." He explained that although the foreign students paid tuition, the poor of the *katchiabaadis* were educated without charge. Yes, he had a Web site. As he spoke, he fielded calls and kept checking the television monitors.

"What do you teach?" I asked.

"Islam, not math or anything else, only Islam." Mufti Naeem called in a number of foreign students. One, a teenage American boy from Los Angeles, explained, "We only study those sciences—such as grammar, Arabic linguistics, and jurisprudence—that help us understand Islam." When I asked the students what they planned to do when they returned home, they all said, "Propagate Islam." Some of the Americans came from Muslim backgrounds; others were Christians who had converted. The Americans agreed that the United States was a land of decadence and materialism for which only the prophet Mohammed had the answer.

The most significant aspect of the *madrassa* was the service it provided for the poor. Here was the one school in Karachi, a local analyst told me, where the children of the *katchiabaadis* were fed, educated, protected, and even loved. Mufti Naeem said, "The state is bathed in corruption. The teachers at the government schools are unqualified. They get their jobs through political connections. We, not the government, are educating the common people. And we are putting all our efforts into training those who will spread Islam."

According to the Human Rights Commission of Pakistan, many of the country's public schools are "ghost schools" that exist only on paper. If there was one thing the military regime could accomplish, I thought, it would be

to force parents, particularly in the backward tribal areas, to send their children, boys *and* girls, to school, and to make the schools decent. But General Musharraf is not doing that. Nor is he being pressured by the West to do it, even as the West spends its political capital here demanding a return to the same parliamentary system that bankrupted the country and resulted in the military coup. Given that the Subcontinent is a nuclear battleground where defense budgets are skyrocketing, and at the same time it is home to 45 percent of the world's illiterate people, I can see few priorities for the United States higher than pressuring governments in the region to improve primary education. Otherwise the *madrassas* will do it. What was so frightening about Mufti Naeem was the way he used Western information-age paraphernalia in the service of pan-Islamic absolutism.

GENERAL MUSHARRAF

PAKISTAN has never been well governed. After the military fought its catastrophic war with India in 1971, hopes were placed on the new democratic leader, Zulfikar Ali Bhutto, a wealthy landlord from Sind. But Bhutto turned out to be a divisive populist who sowed fear with his security service and surrounded himself with sycophants. His 1977 re-election was marred by fraud; riots broke out and Bhutto declared martial law. Soldiers fired on people in the streets. The military wasn't happy; the army chief of staff, Zia ul-Haq, led a coup.

It was Zia who released the fundamentalist genie: though moderate himself, he allied the military with Sunni radicals in order to win support for his new regime. After his death, in 1988 in an air crash that has yet to be explained, democracy returned with the election of Bhutto's daughter, Benazir, as Prime Minister. Though educated at Harvard, Benazir had no political or administrative experience and had made what by all accounts was a disastrous marriage to Asif Ali Zardari, who later became

her Investment Minister. Zardari's large-scale theft of public funds undermined his wife's government. Elections next brought the Punjabi businessman Nawaz Sharif to power. Together with his brother, Shabaz, Sharif ran Pakistan as a family enterprise; the brothers' reputation for taking huge kickbacks and other financial malfeasance outdid even that of Benazir's cabinet. By his second term, reportedly, Sharif was amassing so much money that it was feared that he could perpetually buy off the members of the National Assembly and create a virtual dictatorship. The Sharif and Bhutto governments stand accused of stealing $2 billion in public money, part of some $30 billion smuggled out of the country during democratic rule.

When, last October, General Musharraf toppled Sharif's government in a bloodless coup, the West saw it as a turn for the worse. However, Pakistanis saw the accession of General Musharraf as a rare positive development in a country where almost all trends are bad. The local media are (at least for now) freer under the military than they were under Sharif, whose aides frequently intimidated journalists. Musharraf has initiated no extensive personality cult. He has said more to promote human rights than have the officials of recent democratic governments, working to end such abhorrent tribal and religious practices as "honor killings" and "blasphemy laws" (though radical clerics have forced him to back down on these issues). Mehnaz Akbar, of the private Asia Foundation, in Islamabad, says, "This is the most liberal time ever in Pakistan." Musharraf, an admirer of Mustafa Kemal Atatrk, the founder of the Turkish Republic, is a like-minded modernizer. He shakes hands with women in full public view, and one of the first pictures taken of him after he assumed power shows him holding his two poodles, even though dogs are considered unclean by traditional Muslims. Most important, as one Pakistani journalist told me, "Musharraf speaks with conviction and people believe him, whereas Benazir, though an intellectual, was never believed."

President Bill Clinton's visit to Pakistan in March was not a public-relations success. Clinton, who was opposed to the military take-over, refused to shake hands with Musharraf for the television cameras. A day later Pakistanis saw Clinton, on television in Geneva, clasping the hands of the Syrian dictator Hafez al-Assad—whose regime, they knew, was far more repressive than that of any Pakistani military ruler since the founding of their state.

> ## The former coup leader had read *The Federalist Papers* and Mill's *On Liberty*. "Every single ingredient they say is required for a civil society—you name it, we haven't got it!"

Musharraf is characterized in the West as a dictator who supports fundamentalist terrorists in Afghanistan and Kashmir and who is not moving fast enough to restore democracy. The truth is somewhat different. Musharraf, one of the last British-style aristocratic officers in the Pakistani army, is a man in the middle. The West demands that he stop supporting Islamic militants; his fellow generals, who carried out the coup in his name, are Islamic hardliners, capable of staging another coup if Musharraf puts too much distance between himself and the Taliban and the Muslim fighters in Kashmir. Moreover, some analysts in Islamabad worry that Musharraf might be moving too fast on too many fronts in his drive to reform Pakistan. In addition

to promoting human rights, a free press, and local elections that threaten tribal mafias, he has challenged the smugglers throughout Baluchistan and the North-West Frontier. As the gun battle I saw in Quetta demonstrated, Musharraf has struck hard against various ethnic nationalists and criminal groups. Unlike previous anti-corruption drives in Pakistan's history, Musharraf's has indiscriminately targeted officials from all political parties and ethnic groups. And Musharraf has not relied on fundamentalist organizations like the Maududi-influenced Jama'at-I-Islami ("Islamic Society") for support, as Zia did. He has in fact alienated many vested interests, who have the will and the means to fight back—which is why, despite his liberal instincts, Musharraf may yet declare martial law.

Even if Musharraf's reformist plans succeed, one crucial element will remain: the military itself, which with its own factories, agribusinesses, road-construction firms, schools, hotels, and so on, constitutes a parallel state. No less than the civilian sector, the military is mired in corruption, and yet it is exempt from investigations by the courts. Tanvir Ahmad Khan, a former Foreign Secretary, told me that Pakistan's only hope may be "a genuine hybrid system in which the army accepts responsibility for poverty and illiteracy in return for limited political power." A successful hybrid system, he went on, would "democratize the army." Rifaat Hussain, who chairs the Department of Defense and Strategic Studies at Quaid-Azam University, in Islamabad, agrees: "I will not rule out a formal constitution on the Turkish model in order to create a national-security council and give the army constitutional privileges. We must find a way to legally stabilize civil-military relations."

ATTOCK FORT

PAKISTANI politics have been a circular tale of passion in which one group of people imprisons or persecutes another, only to be imprisoned or persecuted itself once political fortunes

change. Consider the story of Farouk Adam Khan.

In 1973, as a thirty-three-year-old army major, Adam led a coup against the elected Prime Minister, Zulfikar Ali Bhutto. The coup failed when one of the officers deeply involved lost his nerve and reported the details to the Prime Minister himself. Adam spent five years in prison, including, as he puts it, "thirteen months, two days, and six hours" at Attock Fort, fifty miles west of Islamabad, overlooking the Indus River, which was built by the Moguls in 1581 to guard the Afghan frontier. Adam went on to become a lawyer in his native Peshawar, where I met him in 1987. He is now the prosecutor-general of Musharraf's National Accountability Bureau. I saw him again in May, back at Attock Fort, where he was to arraign the former Prime Minister Nawaz Sharif on corruption charges.

After the proceedings in a whitewashed barracks hall—where fans whirred overhead and flies hovered and the unfortunate Sharif pleaded for better food—Adam pointed out the room where he had read *The Federalist Papers* and John Stuart Mill's *On Liberty* in the semi-darkness of solitary confinement. "Those books confirmed my judgment that I was absolutely justified to attempt a coup," he told me. "Every single ingredient that the authors of those books say is required for a civil society—education, a moral code, a sense of nationhood: you name it, we haven't got it! Just look at our history. It sounds authoritarian, but we need someone who will not compromise in order to build a state. It is not a matter of democracy but of willpower."

Adam's interpretation of Mill and the Founding Fathers is certainly questionable. Yet fifty-three years after independence only about one percent of Pakistanis pay any taxes at all: one can empathize with his yearning for a functioning state. But I fear that Adam's dreams may be impossible to realize, under either democracy or the semi-authoritarian conditions he recommends. Musharraf may be better respected by his countrymen than any other Pakistani leader in decades, but there is just too much poverty and ignorance, too many ethnic and sectarian rivalries, too many pan-Islamic influences, too many weapons filtering back from Afghanistan, and too many tribal and smugglers' mafias able to challenge the military. As the Shia leader in Karachi told me, Musharraf may simply be a good man who arrived too late. Atatrk had decades to build Turkey—time Musharraf doesn't have.

From the mottled-ocher battlements of Attock Fort, I gazed down on the Indus River, which marks the geographic divide between the Subcontinent and the marchlands of Central Asia. Mogul, Sikh, and British conquerors, and then the new state of Pakistan, had all rearranged borders, but the river still expressed a certain inexorable logic—evinced by the resentment that the Pashtoons of the North-West Frontier on one bank felt for the more settled

Punjabis on the other. *Here, at this broad and majestic crossing, is where India truly begins,* I thought. A forty-five-minute drive east of Attock lay Taxila, where amid the enervating heat and dust are the ruins of Persian, Greek, Buddhist, and ancient Indian civilizations: a lesson in history's transmutations, with one culture blending with and overturning another. If there is any common thread, it is that India has always been invaded from the northwest, from the direction of Afghanistan and Central Asia—by Muslim hordes like the Moguls, the builders of the Taj Mahal. And given the turbulence within Islam itself, it is hard to believe that this region has seen the last of its transformations—or that Pakistan constitutes history's last word in this unstable zone between mountains and plains.

At the end of my visit to Pakistan, I sat with a group of journalists trying to fathom why Nawaz Sharif, when still Prime Minister, had reportedly turned

down an offer of several billion dollars in aid from the United States in return for agreeing not to test nuclear weapons. A Pakistani friend supplied the simple answer: "India had tested them, so we had to. It would not have mattered who was Prime Minister or what America offered. We have never defined ourselves in our own right—only in relation to India. That is our tragedy."

The feebler the state becomes, the more that nuclear weapons are needed to prove otherwise. At major intersections in the main cities of Pakistan are fiberglass monuments to a rock that was severed in 1998 by underground nuclear tests in the Baluchistan desert—celebrating the achievement of nuclear power. Do not expect Pakistan to pass quietly from history.

On The Atlantic's *Web site, at www.theatlantic.com/rashid, is an interview with the Pakistani journalist Ahmed Rashid, the author of Taliban.*

Article 4

History Today, September 1997

Judith Brown assesses the curious coupling of sage and politician that achieved much—but not all—for Hindu aspirations.

GANDHI AND NEHRU

FRUSTRATED VISIONARIES?

The observer of India in 1997 is rightly struck by the immense stability of this, the world's largest democracy, in contrast with her South Asian neighbours and many other new nation states which emerged out of the former British Empire. But equally striking is the great dichotomy between the reality of India at the end of the century and the vision of the new nation offered by its two greatest leaders at the time of independence, Mahatma Gandhi and Jawaharlal Nehru.

From 1920 at least, India's growing nationalist movement had stressed through its main organisation, the Indian National Congress, the meaning of independence for the poor and disadvantaged. There was to be a new and more egalitarian society, where the state would have a moral obligation to help the poor and under-privileged and provide opportunities to those who for centuries had been despised and deprived. These ideals were enshrined in the new constitution of 1950, whose preamble committed India to securing for all its citizens justice, liberty, equality and fraternity, and were spelt out in the sections of Fundamental Rights and Directive Principles of state policy.

Gandhi and Nehru had, in their different ways, spoken constantly of the moral, social and political regeneration of the country as the true heart of *swaraj,* or self-rule. But despite the seminal role of these two leaders, amongst the greatest visionaries of the post-colonial world, after fifty years of democratic government and economic development, there is still widespread and desperate poverty in India. With inequalities of status, consumption and opportunity as great as any in the world, the economy, having teetered on the edge of international bankruptcy at the start of this decade, now moves towards an open market policy with little ideological framework to distinguish it from Western economies. Moreover, this secular state has at times been rent by sectarian loyalties and violence, and India's religious minorities remain fearful and often profoundly disadvantaged. Why has this happened in place of the Mahatma's spiritual vision, and despite Nehru's eloquent pledge at the moment of independence that India would keep her 'tryst with destiny'?

Gandhi and the younger Nehru were, of course, very different as people and also in their vision of the new India to be created as imperial rule ended. A generation separated them, as did social origin and political experience. The older man came from a far more provincial and less privileged background, had reached professional competence as a lawyer by strict personal discipline and a regime of self-denial and hard work: and he had spent twenty formative years in South Africa, where exposure to a wide range of cultural influences and the experience of racial discrimination refined both his political skills and his religious sensibility.

The younger man had been brought up with everything that money could buy, educated at Harrow and Trinity College, Cambridge, and inducted with ease into the world of Indian public life by a father who was one of India's most successful and respected lawyers. With an effortless sense of superiority and no experience of hardship or personal challenge, he had no religious beliefs worth the name, and little knowledge of the India of the vast majority of his compatriots. It was little wonder that his father, Motilal, greatly feared what would befall his cosseted son, in personal and material terms, as he came under the influence of the homespun Mahatma.

Yet Gandhi and the somewhat aimless Jawaharlal formed a strong attachment and political partnership which was to last for almost three decades, until Gandhi's assassination in 1948. The attachment was partly personal, founded on mutual attraction between two strong and idiosyncratic personalities. It was partly forged out of mutual need, as both needed the other to further their public aims. To Gandhi, Nehru was the symbol of the younger generation, the heart and touchstone of a younger India whom he needed to weld into the nationalist movement. To Nehru, Gandhi was unique in his ability to sense the mind and mood of the vast numbers of uneducated Indians,

and thus essential for the forging of a broad-based nationalist movement to oust the British. But far beyond mutual need the two shared a passionate conviction that India must change radically as independence was won. This was central to the commitment of each man to a public role, and far more than populist rhetoric. Sensing this core of visionary commitment in the other drew them together in a unique way.

Gandhi first worked out his vision of a new India in a small pamphlet published in 1909, entitled *Hind Swaraj* (Indian Home Rule). Here he made plain his belief that true self-rule was far more than mere political independence, or an inheritance of imperial structures of control, but manned by Indians. True *Swaraj* would be founded on a moral revolution of the individual upwards through society as a whole, changing both the pattern of the economy and the nature of political authority. What was needed was a society based on moral individuals who cared for each other and followed spiritual goals, rather than false standards of gain and wealth, imported from the West, along with the means of large-scale production and their potential for the increase of inequality and of violent relations between individuals and groups. After his final return to India in 1915, he never disavowed this early work with its ruthless denunciation of 'modern civilisation' and of Western educated Indians who accepted its values. He persisted in defining *swaraj* in moral and social, rather than political language, affirming that its hallmarks would be a more equal society, mutual tolerance between different religious groups, and a commitment to small-scale economic arrangements which put people before gain.

Above all, the hallmark of new Indians would be a commitment to non-violence in all public and private relationships, as the only moral means of achieving true change. For Gandhi non-violence was the only way to follow after what one perceived as truth without endangering the perception of truth held by others: by its very presence and working it would transform attitudes and relationships, and so begin the process of change at the roots of the individuals who formed the bedrock of society. In this vision a modern state had little role to play. Gandhi was deeply distrustful of the power of the state, and felt that individual self-control was the only true regulatory power which could change society. At the end of his life he advised Congressmen to disband their party, turn their backs on political power and engage in grass-roots social service.

Gandhi drew his inspiration from aspects of Hindu and other religious traditions, and from a wide range of dissenting voices in Western culture who feared for the spiritual and social implications of industrialisation in Western society. Nehru's vision, by contrast, was generated by his contacts with several variants of Western socialist thinking during his years of education in England and later during his European travels (including a visit to the Soviet Union in 1927), and through his wide reading. Despite his 'alliance' with Gandhi, he made plain the differences in their hopes for India's future, for example, in a series of press articles republished as a pamphlet entitled *Whither India?* (1933) and in his subsequent longer writings, including *An Autobiography* (1936). As he wrote in the former:

> India's immediate goal can . . . only be considered in terms of the ending of exploitation of her people. Politically, it must mean independence and the severance of the British connection . . . economically and socially it must mean the ending of all special class privileges and vested interests. . . . The real question before us . . . is one of fundamental change of regime, politically, economically, socially.

The means to this end was first a powerful and broadly-based nationalist movement to oust the imperial ruler; and second, a powerful modern state to redistribute resources more equitably and to manage a modern economy. Nehru had little time for Gandhi's commitments to non-violence and to individual moral 'change of heart' as the route to truly radical change; and he had no sympathy with the Mahatma's religious language and priorities, aiming instead, in more straightforward political terms, for both a secular state and society.

After India's independence the visions of both men were soon dashed on the rocks of reality. In Gandhi's case this was less surprising. He had always known that few Congressmen had shared his very particular moral viewpoint or sympathised with his broad-ranging plans for the reformation of Indians, their society and polity. When Congressmen had begun to gain sufficient power at provincial level under successive constitutional reforms, he had lamented that they were behaving like their imperial predecessors; and he spoke with sad realism of the way they left his 'constructive programme' lying littered on the floor at party gatherings.

Gandhi never held high office in Congress either after the Second World War, when it was clear that independence was imminent, or, later, in the new nation state; he recognised that political power was in the hands of those, like Nehru, who believed in the need for a strong state, both to serve their political ambitions and also to fulfil their genuine hopes for India's economic and social development. After his assassination he was greatly revered: but the only ways in which his vision was even partially enacted was in the legal abolition of the status and practice of untouchability, a gross form of social and ritual discrimination practised against those at the base of Hindu society, and in the encouragement of 'cottage industries' alongside large-scale industrialisation.

Nehru, on the other hand, was India's prime minister without a break from independence until his death in 1964. Yet even his socialist dreams remained unfulfilled. Despite attempts at far-reaching social legislation, he was unable to achieve genuinely radical reform of landholdings on any scale, which would have been a prerequisite for extensive redistribution of resources and abolition of vested interests. He was unable to push through a uniform civil code which would have done much to ameliorate the legal position of women and reduce the entrenched differences between various religious groups. Although there was significant economic development, particularly large-scale industry, planned and partly managed by the state, there was little change in agricultural practices and production, and the incidence of life-threatening poverty, malnutrition and disease remained widespread, making a mockery of the directive principles of the constitution.

Furthermore, India continued to be governed by Nehru in ways which were remarkably similar to those of his imperial predecessors, both in the structure of the state itself, despite the universal adult franchise, and in the style of the administrative services which he had once denounced as anti-national and requiring drastic reform. At the end of his life he was, like Gandhi, frustrated at his inability to achieve so much of his life's dreams. On his desk he kept the words of the poet, Robert Frost:

> But I have promises to keep,
> And miles to go before I sleep

The reasons for the frustrations of these great visionary leaders lay in part in their different, but unique, pathways into Indian political life. Both were to an extent 'apart from' the ordinary world of Indian professional and business life, or that of the nationalist politician. Gandhi had failed as a lawyer in his native Western India and had achieved professional success and personal maturity in another continent, working among the Indian migrant community. Nehru had been insulated, indeed isolated, by the great wealth of his family and by his prolonged period of education in England. Back home in Allahabad with his family he saw for himself no clear role either in politics or in the profession of the law, for which he was destined. On their return to India both found that they had few natural connections with the world of Indian politics, and no groups of allies or supporters with whom to make their mark.

Perhaps more importantly, their exposure to the world beyond India had created in each of them a distinctive and idiosyncratic vision of the meaning and nature of 'nationalism' and the Indian nation as they thought it should become. By contrast most of their contemporaries who saw themselves as nationalists thought primarily in terms either of ameliorating British rule and making more room for Indians within the imperial structures of power, or of removing the British altogether. But few thought beyond independence or had visions of radical change grounded in religious belief or a powerful secular ideology as did Gandhi and Nehru.

Their eruption into the politics of nationalism was therefore unpredictable. Gandhi emerged in 1920 as a leader within the Congress because he offered the party a mode of non-violent protest against the British Raj, at a specific juncture in nationalist politics when constitutional politics seemed to have achieved little and when few were willing to resort to the opposite tactic, namely that of violent protest. In the euphoria which followed, Nehru willingly became involved in politics for the first time, sensing that in Gandhi he had met a leader who would address real social and political problems, would lead Indians in fearless resistance to the imperial ruler, and would do away with the parlour politics of an older generation he had so despised. As he wrote in his autobiography of the heady experience of participating in Gandhi's first nation-wide campaign of non-violent non-co-operation with the Raj:

> Many of us who worked for the Congress programme lived in a kind of intoxication during the year 1921. We were full of excitement and optimism and a buoyant enthusiasm. We sensed the happiness of a person crusading for a cause. . . . Above all, we had a sense of freedom and a pride in that freedom. The old feeling of oppression and frustration was completely gone.

However, the Congress party was never transformed into a band of moral Gandhian enthusiasts, committed to the Mahatma's constructive campaign for the renewal of the nation. Although many Congressmen and many more outside the Party's ranks were attracted by his fearlessness, by his personality and by his Indianness, few accepted his religious vision of man and society, and few were converted to his belief in the rightness and transformative nature of non-violence.

The Congress remained what it had become over the forty years since its inception—a loosely organised association of groups of local men (and a few women), many of high educational and professional background, who were politically active on a full or part-time basis, who wished to gain access to the decision-making and executive power of the state which the imperial authority was creating, and who knew that their hands and arguments would be strengthened by an all-India alliance under the umbrella of the national Congress. It had little full-time and effective party organisation, and depended largely on the co-operative stance of local individuals and groups who used its name—a fact which Gandhi and Nehru both recognised and sought to remedy, because they realised how it reduced the Congress's political effectiveness as a party of direct action or of long-term change.

A further consequence was that Congress had little in the way of a defining and driving ideology, apart from its anti-imperial stance. Ideological compromise was more often the cement which held its members together; particularly as so many of them were comparatively privileged and had social and economic interests to safeguard in the future. Consequently those of its declarations which had a socialist ring were generally little more than vote-catching rhetoric.

In this party Gandhi and Nehru were in their own ways unique, and that uniqueness was both their strength and a long-term weakness in terms of their ability to galvanise Congress into action in pursuit of visionary goals. Gandhi was never a 'leader' in any Western sense of the word. His role from 1920 to the 1940s was more that of an 'expert' to non-violence who could be welcomed and to an extent used by Congress when they felt his particular non-violent strategy of opposition and profoundly moral stance and style suited their purposes; to achieve compromises between different groups within Con-

gress when its internal divisions threatened to rend it apart and destroy the vital unity of the nationalist movement.

Nehru's role was similarly not that of a leader with a natural power base in a locality or in a group of like-minded allies. His 'ticket' in Congress was that of Gandhi's protégé and later heir, a fact which at times caused him embarrassment and distress. In the later 1930s his ideological position was so anti-pathetical to many of the more conservative in Congress that the latter would have made his position in the party impossible if it had not been for Gandhi's presence and watchful eye on the internal dynamics.

As independence became imminent after the end of the Second World War, Congress activists recognised Nehru's skills as a negotiator with the imperial authorities—in part because he spoke their language and had inhabited so much of their mental and political world. But even though he became leader of the transitional government which saw the transfer of power to Indian hands, and subsequently prime minister, Nehru was not secure as the party's undisputed leader and ideologue until some years later.

Although Gandhi lived for a brief period in an independent India, it was Nehru who had to wrestle with the problem of trying to enact his vision of change under the new circumstances—when Congress had become the party of government rather than of nationalist rhetoric and protest, and when he was constrained by the structure of the state and the ability of the administration. For him there were a range of seemingly insurmountable barriers to the achievement of radical change. One continuing example was the nature of the Congress party. Even though he was from the early 1950s its undisputed leader, and though it paid lip service to his vision of a socialist transformation of society, it was now a party which even more than before independence represented the interests of those who had no wish for radical social and economic change. Its very success as a nationalist party had attracted into it many who needed access to power. Increasingly it became the party of the businessman, the prosperous farmer and the professional, those with a stake in the India inherited from the raj and being made more prosperous for those with resources by the actions of an independent government anxious to boost the economy. This rootedness in groups of locally influential people was its great strength at election time, but its weakness as an instrument of change. This Nehru learned the hard way when it came to attempts at land reform and social legislation for the benefit of the deprived.

Moreover, the very structure of the state inhibited change. Just as in imperial India the country had been administered through provinces, often the size of small European countries, now these became the basis of the States within the Indian Union, bound together in a federation. Consequently on many issues legislation had to pass through the legislatures of the States rather than through the Lok Sabha in New Delhi. As in the case of the abolition of great landlords and the redistribution of land into moderate holdings below a certain 'ceiling,' those with vested interests could either get themselves into the State legislature where they could modify or delay reforming measures, or could use the months while legislation was being passed to hire lawyers and so equip themselves to avoid the law. Or in the case of agricultural improvement and the dire need to grow more food, policy implementation was in the hands of the agricultural ministries of the States: and Nehru found it impossible to chivvy them in the way he would have wished. Added to this, the actual tools of government were frustratingly weak and slow.

Independent India inherited an administration structured on an immensely slow bureaucracy, which had made a specialty of generating endless files and pushing them from one level to another with agonising slowness. It was a system where those at lower levels were neither trained nor accustomed to take responsibility and make decisions. At the top it was manned by élite generalists who, though highly educated, were essentially trained to conserve the status quo, to enable the collection of adequate revenue, but not to innovate or manage a social revolution. Nehru as a young nationalist had distrusted and criticised the élite Indian Civil Service, although over half of them were Indian by 1947. He spoke of the need for a total overhaul of the administration and the evolution of a new people-oriented class of administrators. But no administrative revolution occurred, and he found himself increasingly having to rely on the heirs of the service he had castigated, who remained in ethos, background and modes of operation so like their imperial predecessors. It was little wonder that he became increasingly frustrated, and at times bad-tempered, at his inability to 'get things done', despite his own vision and frenetic energy.

The frustrations of the idealisms of India's greatest nationalists, and the pragmatism of the Congress Party, created a profound ideological vacuum in independent India. Into this vacuum have emerged a host of parties in place of the once-great and embracing party which led the country to independence. Many are regional in origin and orientation, fostering the interests of specific areas within the subcontinent.

But they have proved incapable of making a national appeal or providing the base for a stable all-India coalition. Perhaps the one party which has been able to construct a national vision is the revivalist Hindu Party, the BJP, which has emerged as a highly significant political force over the past decade. But this vision of the nation itself endangers the unity of a nation with many religious minorities and cultural diversities, which Gandhi sought to safeguard with his ethical religion and tolerance, and which Nehru hoped to cement and strengthen with a vision of modern secularism and socialism.

India's politicians need to dream dreams and see visions of a tolerant and compassionate India as their nation's fiftieth birthday is celebrated, for their electorate is telling them sober truths about the lack of repute in which they are held, and their need for integrity and a commitment to real change as the country's expanding population grows increasingly sophisticated and aware of the nature of the political system and its departure from the hopes so manifest in 1947. Gandhi and Nehru may have been frustrated in their hopes for India: but they laid down a marker and a standard by which subsequent leaders and aspirant leaders are judged.

FOR FURTHER READING:
A. J. Parel (ed.), *M. K. Gandhi. Hind Swaraj and other writings* (Cambridge University Press, 1997); B. Parekh, *Gandhi's Political Philosophy. A Critical Examination* (MacMillan, 1989); Judith M. Brown, *Gandhi, Prisoner of Hope* (Yale University Press, 1989); S. Gopal, *Jawaharlal Nehru. A Biography* (3 vols. Jonathan Cape, 1975–1984); J. Nehru, *An Autobiography* (The Bodley Head, 1936); R. L. Hardgrave, *India. Government and Politics in a Developing Nation* (Harcourt, Brace, 1970); Robert W. Stern, *Changing India. Bourgeois Revolution on the Subcontinent* (Cambridge University Press, 1993).

***Judith Brown** is Beit Professor of Commonwealth History, at the University of Oxford and author of* Modern India. The Origins of an Asian Democracy *(Oxford University Press, 1984).*

History Today, September 1997

PARTITION

THE HUMAN COST

Mushirul Hasan looks at the reflection of the trauma and
tragedy of partition through literature and personal histories.

*The sun had risen fairly high when
we reached Amritsar... Everytime I
visited Amritsar, I felt captivated. But
the city, this time, presented the look
of a cremation ghat, eerie and stink-
ing... The silence was so perfect that
even the faint hiss of steam from the
stationary engine sounded a shriek.
Only some Sikhs were hanging about,
with unsheathed kirpans which they
occasionally brandished... The brief
stoppage seemed to have lingered into
eternity till the engine whistled and
gave a gentle pull... we left Chhe-
harta behind and then Atari and when
we entered Wagah and then Har-
banspura everyone in the train felt up-
lifted. A journey through a virtual
valley of destruction had ended when
finally the train came to a halt at Platform No. 2—Lahore, the moment was
as gratifying as the consummation of
a dream.*

Mohammad Saeed, *Labore:
A Memoir* (1989)

Few writers reveal such poignancy
and tragedy of nationally-con-
trived divisions and borders. India's partition cast its shadow over many
aspects of state and society. Yet the literature on this major event is mostly inadequate, impressionistic and lacking in
scholarly rigour. Even after fifty years
of Independence and despite the access
to wide-ranging primary source materials, there are no convincing explanations
of why and how M. A. Jinnah's 'two-
nation' theory emerged, and why partition created millions of refugees and
resulted in over a million deaths. Similarly, it is still not clear whether partition
allowed the fulfillment of legitimate as-

pirations or represents the mutilation of
historic national entities.

Part of the reason for this flawed
frame of reference is the inclination of
many writers to draw magisterial con-
clusions from isolated events and to
construct identities along religious lines.
As a result, the discussions tend to be
based on statements and manifestos of
leaders and their negotiations with British officials in Lutyens' Delhi and
Whitehall.

The fiftieth year of liberation from colonial rule is an appropriate moment to
question commonly-held assumptions on
Muslim politics, to delineate the ideological strands in the Pakistan movement, explore its unities and diversities, and plot
its trajectory without preconceived suppo-
sitions. Was there intrinsic merit in relig-
ious/Islamic appeals? Does one search for
clues in British policies (which were tilted
in favour of the Muslims to counter the
nationalist aspirations)—in the ensuing
clash between Hindu and Muslim revivalist movements and in violent contests
over religious symbols (a dispute recently
played out around the Babri Masjid at
Ayodhya)? How and why did the idea of
a Muslim nation appeal to the divided and
highly stratified Muslim communities,
enabling Jinnah and his lieutenants to
launch the crusade for a separate Muslim
homeland?

As a starting point, it is necessary to
repudiate Jinnah's 'two-nation' theory.
Time and again it has been pointed out
that the Hindu and Muslim communities
lived together for centuries in peace and
amity. In fact, their common points of
contact and association were based on
enduring inter-social connections, cross-
cultural exchanges and shared material

interests. Neither the followers of Islam
nor of Hinduism were unified or cohesive in themselves. Their histories, along
with social, cultural and occupational
patterns, varied from class to class, and
region to region.

During his tour in 1946–47 the British
civil servant Malcolm Darling found, in
the tract between the Beas and Sutlej rivers in Punjab, much similarity between
Hindus and Muslims. He wondered how
Pakistan was to be fitted into these conditions? He was bothered by the same
question while passing through the country between the Chenab and Ravi:

What a hash politics threatens to make
of this tract, where Hindu, Muslim
and Sikh are as mixed up as the in-
gredients of a well made pilau... I
noted how often in a village Muslim
and Sikh had a common ancestor. It
is the same here with Hindu and Muslim Rajputs, and today we passed a
village of Hindu and Muslim Gujars.
A Hindu Rajput... tells me that
where he lives in Karnal to the south,
there are fifty Muslim villages converted to Islam in the days of Aurang-
zeb. They belong to the same clan as
he does, and fifteen years ago offered
to return to the Hindu fold, on the one
condition that their Hindu kinsfolk
would give them their daughters in
marriage. The condition was refused
and they are still Muslim. In this area,
even where Hindu and Muslim belong
to different clans, they still inter-
change civilities at marriage, inviting
mullah or Brahmin, as the case may
be, to share in the feasting.

The search for a political explanation
of partition must begin with the fluid
political climate during and after the

First World War, characterised by the drive for power and political leverage that preoccupied all political parties and their followers. This accounts for the swiftness with which the two-nation idea succeeded in becoming actualised; the vocal demand for carving out a Muslim nation summed up the fears of the powerful landed classes and the aspirations of the newly-emergent professional groups in north India and the small but influential industrial magnates of the western and eastern regions.

The bitter and violent contest over power-sharing reveals a great deal about the three major themes that have dominated South Asian historiography—colonialism, nationalism and communalism. What it does not reveal, however, is how partition affected millions, uprooted from home and field and driven by sheer fear of death to seek safety across a line they had neither drawn nor desired.

The history books do not record the pain, trauma and sufferings of those who had to part from their kin, friends and neighbours, their deepening nostalgia for places they had lived in for generations, the anguish of devotees removed from their places of worship, and the harrowing experiences of the countless people who boarded trains thinking they would be transported to the realisation of their dreams, but of whom not a man, woman or child survived the journey.

Most Hindus and Muslims living in harmony and goodwill could not come to terms with the ill-will and hostility that was conveyed through speeches and pamphlets. There were many places in India where the Muslim League's message was received but failed to impress.

Indeed, most Muslims neither understood nor approved of Pakistan, except as a remote place where they would go, as on a pilgrimage. Some left hoping to secure rapid promotion, but not to set up permanent homes there. It did not really matter to the peasants and the mill-workers whether they were physically located in 'India' or 'Pakistan'. Interestingly, for example, the Muslim employees of the East India Railway in a north Indian city decided to stay put in India after having opted for Pakistan, while 8,000 government servants returned to

their homes in March 1948, just a few months after they had left for Pakistan.

In other words, most people were indifferent to the newly-created geographical entities, and were committed neither to a Hindu homeland, nor to an imaginary world of Islam. They were unclear whether Lahore or Gurdaspur; Delhi or Dacca would remain in Gandhi's India or Jinnah's Pakistan. They were caught up in the cross-fire of religious hatred—the hapless victims of a triangular game-plan masterminded by the British, the Congress and the Muslim League. 'The English have flung away their Raj like a bundle of old straw', one angry peasant told a British official, 'and we have been chopped in pieces like butcher's meat'. This was a telling comment by a 'subaltern' on the meaning attached to the Pakistan movement.

Saadat Hasan Manto, the famous Urdu writer, captures the mood in 'Toba Tek Singh', one of his finest stories:

> As to where Pakistan was located, the inmates knew nothing . . . the mad and the partially mad were unable to decide whether they were now in India or Pakistan. If they were in India where on earth was Pakistan? . . .

Pakistan, a prized trophy for many Muslims, was won, but people on both sides of the fence were tormented by gruesome killings, by the irreparable loss of lives, and by the scale and magnitude of an epic tragedy. There can be no doubt that from a purely liberal and secular perspective, the birth of Pakistan destroyed Mohammad Iqbal's melodious lyric of syncretic nationalism—*Naya Shivala* (New Temple)—once the ideal of patriots and freedom-fighters. The vivisection of India severed cultural ties, undermined a vibrant, composite intellectual tradition and introduced a discordant note in the civilisational rhythm of Indian society.

Indeed, the birth of freedom on that elevated day—August 14th, 1947, for Pakistan and August 15th, for India—did not bring India any 'ennobling benediction'. On the contrary, the country was shaken by 'a volcanic eruption'. There was little to celebrate at the fateful midnight hour. In the words of Faiz Ahmad Faiz, the renowned Urdu poet,

This is not that long-looked-for break of day
Not that clear dawn in quest of which those comrades
Set out, believing that in heaven's wide void
Somewhere must be the star's last halting place
Somewhere the verge of night's slow-washing tide,
Somewhere an anchorage for the ship of heartache.

So, which country did poets like Faiz and writers like Manto belong to? Manto, for one, tried in vain to 'separate India from Pakistan and Pakistan from India'. He asked himself: 'Will Pakistan literature be different—and if so, how? To whom will now belong what had been written in undivided India? Will that be partitioned too?'. The uppermost question in his mind was: 'Were we really free'?

Manto's anguish and dilemma was shared by the silent majority on both sides of the fence, including those 1,000 persons who, after eighteen months of separation, met at the Husainiwala customs barrier in February 1949. They did not pull out daggers and swords but affectionately embraced one another with tears rolling down their cheeks. Their sentiments were reflected neither in the elegant exchanges between the Viceroy and Secretary of State, nor in the unlovely confabulations between the Congress and the League managers.

Today the curtain is drawn on the Husainiwala border; small groups from Pakistan and India congregate at Wagah to witness a colourful military parade that is held every evening to mark the closing of the iron gates on both sides of the fence. Their expressions seem to echo the widespread feeling in the subcontinent that never before in its history did so few divide and decide the fate of so many in so short a time.

'What a world of loneliness lies upon Shabbir (Husain, grandson of the Prophet of Islam) this day!' Everyone who heard these lines in Gangauli village, the setting for the Rahi Masoom Reza's novel *Aadha-Gaon* (Half-a-Village), wept bitterly. They did so to mourn Husain's martyrdom in Karbala centuries ago, but also because 'the cut umbilical cord of Pakistan was around their necks like a noose, and they were all suffocating'. Now they knew what 'a world of loneliness' meant.

Independence and partition brought varied moods of loneliness. Every individual in Gangauli 'had found himself suddenly alone'. All of them turned, just as they did every day of their existence, to Husain and his seventy-two companions for strength, confidence and spiritual comfort. 'There was a desire to dream, but what was there safe to dream about?' The atmosphere was foul and murky all around. 'The blood of one's veins was wandering hopelessly in Pakistan, and the relationships and mutual affections and friendships... were breaking, and in place of confidence, a fear and deep suspicion was growing in people's hearts'.

Today we saw for ourselves something of the stupendous scale of the Punjab upheaval. Even our brief bird's-eye view must have revealed nearly half a million refugees on the roads. At one point during our flight Sikhs and Moslem refugees were moving almost side by side in opposite directions. There was no sign of clash. As though impelled by some deeper instinct, they pushed forward obsessed only with the objective beyond the boundary.

Alan Campbell-Johnson,
Government House, New Delhi,
Sunday, September 21st, 1947

The partition of the subcontinent led to one of the largest ever migrations in world history, with an estimated 12.5 million people (about 3 per cent of un-divided India) being displaced or up-rooted. In Punjab, the province most affected by violence and killings, 12 million Hindus, Sikhs and Muslims were involved, and migration of some 9 million people began overnight in an area the size of Wales. In the north Indian state of Uttar Pradesh (UP), nearly 4,000 Muslims a day boarded the train to Pakistan until 1950.

The number of migrants from central and eastern regions was comparatively small, but the proportion of professional migrants was relatively high. Educational institutions were depleted of students and teachers overnight. Enrolment figures at the famous seminary in the city of Deoband were down from 1,600 to 1,000 in 1947–48. Income dwindled,

as large numbers of students and patrons migrated to Pakistan. The Aligarh Muslim University was rudderless without some of its distinguished teachers who searched for greener pastures in Karachi, the eventual homeland of the *muhajirin* (migrants).

In Bihar, emigration began in November–December 1946 as a sequel to rioting in many places. Peace was soon restored and the movement stopped just before partition. There was fresh migration after August 1947 mainly for economic reasons and because of the acute food shortage in North Bihar, which had a common frontier with East Pakistan. Migrants totalled 4–500,000, although some returned to their homes during 1950–51.

The Princely State of Hyderabad had received a continuous migration of Muslims in their thousands, particularly since 1857, from the rest of India. In 1947 the numbers increased to hundreds of thousands. Drawn from both the rural and urban areas, there were traders, artisans, domestic and government servants, agriculturists and labourers. However, the influx came to an abrupt end on September 13th, 1948, the day the armed forces of India moved into the state 'in response to the call of the people'. Almost immediately a reverse movement started: a number of Hyderabadi Muslims left for Pakistan, while others returned to places they had originally come from.

Elsewhere, nearly 450 Muslims a day continued their trek across the Rajasthan-Sind border. From January to November 1st, 1952, 62,467 Muslims went via Khokhropar to Sind in West Pakistan. 'Some hundreds go daily and have been going, in varying numbers, for the last three-and-a-half years', Nehru informed his chief ministers. 'The fact that they go there itself indicates that the conditions they live in are not agreeable to them and the future they envisage for themselves in India is dark'. But quite a number of established and prosperous professionals from UP, Bihar and the Princely States of Hyderabad, Bhopal and Rampur also left.

Men in government and the professions from Delhi, UP and Bihar formed the core of muhajirin. The Delhi police was depleted of its rank and file because of 'mass desertion'. All the three subor-

dinate judges in the Delhi court rushed to Pakistan. People employed with local and provincial governments also opted for Pakistan, although some changed their minds later and returned to India. Poets and writers, Josh Malihabadi being the most prominent, joined the trek at different times. Some landlords, including Jinnah's lieutenant, Nawab Liaquat Ali Khan, were among the muhajirin. The Raja of Mahmudabad left his family behind in the sprawling Mahmudabad House in Qaiser Bagh, Lucknow, to undertake the mission of creating an Islamic state and society in Pakistan.

Many prominent Muslims stayed, including those who headed the Muslim League campaign. Landlords like Nawab Ismail, Nawab Jamshed Ali Khan, the Nawab of Chattari and the Rajas of Salempur, Nanpara, Kotwara, Pirpur and Jehangirabad clung to their small estates. Ismail was elected to the vice-chancellorship of Aligarh Muslim University in September 1947, but relinquished the post on November 14th, 1948. Several others retained their public positions, although they had lost face with their supporters.

Others felt overwhelmed by the climate of hostility, suspicion and distrust. They had a litany of complaints—recurring Hindu-Muslim riots, discrimination in employment and official neglect of Urdu. Syed Mahmud, Nehru's friend and minister in Bihar, protested that Muslims faced harassment and were treated as 'a body of criminals'.

Thirty-one Muslims were jailed for anti-governement activities in addition to many more detained under the Public Safety Act. Muslims in Agra were required to register themselves with the district magistrate. Their houses were searched and a former legislative assembly member, Shaikh Badruddin, was arrested for possessing unlicensed arms. Muslims in Kanpur had to obtain a permit before travelling to Hyderabad; their relatives there had to register at a recognised hotel or a police station in order to visit them.

Muslim officers on the railways in Kanpur, some of whom had served for more than ten years, faced suspicion and dismissal. Aligarh's district magistrate was severe on university students and teachers who had already incurred the wrath of the local leaders for their involvement in the Pakistan movement. The university, threatened with closure, was eventually saved by Nehru's intervention. Zakir Husain, the newly-appointed vice-chancellor, placed it on a firm footing with the active support of Azad, free India's first education minister. Liberal and socialist teachers staged a rearguard action to combat the influence of communal tendencies. In general, however, Mohanlal Gautam, the leading Congressmen touring UP, found 'an all-pervading sense of fear' among the Muslims.

The Evacuee Property Laws, which restricted business opportunities and disabled large numbers of Muslims, were most inequitable. Most Muslims could not easily dispose of their property or carry on trade for fear of the long arm of the property law. A number of old Congressmen continued to send small sums of money to their relatives in Pakistan. They were promptly declared evacuees or prospective evacuees. Nehru was personally distressed by all this, as he was by the spate of communal violence in UP:

People die and the fact of killing, though painful, does not upset me. But what does upset one is the complete degradation of human nature and, even more, the attempt to find justification for this.

By contrast, some of Nehru's colleagues were unrepentant. A powerful section retorted, in answer to the criticism of its murky conduct in handling the civil strife, that the strong anti-Muslim sentiments were generated by bitter and painful memories of partition. These responses angered Nehru and his liberal and socialist comrades, and dismayed Muslims.

The real pinch was felt in Delhi, UP, Bihar and Hyderabad, the area most affected by riots, the exodus to Pakistan and the extensive skimming-off from the professional classes. 'Partition was a total catastrophe for Delhi', observed one of the few surviving members of Delhi's Muslim aristocracy. 'Those who were left behind are in misery. Those who are uprooted are in misery. The peace of Delhi is gone. Now it is all gone'. In UP and Bihar very few Muslims were left in the Defence services, in the po-

lice, the universities, the law courts, or the vast Central Secretariat in Delhi. Large-scale immigration of mostly educated upper-caste Hindus in Lucknow—70 per cent of the total immigrant figure—gradually reduced Muslim influence in government, business, trade and the professions.

In Hyderabad, Muslims constituted 10 per cent of the population before 1947–48. Muslim government servants held, as in UP, a much higher percentage of posts. But their fortunes dwindled following Hyderabad's merger with the Indian Union. Urdu ceased to be the official language. The abolition of *jagirdari* affected over 11 per cent of the Muslim population, three-quarters of whom inhabited about a dozen urban centres. Smaller *jagirdars,* in particular, faced a bleak future due to retrenchment in government departments, recession in industry after 1951, and a sharp fall in agricultural prices. The old nobles and the absentee landowners started selling their remaining lands and spacious houses to make ends meet.

The dissolution of the Princely States impoverished a large percentage, if not the majority, of the upper classes and the bourgeoisie as well as a large number of peasants, artisans and retainers who lost the patronage networks. Nearly half the population of Hyderabad depended on the Nizam for their livelihood, and thus with sources of patronage rapidly drying up this section was worse off.

The rulers of Rampur, Bhopal and Hyderabad were not turned into paupers overnight; they simply lacked the initiative to convert their wealth into more secure and tangible assets. They squandered their inherited resources to maintain their standard of living and allowed properties to be grabbed by unscrupulous land dealers. Their mango orchards, which had yielded vast revenues, were generally converted into uneconomic farm lands. Few ventured into business, trade or industry, or realised which way the wind was blowing. They continued living in their decaying palaces surrounded by a retinue of servants, wives, eunuchs and hangers-on. Wallowing in nostalgia for the bygone era, they cursed the *khadi*-clad politicians for bringing to an end the *angrezi sarkar* (British Raj).

Accustomed to framing their own laws, codes and regulations, they were irked by the presence of local bureaucrats—the district magistrate, superintendent of police and revenue officials—who were visible symbols of political change. Insulated from the populace and blissfully unaware of the changes that were visibly taking place in urban and rural areas, their public contacts were limited to *Id* celebrations at the close of a month's fast or Muharram observances when the *imambaras* were lit up and the mourners turned up at the desolate Nizam's palace in Hyderabad or the Khas Bagh in Rampur. The memory of the suffering of Husain and his companions at Karbala reminded them of their own trials and tribulations.

The abolition of the zamindari (land holding) system in 1951 stripped the large landlords of the bulk of their estates and awarded the land to the cultivators. The rural influence of the former Muslim landlords was reduced, even more than that of their Hindu counterparts. Many former Hindu rentiers and landowners migrated to places like Kanpur, Gorakhpur and Lucknow in search of new sources of livelihood. Muslim zamindars and taluqdars were bereft of such ideas. Muslim immigration was a mere 16.28 per cent between 1947–55 from rural areas as compared to 68 per cent among upper and intermediate Hindu castes.

The bigger Muslim taluqdars suffered more than their Hindu counterparts also because of families being divided, one branch migrating to Pakistan. Such was the fate of the taluqdari in Mahmudabad. The Raja left behind his estates in Barabanki, Sitapur and Bahraich districts to be looked after by his brother. He may have wished to return to his place of birth, but the India-Pakistan war in September 1965 would have thwarted his plans. His huge assets were declared 'enemy property'.

The Awadh taluqdars, accustomed to supporting themselves from the rental income of their estates, were greatly traumatised by zamindari abolition. Some left for Pakistan, and others retired to anonymity in their villages. Those who stayed found the going hard. 'The abolition of zamindari removed our clientele in one fell swoop. All of a sudden the economy changed. And the

English customers left. Our shop was "by appointment" to several governors of the province'.

Some of the smaller zamindars managed to keep their status intact by moving into nearby towns and cities in search of better opportunities. A few families in the Barabanki district, living in close proximity to Lucknow, did well. Some reaped the rewards of being close to the Congress. They obtained private and government contracts, licenses and positions. Mubashir Husain (1898–1959), of Gadia and son of Mushir Husain Kidwai (b. 1878), the pan-Islamic ideologue in the early 1920s, was a judge at the Allahabad High Court until 1948. Begum Aijaz Rasul, the wife of the former taluqdar of Sandila in Hardoi district and mother-in-law of the novelist Attia Hosain, did quite well for herself, being elected to the UP assembly and the Rajya Sabha and holding ministerial positions until 1971. There were other successes too.

For the small Awadh taluqdars, however, the overall scene was discouraging. They lost much of their land to the tenants who acquired legal rights over what they cultivated. They were estranged from the 'new men', rustic and entrepreneurial, who thronged their bazaar and streets and disturbed their social poise and harmony.

For the zamindars their universe had suddenly collapsed: they had no 'land left equivalent even to the hub of the great wheels which was once their zamindaris'. In just a few moments they collapsed like the tomb of Nuruddin the Martyr, a familiar landmark in Gangauli village. In their prayers they cursed the Congress Party. The Syeds, who for centuries had made Gangauli their home, realised that they no longer had any links with the village they had called their own. Whether Pakistan was created or not had no meaning to them, but the abolition of zamindari shook them to the

core. Now it was all the same whether they lived in Ghazipur or in Karachi.

The zamindars of western UP, on the other hand, were not too badly off. Many switched allegiances to the Congress, and some enjoyed a measure of local goodwill because they had implemented certain provisions of agrarian legislation. Most moved to Aligarh to educate their children. They built or renovated their mansions, developed an interest in local politics and used the university—which they treated as an extension of their estates—as a political arena. It satisfied their pride to serve on the university court or the executive council, be involved in the selection of senior office-holders and turn up dutifully at the railway station to greet visiting dignitaries. But when they retired to the privacy of their homes they recounted the harsh encounters in a world that was not their own.

By the early 1960s some smaller zamindars were still struggling to eke out a living. There were those who had limited resources to live on; others relied on inherited charitable endowments or even pawned their family jewellry to maintain the façade of high living. Their crumbling houses on Aligarh's Marris Road bear testimony to their steady impoverishment. The luckier ones, such as the Chattari clan, moved out of Aligarh in search of professional careers. The sherwani-clad Nawab lost the vigour and determination which he displayed during his extended public life, now that he had to cope with harsh realities.

Attia Hosain's novel, *Sunlight on the Broken Column*, describes the faded fortunes of the landed aristocracy and captures the sense of an era having passed once and for all:

He [the Raja of Amirpur] lived in retirement at Amirpur, dignified and aloof, bearing the landslide of adversities with courage. His palace in the city had been requisitioned as a gov-

ernment hospital for legislators, and the huge rambling house at the outskirts, with its ornamental gardens divided into building plots, was the centre of the new colonies for the refugees.

The last occasion on which he appeared in public was four years after independence, when he welcomed the President of the Republic to a reception given in his honour by the Taluqdars.

There were no illuminations, no fireworks, no champagne, no glitter of precious gems, orders, silks, brocades and ceremonial uniforms. This last reception of the Taluqdars was a staid tea-party given by hosts who were soon to have their 'special class' and 'special privileges' abolished.

Dusty portraits and marble statues of stately ex-Presidents of their Associations, and of Imperial representatives, looked down with anachronistic grandeur on tea-tables bearing tea becoming tepid, cakes tasting stale, and Indian savouries growing cold. Guests in *Khaddar* (loin-cloth) outnumbered those in more formal attires.

With grace and courtesy Amirpur presided over this swan-song of his order, while those who had habitually bowed before authority hovered round their gentle, dignified guests still hoping for manna from Heaven.

FOR FURTHER READING:
C. H. Philips & M. D. Wainwright (eds.), *The Partition of India, Policies and Perspectives* (Allen & Unwin, 1970); Leonard Mosley, *The Last Days of the British Raj* (Weidenfeld & Nicolson, 1962); Ayesha Jalal, *The Sole Spokesman: Jinnah, the Muslim League and the Demand for Pakistan* (Cambridge University Press, 1985); Mushirul Hasan, *Legacy of a Divided Nation: India's Muslims Since Independence* (C. Hurst, 1997) and *India's Partition: Process, Strategy and Mobilization* (Oxford University Press, 1997); and his anthology of fiction and poetry on Partition, *India Partitioned: The Other Face of Freedom* (Delhi, 1997), in two volumes.

Mushirul Hasan is Professor of Modern Indian history at the Jamia Millia Islamia University, Delhi.

Article 6   *World Watch*, July/August 1998

What Does India Want?

The government in New Delhi sent a defiant message when it began setting off nuclear bombs in May. But hundreds of millions of Indians, if they had a voice, might have sent a very different message. The threat they feel most acutely—the destruction of their natural support systems—does not come from Pakistan or China but from within their own country.

by Payal Sampat

It's safe to make just one generalization about India— which is that every other time you generalize about India, you're probably wrong. With over 400 living languages, 85 political parties and a 5,000-year-old cultural and intellectual history, India is defined by its heterogeneity. "All the convergent influences in the world run through this society," wrote historian E. P. Thompson. "There is not a thought that is being thought in the West or East that is not active in some Indian mind."

Perhaps the most noted modern representatives of this diversity of thought were Mahatma Gandhi and Jawaharlal Nehru, who worked together in the first half of this century to get the British to "quit India," but differed sharply in their vision of what an independent nation should look like. At that time, their debate pertained only to the future of a former colony facing the challenges of self-governance. Today, the echoes of that famous debate still resonate—now in the accelerating development of the second-most populous nation, and with large implications for the world as a whole.

Nehru aspired to make India a leading industrial society, a *force to reckon with* in the global economy; it would be powered by modern machinery and giant dams—he called these the "new temples of modern India." Gandhi's hope, in contrast, was to strengthen India's grassroots village economies by promoting local self-reliance, and by using what would today be called "appropriate technology"—the kind of tool that in-creases a worker's productivity, but does not devalue or replace him.

In recent years, the intellectual successors to Nehru and Gandhi have polarized the issue in a way those early leaders may never have intended. The debate has taken different forms in the half-century since India's independence in 1947, but the tensions it expresses—over modernism and tradition, globalization and community, economic prosperity and voluntary simplicity—are now as familiar in Mexico, Nigeria, and Japan as they are in India.

Giving added urgency to the debate today is the fact that these issues are matters not only of political philosophy, but also of biological and economic survival. India's physical environment is deeply threatened, and so, as a result, are the one billion people and the economic activities that it supports. At a time when homogeneous prescriptions for economic development are being called into question, the sprawling diversity that has kept people debating for the past half-century may hold answers for India's biggest challenge yet: balancing the needs of its people with the natural systems that sustain them.

Fifty Years in the Making

At the time the British left India in 1947, the newly independent nation faced human deprivation of staggering dimensions. Nehru, as the nation's first prime minister, guided the country's development along the lines of the Soviet Union, a

The illustrations for this article were done by artists of the indigenous Warli tribe of Maharashtra, north of Bombay. They illustrate folk stories based on the activities of traditional village life, as identified on each page. Above: Tree of life. Title page: Piper calling villagers to dance.

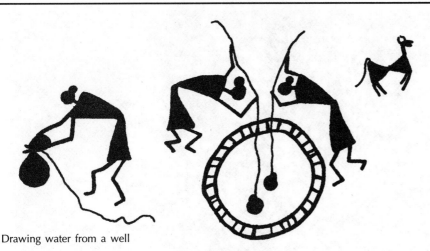

Drawing water from a well

model that suited both his industrial aspirations and the need to overcome this poverty. Like the state planners of China and the Soviet Union, Nehru envisioned development on a grand scale. His government and its successors undertook an ambitious, ongoing campaign to construct dams, transcontinental highways, and nuclear power plants. Unlike the Soviet and Chinese regimes, however, the Indian government encouraged private ownership. In keeping with its long tradition of ideological plurality, it embraced a "mixed economy": although the state controlled some key sectors (electricity utilities, telecommunications, aviation, and mining, among them), private enterprise continued to be a vital part of the economy.

While Nehru's vision prevailed most visibly, Gandhi's ideas shaped the economy as well. His idea of *swadeshi,* putting emphasis on things "indigenously produced," played an important role in India's freedom struggle, and has strongly influenced India's economic philosophy—and its citizens' psyche—ever since. The idea was to empower ordinary people by fostering pride in what they produced themselves, and by encouraging self-reliance through activities like spinning cotton and growing food for their own consumption. By extension, *swadeshi* led to a policy of national self-sufficiency in food production. However, the means that were used to enact this policy—the "Green Revolution" with its heavy dependence on mechanization, agrochemical applications and centralized seed banks—had a decidedly Nehruvian spin. While bureaucrats in New Delhi have continued their pursuit of large-scale development, much of Gandhi's legacy has evolved in less conspicuous venues—in the rural villages and in India's 25,000 non-governmental organizations and grassroots movements involved in environmental and social reform.

Over the past decade, a third voice—promoting free-market policies—has been introduced to the old debate, and has brought rapid changes. The shakeup began in 1991, when India's economy faltered. A weak monsoon that year hit farmers hard. Since agriculture is the backbone of the Indian economy (providing a third of the country's GDP and 70 percent of its jobs), the blow to agricultural growth sent repercussions throughout the economy. Later that year, the Soviet Union dis-

integrated and India lost its primary export market—and oil supplier. India's GDP, which had grown at about 5.5 percent per year throughout the 1980s, flattened to a growth of less than 1 percent in 1991. At the time, the country owed $90 billion in foreign loans it had taken out to finance its many infrastructure projects. With under $1 billion in foreign reserves, India found itself in a dangerously vulnerable position.

At that point, the International Monetary Fund stepped in with an offer to bail India out—on the condition that the country abandon its socialist planning for free-market policies. Like several other developing countries around the same period—Mexico and Vietnam, for example—India agreed to "liberalize" its economy: to reshape its laws to encourage foreign investment, to privatize certain state enterprises, and to dismantle trade barriers that protect domestic industry. These reforms met with hostility in a nation built on the concept of local self-determination. But economists, who had long complained about the inefficiencies of their country's protectionist policies, were relieved that India was finally poised to become a competitive force in the global economy.

Draining Groundwater

In the 50 years since its independence in 1947, India's economy has grown ninefold. While its population in that time has doubled, its grain production has nearly quadrupled—on the surface, an extremely good ratio. And during the same period, the country's electricity generation capacity has expanded 50 times. But much of its material progress has neglected—and often come at the devastating cost of—the natural resources that have fueled it.

Hunting

In its efforts to jumpstart industry and agriculture, India offered virtually free access to those natural resources—fresh water, forests, and minerals—that are the basic materials of a modern industrial economy. It offered high energy subsidies for electricity and diesel fuel. (Electricity subsidies amount to 1.5 percent of India's GDP.) It assumed the costs of expanding roads and railways into previously remote areas, making it cheaper and easier still to take out timber and other resources. These subsidies have allowed increasingly wasteful use of these resources.

This imprudence appears particularly costly in the way India has squandered its freshwater. Highly subsidized electricity rates have encouraged the extraction of increasing quantities of water from underground aquifers. During the 1960s, the Green Revolution spurred a huge increase in the use of shallow tube-wells, whose numbers have grown from 360,000 to 6 million in the last thirty years. (Robert Repetto, an economist at the World Resources Institute, has dubbed this development "the tube-well revolution.") With that many punctures in its skin, it's not surprising that India is dehydrating at an alarming rate: the country's National Environmental Engineering Research Institute reports that in several states groundwater is being drawn faster than its rate of recharge. Farmers in semiarid northern Gujarat say they have to lower their pumps by 3 meters every two years to keep up with falling water levels. Most notably, in some parts of Punjab and Haryana, the "breadbasket" of India where almost a third of the country's wheat is grown, water tables have fallen over 4 meters in the last decade.

In some areas, much of the water that is extracted is not efficiently used: according to the Tata Energy Research Institute in New Delhi, 45 percent of all irrigation water (mostly from canals) seeps through unlined field channels. Some of the seepage causes waterlogging, depriving plant roots of oxygen and reducing their productivity. In warm areas, most of the water evaporates, leaving excessive salt deposits in the soil, rendering it less productive still. As a result, some 10 million hectares are now salinized; another 12 million hectares are waterlogged.

Meanwhile, traditional techniques of water harvesting that were tailored to regional variations in rainfall and water availability have been cast aside. Until about a century ago, the southern city of Bangalore obtained its water from an intricate system of interconnected stone tanks that capture rainfall runoff. These systems also irrigated surrounding farmland. Now India's fastest-growing city and high-technology capital, Bangalore has built football stadiums and apartment buildings over some of its tanks, reports the New Delhi-based Centre for Science and the Environment. The water for Bangalore now has to be carried from the Cauvery River, which means lifting it 1,000 meters in elevation and transporting it a distance of 100 kilometers. It now costs more to supply water to Bangalore than to any other city in South Asia (although Bangalore's

residents foot just 5 percent of this bill), and shortages have become routine.

Several other regions also experience chronic water shortages. Every day, diesel-fueled tanker trucks haul water to the city of Madras in the southern state of Tamil Nadu. (Groundwater levels in Tamil Nadu reportedly fell between 25 and 30 meters over a decade due to overpumping.) Even heavier costs have been exacted in western India, where 30 large dams, 135 medium-sized ones, and 3,000 small dams are planned on the Narmada River. One of the primary beneficiaries will be the textile-manufacturing city of Ahmedabad in Gujarat, where the water table fell by over 20 meters in the 1980s. Yet, the project has become one of the world's most notorious examples of a rob-Peter-to-pay-Paul system of resource management. Critics note that 70 percent of Gujarat's drought-affected areas will not receive water from this scheme. The centerpiece of the project—the now-halted Sardar Sarovar dam—has alone displaced some 100,000 tribal villagers, and if completed, its reservoir will submerge some 37,000 hectares of forests and farmland.

Even so, the worst could be yet to come. The International Food Policy Research Institute projects that India will step up its water demand by 50 percent over the next 20 years. Its water demand will grow from just over 600 billion cubic meters in 1995 to over 900 cubic meters by 2020—the highest absolute increase for any nation over that span. Most of this increase will go to industrial and domestic users, with each projected to quadruple its current demand. By that year, it is estimated that most regions in India will be "water-stressed," meaning that water shortages could become chronic and widespread, and that the quantity available to each person will have fallen to 1,700 cubic meters or less—down from 2,200 cubic meters today, already just a third of the global average. (By comparison, the per person availability is 9,200 cubic meters in the United States and 12,800 cubic meters in Indonesia.)

India has prided itself on its self-sufficiency in food production, a task that will be rendered increasingly difficult by projected water depletion. (Although the country is a net exporter of food, on average one-third of its households do not get adequate nutrition.) Declining soil quality could make this task harder still. About half of India's farmland—some 80 million hectares—suffers from some form of degradation. At a conservative estimate, says a World Bank report, soil degradation reduces agricultural output by between 4 and 6 percent a year; other studies have placed this annual loss at as high as 26 percent.

Putting higher prices on water and electricity to cover the real costs of their production could slow the water decline. This would encourage water-intensive industries like steel, fertilizers and textiles to leapfrog to more efficient production practices, and could prompt municipalities to revive local systems of rainwater harvesting and storage. It would also spur farmers to reconsider crop choices (sugarcane, for instance, is very demanding of water, and uses half of Maharashtra's irrigation water, although it is grown on just 10 percent of its cropland). It would also encourage them to maintain and improve bunding systems (barriers built along contour lines that prevent water runoff and spread rainwater evenly across fields), and to shift to more efficient irrigation practices. Since three-fourths of India's 4,000 cubic meters of rainfall is concentrated in 3 monsoon months, irrigation during the dry months is vital. In the northeastern state of Meghalaya, drip irrigation systems are constructed by stringing together split bamboo sticks that carry spring water over hundreds of meters to betel and black pepper orchards. In mountainous Himachal Pradesh, vegetable farmers hope to double their planted area by stretching their water supply with drip systems during the dry winter months. Introduced by non-profit International Development Enterprises, each system costs $100 per acre of land irrigated. And some villages in Maharashtra manage water resources collectively. This motivates individual farmers to use this limited resource frugally rather than assuming that if they don't take as much as they can, some competitor will.

Climbing for coconuts

Disappearing Forests

India has one of the world's highest shares of arable land: more than half of its land is cultivated. (By comparison, 20 percent of land in the United States, and 10 percent of China's land—the world's other major food producers—is arable). Unlike other populous countries such as Egypt, Ethiopia, or even China, it does not have vast areas of barren or mountainous territory from which little productivity can be gleaned. Another 20 percent of its land is forested, and 4 percent is pastureland. Although much of rural India lives alongside its farms and forests (3 million people live *inside* its forests), most of the country's people and industries are spread out over a remaining area a little larger than the state of Texas. As India's population and economy swell, and its cities and industries expand into the countryside, it faces critical decisions about how to allocate its land. A key question is what will become of the four-fifths of India's land that is still not urbanized or industrialized.

Of the one-fifth of India's land that is forested, just 40 percent (or 8 percent of the country's land overall) is intact, dense forest. Plantations, which have displaced natural ecosystems with monocrops, cover almost a quarter of the land designated as "forested." (A third of these plantations cultivate eucalyptus, a fast-growing, non-indigenous species that is very demanding of soil moisture.) At 15 million hectares, India has the largest plantation area in the tropics. The natural forests that remain are fragmented and consist of more sparsely covered tracts.

Less than a century ago, 40 percent of India was forested. Large tracts of deciduous and tropical rainforest were destroyed over the past century as the British expanded India's railway network across the country. Then, between 1951 and 1976, some 15 percent of the nation's land area was converted to cropland, and much of this came from natural forest. Today, though most of India's natural forests are protected by national law, 43 of its 521 protected areas are endangered by conversion to industrial uses. In the country's most forested state, Madhya Pradesh, in the very center of the subcontinent, diamond and sandstone mines have taken over parts of the Panna Tiger Reserve, one of the last homes of the tiger. The mines routinely dump contaminated tailings into the Ken River, which flows through the tigers' habitat. And one-third of the Melghat Tiger Reserve in Maharashtra has been "de-reserved" to make way for dam construction and industrial timber harvesting.

Forests are strained by increasing demand for their resources. As human and livestock populations swell and forests shrink, the relationship between rural communities and forests has become increasingly precarious. Nearly 90 percent of the wood taken from the forests is used as fuel. And India's forests provide fodder for some 100 million head of cattle that trample and denude undergrowth as they graze.

According to the U.N. Food and Agriculture Organization, the area allotted to plantations in India has been increasing at an average of 15 percent a year. At that rate, if all the plantations were taken from existing forests, all of India's natural forests—even the sparsely covered tracts—would be destroyed in less than a quarter-century. Yet, India's natural forests provide it with some extremely vital services: they protect topsoil from wind and water erosion, regulate temperatures, replenish aquifers, store genetic diversity, offer recreational relief to an increasingly crowded human population, and provide a number of valuable products other than wood—including medicines and food.

Biologically, India's forests are exceptionally diverse: they range from the world's most extensive mangrove forests, the Sunderbans in West Bengal, to evergreen rainforest in the Andaman and Nicobar Islands, and dry alpine forest in the Himalayan foothills. Together, India's forests house some 45,000 plant species, 372 species of mammals, 1,250 bird species, and

399 species of reptiles. But this diversity is eroding precipitously, as natural habitat is cleared for new plantations or farms, bulldozed for mines or dams, or picked over for firewood. One in four of India's mammal species are threatened, says the International Union for the Conservation of Nature. India is one of ten countries with the highest percentage of threatened mammal, bird, *and* plant species. Endemic species—species that are found nowhere else

Moving—displaced by development

in the world—are particularly vulnerable. Just 4,000 lion-tailed macaques, 2,000 Nilgiri *tahrs* (a kind of mountain goat), and 300 grizzled mountain squirrels now remain in India's Western Ghats, a southwestern mountain range designated one of the world's 19 "biodiversity hotspots" by Conservation International. Other distinctive fauna, such as the pink-headed duck, are already extinct.

In some areas, local communities have teamed up with state agencies to manage and regenerate forests. In West Bengal, 150,000 villagers tend to 350,000 hectares of *sal* forest (*sal* is a high-value hardwood somewhat similar to teak), some of which was badly degraded before the state Forest Department initiated the project in 1972. No money was exchanged for this service, but it has turned out to be an important economic transaction nonetheless: the revived forests supply the villagers with medicinal products, food and fuel, and officials no longer need to invest in policing the *sal* groves. Similar partnerships, involving some 15,000 villages in all, have been initiated in other states. Since an estimated one-half of India's forest land is degraded to some degree, and the areas bordering forests are often unproductive marginal lands, such projects offer immense potential for regeneration of lost forest cover. Elsewhere, biogas plants (which convert organic waste like cow dung into a methane-based fuel) have offset firewood demand for some 10 million rural Indians—and have reduced the health risks of burning wood and dung cakes indoors.

Increasing Pollution

At current prices, about half of India's economic growth over the past half-century has been concentrated in the seven years since liberalization. Although the nation's notorious bureaucracy has daunted international investors, the prospect of finding hundreds of millions of new customers for their cars, colas, and cosmetics has proved irresistible. Nine of the world's major auto makers have set up shop in India in the last few years, as have Coca-Cola, Kellogg, Revlon and other international vendors of consumer wares. India has now

opened up its natural resources to foreign investors, welcoming international oil giants Shell, Exxon and Mobil, and mining companies like Australia's BHP Minerals and South Africa's De Beers Group.

But the years since the new economic boom have also brought a spate of environmental problems—over and above resource depletion—of an enormity that India was unprepared for. Perhaps the most pervasive problem is that the building of productive capacity has run far faster than the building of any accompanying protections for environmental and public health. Where environmental laws do exist, they are largely unenforced: just 7 percent of Indian industries comply with pollution control guidelines, says the Asian Development Bank. The mounting risks that result from this course of action have been compounded by rising consumer demands, and population growth that is now the equivalent of adding the entire population of Australia to India's already crowded land each year.

In the past ten years, the number of vehicles on Indian roads has increased threefold. With vehicles contributing over 70 percent of the country's urban air pollution, the consequences have been alarming: by one estimate, the average resident of Bombay or New Delhi has the lung capacity of a two-pack-a-day smoker. Most of the new automobiles are diesel powered (diesel is cheaper in India than anywhere else in the world), and only a fraction were equipped with pollution control devices when built. Diesel's sooty emissions aggravate asthma and other breathing disorders, and recent studies have linked diesel exhaust with increased cancer rates. Although new gasoline vehicles (1995 and later) are required to have catalytic converters, most are still tanked with fuel that contains lead, since the unleaded variety is hard to find at gas stations. Leaded gasoline damages the catalytic converters—and human nervous systems. According to the Tata Institute, air pollution in India caused an estimated 2.5 million premature deaths in 1997—equivalent to wiping out the entire population of Jamaica or Singapore. In 1995, 25 million people in India's major cities were treated for respiratory diseases like asthma and bronchitis.

Indian cities also churn out rising amounts of solid waste, much of which consists of substances that are hard to compost or return to the environment. In the last decade, for example, plastics consumption has increased ten-fold. Plastic bags litter the last remaining mangroves that line Bombay's western coast, while other inorganic waste clogs the creeks and lakes that supply the city's drinking water. India also generates 48 million tons of solid waste each year, most of which is disposed of in unsafe ways: burned, dumped into oceans and other water bodies, or land-filled. Chemicals leak out of landfills, contaminating agricultural land and groundwater supplies. In a country this densely inhabited, landfill space comes at the expense of valuable cropland or forests.

Another outfall of the widening gap between population growth and the building of suitable environmental protections is that only ten percent of all sewage in India is treated. One result is that about one-fifth of all communicable disease in India is transmitted through contaminated water. And only a fraction of industrial wastewater is treated, although industries contribute half of the pollutant load.

India clearly cannot afford the costs of its continued inaction: a study by the World Bank pegs the health costs from air and water contamination at $7 billion a year. By one estimate, Indian industries will need to spend $3 billion on pollution control equipment by the year 2000. This demand will grow by 25 percent a year as industries expand and generate more waste. And fewer than one in three Indians have access to basic sanitation services. As Indian cities explode in the next few decades, municipalities will be hard pressed to meet these needs without private-sector assistance.

India can channel its influxes of foreign investment in ways that benefit, rather than impose on, its environment and people. In some areas it already has. For instance, with the help of Danish, German and Dutch know-how, India has become the world's fourth largest producer of wind power—forerunner to a decentralized renewable energy system that can help the country begin to phase out its heavily polluting, climate-threatening, and health-damaging dependency on coal. Because coal is abundant and its production heavily subsidized, 70 percent of India's power has come from this fossil fuel. The new market-based economy can help streamline environmentally harmful inefficiencies in the state-controlled model. For example, in the first five years of liberalization, India cut back its coal subsidies from $3.3 billion in 1990–91 to $1.9 billion in 1995–96.

Herding

And Another Kind of Impoverishment

India's ecological self-destruction has drained its key resources and undermined the health of its citizens. But the hardest hit, even though statistics may not always show it, are probably those who live closest to their ecological roots: an estimated 400 to 500 million rural Indians who depend directly on their natural environment for their sustenance. Eco-historians Madhav Gadgil and Ramachandra Guha of the Indian Institute for Science describe these subsistence farmers, herders, fisherfolk, artisans and indigenous communities as "ecosystem people." India's natural resource commons have produced their food, traditional medicines, housing material and fuel. In terms of their sheer numbers—and the vital role they can play in preventing the erosion of India's natural systems—India's ecosystem people may hold an important key to its sustainable future.

Since industrial India has appropriated a large part of the nation's natural resource commons to generate its power, build its skyscrapers and discard its waste, four-fifths of the nation's villages are now not just income-poor, but natural resource-poor. In Kumaun, the hilly region to the west of Nepal, forests and pastureland have been cooperatively managed by local ecosystem communities for centuries. Soapstone and magnesite (magnesium carbonate) quarries have since taken over these commons. Be depriving the local people of large tracts of their forest- and pasture-based livelihoods, the mines have cast them into profound impoverishment.

As the commons diminish and populations increase, a destructive treadmill is set in motion, and the resource-poor are forced to use their limited resources in increasingly unsustainable ways. And some of the most resource-abundant states house the largest numbers of India's poor—coal-rich Bihar, or *sal*-forested Meghalaya, for example, where extractive industries have displaced thousands of resource-dependent communities. Ironically, much of this destruction has been rewarded by the state, as investments in "backward" regions come with enormous tax benefits; of the top ten "zero-tax" payers in India, three are mining companies. As local people are pushed onto unproductive soils and arid hillsides which cannot support their needs, they have to seek out new sources of fuelwood, food, and fodder (livestock feed).

Grassroots movements have long protested the impoverishment of India's ecosystem people. Those movements have included, for example, the widely publicized protests against the Narmada and Tehri dams, and the Chipko opposition to deforestation in the Himalayas. Several of these grassroots groups recently banded together to form a National Alliance of Peoples' Movements. And there are signs that the authorities are listening. The southwestern states of Maharashtra, Goa, Karnataka, and Kerala banned mechanized trawling in their coastal fisheries during the monsoon months when fish breed, after local fishing communities complained that trawling was rapidly depleting fish populations.

This has proved to be a sound resource management practice: harvests in Kerala have significantly rebounded since the seasonal ban was introduced in the late 1980s. And the government has seen clear demonstrations, in joint forestry projects like the ones in West Bengal, that traditional knowledge can be an invaluable factor in protecting natural resources and supporting local communities. But these efforts are still largely piecemeal, and the link between natural resource protection and peoples' well-being has thus far been given short shrift by policymakers.

And despite the social spending policies set in motion by Nehru and kept up by his successors, income poverty, not to mention resource-poverty, is still pervasive. Poverty rates have declined slowly in the years since independence—from 45 to 36 percent of the population. In absolute numbers of people trapped in poverty, India is still the world's poorest nation—more than 500 million Indians earn less than $1 a day (many of them less than five or ten cents a day) in purchasing-power terms, says the U.N. Development Programme (UNDP). Meanwhile, the number of "super rich" Indians—those who earn over half a million dollars a year in purchasing power terms—quadrupled from 10,000 to 39,000 in the past 3 years. In short, the benefits of the country's impressive gains in GDP have not been well distributed. In India, the absence of comprehensive land reforms, and persistent inequalities like the legacy of the caste system, have perpetuated these injustices; some government policies have intensified them. Writes WRI's Robert Repetto about the nation's water subsidization policies: "In India, the rights to an immensely valuable resource were distributed gratis in a pattern even more unequal than land distribution, reinforcing rural inequalities in income and wealth."

India needs the benefits—health care, sanitation, education, clean water, and energy—that come with economic prosperity. Yet it also needs to address the inequities that undermine this progress. The *New York Times* quotes a bricklayer who earns less than $1 a day, responding to the promise of India's economic expansion: "I was poor before, and I am poor now. I suppose I will always be poor." And the gap between the urban affluent and rural poor threatens to widen. A study by the New Delhi-based National Council of Applied Economic Research forecasts that in the next decade, the share of India's poor living in its villages will rise from 75 percent to 95 percent.

Mahbub Ul Haq, formerly Pakistan's Finance Minister, and advisor to the World Bank and UNDP notes that "experience in many countries has taught us that economic growth does not translate into human development: a link between growth and human lives must be created through conscious national policies." Policies in the state of Kerala demonstrate the role that good governance—comprehensive land reform, and targeted spending on education, health care, and access to family planning, in this case—can play in overcoming human deprivation and unequal distribution. Almost all its citizens are literate, there is no population growth, it has the highest ratio of working women in all of India, and people live as long as their counterparts in industrial countries—on a seventieth of the income. And Kerala's achieve-

School

ments are relatively recent: from being India's second poorest state in 1960, by 1990 it was ranked among the five most prosperous, according to World Bank researchers Martin Ravallion and Gaurav Datt. Kerala's success provides a powerful model for improving human development and curbing population growth in other regions in India.

What's Next?

India's natural resource wealth—its coal, iron ore, arable land, forests, and freshwater supplies—can be viewed myopically as the fuel that drives its economy. It provides the commodity exports that bring in foreign exchange, and the cheap raw materials needed to build a domestic industrial sector fast. From a longer viewpoint, however, the rapid depletion of these resources is clearly unsustainable. By all indications, India's natural systems are already showing signs of collapse—as seen in falling water tables, deforestation, degraded soils, and dangerous pollution levels. At a conservative estimate, says a World Bank study, the latter three forms of damage alone cost India 4.5 percent of its GDP each year.

India's massive expansion, both human and economic, will place tremendous demands on this already stressed natural resource base. In the next 50 years, its population is projected to increase by 700 million—equivalent to adding the entire population of Africa to its already huge numbers. Almost all of this increase will be in cities, projected to triple in size from today's 250 million to 750 million by 2050, when almost half of India's population will be urban. In the same period, says the Tata Institute, at an estimated 5 percent economic growth a year, industrial production will increase at staggering rates: steel production will grow 10-fold, cement 15-fold, and cotton textiles 8-fold. Without radical changes in the way natural resources are managed, the collective impact of this expansion on air and water pollution, water scarcity, habitat destruction, human health, and rural livelihoods—and the national economy—could be devastating.

If India's grassroots communities and urban victims of pollution—to whom the impacts of this resource destruction are painfully apparent—could frame the national agenda, compet-

ing in the international arms race would probably not feature on their list of priorities. They might tell a different story: that the future of this giant nation depends on its ability to protect its natural support systems. India can harness its unique combination of biological and intellectual diversity in this effort, rather than shrink and marginalize it. Its success in this task will have profound implications for the world as a whole.

Payal Sampat is a staff researcher at the Worldwatch Institute.

Article 7

The New Republic, September 25, 2000

Forgetting the moral and the prudential.

India and the bomb

By AMARTYA SEN

I.

WEAPONS OF MASS destruction have a peculiar fascination. They can generate a warm glow of strength and power that is carefully divorced from the brutality and the genocide on which the potency of the weapons depend. The great epic—from the *Iliad* and the *Ramayana* to the *Kalevala* and the *Nibelungenlied*—provide thrilling accounts of the might of special weapons, which not only are powerful in themselves, but also greatly empower their possessors. As India, along with Pakistan, goes down the route of cultivating nuclear weapons, the imagined radiance of perceived power is hard to miss.

But perceptions can deceive. It has to be asked whether powerful weapons in general, and nuclear armament in particular, can really be expected—invariably or even typically—to strengthen their possessor. An important prudential issue is involved here. There is the question of ethics, of course, and in particular the rightness or the wrongness of a nuclear policy. That important issue can be distinguished from the question of the practical benefit or loss that a nation gains or suffers from a particular policy. We have good grounds to be interested in both questions, the moral and the prudential; but we also have reason enough not to see the two issues as disparate and totally delinked from each other. Our behavior towards each

other cannot be divorced from what we make of the ethics of one another's pursuits, and the reasons of morality have, as a result, also a prudential importance. It is in this light that I want to examine the challenges of nuclear policy in the subcontinent in general and in India in particular.

Whether, or to what extent, powerful weapons empower a nation is not a new question. Indeed, well before the age of nuclear armament began, Rabindranath Tagore expressed a general doubt about the fortifying effects of military strength. If "in his eagerness for power," Tagore argued in his book *Nationalism* in 1917, a nation "multiplies his weapons at the cost of his soul, then it is he who is in much greater danger than his enemies." Tagore was not as uncompromisingly a pacifist as Mahatma Gandhi, and his warning against the dangers of alleged strength through more and bigger weapons related to the need for ethically scrutinizing the functions of these weapons and the exact uses to which they are to be put, as well as the practical importance of the reactions and counteractions of others. The"soul" to which Tagore referred, as he explained, includes the need for humaneness and understanding in international relations.

Tagore was not merely making a moral point, but also one of pragmatic importance: he wished to take into account the responses from others that would be generated by one's pursuit of military might. His immediate concern in the statement that I have cited was with Japan before the Second World War.

Tagore was a great admirer of Japan and the Japanese, but he was very disturbed by the country's shift from economic and social development to aggressive militarization. He did not live to see the heavy sacrifices that were forced on Japan later, through military defeat and nuclear devastation (he died in 1941), but they would have only added to Tagore's intense sorrow. Yet the conundrum that he invoked, about the weakening effects of military power, has remained active in the writings of contemporary Japanese writers, perhaps most notably Kenzaburo Oe.

II.

THE LEADING ARCHITECT Of India's ballistic missile program, and a central figure in the development of nuclear weapons, is Dr. Abdul Kalam, a scientist of great distinction. Kalam comes from a Muslim family, and has a very strong commitment to Indian nationalism. His philanthropic concerns are strong, and he has an impressive record of helping in welfare-related causes, such as charitable work for mentally impaired children in India.

Kalam expressed his proud reaction as he watched the Indian nuclear explosions in Pokhran, on the edge of the Thar desert in Rajasthan, in May 1998: "I heard the earth thundering below our feet and rising ahead of us in terror. It was a beautiful sight. It is rather remarkable that the admiration for sheer power should figure so strongly in the reactions of so kind-hearted a person, but perhaps the force of nationalism played a role here, along with the general fascination that powerful weapons seem to generate. The intensity of Kalam's nationalism may be well concealed by the mildness of his manners, but it was evident enough in his statements after the blasts ("for 2,500 years India has never invaded anybody") and in his unequivocal joy at India's achievement ("a triumph of Indian science and technology").

This was, in fact, the second round of nuclear explosions at the same site, in Pokhran. The first occurred in 1974, under the government of Indira Gandhi. At that time the whole event was kept under a shroud of secrecy, partly in line with the government's ambiguity about the correctness of the nuclearization of India's arsenal. While China's nuclearization clearly had a strong influence on the decision of the Gandhi government to develop its own nuclear potential (between 1964 and 1974 China had conducted fifteen nuclear explosions), the official Indian position was that the explosion in Pokhran in 1974 was strictly for "peaceful purposes," and that India remained committed to doing without nuclear weapons. Thus the first Pokhran tests were followed by numerous affirmations of India's rejection of the nuclear path, rather than any explicit savoring of the destructive power of nuclear energy.

IT WAS VERY different in the summer of 1998, following the events that have come to be called Pokhran-II. By then there was strong support for nuclearization from various quarters. This included, of course, the Bharatiya Janata Party (BJP), which had incorporated the development of nuclear weapons in its electoral manifesto, and led the political coalition that came into office after the elections in February 1998. While previous Indian governments had considered following

the blast of 1974 with new ones, they had stopped short of doing so; but with the new—and more intensely nationalist—government the lid was lifted, and the blasts of Pokhran-II occurred within three months of its coming to power.

The BJP, which has built up its base in recent years by capturing and to a great extent fanning Hindu nationalism, received in the elections only a minority of Hindu votes, and of course an even smaller minority of total votes in the multi-religious country. (India has nearly as many Muslims as Pakistan and many more Muslims than Bangladesh, and its population includes also Sikhs, Christians, Jains, Parsees, and other communities.) But even with a minority of parliamentary seats (182 out of 545), the BJP could put together and lead an alliance of many different political factions, varying from strictly regional parties (such as the AIADMK, the PMK, and the MDMK of Tamil Nadu, the Haryana Lok Dal and the Haryana Vikas Party of Haryana, the Biju Janata Dal of Orissa, and the West Bengal Trinamool Congress of West Bengal) to specific community-based parties (including the Akali Dal, the party of Sikh nationalism), and some breakaway factions of other parties. As the largest group within the coalition, the BJP was the dominant force in the Indian government in 1998 (as it is in the present coalition government, following the new elections that had to be called in late 1999), which gives it much more authority than a minority party could otherwise expect to enjoy in Indian politics.

The BJP's interest in following up the 1974 blast by further tests, and in actually developing nuclear weapons, received strong support from an active pro-nuclear lobby, which includes many Indian scientists. The advocacy by scientists and defense experts was quite important in making the idea of a nuclear India at least plausible to many, if not quite fully acceptable yet as a part of a reflective equilibrium of Indian thinking. As Praful Bidwai and Achin Vanaik put it in their well-researched and well-argued book *New Nukes: India, Pakistan and Global Nuclear Disarmament,* "The most ardent advocates of nuclear weapons have constantly sought to invest these weapons with a religious-like authority and importance—to emphasize the awe and wonder rather than the revulsion and horror—to give them an accepted and respectable place in the mass popular culture of our times."

Abdul Kalam's excitement at the power of nuclear explosions was not unusual, of course, as a reaction to the might of weapons. The excitement generated by destructive power, dissociated from any hint of potential genocide, has been a well-observed psychological phenomenon in the history of the world. Even the normally unruffled J. Robert Oppenheimer, the principal architect of the world's first nuclear explosion, was moved to quote the two-millennia old *Bhagavad Gita* (Oppenheimer's Sanskrit was adequate enough to get his *Gita* right), as he watched the atmospheric explosion of the first atom bomb in an American desert near the village of Oscuro on July 16,1945: "the radiance of a thousand suns . . . burst into the sky." Oppenheimer went on to quote further: "I am become Death, the shatterer of worlds."

That image of death would show its naked and ruthless face the following month in Hiroshima and Nagasaki (what Kenzaburo Oe has called "the most terrifying monster lurking in the darkness of Hiroshima"). As the consequences of nuclearization became clearer to Oppenheimer, he went on to campaign against nuclear weapons, and with special fervor against the hydrogen bomb. But in the experimental station in the desert, called Jornada del Muerto, which is translatable as "the Tract of Death, there was only sanitized abstractness firmly detached from any actual killing.

III.

THE THOUSAND SUNS have now come home to the subcontinent to roost. The five Indian nuclear explosions in Pokhran on May 11, 1998, and May 13, 1998, were quickly followed by six Pakistani blasts in the Chagai hills the following month. "The whole mountain turned white," was the charmed response of the Pakistani government. The subcontinent was by now caught in an overt nuclear confrontation, masquerading as the further empowerment of each country.

These developments have received fairly uniform condemnation abroad, but they have been regarded with considerable favor inside India and Pakistan, though we must be careful not to exaggerate the actual extent of domestic support. Pankaj Mishra did have reason enough to conclude, in *The New York Review of Books,* two weeks after the blasts, that "the nuclear tests have been extremely popular, particularly among the urban middle class. " But that was too soon to see the long-run effects on Indian public opinion. Also, the enthusiasm of the celebrators is more easily pictured on television than the doubts of the skeptics. Indeed, the euphoria that the television pictures captured on the Indian streets immediately following the blasts concentrated on the reaction of those who came out into the streets and rejoiced; but there were a great many people who took no part in the festivities, who were filled with doubt and anger and regret, who did not figure in the early television pictures. Their opposition found increasingly vocal expression over time.

As the novelist Amitav Ghosh noted in his extensive review of Indian public reactions to the bomb (he later expanded his observations and his arguments in his book *Countdown*), "the tests have divided the country more deeply than ever." It is also clear that the BJP, the main political party that chose to escalate India's nuclear adventure, did not get any substantial electoral benefit from the Pokhran blasts. The political result was quite the contrary, as the analyses of local voting since the nuclear explosions of 1998 tend to show. By the time India went to the polls again, in September 1999, the BJP had learned the lesson sufficiently to forego almost any mention of the nuclear tests in its campaign with the voters. And yet, as N. Ram, the political commentator and editor of *Frontline,* has cogently argued in his antinuclear book *Riding the Nuclear Tiger,* we "must not make the mistake of assuming that since the Hindu Right has done badly out of Pokhran-II, the issue has been decisively won."

Indian attitudes towards nuclear weaponization are characterized not only by ambiguity and moral doubts, but also by some uncertainty as to what is involved in making gainful use of these weapons. It may be the case, as several opinion polls have indicated, that public opinion in India has a much smaller inclination, compared with public opinion in Pakistan, to as-

sume that nuclear weapons will ever be used in a subcontinental war. But since the effectiveness of these weapons depends ultimately on the willingness to use them in some situations, there is an issue of coherence of thought that has to be addressed here. Implicitly or explicitly, the eventuality of actual use has to be one of the scenarios that must be contemplated, if some benefit is to be obtained from the possession and the deployment of nuclear weapons.

To hold the belief that nuclear weapons are useful but must never be used lacks cogency. Indeed, such a belief may be a result of the odd phenomenon that the writer Arundhati Roy has called "the end of imagination." As Roy has observed, the nature and the results of an actual all-out nuclear war are almost impossible to imagine in a really informed way. This is how she describes the likely horror: "Our cities and forests, our fields and villages will burn for days. Rivers will turn to poison. The air will become fire. The wind will spread the flames. When everything there is to burn has burned and the fires die, smoke will rise and shut out the sun" It is hard to think that the possibility of such an eventuality can be a part of a wise policy of national self-defense.

IV.

ONE OF THE problems in getting things right arises from a perceived sense of the inadequacy of any alternative policy that would be entirely satisfactory and would thus help to firm up a rejection of nuclear weapons through the transparent virtues of a resolutely non-nuclear path (as opposed to the horrors of the nuclear route). This is perhaps where the gap in perceptions is strongest between the disgust with which the subcontinental nuclear adventures are viewed in the West and the ambiguity that exists on this subject in India (not to mention the support of the nuclear route that comes from the government, the BJP, and India's pro-nuclear lobby). It is difficult to understand what is going on in the subcontinent without placing it solidly in a global context.

Nuclear strategists in South Asia tend to resent deeply the international condemnation of Indian and Pakistani policies and decisions, because it does not take note of the precarious nuclear situation in the world as a whole. They are surely justified in this resentment, and they are also right to question the censoriousness of the Western critics of subcontinental nuclear adventures who fail to examine the ethics of their own nuclear policies, including the preservation of an established and deeply unequal nuclear hegemony, with very little attempt to achieve global denuclearization. George Fernandes, the Defence Minister of India, told Amitav Ghosh: "Why should the five nations that have nuclear weapons tell us how to behave and what weapons we should have?" This was exactly matched by the remark of Qazi Hussain Ahmed, the leader of Jamaat-eIslami (Pakistan's principal religious party), to Ghosh: " . . . we don't accept that five nations should have nuclear weapons and others shouldn't. We say, 'Let the five also disarm.'"

THE INQUIRY INTO the global context is indeed justified; but what we have to examine is whether the placing of the subcontinental sub-story within the general frame of the global story really changes the assessment that we can reasonably make of what is going on in India and Pakistan. To argue that their nuclear policies are deeply mistaken does not require us to dismiss the widespread resentment in the subcontinent of the smugness of the dominant global order. Those complaints, even if they are entirely justified, do not establish the sagacity of a nuclear policy that dramatically increases uncertainties within the subcontinent without achieving anything at all to make each country more secure. In South Asia, indeed, the safest country in which to live now is probably Bangladesh.

There are, I think, two distinct issues, which need to be carefully separated. First, the world nuclear order is extremely unbalanced, and there are excellent reasons to complain about the military policies of the major powers, particularly the five that have a monopoly over official nuclear status as well as over permanent membership in the Security Council of the United Nations. The second issue concerns the choices that other countries—other than the Big Five—face, and this has to be properly examined, rather than being hijacked by resentment of the oligopoly of the power to terrorize. The fact that other countries, including India and Pakistan, have ground enough for grumbling about the nature of the world order, sponsored and supported by the established nuclear powers without any serious commitment to denuclearization, does not give them any reason to pursue a nuclear policy that worsens their own security and adds to the possibility of a dreadful holocaust. Moral resentment cannot justify a prudential blunder.

There is also the issue of the economic and social costs of nuclearization, and the general problem of the allocation of resources. That issue is important, of course, even though it is hard to find out exactly what the costs of the nuclear programs are. The expenses are carefully hidden in both India and Pakistan. Even though it is perhaps easier to estimate the necessary information in India (given a greater need for disclosure in Indian politics), the estimates are bound to be quite rough. Recently C. Rammanohar Reddy, a distinguished journalist at the major daily *The Hindu,* has estimated that the additional cost of nuclearization of the Indian military is something around half a percentage of the gross domestic product per year.

This might not sound like much, but it is large enough if we consider the alternative uses of these resources. It has been estimated, for example, that the additional costs of providing elementary education for every child with neighborhood schools at every location in the country would cost roughly the same amount of money. The proportion of illiteracy in the adult population of India is still about 40 percent, and it is about 55 percent in Pakistan. And there are other costs and losses as well, such as the deflection of India's scientific talents toward militaryrelated research, and away from more productive and more urgent lines of research, and also from actual economic production. The prevalence of secretive military activities also restrains open discussions in Parliament, and tends to subvert traditions of democracy and free speech.

Ultimately, however, the argument against nuclearization is not primarily an economic one. It is, rather, the increased insecurity of human lives that constitutes the biggest penalty of the subcontinental nuclear adventures. This question—the question of nuclear deterrence as a policy of national security—needs further scrutiny.

V.

WHAT OF THE argument that nuclear deterrence makes war between India and Pakistan less likely? Why would the allegedly proven ability of nuclear balance, which is supposed to have kept peace in the world, not be effective also in the subcontinent? I believe that this question can be answered from four different perspectives.

First, even if it were the case that the nuclearization of India and Pakistan reduces the probability of war between the two states, there would be a trade-off here between a lower chance of conventional war against some chance of a nuclear holocaust. No sensible decision-making can concentrate only on the probability of war without taking note of the size of the penalties of war should it occur. Indeed, any significant probability of the scenario captured by Arundhati Roy's description of "the end of imagination" can hardly fail to outweigh the greater probability, if any, of the comparatively milder penalties of conventional war.

Second, there is nothing to indicate that the likelihood of conventional war is reduced by the nuclearization of India and Pakistan. Indeed, hot on the heels of the nuclear blasts, the two countries underwent a major military confrontation in the Kargil district in Kashmir. The Kargil conflict, which occurred within a year of the nuclear blasts of India and Pakistan, was the first military conflict of that size between the two states in nearly thirty years. Many Indian commentators have argued that the confrontation, which was provoked by separatist guerrillas coming across the line of control from Pakistan (in their view, joined by army regulars), was helped by Pakistan's understanding that India would not be able to use its massive superiority in conventional forces to launch a bigger war in retaliation, precisely because it would fear a nuclear holocaust. Whether or not this analysis is right, there is clearly substance in the general reasoning that the enemy's fear of nuclear annihilation can be an argument in favor of military adventurism without expectation of a fuller retaliation from the enemy. Be that as it may, the proof of the pudding is in the eating, and no matter what the explanation, nuclearization evidently has not prevented non-nuclear conflicts between India and Pakistan.

Third, the danger of accidental nuclear war is much greater in the subcontinent than it was in the cold war between the United States and the Soviet Union. This is not only because the checks and the controls are much looser in the arsenals of the subcontinent, but also because the distances between India and Pakistan are so small that there is little time for deliberation and discussion if a crisis were to occur and a first strike were feared. Also, the much discussed hold of fundamentalist jihadists within the Pakistani military, and the absence of democratic control in Pakistan, add to the fear of a sudden flashpoint.

Fourth, there is a need also to assess whether the peace that the world enjoyed with nuclear deterrence during the cold war was, in fact, predictable, and causally robust. The argument for the balance of terror has been clear enough for a long time.

It was most eloquently expressed by Winston Churchill in his last speech to the House of Commons on March 1,1955. His ringing words—"safety will be the sturdy child of terror, and survival the twin brother of annihilation"—have a mesmerizing effect; but Churchill himself did make exceptions to his rule. He also said that the logic of deterrence "does not cover the case of lunatics or dictators in the mood of Hitler when he found himself in his final dug-out."

DICTATORS ARE NOT unknown in the world, even in the subcontinent; and at least partial lunatics can be found with some frequency in both India and Pakistan, judging by what some commentators write on the nuclear issue itself. Perhaps more importantly, we have reason to note that risks have been taken also by people with impeccable credentials for sanity and lucidity. To give just one example, and a rather prominent one: in choosing the path of confrontation in what has come to be called the Cuban Missile Crisis, President Kennedy evidently took some significant risks of annihilation on behalf of humanity. Theodore Sorenson, in a passage generally admiring of the president, put the facts thus:

> John Kennedy never lost sight of what either war or surrender would do to the whole human race. His UN Mission was preparing for a negotiated peace and his Joint Chiefs of Staff were preparing for war, and he intended to keep both on rein . . . He could not afford to be hasty or hesitant, reckless or afraid. The odds that the Soviets would go all the way to war, he later said, seemed to him then "somewhere between one out of three and even."

Well, a chance of annihilation between one-third and one-half is not an easy decision to be taken on behalf of the human race.

We have to recognize, I think, that the peace of nuclear confrontation in the cold war resulted partly from luck, and may not have been preordained. To take *post hoc* to be *propter hoc* is a luxury that can be quite costly for charting our future policies in the nuclear (or in any other) field. We have to take account not only of the fact that circumstances are rather different in the subcontinent compared with what obtained during the nuclear confrontation in the cold war, but also that the world was actually rather fortunate to escape annihilation even in the cold war itself.

The dangers of extermination do not come only from lunatics or dictators. For this reason, too, we must conclude that the nuclearization of the subcontinental confrontations need not reduce the risk of war (either in theory or in practice), and it escalates the penalty of war in a dramatic way. The unjust nature of the world military balance does not change this crucial prudential recognition.

VI.

I COME NOW to a question of rather limited interest, but one which is asked often enough, particularly about India. Even if it is accepted that the subcontinent is less secure as a result of the tit-for-tat nuclear tests, it could be the case that India's own self-interest has been well served by the BJP-led government's nuclear policy. India has reason to grumble, it is argued, for not being treated as seriously as one of the largest countries in the world should be treated. There is unhappiness also in the attempt by some countries, certainly by the United States, to achieve some kind of a "balance" between India and Pakistan, whereas India is nearly seven times as large as Pakistan and must not be taken to be at par with it. A more appropriate comparison, it is argued, should be with China; and to this cause—along with other causes such as getting India a permanent seat in the Security Council—India's nuclear might could be expected to make a contribution. The subcontinent may be less secure as a result of the nuclear developments, but surely, it is argued, India did get some benefit.

How sound is this line of argument? I have some difficulty in pursuing this inquiry. Even though I am citizen of India, I do not really think I can legitimately inquire only into the advantages that India alone may have received from a certain policy, excluding the interests of others who were also affected. Still, it is possible to scrutinize the effects of a certain policy in terms of the given goals of the Indian government, including the attainment of strategic advantages over Pakistan and the enhancement of India's international standing, and ask the cold "scientific" question ofwhether those particular goals have been well served by India's recent nuclear policy. We do not have to endorse these goals to examine whether they have been better promoted by India's nuclear program.

There are good reasons to doubt that these goals have indeed been better served by the sequence of events at Pokhran and Chagai. First, India enjoys massive superiority over Pakistan in conventional military strength. Surely this strategic advantage has become far less significant as a result of the new nuclear balance. Indeed, since Pakistan has explicitly refused to accept a "no first use" agreement, India's ability to count on conventional superiority is now much reduced (along with increasing the level of insecurity in both countries).

In the Kargil confrontation, for example, India could not even make use of its ability to cross into the Pakistaniadministered Kashmir to attack the intruders from the rear, which military tacticians seem to think would have made much more sense than trying to engage the intruders by climbing steeply up a high mountain from the Indian side to battle the occupants at the top. This not only made the Indian response less effective and rapid, it also led to more loss of Indian soldiers (1,300 lives according to India's estimate, 1,750 lives according to Pakistan's estimate); and it added greatly to the expenses of the war conducted from an unfavored position ($2.5 billion in direct expenses). With the danger of a nuclear outburst, the Indian government's decision not to countercross the line of control in retaliation was clearly right, but it had no real option in this respect, given the strategic bind that it had itself helped to create.

MORE OVER, THE FACT that India can make nuclear weapons was well established before the present tit-for-tat nuclear tests were conducted. Pokhran-I in 1974 had already made the point, even though the Indian official statements tried to play down the military uses of that blast a quarter of a century ago. After the recent set of tests, India and Pakistan's position seem to be much more evenly matched, at least in international public perception. As it happens, Pakistan was quite modest in its response. I remember thinking, in the middle of May 1998, following the Indian tests, that surely Pakistan would now explode a larger number of bombs than India's five. I was agreeably impressed by Pakistan's moderation in blasting only six, which is the smallest whole number larger than five. The government of India may deeply dislike any perception of parity with Pakistan, but it did its best to change a situation of acknowledged asymmetry into one of perceived parity.

Aside from perceptions, and considering only the scientific requirement for testing, Pakistan clearly had a greater case for testing, never having conducted a nuclear test before 1998. This contrasted with India's experience of Pokhran-I in 1974. Also, with a much smaller community of nuclear scientists, and a less extensive development of the possibilities of computerized simulation, the scientific need for an actual test may have been much greater in Pakistan than in India. While Pakistan was concerned about invoking the condemnation of the world community by testing on its own, the Indian blasts in May 1998 created a situation in which Pakistan could go in that direction with comparative impunity, without being blamed for starting any nuclear adventure. As Eric Arnett has written, in the SIPRI Yearbook 1999:

In contrast to its Indian counterparts, Pakistan's political elite is less abashed about the need for nuclear deterrence. Military fears that the Pakistani nuclear capability was not taken seriously in India combined with a feeling of growing military inferiority after being abandoned by the USA after the cold war created an imperative to test that was resisted before May 1998 only because of the threat of sanctions. The Indian tests created a situation in which the Pakistani leadership saw an even greater need to test and a possible opening to justify the test as a response that was both politically and strategically understandable.

The thesis, often articulated by India's pro-nuclear lobby, that India was in a greater danger of a first strike from Pakistan *before* the summer of 1998, lacks scientific credibility as well as political plausibility.

NOR WAS THERE much success in getting recognition for India as being in the same league as China, or for its complaint that inadequate attention is paid to the dangers that India is supposed to face from China. Spokesmen of the Indian government were vocal on these issues. A week before the Pokhran tests in 1998, George Fernandes said in a much quoted television interview: "China is potential threat number one. . . . The potential threat from China is greater than that from Pakistan." In the short time between the tests on May 11 and May 13, Prime Minister Vajpayee wrote to President Clinton to point to the Chinese threat as the motivation for the tests. This letter, which was was leaked and published in *The New York Times,* did not name China, but referred to it in very explicit terms:

We have an overt nuclear weapon state on our borders, a state which committed armed aggression against India in 1962. Although our relations with that country have improved in the

last decade or so, an atmosphere of distrust persists mainly due to the unresolved border problem. To add to the distrust that country has materially helped another neighbour of ours to become a covert nuclear weapons state.

As a result of the tit-for-tat nuclear tests by India and Pakistan, however, China had the opportunity to stand above India's little grumbles, gently admonishing it for its criticism of China, and placing itself in the position of being a subcontinental peacemaker. When President Clinton visited China in June 1998, China and the United States released a joint statement declaring that the two countries would cooperate in non-proliferation efforts in the subcontinent. Mark Frazier's assessment of the gap between the government of India's attempts and its achievement in this field captures the essence of this policy failure:

Had it been India's intention to alert the world to its security concerns about China as a dangerous rising power, the tests managed to do just the opposite they gave the Chinese officials the opportunity to present China as a cooperative member of the international community seeking to curb nuclear weapons proliferation. Far from looking like a revisionist state, China played the role of a status quo power, and a rather assertive one at that.

NOR DID THE explosion of the Indian devices advance the cause of India's putative elevation to a permanent membership of the Security Council. If a country could blast its way into the Security Council, this would give an incentive to other countries to do the same. Moreover, the new parity established between India and Pakistan after Pokhran-II and Chagai Hills also militates against the plausibility of that route to permanency in the Security Council; and this, too, could have been predicted. I do not, myself, see why it is so important for India to be permanently on the Security Council. (It may be in the interest of others for this to happen, given India's size and growing economic strength, but that is a different issue.) To be sure, the Indian government clearly attaches importance to this possibility, but then it would have been wiser to emphasize its restraint in not developing nuclear weapons despite its proven ability to do so, and also to use the asymmetry with Pakistan that existed before 1998, in contrast with the symmetry that was provoked—by the Indian government's own initiative—after Pokhran-II and Chagai.

Indeed, a scrutiny of Indian official perceptions reveals the extent to which the Indian government underestimates India's importance as a major country, a democratic polity, and a rich multi-religious civilization, with a well-established tradition in science and technology (including the cutting edge of information technology), and with a fast-growing economy that, with a little effort, could grow even faster. The Indian government's overestimation of the persuasive power of the bomb goes hand in hand with its underestimation of the political, cultural, scientific, and economic strengths of the country. There may be pleasure in official circles at the success of President Clinton's visit to India and the favored treatment that it received in that visit compared to Pakistan, but the tendency to attribute that asymmetry to Indian nuclear adventure, rather than to India's large size, democratic politics, and growing industrial economy and technological capability, is difficult to understand.

VII.

IT IS EXTREMELY important, then, to distinguish between two problems, both of which have a bearing on nuclear policies in the subcontinent. First, the world military order needs a change, and in particular it requires an effective and rapid disarmament, particularly in its nuclear arsenals. Second, the nuclear adventures of India and Pakistan cannot be justified on the ground of the unjustness of the world order, since the people whose lives are made insecure as a result of these adventures are primarily the residents of the subcontinent themselves. Resenting the obtuseness of others is not a good ground for shooting oneself in the foot.

This does not imply, of course, that India or Pakistan has reason to feel happy about the international balance of power that the world establishment seems keen on maintaining, with or without further developments such as an attempted "nuclear shield" for the United States. Indeed, it must also be said that there is an inadequate appreciation in the West of the extent to which the role of the Big Five arouses suspicion and resentment in the developing world, including the subcontinent. This applies not only to the monopoly over nuclear armament, but also, on the other side, to the "pushing" of conventional, non-nuclear armaments in the world market for weapons.

As the Human Development Report 1994 (prepared under the leadership of the visionary Pakistani economist Mahbub ul Haq) pointed out, not only were the top five arms-exporting countries in the world precisely the five permanent members of the Security Council of the United Nations, but they were also responsible for 86 percent of all the conventional weapons exported between 1988 and 1992. Not surprisingly, the Security Council has not been able to take any serious initiative that would really restrain the merchants of death. It is not hard to understand the skepticism in India and Pakistan (and elsewhere) about the responsibility and the leadership of the established nuclear powers.

As far as India is concerned, these two policies—nuclear abstinence and the demand for a change in the world military order—can be pursued simultaneously. Nuclear restraint strengthens rather than weakens India's voice. To demand that the Comprehensive Test Ban Treaty be redefined to include a concrete timetable for denuclearization may well be among the discussable alternatives. But making nuclear bombs, not to mention deploying them, and spending scarce resources on missiles and what is euphemistically called "delivery," can hardly be seen as sensible policy. The claim that subcontinental nuclearization would somehow help to bring about world nuclear disarmament is a wild dream that can only precede a nightmare. The moral folly in these policies is substantial, but what is also clear and decisive is the prudential mistake that has been committed. The moral and the prudential are, in fact, rather close in such a world of interrelations and interactions, for reasons that Rabindranath Tagore discussed nearly a hundred years ago.

Finally, no country has as much stake as India in having a prosperous and civilian democracy in Pakistan. Even though the government of Nawaz Sharif was obviously corrupt in certain ways, India had no particular interest in undermining civilian rule in Pakistan, nor in seeing it replaced by military leaders. Also, the encouragement of across-border terrorism, of which India accuses Pakistan, is likely to be dampened rather than encouraged by Pakistan's economic prosperity and civilian politics. It is particularly important in this context to point to the danger of the argument, often heard in India, that the burden of public expenditure would be more unbearable for Pakistan, given its smaller size and relatively stagnant economy, than it is for India. This may well be the case, but the penalty that can visit India from an impoverished and desperate Pakistan in the present situation of increased insecurity is unsettling to contemplate. The enhancement of Pakistan's stability and well-being has prudential importance for India, in addition to its obvious ethical significance. Once again, the connection between the moral and the prudential, must urgently be grasped.

AMARTYA SEN is Master of Trinity College, Cambridge and the winner of the Nobel Prize in Economics in 1998. A version of this essay was recently delivered as the first Dorothy Hodgkin Lecture at the Annual Pugwash Conference in Cambridge, England.

Article 8   *Harvard International Review,* Winter 1998/1999

Green Growth
India's Environmental Challenge

BY SURESH PRABHU

Around the world, leaders are struggling to meet the imperatives of development in an environmentally sustainable way. India, cognizant of the importance of environmental regulation, has faced the challenge with a set of new policy initiatives. After the parliamentary elections earlier this year, India's first task was to prescribe a National Agenda for Governance. A key element of this Agenda was the formulation of a comprehensive] national policy to balance economic development with environmental protection. While economic liberation and deregulation have injected vitality into production, manufacturing, and services, they have unleashed some environmental conundrums.

The continuing conflict between the environment and economic development consists of many issues. The National Agenda will address both Indian's long-term potential for growth in light of dramatic increases in economic activity and energy demand, as well as concerns relating to public health, industrial safety, and emergency preparedness. India's existing policy framework for protecting the environment is outlined in three documents: the National Conservation Strategy and Policy Statement on Environment & Development of 1992, the Policy Statement for Abatement of Pollution of 1992, and the National Forest Policy of 1998. The National Conservation Strategy provides the basis for the integration of environmental considerations in the policies and programs of different sectors. It emphasizes sustainable life styles and the proper management and conservation of resources. The Pollution Abatement Policy stresses the prevention of pollution at the source. It encourages the development and application of the best available technical so-

lutions. The policy embodies and approach by which polluters are held financially accountable for the pollution they generate and emphasize the protection of heavily polluted areas and rivers regions. The Forest Policy stresses the maintenance of the environment through the preservation and restoration of India's ecology. This policy seeks to substantially increase the forest acreage in the country.

These policies alone, however, lack cohesiveness-a deficiency that has not escaped public attention. Indeed, the environmental problems are large and multifaceted. They include the growth or urban slum and shortcomings municipal and civic services. Developing and implementing solutions to these environmental quandaries will require cooperation between various branches of government and multiple areas of academia.

In articulating its policies, the Indian government has taken the initial step towards alleviating its environmental problems. While the government's position has been clearly expressed, there are still many barriers to the effective regulation of the environment. India is striving towards strengthening monitoring institutions such as state agencies and regional centers of the Central Pollution Control Board that monitor the environment. Despite these efforts, monitoring and enforcement mechanisms are still in their infancy. Other new environment policies seek to complement the existing monitoring arrangements by involving universities and other educational institutions in corresponding field activities.

The tension between the interests of Indian industry and environmental protection is apparent in India's regulatory measures. Chemical and petrochemicals

industries seek to detract attention from their environmentally harmful activities by focusing preventive efforts in other directions. These companies have been able to deflect the focus of governmental control through redefining problem areas; thus, some industries with high-intensity pollution remain exempt from regulation.

Industry vs. Society

Another common area of contention between the state and industry has been the consumption of energy and the disposal of waste generated by energy production. Any discussion on sustainable development must address the environmental issue originating from the power sector. Over two-thirds of electricity in India is generated by coal fired power stations, followed by hydro sources, oil, nuclear, and ass. Coal will remain dominant in the decades to come, as the nation struggles to meet a rapidly increasing energy demand that already outstrips capacity. The government hopes that the privatization of the energy sector will result in the diversification of energy sources away from coal. Furthermore, mechanisms are being implemented to restruct the dumping of fly ash, and environmentally harmful byproduct of coal-based energy production. Efforts are also being made to facilitate the use of fly ash in manufacturing construction material.

Other policy initiatives relate to the handling of hazardous substances in industry and transportation and the dangers posed by chemical accidents to human life and the environment. The management of hazardous substances has always been a policy focus since the Bhopal gas tragedy of 1984. More recently the mushrooming growth of the private sector has generated a need for more developed enforcement authorities and better regulation. In response, the government has engaged in the collection of clinical, epidemiological, and environmental data to support decision-making related to the assessment and management of risks arising out of hazardous substances. For example, to assess the spread of the hazardous waste problem in the country, several surveys have been made by state governments. An exercise has also been initiated to identify unauthorized hazardous waste producers. State governments are also identifying waste disposal sites where there are useful opportunities for both public and private sector actors to build the tools and frameworks necessary for profitable and attractive environmental investments.

The national government recognizes that the environmental problems facing India are weighty. To address them and to improve the quality of life of the Indian people requires a complex set of policies. The interdisciplinary nature of environmental problems, tempered with the specificity of local issues, has prompted a need for innovative solutions.

Mumbai, India's foremost commercial center, is a useful case study in Indian environmental policy. This metropolis has its peculiar environmental problems related to coastal regulations, lack of housing and amenities, growth of the chemical industry, regulation of hazardous substances, and, of course, vehicular pollution.

Last year, the central government issued a report on the problem with an Action Plan for Delhi, and earlier this year, an Authority of Delhi was constituted to function under governmental supervision. Thanks to the effort of the Authority and a successful media campaign, gasoline in Delhi has become nearly lead free. The authority is now seeking to ensure the phasing out of certain categories of old commercial vehicles. It is expected that such situation-specific Authorities, constituted to combat pollution and arrest environmental degradation in particular jurisdictions will, with experience, gain in specialization and command deference from the concerned wings of government.

The Political Environment

The Indian court system deals heavily with normative environmental principles, the organizational issues which are drawing much attention. There has been much debate on rising of pollution levels in Delhi. The initiative of the government to have an overall comprehensive policy has been prompted, very importantly, by a growing public awareness to protect and improve the environment. But the advantage of India's vibrant democracy is that matters of public interest, particularly those of the environment, also get articulated effectively through a vigilant media, an active and synergized NGO community, and a judicial process which has recognized the citizen's right to a clean environment as a component of the right to life and liberty.

There is an increased need for interaction and communication between the legislative and enforcement mechanisms. In response to this predicament of policy without power, the enforcement tools of the government has also been bolstered. For example, the courts have also elaborated on the concepts relating to sustainable development and the "polluter pays" and "precautionary" principles. Recent laws have established institutions for the judicial administration of environmental laws: the National Environment Tribunal Act of 1995 and the National Environmental Appellate Authority of 1997. The Appellate Authority, headed by a retired Supreme Court judge, hears appeals against the decisions of the Central or State Governments granting Environmental clearances. The Tribunal, which will be headed either by a retired Supreme Court or High Court judge, will begin functioning soon. The Tribunal will adjudicate on the compensation for damages to persons, property, and the environment arising out of any accident occurring while handling any hazardous substance.

India has, however, made concrete progress in other areas such as deforestation and wildlife conservation. In recent months, I have had consultations with the State Forest Ministers and the Chief Ministers about the initiatives to be taken for increasing the country's forest cover and to devise strategies for involving he local population in the

conservation of forests-though it should be noted that very significant and successful endeavors have already been made for expanding the forest cover. Forests are a source of sustenance for the rural poor, particularly the tribal populations, who depend on the forest resources for meeting their energy needs and other requirements. Considerably large areas have been planted during various plan periods. But he survival rate is poor. The focus of reforestation activities in Government forests will be focused allowing people to use forests in a sustainable manner. Institutional arrangements will be made for channeling bank finances to farmers, cooperatives, state forest corporations and other organizations for the rehabilitation of forests. A national perspective plan is being prepared under my close supervision to rehabilitate the forests and non-forest waste land within the country in a period of 20 years.

India understands that its steps for sustainable development help he global environment. But developing countries like India require state-of-the-art, environmentally south technologies, and these have not been forthcoming from the developed countries despite the very clear obligations of developed countries under various multilateral environmental agreements. To illustrate, the UN Framework Convention on Climate Change obliges developed countries to transfer technologies to developing countries to enable implementation of the Convention's provisions. But there has been no headway. Moves are now afoot by developed countries to create a Clean Development Mechanism (CDM) as the main vehicle for addressing technology and resource transfers. This would be a breach of the Convention. The CDM is essentially a newly devised mechanism to help the developed countries attain their greenhouse gas mitigation targets. It cannot subsume the obligation of the developed countries for transfer of technology and other resources. This obligation of the developed countries emanates from the principle of "common but differentiated responsibilities" rooted in the principal responsibility of the developed countries for the global problem.

The full implications of the CDM and of emissions trading between developed countries, a concept introduced in the Protocol to the Convention on Climate Change, need to be understood and communicated in a transparent manner. A critical question is the basis of entitlements. Greenhouse gas reduction commitments do not bestow any entitlement. A fundamental step in emissions trading is the determination and creation of equitable emission entitlements of the parties, without the buying and selling of pollution shares. Principles and modalities have to be discussed and agreed upon. The per capita criterion is central to the determination of emission entitlements and will also provide a direct measure of human welfare. At the foundation of equitable emission entitlements is the right to develop equitably. The entitlements cannot derive from historical emissions which are inequitable. Any precept having the potential of depriving the world's poor from their right to develop must not be allowed.

Despite the fact that India's per capita greenhouse gas emissions are many times below the world average, and far lower than the average of developed countries, we have pursued policies which complement mitigation of climate change. Out efforts include national programs for energy, and fuel substitution and pollution abatement. We have raised the efficiency of our power plants, and industries are taking steps to reduce their energy consumption by cutting production costs. New fiscal policies are promoting low emission technologies. For example, in the automobile sector, new technologies and regulations are reducing emissions. We have a full fledge ministry for non-conventional energy sources which has attained much acclaimed success in the installation of solar and wind generation energy. While coal will continue to be the mainstay of commercial energy, there has been substitution to oil and natural gas.

India is responding to the challenges and opportunities of sustainable development through innovative reforms and restructuring. The goal is to ensure that the needs of the present generation are met without compromising the ability of future generations to meet their own needs. The traditional impediments to environmental regulation persist and must be mitigated to ensure success. Without delegation of duty, effective monitoring, and emphatic enforcement, India's environmental policies are likely to falter. But without international aid in the form of technology transfers, India's environment is destined to fail. It is vital that we find an equilibrium between economic development and the environment without sacrificing those living on the edge of subsistence. A nation cannot be expected to protect the environment when its belly is empty. Though India is taking the necessary steps to protect the environment, it cannot accomplish this overwhelming goal alone. The international community has an interest in fostering environmental protection in developing nations such as India.

SURESH PRABHU is Minister for the Environment and Forestry of the Republic of India.

Article 9

The World & I, August 1998

India's Socioeconomic Makeover

by Richard Breyer

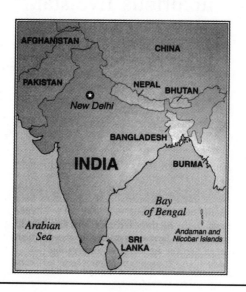

Namaste, Sony Entertainment Television. Please hold. Namaste, Sony . . ."

It's a hectic morning at the corporate headquarters of one of India's leading cable companies—and New Delhi's recent nuclear test explosions haven't caused the pace of business to miss a beat. Inside, secretaries juggle phone calls. Outside, in the crowded reception area, anxious young producers—men and women in their midtwenties—rehearse their pitches and plan power lunches on their mobile phones.

Off to the side, a large television set shows *I Dream of Jeannie.* Jeannie speaks Hindi, out of sync.

This is the new, post-1992 India—young, ambitious Indians in offices of multinational corporations; mobile phones; cable television; and Hollywood stars dubbed in Hindi.

In the old India, there was no cable television or mobile phones. Multinationals had to play by the government's Byzantine rules. Many stayed away.

And before the 1992 economic reforms, the young and the restless were not rehearsing pitches or doing power lunches. They were at the U.S. Consulate applying for a visa to study in the United States, or at the Ministry of Information meeting an uncle who would introduce them to the subsecretary in whose department there was an opening.

Up and Coming India

In 1992, with the Soviet apron strings cut, India began to dismantle its socialist system—part Soviet-style central planning, part British colonial bureaucracy.

The advent of the free market has brought an unprecedented expansion of the middle class, which is now over 200 million strong.

Still, at least 300 million people remain mired in desperate poverty.

But while televisions, jeans, pizzas, and Walkmans have proliferated, Indian families remain large and extended, with at least three generations living in one household—and many marriages are still arranged.

In 1992, India began dismantling its unique brand of socialism—part Soviet-style centrally planned, part British colonial bureaucracy. The country really had no choice. With the fall of the Soviet Union, India lost a major trading partner, political ally, and benefactor.

MIRACLE OF THE FREE MARKET

Before the reforms, most of the pillars of commerce—banks, utilities, airlines, trains, radio, and television—were government owned. High tariffs, inconvertibility of the rupee, limitations on foreign ownership, corruption, and exorbitant taxes kept foreign investors and multinationals away.

Today there are privately owned airlines, phone companies, and television channels. Foreign capital is being invested in India, and foreign corporations are setting up shop. There are more choices, more jobs, more money flowing into the country and into the pockets of the well-educated, well-connected urban middle and upper classes—stockbrokers, airline executives, copywriters, computer programmers, shop owners, and TV producers.

Five years ago it was difficult to find pizzas, jeans and Walkmans in India. Today Domino's, Levi's, and Sony have outlets in most major cities. India's affluent can shop at malls and supermarkets, watch cable television, surf the Internet. Their children have Barbie dolls, *Star Wars* action figures, and video and computer games. To put it simply, India appears to be becoming more Western.

Is this good or bad? It depends on whom you talk to. The upper 5 percent, whose horizons are broader and pockets are deeper as a result of this trend, are very pleased. Followers of Mahatma Gandhi give it a thumbs down, arguing that Walkmans and pizza have little to do with self-sufficiency and simplicity.

Others are concerned that a relative few will benefit from these changes. India's population is nearing a billion. A third are poor—some very poor. The saddest cases are in cities, where millions live in, to Western eyes, garbage heaps.

Bombay, the economic hub of the country, has million-dollar condos and luxurious five-star hotels. It also has slums with sewage running through them

In the new, more open economy, the gap between the haves (200 million at the most) and have-nots (300 million at least) will likely increase. The majority of the poor simply do not have the resources or opportunities to participate in the new order, but the communications revolution will make them more aware of what they're missing.

In Indian cities, at an intersection or stoplight, it is quite common to see a primitive oxcart next to a Mercedes. In the past, the oxcart driver did not envy—and probably did not even see—the Mercedes and its well-dressed owner in the back. If India's consumer-based culture is anything like the West's, however, in the future the poor will want essentially the same things as the rich.

Environmentalists are also concerned about the changes in culture and economy. Currently, Indians consume one-thirtieth of the nonrenewable resources of their counterparts in the West: one-thirtieth the electricity, plastics, and paper products.

In rural India, cow dung is used as fuel and fertilizer and oxen for transportation. There is no refrigeration or packaged goods. Most villagers brush their teeth with neem tree branches. The neem tree has a natural antibacterial sap that works just as well as commercial toothpaste.

GROWING PAINS

In the new India, villagers, especially the young, will probably want Colgate, a Honda motor scooter, a John Deere tractor—someday a Ford. But if India's 1 billion—who live in a country a third the size of the United States—begin to consume like America's 260 million, there will be a catastrophe. India does not have the resources to produce the goods and services required to sustain a Western-style consumer economy.

So with development comes problems, new challenges. What else is new? Like other modern countries, India faces explosions of expectations and threats to its traditional culture. The question is not, will India change? It is, how deeply and how rapidly?

Bombay, the economic hub of the country, is a good place to ponder this question. The city has million-dollar condominiums and luxurious five-star hotels. It also has slums with sewage running through them.

And there are millions of middle-class Indians who will never set foot in a five-star hotel or a slum. But, like middle-class Indians throughout the subcontinent, they will set foot in appliance stores, buy a television set, and pay 200 rupees ($6) a month to have it hooked up to "cable."

The viewing habits of this important sector of society offer clues to what post-1992 India is becoming.

Cable television arrived in India at about the same time the government opened up its markets to the West, in the early 1990s. CNN's coverage of the Persian Gulf War was a key factor in cable's expansion. Indians had thousands of relatives working in the Gulf region, and their well-being was of great interest to their families back home.

After the war, Indians stayed connected. At that time, the only cable channel available in India was Hong Kong-based Star-TV, which offered only English-language programs. After years of being deprived of Western popular culture, urban middle-class Indians could now feast on MTV, *Oprah,* and *Baywatch.*

RESISTING THE HOLLYWOOD CULTURE

The common wisdom among media types was that it would be just a matter of time before English programming, most of it produced in Hollywood, would take over Indian screens and, eventually, its culture—or, at least, the culture of the young. It was just a matter of time, critics warned, before teenagers in New Delhi and Madras would look, sound, and act like VJs on MTV or before young professionals in Bombay and Bangalore would behave like those on *The Bold and the Beautiful.*

However, when Doordarshan, the national broadcasting system, and new cable companies began to offer high-quality programs in regional languages, a different scenario unfolded. Viewers switched to films, musical shows, sitcoms, and soaps in Hindi, Tamil, and other "local" languages.

The only Hollywood-made programs that earn reasonable ratings are those that are dubbed. For example, *Who's the Boss, Dennis the Menace,* and *I Dream of Jeannie* in Hindi have loyal fans, but their numbers are nothing compared with the "channel drivers" produced in Bollywood—the hip name for Bombay, India's film and television capital.

The issue of language is complicated in India. Hindi is the official national

---

India

Official Name: Republic of India.

Capital: New Delhi.

Geography: Area: 1.22 million square miles (about one-third the size of the United States). Location: Occupies the bulk of South Asia's Indian subcontinent. Neighbors: Pakistan on west; China, Nepal, and Bhutan on north; Burma and Bangladesh on east.

Climate/Topography: The highest mountains in the world, the Himalayas, dominate India's northern border. South of that, the wide, fertile Ganges Plain is one of the world's most densely populated areas. Just below is the Deccan Peninsula. About one-quarter of India is forested. The climate ranges from the south's tropical heat to the north's frigid cold. In the northwest is the arid Rajasthan Desert. By contrast, 400 inches of rain fall annually on the northeast's Assam Hills.

People: Population: 970 million. Ethnic groups: Indo-Aryan, 72 percent, Dravidian, 25 percent; Mongoloid and other, 3 percent. Principal languages: Hindi (official), English (associate official), 14 regional languages, hundreds of dialects.

Religions: Hindu, 80 percent; Muslim, 14 percent; Sikh, 2 percent; Christian, 2 percent.

Education: Literacy: 52 percent.

Economy: Industries: textiles, steel, processed foods, cement, machinery, chemicals, mining, autos. Chief crops: rice, grains, sugar, spices, tea, cashews, cotton, potatoes, jute, linseed. Minerals: coal, iron, manganese, mica, bauxite, titanium, chromite, diamonds, gas, oil. Crude oil reserves: 4.3 billion barrels. Arable land: 55 percent. Per capital GDP: $1,500.

Government: Federal republic.

---

language and the tongue of the wealthy north, which includes Bombay and New Delhi, the capital of the country. However, it is only 1 of 14 major languages and hundreds of dialects. Each of the 14 languages is part of a distinct culture with its own traditions and literature, which includes radio and television programs and, in some cases, regional film industries.

There is a Hindi film industry that makes films in Hindi, and there are Hindi cable television channels. There are also cable channels and film industries making and distributing products in other "local" languages—Tamil, Telugu, Gujarati, and so forth.

English is an important linking language, used across the country for business, scholarship, and medicine. Cable companies offer ESPN, CNBC, Discovery, and the BBC in English, but these channels get very low ratings. Most Indians—even those fluent in English—

prefer their music, films, television, and radio in their regional language. Why? Language is the glue that holds together that which is sacred to Indians—family, region, and class.

TRADITIONAL FAMILIES AND MARRIAGES

With few exceptions, Indian families are large and extended, with at least three generations living in one household. Elders have very high status and play central roles in the family. In many cases, they provide the roof over their children's and grandchildren's heads.

It is common for newlyweds to move in with parents rather than go off on their own. "Grannies" raise the young, teaching family traditions and language, while parents pursue their careers.

With one television set per household in India, grandparents also have a great deal of say about what the family watches. This clearly has much to do with the popularity of programs in Hindi, Tamil, and Bengali and the poor ratings of English-language programs.

India's multilingualism is a key ingredient of the nation's rigid class and caste systems—systems that, among other things, help sustain a dependable and inexpensive pool of servants who make the lives of upper-class Indians quite comfortable.

There are few opportunities for members of the lower classes to learn English. Those who attend school are taught only their local language. Employers speak to their cooks, drivers, guards, "tea boys," and nannies in Tamil or Hindi or Bengali. As a result, there is no need or impetus for those in the lower classes to learn English. In fact, in many instances there are pressures for them not to learn a second, "foreign" language, for this would be interpreted as rejecting one's community and culture.

Without English, there is little opportunity for social or economic mobility. A guard, sweeper, or bus driver who speaks only Tamil or Hindi will do the same work all his life. And there is a good chance that his son will do the same work as he.

This is also true for mothers and daughters. A washerwoman, house cleaner, or seamstress who speaks only her regional language has little chance to change her status or the status of her children and move up the economic ladder.

WEARING NIKES BENEATH SARIS

Language plays a very different role in the lives of the middle and upper classes—and their children. They have unlimited opportunities. Because 99 percent know English, they can practice their professions or do business in any region of the country or in most parts of the world. They can also live in both traditional and modern India—yuppies with arranged marriages, enjoying pizza as much as chapati, wearing Nikes under their saris.

Language and regional loyalties are not the only reasons upper-and middle-class Indians stay connected to their traditions. Another factor is that they simply don't need many of the things the West has to offer.

At construction sites, it is common for laborers to crush boulders by hand with sledgehammers to make gravel. This would make no sense in the West—too labor-intensive, too expensive, very inefficient. But in India, this way of doing things provides employment for 40 people who need the work.

Western-style supermarkets, and the culture that goes with them, have little appeal to middle-and upper-class Indians living in neighborhoods where street vendors sell high-quality fruits, vegetables, dairy products, and other staples door-to-door. Labor-saving devices—washing machines, dishwashers, power tools, and the like—are of relatively lit-tle value in a country with hundreds of millions of people willing and able to do manual labor.

But in some sectors, the old ways are changing. To participate in the global economy, India's banks, investment companies, and media have to modernize. Foreign manufacturers and mutual funds are investing in India because they are convinced that 200 million middle-class Indians are about to become Western-style consumers. They may be correct.

In downtown Bombay, New Delhi, and Madras, shoppers use American Express and Visa cards to pay their bills. Bankers sit in front of computer terminals finalizing car loans and home mortgages. Producers edit Pepsi, Nike, and Honda commercials on digital editing systems, then uplink them to satellites. From there they travel to television sets across the country.

These new technologies are changing India—especially urban India—but not such much as to put street vendors, servants, and grandparents, and the culture they help maintain, out of business.

Stay tuned.

Richard Breyer is chairman of the Television, Radio, and Film Department at the S.I. Newhouse School of Public Communications at Syracuse University. He has been a Fulbright scholar to India twice.

Article 10

Far Eastern Economic Review, January 20, 2000

ECONOMIES

India's Awakening

Government stokes the interest of foreign investors with reforms and business-friendly legislation

By Sadanand Dhume in New Delhi,
Hyderabad and Bangalore Issue cover-dated January 20, 2000

Although HSBC Holdings has had a presence in India for a century and a half, there's no time like the present. After decades of waiting to expand its modest branch network, the global banking giant recently won approval to open in three new cities. In addition, its distinctive red bow-tie logo will soon appear on a new asset-management company, a bonds dealership and a nonbanking finance firm. "We've never had a better chance," enthuses Zarir Cama, the bank's country head who has spent most of his 32-year career with HSBC in India. "I am very optimistic."

That sums up the mood of many foreign and domestic investors in India since a business-friendly government led by the Bharatiya Janata Party, or BJP, won a solid majority in October's parliamentary elections and pledged to triple foreign investment and launch an ambitious assault on the remnants of India's decades-old command economy. The government quickly removed onerous foreign-exchange controls and whipped legislation through parliament that opens up the insurance sector to private investors, including foreigners. Additional measures to encourage competition and foreign investment in banking and industry will follow shortly, the government promises.

The foreign business community has responded with enthusiasm. HSBC, the world's third-largest banking group, will invest $14 million in the country in coming months. Swiss-Swedish construction giant ABB and U.S. energy company Enron plan to build power

A NEW INDIA?

Reasons for investor optimism:

- Stable central government committed to economic reform
- State governments that are competing to lure investors
- Strong GDP growth

Reasons for investor caution:

- Bureaucratic bottlenecks
- High fiscal deficit
- Populous heartland states that are slow to embrace reforms
- Perennial tensions with neighbouring Pakistan

Source: REVIEW Data

plants in India, expanding operations in the country. Geneva-based Zurich Financial Services, which saw its insurance operations in India nationalized in 1972, is considering a return. In December, the annual India Economic Summit in New Delhi organized by the World Economic Forum saw a record turnout.

Both domestic and foreign investors are more optimistic about the near-term business outlook than they were a year earlier, says the Confederation of Indian Industry, which conducted a survey in October just after the election. The reasons for the rosy mood: The economy is coming out of a two-year recession, and investors say the new government's policies will ignite record-setting growth. "India could be the next Asian economic miracle," says Prasenjit Basu,

chief economist for Southern Asia at Credit Suisse First Boston in Singapore. "We're looking at an average growth rate of 7.5% over the next five years."

Finance Minister Yashwant Sinha says he hopes to attract $10 billion in foreign direct investment each year, more than triple the annual average of the past decade. Nor is the momentum coming solely from New Delhi. A clutch of reformist states in western and southern India have pioneered investor-friendly policies over the past few years, with spectacular results. Competition among these states to attract new business projects has given economic reform a life of its own.

Of course, India's many investment obstacles won't be eradicated overnight. Bureaucratic red tape, shoddy infrastructure and a runaway fiscal deficit that has driven up the cost of capital all have the potential to spoil the party. Moreover, bright growth projections for the country as a whole disguise the fact that while some states are embracing free markets and globalization, others remain mired in petty caste politics and protectionism. The six states of Delhi, Maharashtra, Karnataka, Tamil Nadu, Gujarat and Andhra Pradesh have cornered most of the $18 billion in foreign direct investment that has flowed into India since 1991. Largely left out are the four states known as the Hindi heartland—Bihar, Madhya Pradesh, Rajasthan and Uttar Pradesh—which are home to nearly a third of India's 1 billion people. The challenge for Delhi is to ensure that the economic reforms take hold even in the poorest states, so that they don't remain a drag on national growth and threaten the hard-won consensus for liberalization.

'The spirit of India has definitely changed and we hope that they can carry this through'

—Robert Sulzer, North Asia and India regional manager for Zurich Financial Services

It is the prospect of stability after three elections in as many years that bolsters investors' confidence. Last October's polls gave the BJP and its allies a comfortable majority in the lower house of parliament, meaning the government can no longer be held hostage by small members of its 24-party coalition. Some key parties supporting the government spearheaded the state-level economic reforms, including Andhra Pradesh's TDP and Tamil Nadu's DMK.

Even the main opposition Congress Party broadly supports the reforms. In December it joined the ruling coalition in approving an end to the state monopoly in insurance—a measure that was hotly debated for six years and came to be considered a litmus test of the government's commitment to reform. That move prompted Zurich Financial Services to think seriously about returning to India this year by entering into a joint venture with a local firm, says Robert Sulzer, Zurich Financial's regional manager for North Asia and India. "The spirit of India has definitely changed and we hope that they can carry this through," Sulzer says. He adds that the company is considering investing as much as $12 million, but will wait to see what detailed regulations follow on the heels of the legislation.

Arun Seth, managing director of British Telecom in India, was impressed when, within two days of taking office, the BJP government implemented a longstanding industry demand:It separated the Department of Telecoms' commercial operations from its policymaking and regulatory functions, thus creating a more level playing field. The government expects to win parliamentary approval soon for replacing high licensing fees with a more business-friendly system of revenue sharing between companies and the government. "I have never seen this much change in this little time," Seth says. "There's greater urgency and more political will than ever before." He says BT is considering investments in mobile telephony, long-distance calling and the Internet.

In recent weeks, parliament also has eased restrictions on most current-account transactions, and lifted a requirement that some foreign companies earn through exports any foreign exchange they wanted to repatriate as dividends. It passed legislation that protects international trademarks and allows trading in derivatives. The government is preparing to send parliament further legislation that would outlaw monopolies and bring Indian patent law up to global standards. The government also has promised to open more sectors to foreign investment, allow foreign law firms to open offices in India, reduce import barriers and press ahead with longstanding plans to reduce state ownership of banks and other enterprises. Currently, about a quarter of India's economy is state-owned.

One reason so many policymakers now accept economic reform is the dramatic growth of India's software indus-

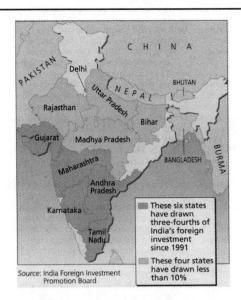

Source: India Foreign Investment Promotion Board

These six states have drawn three-fourths of India's foreign investment since 1991

These four states have drawn less than 10%

try. As a new economic sector, it is relatively free of state involvement and is flourishing. More important, it proved to protectionist politicians that Indian companies can face global competition and win. It also showed foreign investors India has a wealth of entrepreneurial talent.

"The success of software has made fund managers sit up and notice India," says Suresh Rajpal, founder and chief executive officer of eCapital Solutions, a software start-up. "They are beginning to look at other sectors of the economy as well." Rajpal wasn't always bullish. In 1997, as head of Hewlett-Packard's India operations, he told the REVIEW he was concerned about the government's slowness to reform, and said poor logistics caused HP to decide against putting a printer factory in India. Now, he says:"Things have clearly changed for the better."

Much of the current enthusiasm is based on projections of India's market size once its economy takes off and incomes rise. Philip Spender, president and managing director of Ford India, expects India's passenger-car market to double to about 1 million cars a year over the next decade. "Then you're beginning to knock on the door of becoming a major market. India looks very attractive," he says. In the first eight months of the current financial year, passenger-car sales rose 53% from a year earlier to 400,000 units. Ford has invested about half a billion dollars in India over the past three years, including designing a sporty new model, the Ikon, targeted at the growing population of young professionals.

Obstacles still loom large. Stephen Howes, senior economist at the World Bank in New Delhi, says the combined central and state fiscal deficit is hovering at about 9% of gross domestic product, helping keep interest rates high. "Growth won't take off unless you solve the fiscal crisis," says Howes. The central government was aiming to get its portion of the deficit down to 4% of GDP for the year that ends March 31, but the actual figure is expected to be 5.5%, according to SGAsia Securities.

India's bureaucracy also retains its ability to effortlessly choke economic growth. On December 9, Cogentrix of the U.S. and China Light & Power of Hong Kong withdrew from a $1.3 billion project to build a power plant in the southern state of Karnataka, citing inordinate delays in government clearances and multiple lawsuits over the environmental impact that dragged on for four years. But the government's swift response showed a new willingness to battle for investment funds: It offered the project financial guarantees, prompting the companies to say they would reconsider.

However, investors would all like the government to pay greater attention to implementing, not merely announcing, business-friendly policies. "There's a massive amount of regulation and control built into the Indian economy," says Alan Rosling, chairman of the Jardine Matheson group in India. "What India really needs is a deregulation drive and for the government to start working faster."

The single most important move the government could make to encourage more foreign investment would be to create a one-stop shop for project ap-

provals, as countries such as Malaysia have done. Senior government officials in India say turf consciousness among the various ministries remains too strong at the moment for that to happen. Instead, reformers are nibbling at the edges of the often daunting licensing process by expanding the list of sectors in which foreign investment is automatically approved. Foreigners also are being allowed to own bigger stakes in Indian projects: As of January, the ceiling for foreign investment in pharmaceutical firms rose to 74% from 51%.

The government also needs to take steps to bring the new reformist programme to India's poorest states. While strong investment inflows and expanding industries powered a 7.4% average annual growth rate in the western state of Maharashtra from 1991 to 1997, Bihar's economy actually shrank by an average of 0.7% a year, according to the World Bank.

"India's more prosperous states are growing at rates that make them look more and more like East Asian tigers," says Joydeep Mukherji, a New York-based India analyst at Standard and

Poor's. "The trouble is, some others are stagnating like sub-Saharan Africa." P. Chidambaram, a former finance minister of India, blames backward-looking politicians in the less-developed states. "A different breed of political people must come up," he says.

There are signs that the Hindi states are starting to awaken to the challenge. Uttar Pradesh, for example, took the first steps toward the privatization of power by establishing an independent regulator. Kirit Parikh, a Bombay-based economist at the Indira Gandhi Institute for Development Research, says that in just four years Andhra Pradesh went from being among India's laggards to a leader, largely because of the reformist policies of its chief minister, Chandrababu Naidu. Says Parikh: "If Andhra Pradesh can do it, then why can't Uttar Pradesh and Bihar?"

India might look to its neighbours in East Asia and ask itself the same question. If the government continues lifting obstacles that have kept capital out, India can finally join the ranks of the Asian tiger economies.

Article 11

Far Eastern Economic Review, September 14, 2000

The Trouble With Wealth

A rapidly widening gap between rich and poor states and the rise of regional parties could jeopardize hard-won economic reforms

By Sadanand Dhume/NEW DELHI

NEARLY A DECADE into an era of economic reforms designed to dismantle India's command economy, the gap between its relatively rich states and their poor cousins has grown into a gulf.

Parts of India are clocking growth rates as high as those that propelled East Asia to prosperity. But the two largest states, Uttar Pradesh and Bihar, home to one in four Indians, remain backwaters largely untouched by the economic energy

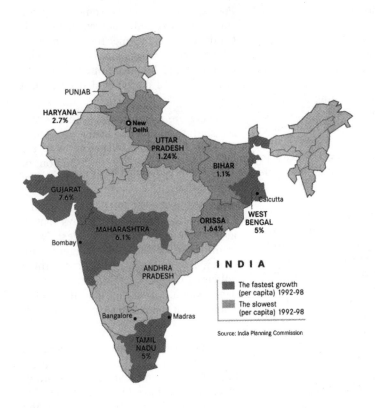

PUNJAB

HARYANA
2.7%

New
Delhi

UTTAR
PRADESH
1.24%

BIHAR
1.1%

GUJARAT
7.6%

Calcutta

ORISSA
1.64%

WEST
BENGAL
5%

MAHARASHTRA
6.1%

Bombay

ANDHRA
PRADESH

I N D I A

The fastest growth
(per capita) 1992-98

The slowest
(per capita) 1992-98

Bangalore

Madras

TAMIL
NADU
5%

Source: India Planning Commission

rippling through other parts of the country. In 1981, Gujarat's per-capita income was about twice that of Bihar; by 1998, the average Gujarati was earning 16,250 rupees a year (about $400 at then exchange rates), roughly three and a half times as much as the average Bihari.

"POOR STATES SHOULD BE given money, but not at the cost of performing states"

CHANDRABABU NAIDU, CHIEF MINISTER,

ANDHRA PRADESH

Not surprisingly, the strain of managing such glaring disparities is beginning to show as rich states grumble loudly about New Delhi's attempts to play Robin Hood.

On August 21, Andhra Pradesh's chief minister, Chandrababu Naidu, led seven other chief ministers and officials of rich states to New Delhi to protest at the decision of a nonpartisan government commission to reduce their shares of the federal tax pie. Naidu complained that "reforming and per-

forming states" were being punished for reducing poverty, building infrastructure and controlling their populations. "Poor states should be given money, but not at the cost of performing states," Naidu says.

Naidu's action is the first shot in what promises to be a drawn-out battle that could jeopardize India's hard-won political consensus on economic liberalization.

Opposition from rich states is not the only problem. Uttar Pradesh and Bihar have benefited little from reform. "The consensus on economic reforms is beginning to crumble," says Yogendra Yadav, a political scientist at New Delhi's Centre for the Study of Developing Societies.

New Delhi's challenge is to maintain a balance between equity and efficiency; in the process, it must also be careful that regional grievances don't spin out of control. "If you are going to give more money for poor states, we will also become poor," Naidu says. "We have to go forward, not backward."

Dramatic changes in the economic and political landscape over the past decade make New Delhi's task even more difficult. States have more economic decision-making power than ever before. And regional political parties have grown more assertive as their voters become more demanding.

States that have seized on the end of licensing and the advent of more liberal rules on investment have profited. One star example is Naidu's Andhra Pradesh, a large state with 76 million people that has slashed red tape and attracted investment from international companies such as Oracle, Microsoft and HSBC.

INVESTORS FAVOUR JUST SIX STATES

Similarly, Maharashtra and Gujarat, with their skilled workforces and relatively high-income consumers, have been the natural destination for much new investment, both domestic and foreign. More than three-fourths of the $20 billion in foreign investment that India has approved since reforms began in 1991 has been concentrated in only six states. And as these states grow, so will lagging states find it increasingly difficult to find investors. Says Bibek Debroy, director of the Rajiv Gandhi Institute: "Who on earth is going to invest in Bihar?"

While the invisible hand of the market has rewarded better-governed states, the strong hand of government has begun to wither. Wrestling with a runaway fiscal deficit, New Delhi has been forced to cut back its commitment to the public sector. This has hurt the ability of populous states to translate their political clout into economic largesse.

The fact that many poor states are also those with runaway population growth hurts even more. India's planning commission says the population of Gujarat, Maharashtra and the four southern states is likely to stabilize by 2014. But Uttar Pradesh, at current growth rates, will continue to add to its 170 million people well past 2100.

India's fractious politics—where regional parties are becoming more and more assertive and politically powerful—

only sharpens the disparity. The current BJP-led government, a patchwork of 24 parties, survives thanks to support from regional heavyweights such as Andhra Pradesh's Telugu Desam Party and Tamil Nadu's DMK. Voters, on both a national and state level, have become more demanding. Single-state parties such as Naidu's TDP aggressively articulate the demands of their state and chief ministers are willing to fight for every rupee. Naidu believes that New Delhi's financial largesse for poor states rewards economic laggards for avoiding often painful reforms. Naidu, for example, faces hunger strikers and rioting protesters opposed to his government's attempts to hike power tariffs.

For now, the spotlight is on a report by the Finance Commission, which decides on the distribution of central taxes and grants to India's 26 states. India is a federation, but the most important taxes and duties—income tax, excise and customs—are collected by the central government. States collect less important levies such as sales tax and motor-vehicle tax.

Thanks to strong GDP growth and a decision by the Finance Commission to pass on more cash to states, the total amount it disburses to states is set to grow to nearly $95 billion (at today's exchange rate) between 2002 and 2007 from about $50 billion between 1996 and 2001. The wealth of a state is determined by a formula that includes per-capita income, population, land area, level of infrastructure development, tax effort and fiscal responsibility, with income by far the most important factor. This means that states with low economic growth and high population growth will continue getting a larger slice of the pie, while the fastest-growing states see their share shrink. For example, Gujarat, one of India's best-performing states, has seen its share fall to 2.75% from nearly 4% in 1995. Poorly performing Bihar's has grown to 13% from less than 11%.

DRAG ON GROWTH

The Financial Commission justifies the changes by pointing out that poorer states need a helping hand. Poor states tend to have spotty tax collection and a hard time attracting investment.

Participants in the negotiations suggest that New Delhi will buy peace with rich states by setting up a special fund for the development of infrastructure. But this won't do anything to solve the underlying problem of balancing equity and efficiency.

Moreover, what New Delhi faces is not just the issue of equity among states, but also of accelerating national growth. According to Montek Singh Ahluwalia, a member of the Planning Commission and one of the architects of India's economic reforms, India will not be able to grow at 8%-9% a year unless laggard states improve their performance. Without accelerated growth, millions of Indians will continue to live in poverty, and the country will remain far behind China and the "miracle" economies of East Asia.

But China, which has its own regional economic disparities, is not a democratic federation. Debroy of the Rajiv Gandhi Institute says "the resentment is going to be much more palpable and difficult to handle" in India than in China. Yadav, the political scientist, adds that the first murmurs of dissent against economic reform have begun, especially in the Hindi heartland. Uttar Pradesh and Bihar control 139 of the 545 seats in India's lower house of parliament. Earlier this year the Congress Party set up a committee to review its position on economic reforms.

So far, Congress remains on board. For the most part, politicians from Hindi-heartland states have been preoccupied with caste and religion and have gone along with economic reforms. But Yadav thinks this could change. Should that happen, the divide between India's rich and poor states will only deepen.

Article 12

Far Eastern Economic Review, August 24, 2000

Gates and Gandhi

In Infosys he created one of India's most successful firms, but Narayana Murthy still lives the simple life and remains committed to battling against poverty

By Nayan Chanda/BANGALORE

IT'S LUNCHTIME at the Bangalore headquarters of software giant Infosys, and a waiter is serving rice and vegetables to the company's chairman and CEO, N.R. Narayana Murthy. As the waiter, Chandrappa, bustles about, Murthy remarks, in answer to a question: "He's worth about half a million dollars."

There aren't many companies in India—or anywhere else—where waiters are worth a fortune. But Infosys isn't like many other Indian companies, and its co-founder and leader, Murthy, isn't like many other businessmen. He has gone from early dabblings in communism to a multibillionaire. He has negotiated a minefield of official hostility to business to create a major software provider. And through it all he has retained a set of principles that mix the drive and ambition of a Gates with the social concern of a Gandhi. "In business he is a completely hard-nosed, free-market capitalist," says Paneesh Murthy (no relation), a U.S.-based Infosys veteran. "In his lifestyle he is a Gandhian."

Today, Narayana Murthy is being a businessman, and earlier today, as he welcomed his visitor to his company's campus, he was a very annoyed businessman. "It's insane," Murthy had screamed into his mobile phone. He had learned that the director of a technology institute who wanted to attend a conference in Germany first needed to get permission from a bureaucrat. "Why the hell should a joint secretary in the ministry get involved," Murthy shouted down the phone.

"POVERTY CANNOT BE SOLVED unless the competent are encouraged to create wealth"

NARAYANA MURTHY

For the visitor, it's a good place to come in. Murthy and Infosys have been waging such battles with bureaucracy for almost two decades, and the history of the company—and the development of Murthy's own philosophies—is inextricably tied up with India's slow and reluctant embrace of the business ethic.

But Murthy's determination to shake up Indian business, and India itself, goes back to before Infosys. Born in 1946 to a poor family, he was a student in the 1960s, and, like many others, was initially attracted to socialism and state intervention as ways of ending poverty. But exposure to the world outside India would change those views. Three years in Paris in the mid-1970s working for a software firm gave him some idea of how free enterprise could create wealth. And a holiday in Soviet-era Bulgaria showed him at first hand the power of states to repress individuals—he was briefly jailed after being "caught" chatting in French to a Bulgarian woman on a train. For Murthy, the solution to India's rampant poverty was clear: "Poverty cannot be solved unless the competent are encouraged to create wealth."

Back home, few in government shared his views. After working in a Bombay software consultancy for several years, Murthy and six colleagues quit in 1981 to set up Infosys Technologies, with seed capital of just 10,000 rupees (then about $1,000). The obstacles they faced were immediate. "It took us 18 months to get the licence to set up the company," Murthy recalls.

In the early days, given the stifling bureaucracy and total lack of infrastructure in India, it made more sense for Infosys to send people overseas to work with clients to design and customize software, rather than do the work at home. The firm struggled on in this way for 10 years until 1991, when the government began liberalizing the economy. "We were preparing ourselves for this day for a long time, almost 11 years," says Murthy. "When it happened, we seized it with both hands."

WHERE NEXT for Infosys?

Since it was founded, Infosys has transformed itself from a provider of cheap software fixes to a designer of complex e-commerce and telecoms software. Today, over 90% of its clients are based in either Europe or the United States, and it's seen as a company that can hold its own on the world stage.

"As an overall IT services firm, their services are equal to if not better than their competitors," says Jackie Moss, research analyst at merchant bank Thomas Weisel Partners in San Francisco. "They've proven themselves time and time again."

Certainly, Infosys has enjoyed some very good years: Earnings rose at an annual rate of 66% in the five years to 1999, to $17.5 million on reviews of $122.1 million. CS First Boston predicts that in a decade, revenues could touch $9 billion.

But like any company, Infosys faces questions of how to manage growth. For Samir Arora, the Singapore-based head of Asian Emerging Markets at Alliance Capital, Infosys has so far "done everything they were supposed to do very well." But, he adds: "Perhaps they have been too cautious in taking over companies."

To date, Infosys—unlke smaller Indian firms such as HCL Technologies—hasn't bought any U.S. companies, although it has taken stakes in some. Industry leaders such as Microsoft and Cisco have grown by acquiring companies in areas where they lag. Analysts believe the failure to buy-in such expertise has prevented some of Infosys's units, like its business consulting division, from taking off. A former Infosys employee comments: "They are comfortable with software programming.

So far, they haven't really gone beyond that."

Moss thinks acquisitions may happen in the future. Infosys has $105 million in cash, she says. "You would think they would be on a hunt simply because of their case position."

Meanwhile, in Bangalore, some say Infosys may yet pay a price for CEO Narayana Murthy's legendary largesse to staff. Industry insiders talk of the "02K" phenomenon—speculating that senior managers may leave the company this October when their stock options mature. Managing Director Nandan Nilekani concedes that a "couple of senior people are leaving," but insists "there is absolutely no risk to the organization."

Dan Biers and Sandanand Dhume

MURTHY'S LAW: Wealth creation, rather than wealth redistribution, is the key to eradicating poverty

Not only did the 1991 reforms remove a lot of bureaucratic cobwebs but also they created the software technology park in Bangalore, offering tax holidays and high-speed satellite links. Now, with the ability to transmit data instantly to almost anywhere in the world, Infosys could provide its software-design and customization services to global customers like Nortel, Aetna and Nordstrom 24 hours a day, seven days a week. At a time when "globalization" had yet to become a buzzword, this was a pioneering move. Today, with a value of $16.9 billion, Infosys is one of India's five biggest companies in terms of market capitalization.

But India has plenty of software companies that have benefited from deregulation. How did Infosys race so far ahead of the pack? To answer that, it's worth going with Murthy on a tour of the company's green, 50-hectare Bangalore campus. Murthy first shows off a newly built, airy, circular building that will serve as a library and offices. Next door can be seen a glass-domed cafeteria sitting atop a gym and a medical centre. Just beyond, workers are digging a swimming pool.

The facilities are here for sound business reasons. In 1992, Infosys was still virtually unknown, even in India, and was in danger of losing people to companies like IBM, which was then returning to India. Infosys studied why people might go to IBM, and found that excellent pay and working conditions were the main reasons. So Infosys followed suit. Today, it's an employer of choice. Last year, 184,000 job-seekers applied to join, from which around 2,000 were hired. From 480 software professionals in 1994, Infosys has grown to employ nearly 6,500.

For Murthy, looking after the staff makes business sense. "Our asset walks out in the evening tired, and we know it is entirely our responsibility that this asset walks back in the morning bright, enthusiastic and energetic."

Dexter Desouza is one of those to have benefited from Murthy's constant calls to "work hard, play hard." The young programmer has formed a band, encouraged by the company with expensive musical equipment. "In terms of benefits like this, Infosys is way ahead of others", he says. Of Murthy, he adds: "He really encourages people to dance, to enjoy themselves."

And over lunch, where we meet the waiter Chandrappa, Murthy talks about the other great Infosys lure: "As of May 27 this year, everybody has stocks in the company, including the sweepers—whoever is on the permanent roll." The ap-

proach looks to be working: With an attrition rate of just 9% last year, Infosys is well below the world industry average of 20%–25%.

In return, though, Murthy asks a lot of staff. "There is no quarter asked, no quarter given," says Mohandas Pai, the company's chief financial officer.

For Murthy, the aim is simple: "What really drives me is to be able to do something that is world class." That has meant pursuing openness and transparency—an approach that hasn't always been popular within the company. In 1995, Infosys lost 22.7 million rupees (then $600,000). Some preferred to keep it quiet, but Murthy overruled them. "We said, 'No, transparency is not showing off your good things alone; transparency is showing things as they are,'" he recalls. "So we said to the shareholders how much we lost. We went to the podium; we said 'Sorry, we committed a mistake and we won't do it again.'"

Technology analyst Yeshwanth Kini of SG Securities in Bombay believes the approach gives Infosys an edge over its rivals. "I feel Infosys scores over the others in transparency, investor-friendliness, access to senior management," he says.

Murthy, though, is not happy just to have created a successful company. In recent years he has stepped back from direct control of Infosys to promote technology in India and the need to create wealth, rather than just redistribute it.

Both within the company and outside, he has tried to lead by example by avoiding the usual trappings of corporate power. In Infosys, he has departed radically from traditional Indian corporate practice by avoiding the usual strict hierarchies. As Desouza says: "What I like about him is the fact that he himself comes and stands in the same line that we all stand in for food in the canteen." Murthy continues to live in the same modest apartment he moved into 20 years ago, washes up after dinner, and—until recently—flew only economy class. Some, though, find Murthy's lifestyle a little incongruous. "I think that he takes his personal economy habit too far," says T.N. Ninan, editor of the *Business Standard* in Delhi. "If you look at his belt, it's frayed and you wished he went out and got himself a new belt. After all, he is the head of a company; but that's the way he is."

"SOFTWARE COMPANIES ARE making profits hand over fist. It is only fair that they pay tax"

NARAYANA MURTHY

But, as Ninan also points out, Murthy's high profile and modest image haven't hurt Infosys. "He realizes that selling is not just going into a room and making a pitch but selling yourself, selling everything about you, selling yourself through secondary publicity and you create a larger-than-life image of a company, which, at the end of the day, is still quite small."

For longtime India specialist Marshall Bouton, executive vice-president of the Asia Society in New York, Murthy has helped transform Indian business. "He has brought a whole new standard to management," Bouton says. "He is a refreshing departure from the *homo hierarchicus* model common in India." And for business people like entrepreneur Arun Maheshwari, CEO of TriVium India Software, Murthy is someone to look up to: "He has inspired a whole generation of Indian entrepreneurs."

Still, they don't always agree with him. Earlier this year, when software firms were grumbling about a government plan to phase out tax holidays for software exports, Infosys shocked its peers by announcing it was ready to pay the tax. "Software companies are making profits hand over fist," Murthy said then. "It is only fair that they pay tax."

Murthy is optimistic about India's future, but insists on the need to privatize state assets. "The government has enough on its hands already," he told a meeting of the Asia Society in Hong Kong. "We must let the marketplace be the ultimate

decider, and unless you can create more and more wealth, you're not going to be able to create more jobs."

He believes the private sector should take the lead in providing and funding health and education services. His company donates 1.25% of its net profits (and plans raising that to 5%) to the Infosys Foundation, a nonprofit body that's building orphanages, schools, libraries and medical facilities for India's poor.

But for all India's progress, Murthy still sees many problems. He denounces what he again sees as the hypocrisy of India's establishment, which sends its children to English-medium schools while insisting that the bulk of the population is educated in one or other of India's many regional languages.

"Eighty-five percent of the population is placed in intellectual slavery," says Murthy. "This is all deliberate. We want the children of lower-income people to be perpetually in that orbit. That way we'll all be safe." For as long as those problems remain, Infosys will be a hi-tech company in a low-wealth country. "We have First World aspirations but we operate from a Third World context," Murthy says. "Twice a day we effect this transfer. We come from the warm womb of home every morning, pass through bad roads, bad pollution, traffic. Once we enter this gate, we leave India out."

Article 13   *Populi*, June 1998

India: Globalized Economy, Victimized Workers?

by Sharmila Joshi

What does a globalized economy mean for India's women workers? A recent study suggests that there are more threats than opportunities for women in the current process of liberalization. Traditionally an underpaid, exploited and unorganized group, women employees in many Indian industries have found that the restructuring of their workplaces has virtually restructured their lives.

Let us take, for instance, Sushama, a skilled worker in an electronics factory in the Okhla Industrial Area of Delhi. In mid-1995, she found that her job, along with that of many co-workers', had been

downgraded to an unskilled, less-paid category. Ratni, Gayatri and Sandhya, from another electronics factory in the area, found themselves locked out, after 20 years of work, along with 200 other workers, some of whom were retrenched with a 'final settlement'.

In the diamond-processing and jewellery industry in Mumbai, the city formerly known as Bombay, women workers have had to juggle household budgets to live through the 1990s decade of rising prices and reduced real incomes. This has included reductions in medical and food expenditure, at great costs to their health.

"Several studies have pointed out, and our study confirms, that in policies like the Structural Adjustment Programme or the Indian version of it, the New Economic Policy, it is often households, and much more often the women of the household, who have to play the role of a buffer," writes Sujata Gothoskar, co-author of an extensive report on the effects of industrial restructuring on women workers, at home and in the workplace. The report is the outcome of a three-year (1993–96) research project which covered 610 women workers in five industries: pharmaceuticals, plastics, soaps and detergents, gems and jewellery in Mumbai and electronics in Delhi. The four researchers—Ms. Gothoskar, Amrita Chhachhi, Nandita Gandhi and Nandita Shah—also interviewed male workers, employers, managers and trade unionists.

The five industries were chosen from available data from the Factory Inspectorate for National Industrial Classification. The choice was based on several factors: industries with significant changes in the proportion of women employees over the years and those employing many women affected by industrial restructuring.

The report examines the effects of an increasingly "flexible" market and points out that newer forms of adjustments now overlap older ones such as lax labour regulations and easy availability of labour. The new flexibility encourages changes in the organizational structure of a firm through subcontracting.

"A major impetus for subcontracting was lower labour costs and an attempt to avoid dealing with a unionized workforce," writes Ms. Chhachhi, who studied Delhi's electronics industry, which employs 45,000 workers, up to 40 per cent of whom are women. The number is expected to grow, according to Ms. Chhachhi, as labour force flexibility increases and industries seek more "exploitable" workers. New forms of flexibility also promote changes in the pattern of production through the manufacture of customized products, automation and changes in job categories; job rotation; and the training of workers for multiple jobs.

The new policies have changed legal regulations and practices to make it easier for management to hire and fire workers. They have further casualized labour and restricted workers' rights to organize themselves. For instance, due to economic reform, the electronics industry was opened almost completely to global competition. "By 1996, domestic manufacturers had begun to change their attitudes towards multinational corporations (MNCs)," writes Ms. Chhachhi. "Now, there is talk of foreign friends, partnership and collaboration. Behind

UNFPA/Vivianne Moos

An Indian electronics factory worker.

the scenes, domestic manufacturers engaged in yet another phase of restructuring to meet the challenge of the MNCs by introducing more 'flexibility' in the organizational structure as well as in the production of items."

The research report reveals that in the five industries, 63 per cent of the workers were non-permanent, with an attendant absence of labour rights. Only 28 per cent had written contracts, while the rest had verbal ones. Besides, 56 per cent had no unions in their workplaces, 14 per cent had some form of informal groups and only 29 per cent worked in unionized units.

In the pharmaceuticals, soaps and cosmetics industries in Mumbai, automation, a ban on new permanent recruitment, the replacement of permanent staff with contract workers, retrenchment and other strategies, have had a direct impact on women workers. "What were earlier stable, well-paying jobs, are now being converted into sweat-shop jobs," writes Ms. Gothoskar.

Who are the women working in these industries? The younger ones are in small- and medium-scale units: women in their 20s, in their first jobs,

neither permanent nor unionized. Older women, with a greater degree of unionization and politicization—because of long years of factory work and a strongly developed worker identity—are being phased out.

Some industries are giving more work to employees at home. "This provides a flexible workforce which can be deployed without any overhead cost to the employer," writes Ms. Shah, who studied the plastics processing industry in Mumbai. Such home-based work includes assembly of toys, switches, toothbrushes and scooter parts. Of the home-based workers, 45.8 per cent spend their own money on equipment and part of the raw materials and 41.1 per cent do not take even a single day's break. "The low pay rate forced employees to work as much as they could. The majority of women were working all year round," writes Ms. Shah.

A casual, unorganized workforce ensures lower wages and benefits, according to the study. In the plastic processing industry, 88.3 per cent of the 180 women surveyed came from families with a per-capita income of less than 950 rupees a month [39.44 rupees:US$1]. As many as 86.7 per cent of the workers received less than the average minimum wage.

"With the tussle between family expenditure and insufficient income, any small or big crises sent these workers over the brink and into debt," writes Ms. Shah. "The price rise has affected 97.8 per cent of households negatively. They had to cut down their expenses."

This included 46.6 per cent who had cut down on food items and 28.3 per cent who were buying cheaper food. In more than 10 per cent of the families, the women were eating less food. All this while coping with work at home and in the factory, and facing an uncertain future.

The three-year study also looks at the job loss experience of 46 workers, men and women, in the electronics industry in Delhi. Most had worked for 10–20 years in the same unit, and 42 per cent were below 30 years of age, contrary to the belief that only older workers are being phased out. Compensation for retrenchment ranged from 9,000 to 65,000 rupees.

"The money for most of the workers disappeared overnight. For over half, it was spent on domestic expenditure," write Ms. Chhachhi and Ms. Gothoskar. As many as 26 per cent of the jobless workers belonged to single-income families. Due to the drastic cut in family income, 43 per cent were buying cheaper food and 48 per cent had reduced the number of meals they ate daily. One worker said: "Earlier, we were two earners, now we can barely get two *rotis* a day."

After two years of job loss, 41 per cent of the workers interviewed were still unemployed, 37 per cent self-employed and 9 per cent had irregular jobs. Only two workers, one man and one woman, had again landed permanent jobs in an electronics factory.

Job loss has also meant loss of identity and dignity. Ms. Gayatri, now in her late 40s, misses the company of other workers and the joy of earning an income. "The future is bleak for us," she said. "Only this house and the tenancy keep us going, and my husband's pension helps. But it's not like working and earning, which had given me so much confidence."

"For retrenched workers from the organized sector, the loss of a regular, stable job with benefits won over years creates a different kind of trauma," write Ms. Chhachhi and Ms. Gothoskar. "They are unable to enter the lower levels of the unorganized sector, given a strong sense of worker identity as organized sector workers."

One worker said: "It is very difficult to run a house with two growing sons. My husband retired at the same time as when our factory closed. I cannot think of working as a domestic servant. After so many years of work experience, I cannot join a new factory only to be dismissed after six months of being a casual worker. I do not know what to do. What is the result of so many years of hard work?"

What, indeed? Years spent labouring, painstakingly juggling incomes and expenditure, hoping for brighter days, have come to nought. Drastic macro-level economic policies have crushed their hopes. For these invisible victims, what are the benefits of a Brave New Economic India, what is the use of better television sets and lipsticks?

Sharmila Joshi is a writer for Women's Feature Service.

Article 14   *The New York Times,* May 3, 1999

Lower-Caste Women Turn Village Rule Upside Down

By CELIA W. DUGGER

CHIJARASI, India—Rani, an illiterate woman from the washermen's caste, changed into her prettiest sari one recent morning. Heavy with child, she boarded a series of crowded, ramshackle buses for the dusty, two-and-a-half hour ride to the bureaucrat who has become her teacher in the art of governing.

Scorned by the upper-caste Brahmins who have long dominated this small village, Rani—who like many lower-caste women goes by only one name—is now head of the village council, or panchayat. "I am the boss," she said boldly.

She is one of almost a million women who have been elected to village governing councils since India adopted a constitutional amendment in 1993 that set aside a third of all panchayat seats and village chiefs' positions for women and set aside a percentage of those for women from the lowest rungs of the caste system.

This epic social experiment is playing out in more than 500,000 villages that are home to more than 600 million people—about 1 of every 10 people on earth. In many North Indian villages like this one, women who are expected to veil their faces and submit to male elders are now challenging centuries-old, feudal hierarchies.

"The Government has turned power upside down," said Alam Singh, a Brahmin farmer who was village head before Rani took over. "The Government is making these people sit on top of us. We are the rulers, but now she is ruling."

"She's stupid, she's illiterate, she doesn't listen to anybody," he said angrily poking the air with his finger.

A new Government-financed study, based on field work in 180 villages in the states of Uttar Pradesh, Rajasthan and Madhya Pradesh and coordinated by the Center for Women's Development Studies in New Delhi, found that while a third of the new women panchayat members are just rubber stamps for their husbands, two-thirds are actively engaged in learning the ropes and exercising power.

Like men, women panchayat leaders, too, are now involved in obtaining village lands for schools, selecting families who will qualify for Government housing and deciding how to distribute brick lanes, latrines and electricity.

But changing deep-rooted social attitudes cannot be accomplished by legal fiat.

In Chijarasi, Rani has assumed the mantle of village chief—but whether she can hold on to it is another matter. While a third of the seats on each panchayat are permanently reserved for women, the panchayat-head slots for women—one third of the total—rotate to different villages every five years, when new elections are held.

In the next election, Rani's seat will no longer be reserved for a low-caste woman. If she seeks re-election, she will have to run against candidates from the land-owning Brahmin elite who have always been in charge. Brahmin men, even those who believe she has done a good job, say they will vote for one of their own next time.

Two Villages

Air of Subversion And Big Obstacles

Generalizing about the experiences of villages—each as individual as a thumb print—is risky, but Government officials say the new rules are having their greatest effects in states where women have already made strides, for example in Kerala, where 9 of every 10 rural women are literate. Change will come more slowly in a state like Uttar Pradesh, India's most populous, where only 35 percent of rural women can read and write, compared with 66 percent of the men.

During six months of periodic visits to Chijarasi and Khoda, two villages in Uttar Pradesh that are almost three miles apart, the subversive nature of the

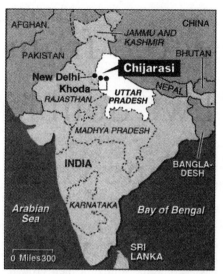

The New York Times

People in Chijarasi say the council leader has done her job very well.

change was apparent in Chijarasi, while the serious obstacles were visible in both places.

In Khoda, Munni Yadav is the pradhan, or village head, but her husband, Bir Bal Singh Yadav, held the job for three decades before he chose her to stand for election when the position was reserved for a woman. Mr. Yadav, regally ensconced on his charpoy—the traditional Indian cot—shooed his wife away to make tea and declared that he would answer all questions. Each time she attempted to speak, he cut her off.

"My lady is illiterate," he said, as his wife—like a ghostly shadow in a pale lavender sari—walked around the courtyard, her silver ankle bracelets tinkling softly. "She has to attend the meetings, but besides that, I do all the work and I explain matters to the authorities."

When the panchayat members gathered for a meeting in January, Mrs. Yadav was sitting on the sidelines, holding her 3-year-old granddaughter on her lap. The only woman in the center of the courtyard with Mr. Yadav and the male panchayat members was wordlessly pouring tea.

Mr. Yadav, who belongs to the middling caste of cowherds, puffed away on bidis—hand-rolled cigarettes—and accepted the greetings of members. They said, bowing respectfully, "Namaskar, pradhanji," which, roughly translated, means "Good day, Mr. Mayor." Even Mrs. Yadav, herself the pradhan, called

her husband by that title and scolded visitors for failing to do so.

"I'm not an educated woman," said Mrs. Yadav, who won election in a field of a dozen women candidates. "I am a village woman. So most of the work is done by my husband. We village women are not supposed to come out of the house and speak with strangers."

Despite her submissive posture, Mrs. Yadav, who is 40, showed flashes of spirit, when she was allowed to speak. She said she would like to do more to educate girls, to attract a bank where women could deposit their own money and to bring flush toilets to the village.

With her husband listening impatiently nearby, Mrs. Yadav said the most remarkable thing that had ever happened to her since she became pradhan was taking place at that very moment: someone was listening to her views.

"Even my husband has not asked me these things," she said.

Here in Chijarasi, Rani, who is 30, is also a traditional village woman. She grew up in a hamlet where only boys were educated. She drops her voice to a hoarse whisper and covers her unflinching, hazel eyes with a veil in the presence of older village men.

But she is nobody's fool. Her whispery voice was loud enough to put a stop to what she and others in the village say was her predecessor's habit of collecting money from peddlers on behalf of the village, then pocketing it for himself.

After the long bus ride, Rani strode into the office of Kamlesh Kumar, the state official who oversees development in 54 villages including hers without benefit of even a telephone. Rakesh Guar, her husband and inseparable teammate in running the village, was there to support her, but Rani did all the talking in her usual animated fashion.

She leaned forward intently with her elbows resting on her knees. The scarf that would have normally shrouded her face was tucked behind one ear as she explained her latest suspicions to Mr. Kumar: A group of influential villagers, in league with a former petty bureaucrat, had told her to hand over the basta—a book that records the panchayat's business.

The Innovation

Setting Goals For Women

She suspected they might be planning to jigger the records so they could personally profit from selling some of the village land that had just been chosen as the site of a new school.

"Do I have to give them the basta?" she said.

Perched on the edge of her chair, Rani awaited Mr. Kumar's reply.

In India, the states are often laboratories of democracy, and it was the southern state of Karnataka that pioneered the use of a women's quota on village councils in the early 1980's as a means of giving village women, who had lagged badly in many statistical measures of well-being, a political toehold in the electoral system.

In the late 1980's, Prime Minister Rajiv Gandhi, son of Indira Gandhi—the first and so far the only woman to be Prime Minister of India—picked up the idea and proposed it on a national level. It was part of a broader constitutional amendment intended to institutionalize democratically elected village councils and decentralize authority to them.

The idea of affirmative action for oppressed, low-caste groups had a long tradition in independent India. The innovation was to apply the approach to women.

It was not until 1992, a year after Mr. Gandhi was assassinated, that Parliament—then 93 percent male—passed a version of the panchayat amendment that retained the one-third set-aside for women, with lower-caste women represented in proportion to their percentage of the population. A year later, it went into effect.

Several recent national Governments have sought to extend the women's quota to Parliament. But such proposals have gotten bogged down in caste and religious politics, as some parties have pushed for quotas, not just for women generally and low-caste women specifically, but for Muslim and intermediate-caste women, as well.

Under the leadership of the Congress Party president, Sonia Gandhi, Rajiv's widow, the party decided last year to set aside a third of all party positions for women, who now fill fewer than 10 percent of them.

The Chief

An Honest Leader Squeezed by Critics

In villages, panchayats have turned into training grounds for women who had been excluded from a role in village politics for millenia.

"It has given something to people who were absolute nobodies and had no way of making it on their own," said Sudha Pillai, joint secretary in India's Ministry of Rural Development. "Power has become the source of their growth."

Other governments and political parties—in Peru and Argentina, Germany and Belgium—are also experimenting with quotas for women's political participation, but India's effort is by far the largest.

"This is one of the best innovations in grass-roots democracy in the world," said Noeleen Heyzer, executive director of the United Nations Development Fund for Women.

Rani, a cheerful, talkative young housewife who follows all the proprieties of her village, seems an unlikely rebel. When she meets an elder woman, Rani falls to her knees, wraps her arms around the woman's legs and touches her feet.

When guests arrive at her home, she disappears on her callused bare feet, silver rings glinting on her toes, and returns to put aluminum pitchers of steaming, sweet tea and frothy cups of buffalo milk on the battered coffee table. She nurses her baby daughter, Parvati, at the slightest whimper.

But when it came time for Chijarasi, a village of 2,500 people, to elect its first woman village head a year and a half ago, it was she who was chosen.

As is common in north Indian villages, politics is dominated by caste-based voting. Chijarasi is divided into thirds: upper castes, middle castes and lower castes. The only way to win a majority is with an alliance.

The male Brahmin elite of the village say they supported Rani as the least of the evils when it was announced that Chijarasi would have to elect as its village chief a low-caste woman. The Brahmins are the village's biggest landowners and dominant caste.

In the caste ranking, Rani came from the upper rung of lower castes. She and her husband are dhobis, people who wash and iron clothes. They do not handle the substances the Brahmins of the village believe exceedingly impure: animal skins, dead bodies and human feces.

Also, the Brahmins knew that the dhobis were neither numerous nor politically assertive in the village. And Rani was illiterate and, they figured, malleable.

In the election, 10 low-caste women sought to be elected pradhan. Two were dhobis and 8 were chamars, from a caste of leather workers formerly considered untouchable. The chamar vote fractured, and Rani prevailed with support from Brahmins and Yadavs, an intermediate cowherd's caste—an alliance that has made her unpopular with other low-caste people in the village.

At dusk one evening, a group of low-caste women gathered in a lane to heap calumnies on Rani. "We want land and houses!" they shouted angrily, and "She has not given them to us!"

Rani replied wearily that 12 Government-financed houses have been built for low-caste families, but there is no money for more. "And we don't have land in the village to distribute to the landless," she said. On the opposite side of the caste divide, Rani has made an enemy of the former pradhan, Alam Singh, whom she believed was corrupt. Mr. Singh—who denies that he ever did anything dishonest—can barely contain his rage when her name comes up.

"Women should be confined to the household and men should be village heads," he said one afternoon, as men crowded around, drawn by the raucous harangue of this almost toothless old man. "The work of a woman is to cook the food and clean the clothes."

So Rani is caught in a sandwich of critics, with the contemptuous former pradhan, a Brahmin, on one side and distrustful lower-caste people on the other.

But people from within and outside the village say she is an honest woman who has done a good job.

On a walk through the quiet lanes in October, past herds of snoozing water buffalo and carts pulled by teams of oxen, Rani pointed to the village hand pump she had gotten fixed. She showed off the new brick lanes, electrical poles and street lights installed on her watch and checked on the progress of a new community hall, being built for 90,000 rupees, or about $2,100.

Mahendra Singh, a Brahmin from another village who has taught in Chijarasi's elementary school for 36 years, said he has seen the local Brahmins try to sabotage her.

"They find it difficult to digest that a lower-caste woman is the village head," he said. "But she's doing a better job than the others. When the village got 90,000 rupees for a community hall, any other pradhan would have taken a cut of the money. She did not."

She has also paid attention to the problems of women. Manju, a 28-year-old factory worker, came to her last year to say that her drunk husband was beating her. Rani asked her own husband to talk to Manju's husband. And Rani called the police and asked them to go to the places in the village where men gather to tell them not to abuse their wives.

Manju said that her husband has since stopped hitting her. "I had complained to the previous village head, but he didn't do anything.", Manju said.

And Rani has lobbied state officials for a medical clinic. She watched help-lessly as five of her seven children died of diseases she only vaguely understood—a curse that she believes might have been avoided had there been a convenient, reliable place in the village to take them for checkups and vaccinations.

"The officials have promised to help," she said. "But they have done nothing yet."

Rani herself says she has learned how to operate as a pradhan in her year-and-a-half on the job. She has gone to meetings in state offices she never knew existed, watched as other pradhans raised their voices to win more resources, then followed their example. "I have gained a lot of confidence," she said.

But she has not tried to do it alone. She relies on her 10-year-old son, Vikram, to read documents aloud, his finger tracing the lines of script as he haltingly says the words. She sends her husband to speak on her behalf to village men. She asks the Brahmin elementary school teacher for advice about how to deal with officials. And she has cultivated Mr. Kumar, the state official who oversees her village.

"The good thing about Rani is she asks for help," Mr. Kumar said.

Most recently, Rani turned to Mr. Kumar with her worry that a group of villagers were trying to tamper with the panchyat record book for their own gain. They had demanded she give it to them for five days. She was unable to read the book's well-thumbed pages, but it was a point of honor with her that they not be falsified.

"They're trying to get my basta," she said.

So she waited fearfully that day for Mr. Kumar's reply to her question: Did she have to hand it over?

"Do not give the basta to anyone," he told her. "And do not sign any paper. They can do nothing to you unless they have a two-thirds majority."

Relieved, Rani smiled. With business out of the way, she, her husband and Mr. Kumar chatted about village matters and the former pradhan's efforts to undermine her.

Then Mr. Kumar grew serious. And as he spoke of her honesty and her pluck, it seemed that Rani sat up a little straighter and held her head a little higher.

"I'm impressed by her courage," he said. "She's fought head on with a very influential man of the upper caste who was head of the village for a decade. And he has been defeated by the grit of this low-caste woman."

With her resolve fortified and her rights established, Rani caught the bus back to Chijarasi to take on her social betters once again.

Article 15   *Commonweal*, October 8, 1999

DOWRY DEATHS IN INDIA

'Let only your corpse come out of that house'

Paul Mandelbaum

On the outskirts of Delhi, in the shadow of the famed Qutab Minar tower, lies the village of Saidulajab. Through its narrow rutted dirt alleyways, a local resident takes me to the home of his onetime neighbor, Manju Singh. It is there that he heard her cries of agony on July 10, 1996.

Enacting an elaborate pantomime, Manju's neighbor indicates, by pointing to the browned leaves of a backyard plant, the spot where he found her and from which he took her, in the back of his bicycle rickshaw, to a local clinic.

The next day, lying in South Delhi's Safdarjung Hospital with burns covering nearly her entire body, the twenty-seven-year-old regained consciousness long enough to tell a local police officer that her husband and in-laws had threatened to beat her the previous afternoon, haranguing her yet again over the inadequacy of her dowry. As she tried to escape—so alleges the police report—her husband and brother-in-law caught hold of her while her mother-in-law doused her with kerosene; then Manju's husband struck the match that would eventually kill her.

Manju's case is one of an alleged six thousand "dowry deaths" a year in India. The term typically refers to a newly-wed bride who, upon moving into her husband's family home, is harassed over the goods and cash she brought to the marriage, leading to her murder or suicide. Antidowry activists claim the actual death toll is much higher, and the British journal *Orbit* recently put the annual figure at fifteen thousand.

Twenty years ago, India's feminist leadership began sounding the alarm. Responding to a groundswell of pressure from women's groups and the media, in the mid-1980s India's Parliament passed sweeping amendments to the largely moribund Dowry Prohibition Act of 1961, as well as the Indian Evidence Act and the penal code. The new laws acknowledged a quasi-manslaughter crime called "dowry death," and placed the burden of proof on the accused in any situation where a bride dies unnaturally during the first seven years of marriage, if a history of dowry harassment can be shown. In the ensuing years, the violence seems only to have escalated.

As late as 1987, high concentrations of dowry-death cases were mostly confined to the corridor connecting Punjab, traditionally a very patriarchal and violent part of northwest India, to Delhi and, further east, Uttar Pradesh. But by the mid-1990s, significant per-capita concentrations of dowry death had infested half of India's thirty-two states and union territories.

Often the conflicts are not so much about material goods *per se* as about the family status such items represent. Sometimes, dowry conflicts may mask other underlying problems—infidelity, sexual incompatibility, for example—that are unthinkably intimate for many families to acknowledge and discuss.

In most cases of dowry death, the physical evidence is murky. Often a bride's death is staged to look like an accident—hence the popularity of burning. Fire can obscure a variety of incriminating details, and the cheap kerosene stoves to which many Indian wives are virtually chained often do explode, providing offenders with a plausible scenario.

In the days before kerosene stoves, writes historian Veena Talwar Oldenburg, Indian brides fell down wells with suspicious regularity. Oldenburg has traced some of the roots of India's dowry problems to the British Raj and the economic pressures imposed by its agricultural tax system, which in turn pitted Indian farmers against one another. The parents of sons, according to Oldenburg, capitalized on the urgency felt by the parents of daughters to arrange a marriage by an acceptably early age. This urgency fueled a climate of extortion. Other cultural observers speculate that such a climate may have arrived earlier, when Hindu parents felt anxiety about protecting their daughters' honor from Muslim invaders.

In any case, modern-day dowry came to corrupt two ancient Hindu customs associated with arranged marriage. The first, *kanyadan,* called for enhancing the virgin bride with an array of jewels. The second, *stridhan,* provided the bride with a pre-mortem inheritance from her parents. These two concepts merged and have mutated into a type of groom-price, now practiced not only by Hindus but also by some of their Muslim neighbors. Even some tribal groups who until recently preferred the inverse custom of bride-price have switched.

Today, Indian brides and their families feel compelled to buy their way into a marriage alliance with "gifts" of cash, jewels, and consumer goods for the in-laws' pleasure. This "marriage settlement" is often calculated in direct relationship to a groom's prospects. Grooms working for the elite Indian Administrative Service can sometimes command dowries equivalent to $100,000 or more. Indian grooms living in the United States seek compensation not only for their own self-perceived worth but for providing access to the American dream. In many cases, dowry is seen by both parties as an acknowledgment of the groom's desirability.

Manju Singh's parents felt obliged to present a significant endowment, even though she held a bachelor's degree from Delhi University while her fiancé was a village shopkeeper. Her father, Nawab Singh, has a thirty-one-item list of the bounty he gave, including 70,000 rupees (close to one year's salary), a scooter, a color TV, 224 grams of gold jewelry, 2 kilograms of silver, bedroom furnishings, and thirty-five suits of clothes for the groom's side. Several months after the wedding, he says, Manju's in-laws demanded a washing machine, a refrigerator, and 50,000 rupees. "So many things," the school teacher recalls for me harriedly over his lunch break. "I tried to give as much as I could." Nonetheless, he alleges, Manju's in-laws began to harass and beat her in a spiral of domestic violence leading to her death. "She was burned by them purposely for dowry," says Nawab Singh.

Even if the last quarter of the twentieth century did not create dowry death, several intersecting social and economic trends seem to have escalated the problem. For one, availability of a host of household appliances, as well as their increasing promotion on television have created a hunger among the lower-middle class and others who lack the purchasing power to afford what they are being encouraged to desire. The families of grooms have seized an opportunity, through negotiation of the customary premarital settlements, to acquire some of these items through dowry, leaving it to the bride's family to worry about the bills. At the same time, some brides' families have been doing quite well, so well that they might wish to hide surpluses of hard currency from the tax authorities. They have seen dowry as a means to invest that money under the table and to secure their daughters a place in higher-status families. Ultimately, these two forms of dowry inflation have increased the likelihood that more and more brides' families will have a harder time fulfilling the terms of the marriage settlements they feel obliged to enter into, setting the stage for dire consequences.

The transience of the modern world has also put other pressures on arranged marriage. In the small southern town of Bangarapet, a village elder recalls for me the dowry negotiation he mediated on behalf of a local family. The prospective groom's father, visiting from New York, objected strenuously to the offer of three *lakhs,* or roughly $8,500, on the following grounds: "What do you think of me? What do you know about my status? I know the president of America. I know the president of India. What will be the state of my prestige if I collect three *lakhs* from you?"

While most Indian marriages are still made by parents as a way of ensuring a suitable match within an appropriate range of subcastes, as more Indians move from the countryside to teeming cities or abroad in pursuit of opportunity, chances have grown that a bride would marry into a family geographically removed from and previously unknown to her own parents.

Increasingly, today's marriage alliances are made blindly through brokers, classified ads, and Internet services. When it was time to marry off his twenty-nine-year-old daughter Sangeeta, who had completed her Ph.D. in solid-state physics, Bimal Agarwal of Kanpur started replying to ads in the *Sunday Times of India.* Turning to the June 27, 1993, classified section, he found one looking for a "beautiful educated match" for a "Kanpur-based handsome boy 29/173/5000 employed leading industrial house only son of senior business executive with own residence. . . ."

Agarwal telephoned the father of this twenty-nine-year-old businessman earning 5,000 rupees per month, and over the next four days the families met several times to negotiate marriage expenditures. On July 1, Sangeeta was engaged.

As her father and I converse on his apartment balcony, I am distracted by the anachronism of a laser eye-surgery center located across a narrow dirt street crowded with sleeping pigs. A passing woman carries atop her head the dried cow chips commonly used for cooking fires. When I get around to asking Mr. Agarwal if his daughter's engagement was decided hastily, he assures me it was quite typical.

Problems, however, began at the wedding itself, when, alleges Agarwal, the groom's family demanded a car. He adds that the ensuing pressure became a nightmare for Sangeeta. One day, roughly five months after her wedding, she and her father met for lunch. "She was weeping," he recalls. "She said, 'Father, go and talk to those people.' " But he had recently tried that, he says, and was reluctant to intervene again so soon.

Two days later, Sangeeta was found dead from "asphyxiation as a result of hanging," according to a postmortem report.

Her husband, Sanjay Goel, points out for me the ceiling fan in his family's middle-class living room. He maintains that Sangeeta committed suicide not because of any dowry demands but possibly because she had no desire to marry him in the first place.

Sangeeta's father, however, alleges that not only did dowry play a role in her death, but that she was murdered. The courts have yet to settle the case. Whatever the outcome, it seems fair to say that Sangeeta Goel, like many Indian women today, was burdened with the worst of two worlds: the marriage mandate of tradition combined with the compassionless anonymity of modern-day life.

Meanwhile, the day-to-day struggles fall to a handful of privately run women's shelters. One of the best known, Shakti Shalini, was formed thirteen years ago by mothers who were grieving for their lost daughters and who wanted to offer a haven to endangered brides. Shakti Shalini also gives counseling sessions designed to restore such troubled marriages, a service not appreciated by everyone.

"They're taking too much of a chance with somebody's life," charges Himendra Thakur, who heads the International Society against Dowry and Bride-Burning in India, an organization he runs from his home in Salem, Massachusetts. "They feel very good when they send somebody back. They think they're saving a home," says Thakur, who maintains that at the first sign of dowry harassment, "the marriage should be dissolved."

But this stance has met great resistance in India. Speaking before a Kanpur civic organization in order to pitch his dream of building a series of "residential training centers" for abused brides, Thakur is confronted by an elderly man in the front row, who stands up and demands, "What about divorce?" This strikes me as an absurd question: How could divorce conceivably approach the tragedy of dowry death? But in the mind of this gentleman and many others in India, divorce is viewed with an alarm difficult to appreciate in the United States.

In general, Hindus face a spiritual imperative to marry and remain married, with nothing less than the salvation of their forebears at stake. Furthermore, the ancient Laws of Manu enjoin a wife to suffer her husband's trespasses (thus, most marital breakdowns are viewed as the wife's fault). Such traditions serve to keep many Indian wives married, even when their safety is in danger.

As indicated by the traditional Hindu parting to a newly wed daughter ("We are sending your bridal palanquin today. Let only your corpse come out of that house."), Hindu parents have long stressed that a married daughter should refrain from returning home. A bride's parents may be especially reluctant to allow her back if there are still maiden sisters whose chances of marrying might be hurt by the reputation of coming from a "difficult" family. Sadly, this reluctance has hardened in recent years, according to Delhi University sociology professor Veena Das. "There is something that has become pathological in India," she asserts. Typically in the case of dowry death, one thing is very shocking: "The girl has gone to her parents repeatedly and says she wants to come back, but the parents refuse to take responsibility for her."

Paul Mandelbaum's journalism has appeared in the New York Times Magazine and elsewhere. He is currently completing a novel about marriage set partly in India, for which he has received a 1999 James Michener/Copernicus Society of America fellowship.

Article 16

The Wall Street Journal, September 21, 1999

Selling Birth Control to India's Poor

Medicine Men Market an Array Of Contraceptives

By Miriam Jordan

Staff Reporter of THE WALL STREET JOURNAL

MIRZAFARI, INDIA

From his outpost behind a wobbly desk under a tree, medicine man Sushil Bharati dispenses everything from cough remedies to advice on bad karma. Like thousands of other medicine men throughout the country, he is at the very heart of village life.

Now he is also part of an elaborate new medicine-man marketing network. Known as "Butterfly," its goal is to revolutionize the way the world's second-largest country curbs its soaring population. In return for advocating a formalized birth-control program, Mr. Bharati receives free radio ads and other benefits, like customer referrals. He also profits from selling condoms, prominently displayed in a jar on his little table, and birth-control pills.

It's a revolutionary concept for a village that is far removed from the modern world. Mirzafari's 10,000 citizens have no electricity, and women are confined to the home. Most men earn about $10 a month, mainly farming or weaving cotton. The average couple has eight children.

Plastered on the wall of Mr. Bharati's makeshift clinic are posters with the bright Butterfly logo—the same one that is displayed on billboards and village walls across the giant state of Bihar. There are butterflies, too, on Mr. Bharati's stationery, referral notes and prescription pad.

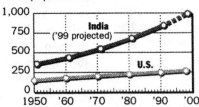

A Giant Keeps Growing

Total population in millions

"We've gone for total branding," says K. Gopalakrishan, the network's director. "This is not only about serving humanity; it's about making money."

That is a significant philosophical shift. For decades, stabilizing population in India amounted to government-ordered sterilization. Policy makers set annual sterilization quotas, which were sometimes achieved by threatening, bribing or otherwise coercing women to participate, other times by fudging the figures. Under pressure from human-rights groups, New Delhi abolished that system three years ago.

Currently, India's census bureau estimates that on May 11, 2000, the nation's population will top one billion. Only China, with 1.2 billion people, is bigger; India is on track to surpass China within four decades. That prospect has spawned Butterfly and other programs—many funded by the U.S. government and U.S. private money—that aim to create networks out of existing commercial enterprises such as the

medicine men. In neighboring Uttar Pradesh state, another program recruits milkmaids at village dairy cooperatives to spread the word on family planning.

The hurdles are huge. "Pills collect in your stomach and cause a cancer to grow," declares Lukoh, a pregnant woman in a pink and orange sari at Kharik village in Bihar, who already has had four children and five miscarriages. Another villager, Bebi, chimes in as she cradles her third child: "I have never taken contraceptives. My husband is my master—he will decide."

The northern states of Uttar Pradesh and Bihar are immense and poor. With 165 million people, if Uttar Pradesh were a nation, it would be the world's fifth largest. In neighboring Bihar, 100 million people eke out a living on 5% of India's land, and more than half live under the poverty line. Fewer than two out of 10 women can read and write.

India has made remarkable strides in slowing population growth in southern states, where female literacy is higher and states devote more money to health and education. Three southern states have achieved a replacement-level fertility rate—2.1 children per couple—or lower.

The risk to India is that soaring northern populations will swallow the economic advances made since India introduced market-oriented reforms earlier this decade. "If Uttar Pradesh and Bihar don't curb their population, India as a nation will no longer be viable," cautions Gadde Narayana, an adviser to Futures Group International, Washington, D.C., which does population research in India.

Butterfly was born two years ago when DKT International, a Washington, D.C., nonprofit group, created an Indian affiliate, Janani, which hatched the idea of using village medical practitioners. DKT invested $1 million and raised another $4 million from private Indian and U.S. groups.

Eight months ago, Mr. Bharati the medicine man and his wife, Sanju, signed on. They boarded an overnight train to the state capital, Patna, for a crash course on reproductive health at Janani's headquarters, where they learned about basic anatomy and the menstrual cycle. Armed with several tall jars of condoms and birth-control pills, supplied by Janani at cost, the couple returned four days later to northern Bihar.

Standing outside his brick hovel in Mirzafari, Mohammed Khurshid, father of 12, says he would prefer not to have any more children. But he won't countenance birth control. "It's in God's hands," he says. His third wife, Birwira, the mother of four of his children, seems to agree. Later, however, Mr. Bharati says that Birwira, 27 years old, regularly buys birth-control pills: "She doesn't skip a cycle."

That some villagers are even aware of birth-control methods other than sterilization is a tribute to Mr. Bharati and his wife. Typically, it takes several encounters to get a woman to consider birth control, so Mrs. Bharati broaches the subject subtly as she performs her daily chores with other women, such as fetching water at a well.

She is openly proud of her new knowledge. "Word is spreading that I have training," says Mrs. Bharati, who is one of the relatively few women who can read here. "Many women are seeking me to help them have fewer children," she says. Some ask to speak with her in the privacy of her family's dirt-floor home. She encourages the women to bring their husbands to Mr. Bharati.

Mr. Bharati, meanwhile, says he discusses family planning with nearly every customer. The condom jar on his desk stands next to another jar full of birth-control pills, in full view of patients, as required by Janani. "Family planning is my new responsibility," says Mr. Bharati, in his sixth year as a medicine man. "It is good for the village and it is good for my business," he says. A woman in a pink and blue sari steps up to buy a pack of pills.

Mr. Bharati charges about 20 cents a customer consultation, and 40 cents for bandaging a cut, but he doesn't charge separately for family-planning advice. In fact he even has to pay an annual $12 fee to be affiliated with Janani. But he makes a tiny profit from selling Janani's Bull brand condoms and Divine Dancer pills. He also receives a $1 commission for every patient he refers to Janani-endorsed doctors for intrauterine devices or abortions.

His practice, which earns him $70 to $90 a month, most of which comes from selling medicine, is thriving thanks to the free radio ads. He claims he is even winning business away from two competing medicine men. To preserve the brand's cachet, Janani affiliates with no more than one medicine man per village.

Janani has trained about 5,400 rural practitioners in 38 of Bihar's 55 districts. That's a drop in the bucket: There are 150,000 to 200,000 medicine men statewide. But encouraging results, such as that about 45% of the condoms and oral pills sold in the state are Janani brands, have prompted the organization to lay the groundwork for similar programs in two other northern states, Madhya Pradesh and Uttar Pradesh.

"We thought that if we could make this work in Bihar, we could make it work anywhere in India," says Mr. Gopalakrishan, the program director.

In neighboring Uttar Pradesh, another approach is under way at one of the world's biggest U.S.-funded population projects. The U.S. Agency for International Development is devoting $325 million over 10 years to an array of grass-roots programs to educate peo-

ple about birth control. Among them is the milkmaid project.

Looking for an avenue into village society, USAID spotted opportunity in the state's countless dairy cooperatives, which provide a livelihood for women and also serve as de facto social centers. "The cooperative has always offered health care for the cows and buffalo of its members," declares Sumitra Singh, chairwoman of Pradeshik Dairy Co-op in Revri village. "Now, it's taking care of the women themselves."

As the early morning sun warms Revri's mud huts, women with cans of buffalo milk line up at the co-op, and Sita Kumari, a co-op member and health worker, canvasses the crowd. Carrying a supply of pills and condoms in her shoulder bag, along with flip charts showing how to use them, she quickly identifies women who might need to restock.

The goods Ms. Kumari gives away are supplied by the government free of charge, though recently she started selling private brands, too.

USAID has trained 4,300 volunteers like Ms. Kumari, and pays them $8 month. In 15 districts of Uttar Pradesh where USAID is operating, the number of couples using family-planning services, such as pills, condoms and IUDs, has nearly doubled in three years.

A few years down the road, the co-op is expected to share the cost of the program by pooling a few pennies each month from members. In the long run, the idea is for each co-op to run the program on its own, and in fact make a profit by sourcing contraceptives for its members to sell.

"Dealing with population in India requires dynamism, flexibility and entrepreneurship," asserts Mr. Narayana of Futures Group. Nevertheless, it may take years before the success of the soft-sell approach can be accurately gauged.

Meanwhile, Ms. Kumari perseveres. Three years into the project, she supplies contraceptives to about 220 out of the 510 couples she has contacted. As for the others, she says, "I keep going back to them with my message."

Article 17

Education About Asia, Fall 1996

Enduring Stereotypes About Asia

India's Caste System

Joe Elder

Joe Elder is Professor of Sociology and South Asian Studies at the University of Wisconsin at Madison. He is also Director of the Center for South Asia.

*F*or decades most United States textbooks dealing with South Asia have contained sections on India's caste system, and most such sections have contrasted India's "immobile caste society" negatively with America's "open and mobile class society." People in India are seen (presumably) as locked forever in birth-determined positions, while people in the United States can (presumably) rise to whatever levels their abilities and good fortune permit. Caste in India is described as a fatalistically-accepted system of discrimination, an inducer of lethargy, and the generator of a mindset that continues to permit a tiny minority of high-caste brahman priests to exploit a large majority of lower-caste farmers and laborers. Implicit—and sometimes explicit—questions in these textbooks are: "When will Indians treat each other more fairly?" and "When will India get rid of its caste system?"[1]

One difficulty in discussing caste in India is that the term itself is applied to several quite different Indian social phenomena. "Casta" was originally a Portuguese word, used in places such as Brazil to describe groups with different proportions of "racial purity" as the Portuguese inter-bred with local Indians and Blacks. The Portuguese applied the term "casta" (inappropriately) to the inter-marrying groups they found in India. The British changed the word to "caste" and incorporated it into their legal documents, where it continues to be used by the post-independence government of India.

Today in India the word "caste" is applied to at least three different social phenomena

---

1 FOUR MYTHICAL CATEGORIES OF HUMANS THAT EMERGED FROM FOUR DIFFERENT PARTS OF PURUSA'S BODY AT THE DAWN OF CREATION. According to the *Rig Veda* (X, 90)[2] four categories of humans emerged from four different parts of the body of the primeval man, Purusa when he sacri-ficed himself on a cosmic funeral pyre at the dawn of creation. In Sanskrit texts, these categories are often referred to by the term *varna*. The dawn-of-creation story had been in circulation for centuries before priestly intellectuals generated different rules for each of the four mythical categories. Such rules were incorporated, for example, in the frequently cited *Laws of Manu*. Central to the *Laws of Manu* were requirements that men and women marry within their category *(varna)* and perform occupations assigned to their category *(varna)*. Thus, members of the brahman *varna* (that emerged from Purusa's mouth) should be priests; members of the ksatriya *varna* (that emerged from Purusa's arms) should be warriors and administrators; members of the valsya *varna* (that emerged from Purusa's thighs) should be producers of wealth; and members of the sudra *varna* (that emerged from Purusa's feet) should serve the other three *varnas*. The *Laws of Manu* describe a fifth "mixed" Varna, the candalas. Candalas were, according to myth, the offspring of brahman women impregnated by sudra men—in gross violation of rules prohibiting such inter-*Varna* sexual relations. According to the *Laws of Manu*, candalas were to be dealt with as social pariahs, excluded from sacred places and events, and required to perform the least pleasant tasks of society, including removing human feces and disposing of the carcasses of dead animals. The mythical candalas may have provided a basis for the more recent identification and segregation of India's "untouchables."

It is unlikely that the mythical four-*varna* society ever historically existed for any extended period of time. However, such a mythical society is described in epics and folk tales, and it serves even today as a point of reference for an idealized harmonious society.

2 HUNDREDS OF PUBLICLY IDENTIFIED KINSHI GROUPS LABELED AS "CASTES" IN CENSUS TRACTS AND OTHER OFFICIAL DOCUMENTS BY PEOPLE IN AUTHORITY.

According to the Government of India, for example, 15 percent of India's population belong to "scheduled castes," and another 7.5 percent belong to "scheduled tribes"—kinship groups, many of them previously considered to be "untouchables" who suffered historic deprivations at the hands of their neighbors—who were often regarded as ritually "polluting," were prevented from using certain temples and wells, and who are now entitled to special governmental benefits.

The government of India's 1960 publication entitled *Scheduled Castes and Scheduled Tribes Arranged in Alphabetical Order*[3] lists 405 scheduled castes and 255 scheduled tribes, for a total of 660 kinship groups (the boundaries distinguishing "castes" from "tribes" are unclear). Indian citizens who can establish their claim to belong to one of these publicly identified "castes" or "tribes" are today entitled to special benefits from the government (e.g., preferential access to government jobs, special representation on elected bodies, etc.). More recently, the government has published lists of "Other Backward Classes"—52 percent of India's population belonging to kinship groups that are also entitled to certain benefits because they are disadvantaged—but generally less disadvantaged than the scheduled

castes and scheduled tribes. The government's 1980 publication entitled *Report of the Backward Classes Commission* (also called the Mandal Commission Report) lists on a state-by-state basis a total of 3,743 castes belonging to "Other Backward Classes" above and beyond the "scheduled castes" and "scheduled tribes" included in the earlier government lists.

As one examines the official government lists of castes, it is clear that considerable arbitrariness went into identifying what comprised any given caste. For example, "scheduled caste no. 186" that is listed as jolaha in the region of Jammu and Kashmir is listed as kabirpanthi, megh, meghwal, or keer in other regions of northern India. The government official who identified "scheduled caste no. 186" provided no evidence why he ultimately gave the same single label to kinship groups with different names in different regions of India.[4]

3 LINEAGES OF RELATED FAMILIES FROM AMONG WHICH PARENTS ARRANGE THEIR CHILDREN'S MARRIAGES.

Historically, a major responsibility of parents in India has been to arrange their children's (especially their daughters') marriages. Typically, the caste into which one is born provides the boundaries within which one's parents' marriage partners were selected, one's own marriage partners are selected, and one will select the marriage partners for one's own children. To marry outside of one's caste is usually to invite serious social opprobrium—and possibly even expulsion from one's caste.

The caste made up of one's own intra-marrying lineages forms one's ultimate base of social support. These are the people to whom one is related, whose food one can eat, whose hospitality one can provide (and benefit from), to whom one can go for financial and other assistance, and on whom one will have to depend for aid in one's old age and for proper disposal of one's body after one's death.

When defined as marriage-pool lineages, hundreds of thousands of such

castes exist today in India. Strong we–they distinctions are often drawn between the members of one's caste and the members of other castes. What from one perspective is standing by one's relatives, from another perspective is favoritism and nepotism. Also higher and lower social distinctions between castes are often perpetuated—or challenged. Certain lineages fall out of favor, are cut off, and become separate castes. Similarly, mergers are possible between castes that see themselves as near social equals. Castes' standings in relation to one another are constantly being renegotiated on the basis of changing wealth, power, status, ritual behavior, sponsorship by important "others," political mobilization, education, and geographical location. One can see parallels between castes as status determiners and marriage pools in India and racial, religious, and ethnic groups as status determiners and marriage pools in the United States.

True or False?

As a consequence of the term "caste" referring to such different social phenomena in India, misconceptions about caste have frequently arisen. Taking "caste" to mean *lineages of related families from among which parents arrange their children's marriages,* here are seven prevalent misconceptions about India's caste system:

1. *The caste into which one is born determines one's occupation.*

False. People in the same caste engage in (and historically have engaged in) a wide variety of different occupations. Confusion arises from the fact that according to the mythical *varna* system of the idealized Hindu law books, everyone is *supposed to* carry out occupations that match their *varnas*. However, the mythical *varna* system and the current caste system are two very different phenomena. Only a very few caste names listed in official publications refer specifically to occupations. Most caste names are merely designations whereby other castes identify a given caste.

2. *Caste designations are changeless.*

False. There are many historical instances of castes changing (or trying to change) their caste names and behavior in order to receive advantageous treatment. Trying to convince someone in authority to label one's caste more highly in a public document is one well-tried way to change one's status. Some efforts to "move up" have succeeded; others have failed. There are instances of castes moving to new areas and thereby changing their names and status. When members of a caste acquire wealth or political leverage, they can sometimes use such resources to upgrade their caste.

3. *Castes relate to each other in mutually accepted hierarchical patterns.*

Frequently false. In any given locality some castes are likely to differ from other castes in their perceptions of what the "correct" local hierarchical patterns are. Disputes regarding the "correct" local hierarchy occur (and have occurred) frequently.

4. *Everyone called by the same caste name is related to everyone else called by that same caste name.*

False. Castes are assigned names by other castes living around them. Labeling coincidences frequently occur. Thus, there are numerous castes, some of whose members perform priestly functions, that are called brahmans by those around them. However, they are not related to all other castes that are called brahmans. There are castes that are called "patels," "deshmukhs," or "rajputs" (honorific civil titles) by those around them that are not related to all other castes called "patels," "deshmukhs," or "rajputs." There are numerous castes, some of whose members make (or did make) pots, that are called "potters" by those around them that are not related to all other castes called "potters." Every "gandhi" is not related to every other "gandhi."

5. *Castes are uniquely Hindu.*

False. In India castes exist among Christians, Jains, Sikhs, Buddhists, and Muslims. Frequently the rules about marrying within one's caste and avoiding interactions with other castes are as strict among Christians, Jains, etc. as they are among Hindus.

6. *Hinduism legitimizes preferential treatment according to caste.*

Occasionally false. In the idealized *varna* system, being born into a high *varna* was seen as a reward for virtue in a previous life. Being born in a low *varna* was seen as punishment for sins in a previous life. However, throughout India's history, movements have appeared within Hinduism criticizing preferential ranking and treatment according to caste (or *varna*). These movements have included Buddhism, Jainism, *bhakti* poets and saints, the Lingayats, Sikhism, and philosophers and intellectuals such as Mahatma Gandhi and Dr. B. R. Ambedkar, the architect of India's constitution.

7. *Castes have been abolished.*

False. India's constitution declares that "untouchability" is abolished and anyone discriminating against "untouchables" can be prosecuted. In addition, India's government now provides certain benefits to members of the "scheduled castes," "scheduled tribes," and "Other Backward Classes." However, India's constitution says nothing about abolishing castes. That would mean abolishing lineages of related families from among which parents select their children's marriage partners, and that would not be possible.

In the United States, discrimination on the grounds of race and gender has been declared illegal. However, the U.S. has no laws abolishing race or gender. Just as race and gender cannot be abolished by laws (although efforts can be made to end discrimination based on race and gender) so castes cannot be abolished by laws (although efforts can be made—and some are being made—to end discrimination based on caste).

Notes

1. For a review of U.S. textbook presentations of India, see Bonnie R. Crown, "Textbook Images of India," in Barbara J. Harrison (ed.), *Learning About India: An Annotated Guide for Nonspecialists* (Albany: Center for International Programs and Comparative Studies, New York State Education Department, 1977), 21–37.

2. Vedas Rgveda, *Rgveda Samhita,* with English translation by Svami Satya Prakash Sarasvati and Satyakam Vidyalankar, vol. XIII (New Delhi: Veda Pratishthana, 1987), 4483–4487.

3. Census of India, Paper No. 2 (New Delhi: Government of India, Manager of Publications, 1960).

4. For a thorough discussion of the Government of India's efforts to improve the lives of the lowest castes and poorest classes, see Marc Galanter, *Competing Equalities: Law and the Backward Classes in India* (Berkeley: University of California Press, 1984).

Bibliography

India (Republic), Backward Classes Commission. *Report of the Backward Classes Commission.* Vols. I–VII. New Delhi: Manager of Publications, 1980.

Manu. *The Laws of Manu.* Trans. by George Bühler. Vol. 25. Sacred Books of the East; reprint New York: Dover, 1969.

Article 18

The World & I, October 1996

Ancient Jewel

From early Greece to the modern civil rights movement, Indian thought and philosophy have had a wide-ranging influence on Western culture.

T. R. (Joe) Sundaram

T. R. (Joe) Sundaram is the owner of an engineering research firm in Columbia, Maryland, and has written extensively on Indian history, culture, and science.

The very word *India* conjures up exotic images in one's mind. Yet this name for the south Asian subcontinent is of Western making, mediated by the Persians and the Arabs. The name used in ancient Sanskrit texts is *Bharat* (for the land of Bharatha, a legendary king), which is also the official name of the modern republic. Other familiar Western words such as *Hindu, caste,* and *curry* are also totally foreign to India. The general knowledge that exists in the West about India, its early history, philosophy, and culture is, at best, superficial. Nevertheless, since it would be impossible in a brief article to do justice to even one of these topics, I shall provide a brief, accurate glimpse into each.

India covers about 1.2 million square miles and is home to a population of 895 million; in comparison, the United States covers 3.6 million square miles and has 258 million residents. Thus, the population density of India is nearly 10 times that of the United States. (The size of classical India—which includes modern-day India, Pakistan, Bangladesh, and parts of Afghanistan—is about two-thirds that of the continental United States.)

But statistics about India can be misleading. For example, while only about one-quarter of the population is "literate," able to read and write, this has to be viewed in light of the strong oral traditions present in India since antiquity. Therefore, while a "literate" American may often be unaware of the collective name of the first 10 amendments to the

Embassy of India

Continuous civilization: Excavations at Mohenjo-Daro and Harappa reveal well-planned towns and a sophisticated urban culture dating back to 2500 B.C.

U.S. Constitution, an "illiterate" Indian peasant would be aware of the history of his ancestors from antiquity to the present day.

Not only is India one of the oldest civilizations in the world, being more than 6,000 years old, but also it may be the oldest continuing civilization in existence; that is, one without any major "gaps" in its history. As the renowned historian A. L. Basham has pointed out,

> Until the advent of archeologists, the peasant of Egypt or Iraq had no knowledge of the culture of his forefathers, and it is doubtful whether his Greek counterpart had any but the vaguest ideas about the glory of Periclean Athens. In each case there had been an almost complete break with the past. On the other hand, the earliest Europeans to visit India found a

culture fully conscious of its own antiquity.

India is a land of many ancient "living" cities, such as, for example, Varanasi. Even at sites like Delhi, many successive cities have been built over thousands of years. Among old buried cities that have been unearthed in modern times by archaeologists are Mohenjo-Daro and Harappa.

Of these cities, the renowned archaeologist Sir John Marshall writes that they establish the existence

> in the fourth and third millennium B.C., of a highly developed city life; and the presence in many houses, of wells and bathrooms as well as an elaborate drainage system, betoken a social condition of the citizens at least equal to that found in Sumer, and su-

Crucible of Learning

- *India's may be the oldest continuing civilization in existence.*
- *To avoid misunderstanding India, it is essential to appreciate three central tenets of Indian thinking: assimilating ideas and experiences, a belief in cycles, and the coexistence of opposites.*
- *India has made numerous contributions to contemporary Western understanding of mathematics, science, and philosophy.*

perior to that prevailing in contemporary Babylonia and Egypt.

Thus, India was the "jewel of the world" long before the Greek and Roman civilizations.

Nor was classical India isolated from developing civilizations in other parts of the world. Clay seals from Mohenjo-Daro have been found in Babylonia and vice versa. Ancient Indian artifacts such as beads and bangles have been found in many parts of the Middle East and Africa. India and Indian culture were known to the Greeks even before the time of Alexander the Great. The Greek historian Herodotus wrote extensively about India during the sixth century B.C. Also, during this period many Greeks, including Pythagoras, are known to have traveled to India.

In Alexander the Great's campaign to conquer the world, his ultimate goal was India; he died without achieving that objective. When Seleucus Nicator, Alexander's successor, tried to follow in Alexander's footsteps, he was soundly defeated by Indian emperor Chandragupta Maurya. A peace treaty was signed between the two, and Seleucus sent an ambassador, Megasthenes, to the court of Chandragupta. Megasthenes sent glowing reports back to Greece about India, and he pronounced Indian culture to be equal or superior to his own, a high compliment indeed, since Greece was then near its zenith.

For the next 1,500 years or so, India—rich in material wealth, scientific knowledge, and spiritual wisdom—enjoyed the reputation of being at the pinnacle of world civilizations. Arab writers of the Middle Ages routinely referred to mathematics as *hindsat*, the "Indian science."

And as is well known now, it was Columbus' desire to reach India that led to the discovery of America. Indeed, the explorer died thinking that he had discovered a new sea route to India, while he had merely landed on a Caribbean island. Columbus' mistake also led to the mislabeling of the natives of the land as "Indians," a label that survived even after the mistake had been discovered.

The Upanishads

Indian philosophy is almost as old as Indian civilization, and its zenith was reached nearly 3,000 years ago with the compilation, by unknown sages, of 108 ancient philosophical texts known as the Upanishads. These texts reflect even older wisdom, which was passed down from generation to generation through oral transmission. A Western commentator has remarked that in the Upanishads the Indian mind moved from cosmology to psychology, and that while most other contemporary civilizations were still asking the question "What am I?" the Indian mind was already asking, "Who am I?"

India was the "jewel of the world" long before the Greek and Roman civilizations.

Sixth century B.C. was a period of great religious and philosophical upheaval in India. Hinduism was already an established, "old" religion, and reform movements were beginning to appear, such as one by a prince known as Siddhartha Gautama, who later came to be known as the Buddha. The religion that was founded based on his teachings spread not only throughout Asia but also to many parts of the world, including Greece, and it helped spread Indian culture in the process.

Embassy of India

A terra-cotta toy cow: Ancient Indian civilizations featured highly talented artisans and craftsmen.

When translations of the Upanishads first became available in the West in the nineteenth century, the impact on European philosophers such as Goethe and Schopenhauer and on American writers such as Emerson and Whitman was profound. "In the whole world," wrote Schopenhauer emotionally, "there is no study as beneficial and as elevating as the Upanishads." Emerson wrote poems based on the texts.

One of the principal underlying themes in the Upanishads is the quest for a "personal reality." This quest began with the conviction that the limitations of our sensory perceptions give us an imperfect model to comprehend the real world around us; this is known as the concept of *maya*. Since individual perceptions can be different, different people can also have different "realities."

For example, a happy event for one individual may be an unhappy one for another. Recognition and perfection of our personal reality is the quintessential goal of Indian philosophy and is also the basic principle behind yoga. Indeed, the literal meaning of the Sanskrit word *yoga* is "union," and the union that is sought is not with any external entity but with one's self. This is, of course, also the principal tenet of modern psychoanalysis.

From a Western perspective, to avoid misunderstanding India in general, and Indian philosophy in particular, it is essential to appreciate three central tenets of the Indian way of thinking. These are:

Assimilation. In the Indian way of thinking, new experiences and ideas never replace old ones but are simply absorbed into, and made a part of, old experiences. Although some have characterized such thinking as static, in reality such thinking is both dynamic and conservative, since old experiences are preserved and new experiences are continually accumulated.

Belief in cycles. Another central tenet of the Indian character is the belief that all changes in the world take place through cycles, there being cycles superimposed on other cycles, cycles within cycles, and so on. Inherent in the concept of cycles is alternation, and the Upanishads speak of the two alternating states of all things being "potentiality" and "expression."

Khorrum Omer/The World & I

Indian music has influenced Western artists, particularly in modern times. The beat of the tabla (above) can be heard in pop music ranging from the Beatles to Michael Jackson.

Acceptance of the coexistence of opposites. Early Western readers of the Upanishads were puzzled by the apparent inherent ability of the Indian mind to accept the coexistence of seemingly diametrically opposite concepts. Belief in, and acceptance of, contradictory ideas is a natural part of the Indian way of life, and the logical complement to

the tenets already mentioned. It is an indisputable fact that birth (creation) must necessarily be eventually followed by death (destruction). Creation and destruction are inseparable alternations. Even concepts such as "good" and "evil" are complementary, as each of us may have within us the most lofty and divine qualities and at the same time the basest qualities. We ourselves and the whole world can be whatever we want to make of them.

These three tenets are responsible for the amazing continuity of the Indian civilization, its reverence for the elderly, and the acceptance of the aging process without a morbid fear of death.

Ironically, the culture that taught of the need to renounce materialistic desires also produced some of the most pleasurable things in life. The intricacies and highly developed nature of Indian art, music, dance, and cuisine are examples. And the Kama Sutra is perhaps the oldest, and best known, manual on the pleasures of love and sex.

From Pythagoras to King

Throughout history, India's contributions to the Western world have been considerable, albeit during the Middle Ages they were often felt only indi-

Khorrum Omer/The World & I

Melodic inspiration: Performing traditional dance and music in Orissa.

rectly, having been mediated by the Middle Eastern cultures.

After the early contacts between Greece and India in the sixth and fifth centuries B.C., many concepts that had been in use in India centuries earlier made their appearance in Greek literature, although no source was ever acknowledged. For example, consider the so-called Pythagorean theorem of a right triangle and the Pythagorean school's theory of the "transmigration of souls"; the former was in use in India (for temple construction) centuries earlier, and the latter is merely "reincarnation," a concept of Vedic antiquity. There was also a flourishing trade between the Roman Empire and the kingdoms in southern India, through which not only Indian goods but also ideas made their journey westward.

During the Middle Ages, the Arabs translated many classical Indian works into Arabic, and the ideas contained in them eventually made their way to Europe. A principal mission of the "House of Wisdom" that was established by the caliph in Baghdad in the eighth century was the translation of Indian works.

Among the major Indian ideas that entered Europe through the Arabs are the mathematical concept of zero (for which there was no equivalent in Greek or Roman mathematics) and the modern numerical system we use today. Until the twelfth century, Europe was shackled by the unwieldy Roman numerals. The famous French mathematician Laplace has written: "It is India that gave us the ingenious method of expressing all numbers by ten symbols, each receiving a value of position as well as an absolute value, a profound and important idea which appears so simple to us now that we ignore its true merit."

India's contributions to other areas of science and mathematics were equally important. The seventh-century Syrian astronomer Severus Sebokht wrote that "the subtle theories" of Indian astronomers were "even more ingenious than those of the Greeks and the Babylonians."

The scientific approach permeated other aspects of Indian life as well. For example, classical Indian music has a highly mathematical structure, based on divisions of musical scales into tones and microtones.

In modern times, Indian music has had a considerable influence on Western music. Starting in the 1960s, the famous Indian sitar virtuoso Ravi Shankar popularized sitar music in the West, and now the melodic strains of the sitar, as well as the beat of the Indian drum known as tabla, can be heard in the works of many pop-music artists, ranging from the Beatles to Michael Jackson. The movies of the Indian filmmaker Satyajit Ray have also made a significant impact on the West.

Th contributions of many modern Indian scientists have been important to the overall development of Western science. The mathematical genius Srinivasa Ramanujan, who died in 1920, has been called "the greatest mathematician of the century" and "the man who knew infinity." The discovery by the Nobel Prize–winning Indian physicist Chandrasekhara Venkata Raman of the effect (which bears his name) by which light diffusing through a transparent material changes in wavelength has revolutionized laser technology. The theoretical predictions by the Nobel Prize-winning astrophysicist Subrahmanyan Chandrasekhar on the life and death of white-dwarf stars led to the concept of "black holes."

In the literary area, the poetry of Nobel laureate Rabindranath Tagore and the philosophical interpretations of the scholar (and a former president of India) Sarvepalli Radhakrishnan have inspired the West. Albert Einstein was one of the admirers of the former and corresponded with him on the meaning of "truth."

In terms of our daily dietary habits, many vegetables such as cucumber, eggplant, okra, squash, carrots, many types of beans, and lentils were first domesticated in India. Rice, sugarcane, and tea, as well as fruits such as bananas and oranges, are of Indian origin. The name orange is derived from the Sanskrit word narangi. Chicken and cattle were also first domesticated in India, albeit the latter for milk production and not for meat consumption. Cotton was first

For all India's material contributions to the world, it is its spiritual legacy that has had the widest impact.

domesticated in India. The process of dying fabrics also was invented in India. Indian fabrics (both cotton and silk) have been world renowned for their quality since antiquity. The game of chess was invented in India, and the name itself derives from the Sanskrit name Chaturanga.

India's most popular modern exports have been yoga and meditation. Hatha yoga, the exercise system that is a part of yoga, is now taught widely in America, in institutions ranging from colleges to hospitals. Many scientific studies on the beneficial effects of yoga practice are now under way. A similar state of affairs is true of Indian meditation techniques, which people under stress use for mental relaxation.

Finally the Rev. Martin Luther King, Jr., repeatedly acknowledged his debt to Mahatma Gandhi for the technique of nonviolent civil disobedience, which he used in the civil rights movement. For all India's material contributions to the world, it is its spiritual legacy that has had the widest impact. The ancient sages who wrote the Upanishads would have been pleased.

Additional Reading

A. L. Basham, *The Wonder That Was India*, Grove Press, New York, 1959.

———, *Ancient India: Land of Mystery*, Time-Life Books, Alexandria, Virginia, 1994.

Will Durant, *the Story of Civilization: Part I, Our Oriental Heritage*, Simon and Schuster, New York, 1954.

Article 19

The New York Times, May 11, 1998

Though Illegal, Child Marriage Is Popular in Part of India

By JOHN F. BURNS

MADHOGARH, India—If a wedding is supposed to fulfill a girl's earliest dreams, Hansa's in this tiny hamlet in Rajasthan State seemed more like a nightmare.

Early in the starlit evening, the smoke from the sacred fire began searing her eyes. The rituals pushed the ceremony deep into the night, in a crucible of heat and haze. After the first two hours, Hansa was quietly sobbing. By midnight, with Hindu priests leading Hansa and her new husband, Sitaram, in the climactic ritual, involving seven purifying circuits of the wood-burning fire, Hansa's wailing was drowning the rhythmic mantras of the priests.

"I want to go to bed," she cried. "Please, Mama, Papa. Let me sleep!"

Bafflement can only have worsened the ordeal, since Hansa, the youngest of six sisters being married in a joint ceremony to boys from other villages, was only 4. Her husband was 12.

Such weddings are common in Rajasthan, a state known for its desert landscapes, hilltop forts and maharajahs' palaces, as well as its persistence in feudal traditions, including child marriages, that have kept Rajasthani women among the most socially disadvantaged in India.

Indian law sets 18 as the minimum age for a woman to marry and 21 for a man. When India's Parliament adopted the Child Marriage Restraint Act in 1978, legislators hoped that the statute

would curb child marriages and the social ills they perpetuate.

Concern focused on an arc of populous northern states where child marriages are most deeply rooted: Rajasthan, Madhya Pradesh, Uttar Pradesh, Bihar and West Bengal, with a combined population of 420 million, about 40 percent of all Indians.

According to decades of research, child marriages contribute to virtually every social malaise that keeps India behind in women's rights. The problems include soaring birth rates, grinding poverty and malnutrition, high illiteracy and infant mortality and low life expectancy, especially among rural women.

In Rajasthan, a survey of more than 5,000 women conducted by the national Government in 1993 showed that 56 percent had married before they were 15. Of those, 3 percent married before they were 5 and another 14 percent before they were 10. Barely 18 percent were literate, and only 3 percent used any form of birth control other than sterilization.

Large families and poor health for children and mothers were among the results. The survey showed that of every 1,000 births, 73 children died in infancy and 103 before they reached age 5. Sixty-three percent of children under 4 were found to be severely undernourished. Average life expectancy for women was 58.

In every case, the figures were among the worst for any Indian state.

Social workers say many husbands tire of their marriages after the third, fourth or fifth child, when their wives are still teen-agers. Alcoholism contributes to domestic violence, with sometimes fatal beatings.

In some cases, husbands sell their wives, and even their unmarried daughters, as sexual partners to other men. In scores of cases every year, village women strike back by killing their husbands, only to face long terms in prison.

"It is a tragedy for these little flowers, and for our country, that they are snatched away into marriage before they even have a chance to bloom," said Mohini Giri, 60, chairwoman of the National Commission for Women, a Government agency established in the early 1990's that has become a driving force for raising awareness about the plight of women.

In Rajasthan, child marriages remain so popular that virtually every city, town and village takes on a holiday atmosphere ahead of the day set by astrologers for the annual Akha Teej festival—the moment judged most auspicious for marriages.

On the day of the festival, usually in late April or early May, roads are choked with tractors pulling trailers filled with gaily dressed wedding guests. On the outskirts of every settlement there are open-sided wedding tents in brightly patterned fabrics known as pandals.

Each year, formal warnings are posted outside state government offices stating that child marriages are illegal, but they have little impact.

Three strangers arriving at Madhogarh, the village where Hansa was married, had only to pull off the main road running south from the town of Alwar, 125 miles southwest of New Delhi, and drive a mile to spot a wedding pandal.

Villagers were unhesitating in their welcome, even when one of the visitors was introduced as a reporter.

"Of course, we know that marrying children is against the law, but it's only a paper law," said Govind Singh Patel, a village elder in the cattle-herding Gujjar community, which is among the poorest in Rajasthan and the most resistant to social change.

Sociologists say the Gujjars and similar groups trace the origin of child marriages to Muslim invasions that began more than 1,000 years ago. Legend has it that the invaders raped unmarried Hindu girls or carried them off as booty, prompting Hindu communities to marry off their daughters almost from birth to protect them.

Today, the stories have an echo in the local view that any girl reaching puberty without getting married will fall prey to sexual depredations, some from men imbued with the common belief that having sex with a "fresh" girl can cure syphilis, gonorrhea and other sexually transmitted diseases, including the virus that causes AIDS.

Tradition has been reinforced by necessity. In villages like Madhogarh, a family can be fortunate to have an annual income of $500, less in years when there is drought or flood. Securing early marriages for daughters can mean the difference between subsistence and hunger.

Traditionally, this has meant seeking grooms in neighboring villages, since the fear of inbreeding has generated a taboo against marriage between boys and girls from the same village.

Hansa's father, Shriram Gujjar, 40, works an acre of land beside the family's thatched home of mud and straw, with three cows to supplement his crop of mustard and wheat. Villagers say his troubles were compounded when his wife, Gyarsi Devi, gave birth to seven daughters but no sons.

But Mr. Gujjar's fortunes improved when a network of community contacts found husbands for the first six daughters, ranging in age from 4-year-old Hansa to Dohli, 14. An infant girl of 18 months, and another child on the way, will await another marriage ceremony in the future.

Mr. Gujjar, a fierce-looking man with a handlebar mustache and a luxuriant white turban, said he had borrowed about 60,000 rupees, about $1,500, to pay for the dowries required by the grooms' families and for the wedding festivities. While the loan will be a problem for years, he said, the weddings mean that he can now look forward to growing old without being trapped in penury by the need to support his daughters.

"Tonight I am a free man again!" he said, grinning as he circulated proudly among the scores of wedding guests seated cross-legged beneath the pandal.

After a moment to check the register in which cash donations from the guests were being entered, he returned, thrust his hands into the air in a gesture of release and added, "Thanks to God, the heaviest of my burdens has been lifted."

The brides spend the night of their weddings in their homes, then join their husband's families the next day for a journey to their in-laws' village.

In Hansa's case, this entailed traveling half a day by oxcart and bus to a village 25 miles away. After a few days there, tradition required that she return to her family in Madhogarh and await the onset of puberty, when another ceremony known as the Gauna would mark her fitness to join her husband's family.

But not all grooms' families are prepared to wait for puberty. In many cases documented by sociologists, girls as young as 6 or 7 have been taken away by their husbands' families to begin working as servants or field hands.

"With the addition of a girl to the household, the in-laws get a laborer, someone who will feed the cattle and clear the house, a servant who comes free of cost," said Ratan Katyani, a social worker in the Rajasthan city of Jaipur.

In 1994 the National Commission for Women urged the national Government, then headed by Prime Minister P. V. Narasimha Rao, to consolidate the separate marriage laws that exist for each of the major religious communities—Hindu, Muslim and Christian—and to include a provision requiring that all marriages be legally registered. That, the commission reasoned, could be used to bar under-age marriages.

But the Government rejected the proposal, as did its successor, headed by Prime Minister H. D. Deve Gowda, in 1996.

"It has been the consistent policy of the Government not to interfere in the personal laws of the distinct communities unless the initiative comes from the communities themselves," the Government said in a statement. "The Government is of the view that it is only through social and economic upliftment of these sections of the community that the practice can be eradicated."

Article 20

Ms., September/October 1998

In India, Men Challenge A Matrilineal Society

By Kavita Menon

Meghalaya, a district tucked away in the remote northeastern corner of India, is home to the Khasi, one of the largest surviving matrilineal societies in the world. In this hill tribe of nearly 650,000, descent is traced through the mother's line and women have an honored place in the society. Here, baby girls are quite welcome, and, some argue, even more highly prized than boys. Since the woman's family holds the cards when arranging a marriage, the question of dowry—paying a man's family for accepting the "burden" of a wife—would never even arise. No social stigma is attached to women, whether they choose to divorce, remarry, or stay single.

Anthropologists say the Khasi matriliny developed as a practical measure: the men were often away fighting in wars, so it made sense for the women to hold all that was precious to a family. Money, land, and lineage were passed from youngest daughter to youngest daughter, since it was expected she would be the last to marry.

But a growing number of Khasi men are not interested in the logic of the old system. They say the matriliny has empowered women at the expense of men and the community as a whole. The epicenter of this dissent is a tiny office in a pleasant residential neighborhood in Shillong, Meghalaya's capital city. This is where the Syngkhong Rympei Thymmai (SRT)—which means "organization

for the restructuring of Khasi society"—has its headquarters. The SRT, which was formed eight years ago and has a membership of about 400, including a handful of women, aims to dismantle the matriliny. It wants property to be equally divided among all the children in a family, and children to carry their father's surname.

> Men's roles are less of an issue in the villages where the traditional system still serves people's needs.

"We believe that children should take their father's name because 90 percent of the blood comes from the male," says Johnny Lyngdoh, an active member of the SRT. Many SRT members, like Lyngdoh, believe it is both a biological and a divine imperative for a man to be the head of the family. They argue that it is the man who plants the seed that becomes the child and that for this reason almost all children resemble their

fathers. For many, passing on their titles—or establishing ownership of their children and their wives—is even more important than the matter of inheritance.

SRT members believe the Khasi matriliny has favored the development of Khasi women to the detriment of the men. "Women have all the inheritance and therefore all the power," says SRT vice president Pilgrim Lakiang. "They are making more progress than the men and boys."

Women are indeed prominent in Khasi life. There are more Khasi women doctors than men, more Khasi women graduating from colleges, more Khasi women conducting business in the marketplaces. Women are now even seen in the traditional governing bodies, or durbars, which were once off-limits to them.

In contrast, Khasi men are said to be drinking too much, and are increasingly worried about losing their jobs, their land, and their women to migrants from West Bengal and Bangladesh. "Well-to-do families give their daughters to nontribals instead of to Khasi boys, and property and other assets that belong to the Khasi society pass to them," bemoans the writer of an article in one SRT booklet.

Others in the community, like Sweetymon Rynjah, a retired civil servant, believe the men have only themselves to blame for their problems. "The males have become degraded in the performance of their duties," she says. "They haven't understood their own customs. They have only read the customs of other people."

By "the customs of other people" Rynjah means Christianity. European missionaries introduced the Christian faith to Meghalaya in the 1800s. Many tribe members have since replaced Ka Iawbei, the original grandmother from whom all Khasi clans trace their ancestry, with the Father, Son, and Holy Ghost. About half the Khasi population is Christian, as against almost the entire SRT membership.

Donakor Shanpru is a single woman in her late forties whose family home is situated on the same block as the SRT headquarters. She lives in the home of her youngest aunt, who is also unmarried, with other members of the extended family including her father, a widower; a brother, who has left his wife and child; and two sisters (whose husbands have both left them, then tried to return, only to be turned away) and their children.

Shanpru, who teaches Khasi literature at one of Shillong's four women's colleges, has no patience with the SRT or its views. As far as she's concerned, it is a minority group expressing a minority position, and she's happy to let you know that its president has been kicked out of her house three times for "talking nonsense." For all the SRT's huffing and puffing, Shanpru says, Khasi men have been invested with important duties, as husbands, fathers, and maternal uncles in the clan. Maternal uncles in particular exercise a lot of clout—though the youngest daughter holds the purse strings and her opinions matter, it is typically the oldest maternal

uncle who decides when and how to spend the clan's money.

But while the SRT positions are seen as extremist by some, they do fit into a larger debate within the society and attract some unexpected sympathizers. Patricia Mukhim, a journalist from Shillong, agrees to some extent with what the SRT is saying. She believes that giving boys an equal share of the family property will boost their self-esteem and encourage them to be more responsible, industrious husbands and citizens. Mukhim also blames the matriliny for making Khasi marriages "very brittle." Divorce has become too easy, she says, because husbands and wives can always return to their respective clans.

Where Mukhim disagrees with the SRT is in the speed of change. "We can't turn the system inside out so suddenly," she says. But change must come, she feels, since the problems that the men are facing affect everybody in the end.

A traditional society is being pressured to adjust to a modern world that is increasingly urban, and one in which families are smaller and more distant. Although the men's movement and the anxiety it expresses are city-based—men's roles are less of an issue in the villages where the traditional system still serves people's needs—the debate is widespread. The extent of it was made clear recently when the Khasi Social Custom of Lineage Bill, which seeks to codify Khasi customary law, and maintain matriliny, was put on hold.

The bill stalled following disagreements voiced by various factions that

don't necessarily hold to the old way—many of the most respected Khasi intellectuals already use the clan title of their fathers, according to *Grassroots Options*, a magazine that covers the Indian northeast. If the bill is passed, those who don't adhere to all the traditions would have to relinquish Khasi status—and the privileges that go with it. Minorities in India are entitled to special benefits, including quotas for places in universities and jobs in the government.

Even though the matriliny has been the norm in Khasi society, that doesn't mean there are no gendered roles. In one traditional Khasi dance, for instance, the women are required to creep slowly forward by wriggling their toes like inchworms. They move in large groups, chins upturned and eyes downcast, looking very regal in their elaborate headdresses and long gowns. The role of the men is to "protect" the women—and they look like they're having great fun galloping, skipping, and spinning in circles around the women, while madly waving long, feathered whisks.

In the dance, the women are locked into the lines and circles assigned them, a reminder that in addition to being doctors and teachers and shopkeepers, they are still expected to be dutiful daughters, good mothers, and patient wives. And, for all the SRT members' talk of being downtrodden, men in a traditional Khasi home are still served the top of the rice bowl as a blessing on the family—and they very rarely cook or clean.

Kavita Menon, a writer, works at the Committee to Protect Journalists, in New York City.

Article 21

The Christian Science Monitor, May 13, 1998

India's Parsi community may have to change customs in order to grow.

Oldest Prophetic Religion Struggles For Survival

By John Zubrzycki

Special to The Christian Science Monitor

BOMBAY

DEEP in the heart of downtown Bombay, a century-old blue-granite building stands like a silent sentinel to an ancient community in rapid decline. The dilapidated building houses the Parsi Lying-in Hospital, established in 1893 as a maternity unit for the city's once-thriving Parsi community. Built to accommodate 40 beds, its wards are almost empty today. "We get only four or five patients a month," says Zarin Langdana, the doctor-in-charge. "And most of them are not Parsis."

As India's population expands steadily, the country's Parsi community faces extinction. Emigration, falling birthrates, the growing tendency to marry outside the community, and an injunction against accepting converts is threatening to erase Zoroastrianism, the world's oldest prophetic religion, and its followers from the map of India. "We are an endangered species, just like the tiger and the lion," says Jamshed Guzdar, chairman of the Parsi Panchayat, or council.

A recent demographic study predicts that by 2021, when the population of India will be 1.2 billion, the number of Parsis will drop from their current level of 60,000 to just 21,000.

Bombay legacy

Parsis once dominated Bombay's commercial life. Almost every major municipal building built in the 19th century had the bust or statue of a Parsi benefactor perched on a pedestal outside. Parsis started the city's first hospital, university, and municipal corporation. The city's best-known landmark is probably the Taj hotel, built by Jamshetji Nusserwanji Tata in 1903 after he was refused entry into the exclusive Green's Hotel because he was a native.

Zoroastrian activist Smiti Crishna says, 'The religion has to undergo a change in order to protect and propagate the community.'

Mr. Jamshetji's great-grandson Ratan controls India's largest industrial conglomerate, the Tata group. "Now the Parsi population's outlook has changed," laments Mr. Guzdar. "There is on urge to step forward and create for themselves high positions in business and industry. Now they find they cannot meet the competition."

For most communities, the prospect of extinction would unite members, but it has divided the Parsis. In Bombay, the world's Parsi "capital," the gulf between those who refuse to question orthodox Zoroastrianism and those clamoring for reform is breaking apart a once close-knit community.

Perhaps the most divisive issue is whether the children of a Parsi woman who marries outside the community can be considered Zoroastrian. "It's a very emotional issue," says Jehangir Patel, editor of the monthly magazine Parsiana. "As the community gets smaller, your chances of finding a Parsi spouse to your liking are dwindling. More and more families are being touched by this problem."

Questioning Zoroastrianism

With almost 1 in 4 women marrying outside the community and almost as many not marrying at all, the mixed-marriage bias is being challenged. "People are questioning the faith much more," says Smiti Crishna, vice chairperson of the Association of Intermarried Zoroastrians. "The religion has to

Persian Roots of Zoroastrian Faith

Area of ancient Persia

BOMBAY

The Zoroastrian religion was expounded sometime before 600 BC by the ancient Persian prophet, Zarathustra, who lived in what is now eastern Iran. Some scholars, however, say the prophet, whose name means "rich in camels," dates back as far as 1200 BC.

Central to the religion is a concept of righteousness or natural law, the notion of a supreme all-knowing and benign God, and the rejection of polytheism. The word Parsi is thought to be derived from Fars, the name of the port in Persia from which the Parsis fled in the 10th century AD to protect their religion from Islamic persecution.

The first Parsi settlers soon arrived on the coast of Gujarat, taking with them the sacred fire that, according to the legend, has burned continuously in their temples ever since. Like earth and water, fire is sacred to the Zoroastrians and symbolizes *asha,* the concept of truth, order, and righteousness.

When Bombay became a trading center under the British in the 17th century, the Parsis moved to the city in large numbers, quickly establishing a reputation for hard work, entrepreneurship, and honesty. Their ability to adapt to Western ways made them into a colonial elite, and they flourished under British patronage. While the Parsis are unique to India and remain the largest contingent of the Zoroastrians today, pockets of followers remain in Iran as well as in other parts of Asia, the United States, and Canada. —*J.Z.*

undergo a change in order to protect and propagate the community."

A member of the wealthy Godrej family of Parsi industrialists, Ms. Crishna broke the taboo on intermarriages when she wed a Christian businessman. According to the orthodox keepers of the faith, her two daughters cannot undergo a *navjote,* or baptism ceremony, or enter a Zoroastrian fire temple. "Women like us are ostracized," Crishna says. "Why should people look down on us when there is no injunction against intermarriage in our holy books?"

That's wrong, retorts Dastur Firoze Kotwal, one of the religion's eight high priests, who leafs through a religious text in his south Bombay flat. According to Dastur Kotwal, the Zoroastrian scriptures outlaw all intermarriages. He also dismisses demands that the ban on conversions be lifted to swell the community's numbers, a stand that has put him at loggerheads with the normally conservative Parsi Panchayat. "Zarathustra never said you can't convert. If you don't allow conversions, how does the community grow?" asks Guzdar of the Parsi Panchayat.

> Dastur Firoze Kotwal, a Parsi high priest, dismisses demands that a ban on conversions be lifted to swell the community's numbers.

Alarmed by the steady demographic decline of the Parsi population, Guzdar persuaded the Panchayat to sponsor the third child of every Parsi couple to encourage larger families. The Panchayat now looks after the material and educational needs of 45 children. "I thought to myself, I cannot let my community perish," Guzdar says. "I hope that by doing something like this, the population will increase."

A successful businessman who established India's first air freight business in the 1940s, Guzdar plans to set up a venture-capital fund to encourage young Parsi entrepreneurs to start businesses in India rather than moving abroad.

The disappearance of the Parsis would not just be a loss for Bombay. This small but talented community has produced composers like Zubin Mehta, novelists like Rohiton Mistry, and the late rock star Freddie Mercury, the former front man of the band Queen. "Last year when I was asked to become the chairman of the National Foundation for Social Affairs and Family Planning, I was told, 'Do all you can to control India's population but make sure the Parsis increase in number,'" chuckles Guzdar.

Article 22

The World & I, October 1996

A Celluloid Hall of Mirrors

*The world's largest film industry churns out wildly popular music
and dance extravaganzas that have roots deep in Indian culture,
but a number of films reflect more complex realities.*

Somi Roy

Somi Roy is a film curator based in New York City. His articles have appeared in a number of national magazines, including Asian Art, Artforum, *and* Wide Angle.

As filmmakers in countries from France to Japan lament that their country's top-grossing films come from Hollywood, the Indian film industry is more than holding its own. Indeed, it might be ventured that within India itself, the popular Indian film, along with its inescapable music, is perhaps the single most important modern force—cricket being a distant second—that has held together this incredibly diverse nation of 850 million people with well over 200 languages.

Remarkably independent of Hollywood and other major film centers, the popular Indian film has its own body of cinematic conventions and stylistic signatures. If one has seen the spectacular song-and-dance melodrama that is the run-of-the-mill Indian film, one might wonder why these films have such tremendous appeal, not only in India but throughout the geographic area that stretches from Morocco to Indonesia.

To begin with, it is all rather awe-inspiring and numbing. Credits and title music blast your eyes and ears. The hero takes on the food hoarder, dances with the heroine on a hilltop, engages a gang of hooligans in a choreographed fight. There is applause, wolf whistles, singing, and dancing in the aisles. Outside, three-story-high movie posters with film stars painted in poisonous green, neon blue, and lurid pink scream: "Every Sinner Has to Pay the Price!" "A Saga of Love, Hate, and Desire!" and "He Sings, He Dances, He Kills, Too!"

The typical film is a star-studded affair with household names like Amitabh Bachhan, Sanjay Dutt, Sridevi, and Madhuri Dixit. (Some stars, like Bachhan and Rajesh Khanna, are so popular they are elected to political office.)

Structurally, the usual popular film essentially strings together six or seven extended sequences of song and dance with bits of melodramatic plot sandwiched between. Emphasis is not on the linear unfolding of a story line (unlike the popular films of the West, with their novelistic narrative); plots are interrupted by lengthy music, dance, fight, or comedy sequences that may have nothing to do with the plot. In a typically three-hour film, the plot may be introduced at the beginning but may not reappear until after the intermission.

accounts for the immense popularity of these films in India, but it also may explain their appeal in countries that have similarly ancient yet still vital folk cultures.

Stories and themes are repeated in film after film: good triumphing over evil, the struggle of the poor, the sins of the big city, the destruction of family. Actors declaim stylized dialogue underscored by near-constant background music. The result is a heady mixture of fantasy and exaggerated melodrama that packs in the crowds. In India, every showing of these popular-audience films attracts throngs like *Independence Day* did at its U.S. opening, even though in large cities theaters seat several thousand. The biggest blockbuster, *Sholay* (1975), ran for five years in one Bombay theater alone.

While the popular Indian film con-

Reflections in Cinema

- Most popular Indian films are music and dance extravaganzas with roots in ancient traditions.
- "All-India" films, made to reach the broadest audience, are a force for cultural and linguistic unity.
- Since the late 1960s, filmmakers of the New Indian Cinema have striven to reflect daily life realistically and to create serious art films.

The roots of this burlesquelike approach lie in traditions of folk theater and performance that stretch back 2,000 years, traditions that developed from dances performed at religious festivals. The fact that popular Indian cinema uses these as the basis of its film grammar

sists of musical extravaganzas, the film industry also produces other kinds by internationally recognized artists like Satyajit Ray, who was awarded a Lifetime Achievement Oscar in 1992 for masterpieces such as *Pather Panchali* (1955) and *Jana Aranya* (1975). Directors including Ray, Shyam Benegal, and Adoor Gopalakrishnan make independent films that, like the independent "art films" in the United States, are seen by smaller, more discriminating audiences.

Films by these independent directors, being the work of individualistic artists, don't fall into easily identifiable genres. But popular Indian cinema, manufactured as commercial entertainment, has enthroned a handful of reigning genres.

This was true from the beginning. Dadasaheb Phalke, an amateur magician and theater buff, made *Raja Harishchandra,* the first Indian feature, in 1912. Released to an enthusiastic audience the following year, it cannily took a story from Indian mythology well known to the national collective mind. It was the beginning of a hardy and perennially popular genre of Indian cinema: the mythological film—usually based on episodes from religious epics such as the Ramayana and the Mahabharata—and its cousin the devotional film, about the lives of Indian saints.

Historical films about familiar figures, like *Razia Begum* (1924), soon followed. And as film came to India at a time when the country was poised to embark on major social and political reforms, a more realistic genre called the social film emerged, with its cautious critiques of social evils like dowries and polygamy.

Thus, Indian cinema was truly Indian from the start. The mythological, devotional, historical, and social genres still survive, sometimes in new, surprising mutations.

In fashioning their films, Indian filmmakers were basically exercising good business sense. The industry is big business: About $270 million is invested in films annually. It is the largest film industry in the world (almost three times bigger than that of Hollywood), producing over 800 films on average every year. The budget of a film usually runs to about 30 million rupees, or about $1 million.

A major film issues only 100 to 150 prints—compared with Hollywood's 3,000 or so for a major release—since there are only about 13,000 cinemas in India, one-third of which are touring cinemas that screen movies in outdoor tents. Still, five billion tickets are sold every year to 300 million moviegoers. Tickets are relatively cheap—a ticket in an air-conditioned Bombay theater may cost as much as 20 rupees, about 80 cents, and in a touring cinema it may be as little as 2 rupees, less than a dime.

Superstar actresses work on up to six films a day, in six different shifts, shuttling from one studio to another.

The all-India film, also called the Hindi film, is made in Bombay, a city the size of New York, and is seen pretty much throughout India. It also receives international distribution to the geographic swath mentioned earlier. Yet, in this country of so many different languages and dialects, there are in addition five major film production centers in five different states, each making films in one of five major languages: Tamil, Malayalam, Telugu, Bengali, and Kannada. These generally do not receive international distribution. The all-India film and the five others all follow the formulaic approach outlined above, though some younger regional filmmakers have forsaken formulas for more authentic reflections of local life.

As for the stars, many sign on for up to 20 films at once. Superstar actresses like Sridevi work on up to six films a day, in six different shifts, shuttling from one studio to another—a practice that has earned them the name "taxi stars." Over 600 film magazines, with names like *Stardust* and *Film fare,* breathlessly cover the lives and careers of these stars for hungry fans.

Characteristics and Impact

Because it is such big business, the popular Indian film has evolved several characteristic features. It is these features—formulaic filmmaking (collo-quially referred to as *masala* filmmaking, a term derived from the mix of spices that go into an Indian curry), melodrama, nonspecificity as to regional cultures, nonsectarianism, and music and dance—that have made the film industry so powerful in India today.

The perfunctory attention often paid to the script and the resultant formulaic quality of the films is very much a response to India's postindependence economic policies, which financed social programs for education, industry, and agriculture with high taxes and tight controls on industry. As much as 60 percent of all box-office receipts went into taxes of one sort or another. At the time there was no credit financing and, under these heavy taxation rates, producers were forced to turn to distributors to finance films. They would sell distributors regional rights to films, but the distributors in turn demanded tried-and-true formula films: major stars, six dances, seven songs, and so on. Popular stars began working in several films at once, script values began to suffer, and the melodramatic formula film became ascendant. The resulting masala film made for high entertainment values and reliable escapist fare for the average audience.

What the Indian film provides without parallel are Indian dreams based on Indian situations acted out by Indian character archetypes.

('Twas not ever thus. During the time when India was struggling to shake off the British, many Indians felt it was vital to modernize. In the 1930s and '40s filmmakers made movies that, though still melodramatic, took up extremely powerful social themes with solid scripts and strong story lines. Classics such as *Achhut Kanya* (1936) and

Duniya na Mane (1937) may have had some elements of song and dance, but the result was not the pastiche that is so prevalent today.)

Melodrama itself—with its sensational, emotionally overwrought, romantic, and violent character—is eminently suited to being the prime form for popular entertainment everywhere. The average Hollywood product (especially thrillers), or any soap opera worth its salt in tears, provides as much. What the Indian film provides without parallel are Indian dreams based on Indian situations acted out by Indian character archetypes. In a popular film such as Maui Rathnam's *Bombay* (1994), a Hindu boy and a Muslim girl who fall in love are forced to escape their village for the relative secular anonymity and safety of Bombay, which later explodes in religious riots. The familiar Indian archetypes—such as, in this film, young star-crossed lovers, complaining in-laws, a family ruptured by an intolerant and violent society, and the contrast of intimate village life with the anonymous and decadent city—make it easy for a broad spectrum of people to identify with the characters and situations.

Because the Indian film is designed to attract the largest number of viewers, and mainly in towns and cities, the all-India film shows no regional specificity. Its story, sets, costumes, and language are devoid of the cultural distinctions of the different linguistic and ethnic regions—say Bengal or Kerala—that actually make up the country, although all these aspects in fact tend to be dominated by the numerically dominant culture of northern India. Though generally called the Hindi film, the all-India is actually in Hindustani, a vernacular mix of Hindi and Urdu, effectively making this north Indian hybrid the country's lingua franca. As this film is seen pretty much all over India, it contributes to the linguistic unification of the country.

The fact that the all-India film is made for a national market has resulted in the espousal, in these films, of a near nonsectarianism. This creates a sort of demilitarized zone in a country where religion is extremely important and often divisive. Most all-India films are made by Hindus, but apart from the religious themes of mythologicals, most of the films' charac-

ters have only a broad identification with Hinduism, the overwhelmingly predominant religion. Many of these films—such as *Amar, Akbar, Anthony* (1977), about three brothers separated as children to be brought up as a Hindu, a Muslim, and a Christian, making the point that we are all brothers under the skin—espouse communal and religious harmony. This is done to give these films the widest possible reach and ensure a stable environment for business, and it effectively serves as a unifying cultural force.

Music often stands in for the kiss in a society where public displays of intimacy are frowned upon.

The use of music and dance is perhaps the most distinctive feature of the Indian film. Creating songs that dominate the music industry, the film industry is like Hollywood and the rock music industry rolled into one huge behemoth. Because of the absence of differentiation between the two industries, the signing up of singing stars like Lata Mangeshkar and Asha Bhosle is essential to ensure investment in a film. The soundtrack, often released before the film itself, determines to a great extent the film's performance at the box office.

The songs are composed by hot music directors such as A. R. Rahman and Rahul Dev Burman, and are set to lyrics by some of the country's finest poets, such as Kaifi Azmi and Gulzar. The very enjoyment of music and dance in an Indian film is often based on the use of classical Indian dance, traditionally performed in temples or royal courts (where they could not be seen very well by the common people), or the ring of familiarity of a raga-based song. In a masala film today, sitars, synthesizers, pianos, and violins provide a score that moves effortlessly from classical Indian ragas to Mozart to hip-hop and rap mu-

sic. Every taste is catered to, while creating a bridge between East and West, and between traditional and contemporary cultures.

Music in Indian cinema not only entertains the audience but establishes dramatic development, emotional continuity and emphasis—and often stands in for the kiss in a society where public displays of intimacy are frowned upon. Ironically, to skirt an actual ban on kissing, many Indian films evolved extended "wetsari" sequences and the like, which are infinitely more suggestive. And now that the ban has been revoked, these sequences still persist, as they have become established conventions.

When it comes to using songs to advance plots, director S.S. Vasan's 1948 *Chandralekha,* though it used Busby Berkeley-inspired choreography, actually preceded Hollywood's use of songs in this way, says noted American critic Elliott Stein. When filmmaker Ketan Mehta made his version of *Madame Bovary*—*Maya Memsahib* (1992)—without songs for non-Indian audiences, a noted critic mused that it no longer had a place for the eyes and ears to rest.

Mirrors Trick and True

Spectacle, music, melodrama, romance, and action go only a little way in explaining the allure of the Indian film, however. A typical Hollywood studio product provides as much.

More to the point, perhaps, popular Indian films tell stories of good triumphing over evil in a distinctly Indian context. Mythological works, like the extra-ordinarily successful *Ramayana* and *Mahabharata* epics on television in recent years, are direct extensions of the ritualistic oral tradition of Hinduism into the medium of the moving picture. But even an average musical melodrama unconsciously but powerfully reflects a basic Indian reality, however distorted. Manufactured as commercial entertainment and based on tried-and-true formulas, the Indian film is inevitably the product of contemporary Indian psyches and is a psychological index of a society.

Ray opened the eyes of young aspiring filmmakers in India to films that were true to an Indian reality and possessed artistic integrity.

Often what is portrayed, however, is a reflection of what simmers beneath the surface. The Indian screen, for instance, often depicts romantic love and alliances, whereas in real life, society severely restricts romantic behavior and most marriages are arranged. In this case film does not so much mirror reality as make an inverse reflection of Indians' desires.

But some films explore both reality and desire quite penetratingly. It is in the internationally better-known cinema of artists like Satyajit Ray, Ritwik Ghatak, and Shyam Benegal that we see a conscious exploration of these psychological states and social phenomena. Ray's *Devi* (1960), for example, is a richly perceptive and nuanced Freudian tragedy about a wealthy Hindu man who begins to perceive his young daughter-in-law as the incarnation of a goddess. The film was controversial when it first came out because of its depiction of Hinduism and the disturbing effect it can have on individual lives. The man "sublimates" his sexual attraction to his daughter-in-law by venerating her as a deity; the girl takes part in his religious rituals, begins to hallucinate, and winds up losing her mind—a pointed commentary on how Indian women are made to sacrifice themselves uselessly for religious obsessions.

Starting with his famous Apu Trilogy, Ray opened the eyes of young aspiring filmmakers in India to films that were true to an Indian reality and possessed remarkable artistic integrity. For his films, Ray dug deep into the immense riches of Bengali literature, Indian classical music, and international cinema—in particular post–World War II Italian Neo-Realism's humanism, style, and use of outdoor locations, amateur actors, and inexpensive technology. (Other international influences were undoubtedly the lyric realism of Jean Renoir and John Ford's use of sound and straightforward, simple, but well-composed camera angles.)

Yet Ray's films appeal basically to only the urban elite of India. When the commercial film industry was attacked by Ray's disciples for creating trash, the commercial producers replied that they felt Ray's truthful depiction of the realities of Indian society, as in his celebrated *Pather Panchali,* only provided despair for the average filmgoer, who actually needed escapist entertainment.

It was in reaction against popular cinema's escapism and portrayal of a fictional India that this new generation of filmmakers, inspired by Ray, sought to deal directly with the realities of modern India. These filmmakers of the New Indian Cinema strove to portray recognizable but distinctly individual characters with inner complexities in situations close to life. Some chose to work in regional Indian cinema to create films true to specific locales, like Adoor Gopalakrishnan in his *Elippathayyam* (1981), set in his native Kerala. Others, like Shyam Benegal, chose a sort of middle way, making classics such as *Bhumika* (1977) in Hindi—the language of popular film—retaining and reworking the familiar elements of song and dance. The difference is that for once there is a conscious effort to weave these elements into the story and characters of the film. And in a third skein, filmmakers like Mani Kaul, with films such as *Siddeshwari* (1986), and Kumar Shahani, whose latest film is *Bhavantaran* (1996), display a consummate experimental style.

The New Indian Cinema, which started in the late 1960s, is basically the cinema of the urban, educated baby boomers of India. Their films, both in form and content, tend to be politically progressive, interpreting and reflecting the world around them through the eyes of the modern Indian. The social critiques in these films—of, say, lingering feudal values or the oppressed status of women—reflect the modernizing ideology of post-independence India. Because many of these filmmakers such as Benegal incorporate elements from the popular cinema, it is no surprise that many of their films get funding from India's state film corporation or state television.

An emerging alternative, especially for New Indian Cinema filmmakers who are based abroad or have been educated in the West, is to secure international financing from Europe, Britain, the United States, or even Japan, to produce films that appeal not only to their traditional urban constituency in India but also to the international art film market.

As might be expected, many of these international coproductions have favored certain subjects and treatments of Indian themes that would be easily recognizable as such by an international audience. The fact that certain images of India are widely prevalent in the West—including poverty, exoticism, and the caste system—was probably not lost on the international financers of Mira Nair's *Salaam Bombay* (1988), about street children, or *Kama Sutra,* her forthcoming erotic fantasy, or Shekar Kapur's *Bandit Queen* (1994), which explores the exploitation of a low-caste woman. The Merchant Ivory team built its early career on the clash of Eastern and Western worlds in *Shakespeare Wallah* (1965), a film about a traveling English theater troupe in India, and *The Guru* (1969), a satire about Westerners coming to India—a subject that was given an updated spin in Pradip Krishen's *Electric Moon* (1992).

The Indian film industry today is an immensely and increasingly varied world, with filmmakers such as Maui Rathnam and Ketan Mehta at one end of the spectrum, creatively using hallowed conventions of the popular cinema while dealing with actual contemporary political situations (as in Rathnam's *Bombay),* and at the opposite end, thinkers in film like Maui Kaul extending and recreating the boundaries of film. A broad range of styles, conventions, and schools of realism and experimentation now exist, together with the glitter and gloss of the ever-popular musical melodramas, to make up the great Indian film bazaar.

Article 23

The Economist, May 27, 2000

The wiring of India

India's cable-television industry has thrived on chaos.
Now it needs order if it is to become that country's main link to the Internet

DELHI AND MUMBAI

CABLE television is a rough business in India. Earlier this month, the news that a gang in the southern state of Kerala had set fire to the office of a cable operator, immolating two of its employees, rated a one-sentence item in the national press. That sort of thing sits ill with India's vision of itself as a knowledge-industry superpower, which expects cable to deliver much of the data and entertainment needed to justify that ambition. When international investors, such as Intel, are putting money behind the vision, the murder, piracy and cable-cutting that characterise the industry have become positive embarrassments.

Up to now, chaos has had its virtues. The land of the "licence raj" somehow forgot to regulate cable. Anybody could run wires to a few hundred houses, beam programmes and collect money. The result was a boom. Like most Indian statistics, measures of the cable industry's size are disputed, but it is certainly big. The Cable Operators Federation claims to represent 60,000–70,000 firms; others say consolidation has cut that number to around 30,000. By some estimates, India has more cable connections (about 30m) than telephone lines (about 20m).

Now big firms are beginning to attach fibre-optic wires to this snarl, to give households and businesses broadband Internet connections. And India's disparate cable operators are being pulled together into alliances which are more likely to have the money and organisation to equip the country with an up-to-date communications infrastructure. Credit Lyonnais Securities Asia reckons that the number of Internet users in India will rise 15–20-fold by 2004 to 30m, fewer than in China but many more than in any other mainland Asian country. And the key driver after 2001, the brokerage firm predicts, will be cable television.

The incentive will be the difficulty of making money from cable television as it is now structured. At present, the cable industry has the pile-'em-high, sell-'em-cheap approach of down-at-heel discount shops. Subscribers get as many as 75 channels, with new ones coming all the time (recently, HBO, an American movie channel). But, since India lacks set-top boxes that can direct programmes to subscribers who are willing to pay extra for them, most households pay a flat fee of only around 100–150 rupees ($2.30–3.40) a month for their televisual cornucopia.

In this cut-throat market, cable operators grumble that customers demand new channels but refuse to pay more for them. Broadcasters say the operators cheat by drastically understating their subscriber numbers. Multi-systems operators (MSOs), middlemen who take signals from broadcasters and pass them on to local operators, complain that neither pays them adequately. The local operators are probably the best off. They keep nearly 90% of the 40 billion-42 billion rupees of subscription revenue that they collect annually, reckons Bharat Parekh, an analyst at DSP Mer-

rill Lynch in Mumbai. MSOs get 5–6%, which leaves 4–5% for broadcasters.

Not surprisingly, the MSOs are leading the drive to send more expensive services down the cable—and they want to claim a larger share for themselves. Two prerequisites are needed if they are to succeed: the communications infrastructure must improve, and the gaggle of local operators must be wielded into obedient alliances.

Order from chaos

The need for better communications infrastructure, and not just for cable, was noted this month by the National Association of Software and Service Companies (NASSCOM), which launched "operation bandwidth", a campaign to boost Internet bandwidth 80-fold by 2003, and to remove regulatory obstacles, such as a 49% cap on foreign ownership of telecoms ventures and a ban on Internet telephony. It has the backing of many large companies, foreign and domestic. Enron, an American energy firm, wants to install at least ten gigabits of bandwidth among seven cities within the next 18 months, by itself about a tenth of NASSCOM's bandwidth target. Hughes Tele.com, a joint venture that is part-owned by General Motors, plans to spend $750m on a fibre-optic network for business communications in Maharashtra and Goa: it already offers basic telephone service there. Last week Reliance Industries, India's biggest private industrial company, offered to raise its stake in BSES, a big power producer and distributor, from 15% to 35%: BSES's fibre-optic network in Mumbai seems to be part of the attraction.

As for the local cable operators, since the mid-1990s, MSOs such as IN Cable-Net, owned by the Indo-European Hinduja family, and SitiCable, part of Zee Telefilms, India's biggest private broadcaster, have been enlisting thousands, supplying them with equipment and signals and sharing their revenues. Now they are trying to turn these ramshackle federations into alliances bound together with new broadband cable that can carry two-way traffic and deliver sports, movies, online shopping and other luxuries to consumers who are willing to pay extra for them.

Thus the Hindujas' IN CableNet plans to invest up to $500m of fresh money in upgrading cable networks in 75–100 cities, and buying content to take advantage of them. It has moved fastest in Mumbai, where it has laid 150 km of fibre-optic cable and is now offering speedy Internet access to the first of its 1.9m customers in the city. Intel, the biggest chip maker, is impressed enough to have invested $49m, valuing IN CableNet at $1.5 billion. SitiCable plans to offer Internet access over cable in a dozen cities within the next six months and is pondering ways to raise the money. It claims to be worth $3.5 billion.

Such lofty valuations are based in part on the assumption that the MSOs can whip local cable operators into line. They have had some success. Thus, in Mumbai, the Hindujas have an alliance of some 900 local operators who have become little more than agents, collecting the basic subscription fees and handling customers' problems. Such practices as cable-cutting and amplifier stealing have "stopped completely", says Dileep Gupte, who runs the company's broadband services. To build such alliances, MSOs are carrying the cost of upgrading the networks, sometimes including the last mile, which the cable operators usually control.

But plenty of operators retain their wild ways. Earlier this month Bhopal, capital of the state of Madhya Pradesh, lost cable service for a week because of a dispute between an operator affiliated

Wedding bliss

WHEN asked to find a decent caterer for a friend's wedding last December, Krishna Allavura thought he would see what he could find on the Internet. As one of India's first information-technology lawyers, he wanted to avoid the usual resort of asking his mother for suggestions. He failed, but his search made the 28-year-old Mumbai lawyer realise the opportunity that lay in the $11 billion that Indians spend annually on weddings. Mr Allavura left his job to set up shaadis.com (*shaadis* is Hindi for weddings), which was launched last month.

Other Internet sites already compete with the advertisements that Indian families place in the newspapers, requesting fair-skinned, slender, domesticated, convent-educated Brahmin girls in their early 20s for their 30-something, tall engineer sons with a five-figure salary. Shaadis.com will offer more than match-making. It has a tie-up with ETC Highlight, an event-management company that specialises in arranging weddings, including theme weddings (a Thai temple, a rural village) that upper-middle-class Indians like. Because Indian couples are used to getting dozens of identical presents from their hundreds of guests, Mr Allavura also offers a gift registry. That, and links to suppliers of wedding services, should bring in money from commissions paid by companies linked to the site.

Mr Allavura has already stumbled against many of the obstacles that beleaguer so many Indian Internet entrepreneurs. Lack of bandwidth has forced the company to abandon its plans to carry on its site videos of weddings that it has organised. Precedents in America are not promising: even after five years in business, most American online wedding-service providers are still losing money. But Indians may soon have a special reason for turning to an online wedding site: the company wants to do a deal with one of the large portals through which the Indian diaspora looks for partners back home.

Meanwhile, Mr Allavura's toughest competition is likely to come from the formidable ranks of Indian mothers, unwilling to give up their traditional role. Until Indians learn to look online, the fastest way to find a wedding caterer may still be to ask Mum.

with Siticable and a local MSO. The police brokered a truce. Roop Sharma, president of the Cable Operators Federation, scoffs that an MSO is "just a signal provider". She sees little reason for her constituents to upgrade their networks: "Why should cable operators spend when consumers only give 100 rupees a month?"

Sceptical operators are not the only risk that the MSOs face. They are pioneers in a market with low incomes, poor technology and excessive regulation. Interactive digital television has yet to arrive in India, so the first customers for the Internet over cable will be users of its 3m–4m computers. Although MSOs expect the cost of the service— 1,500 rupees a month, or ten times what most subscribers pay for cable TV—to fall quickly, along with that of cable modems, for the moment it is out of reach of all but the rich.

The quality of the service that MSOs can offer depends in part on bits of the wires that they do not control. Most Internet traffic comes from outside India, and thus hits the bottleneck of India's publicly owned telecoms companies, which have a monopoly of long-distance telephony and international data exchange. The data monopoly is about to end, and private operators will soon carry Internet traffic via satellite. But the state monopoly is keeping its grip over access to ultra-high capacity submarine cables.

Yet MSOs have one great advantage, which telcos cannot rival. They already have broadband connections with millions of homes, which they can now upgrade and use to promote their new services. If they succeed, India could yet be the country that proves the Internet can benefit the poor world, and not just the rich.

Article 24

The UNESCO Courier, November 1993

Making Something Out of Nothing

By inventing the zero, India became the birthplace of modern arithmetic

Pierre-Sylvain Filliozat

Pierre-Sylvain Filliozat, of France, is a specialist in Indian studies. He is a director of studies at the Ecole Pratique des Hautes Etudes in Paris.

In India mathematics has not always been linked to writing. The earliest surviving written document dates from the third century B.C., but India certainly had an advanced civilization many centuries before that, and scientific knowledge formed part of it. Most knowledge was transmitted orally. This ancient learning preserved in human memory makes up the corpus of the great religious texts known as the Vedas, which incidentally contain evidence of mathematical knowledge. The Vedas are written in an archaic form of Sanskrit. Like all Indo-European languages, Sanskrit has decimal numerals and individual names for the nine units, as well as for ten, a hundred, a thousand and higher powers of ten (figure 2).

The names of the tens are derived from those of the units, somewhat modified and with the addition of a suffix. Examples are *vimçati* 20, *trimçat* 30, *catvârimçat* 40. The other numerals are formed from these components. The names for the hundreds, thousands and so on consist of a unit name followed by *çata* or *sahasra*. *Dve çate* (dual), for example, means 200, and *trini-sahasrani* (plural), 3,000.

In Sanskrit grammar the qualifier in a compound word precedes the qualified. In the case of compound numerals the number of the higher order is regarded as qualified by the lower. Eleven, for example, is ten qualified by the addition of one, giving the compound *ekâ-daça,* and similarly *dvâ-daça* is 12, *trayas-trimçat* 33 and so on. The number is divided into components, with the smallest coming first. Units are followed by tens and so on.

The advent of writing

We do not know when, how or by whom writing was introduced into India. All we know is that as early as the third century B.C. two scripts were in use. One, called *kharoshtî*, was derived from Aramaic. It was used in the extreme northwest of the sub-continent, but soon fell into disuse. The other, known as *brâhmî*, seems to have originated in India itself. It is the forerunner of all the scripts now in use in the Indian sub-continent and in southeast Asia. The earliest records (from between the third century B.C. and the third century A.D.) of figures transcribed into this script reveal a notation system that corresponds fairly closely to the pronunciation system.

There is one sign for each digit, and so there are nine signs for the nine units, an entirely different sign for each of the tens (10, 20, etc.), another sign for 100 and yet another for 1,000. Compound numbers are represented by combinations of symbols. The *brâhmî* script reads from left to right, and combinations of signs are written in that direction, starting with the highest value. Here there is a difference between the written and the spoken language. The scribe starts with the highest component, whereas the speaker starts with the lowest. For example, the number 13 is pronounced *trayo-daça,* or "three-ten", but is written "ten-three".

Combinations of components are usually produced by juxtaposing signs, in some cases by ligatures. Whereas there are different signs for each of the tens, for the hundreds there is just the sign for 100 plus the sign for the number of hundreds, and likewise with the thousands.

At this stage we cannot yet speak of positional notation. There is a juxtaposition of the numeral signs which when

Numerals	Value	Numerals	Value
○< ͋	12	—	1
—	1	○< ͋	12
T ꙅꙄ	1700	Ŧ○T	21,000
ꙅ ⊕7	189	—	1
○< 7	17	Ŧ	60,000
Ŧ○< T	11,000	Ŧ○< —	10,001
T	1,000	ꙅ —	101
○< ͋	12	T ꙅ	1,100
—	1	ꙅ	100
Ŧ○ T+ ꙅꙄ	24,400	ꙅ —	101
Ŧψ	6,000	T ꙅ —	1,101
—	1	T ꙅꙄ —	1,101
—	1	ꙅ —	101
—	1	T ͋	1,002
ꙅꙄ	100	T —	1,001

Figure 1
Numeral signs and their values as attested by the Nâneghât inscriptions (first century B.C.)

added together give the desired number. This is exactly in keeping with the structure of the language (figure 1).

The zero and positional numeration

In the decimal positional system of numeration the tens, hundreds and thousands are not represented by different signs but by the same digit signs placed in different positions. Only then does position become significant. It alone shows which are the tens, which the hundreds and which the thousands. Such a system needs only ten signs, the digits from 1 to 9 and a zero—or at least a blank space.

There is no satisfactory documentary evidence as to how and in what exact period this system was discovered in India, and how it developed. The earliest reference to a place-value notation is a literary one. Vasumitra, a Buddhist writer and leading figure at a great religious council convened by King Kanishka (who reigned over the whole of north and northwest India at the end of the first or the beginning of the second century A.D.), maintained in a book on Buddhist doctrine that if a substance that exists in all three time dimensions (past, present and future) is regarded as something different every

time it enters a new state, this change is due to the alterity of the state, not to its own alterity. He illustrated this idea by speaking of a marker which in the units position counts as a unit but in the hundreds position counts as a hundred. He did not specify the nature of the marker.

This may be a reference to a kind of abacus. The marker might have been an object that could be placed in a column or square, where its position gave it the value of a power of ten. Or it could be a mark in the sand, in the case of sums written on the ground. Indian accounts are known to have liked the simplicity of this method. In some parts of southern India village astrologers can still be seen doing calculations by placing cowrie shells in columns drawn in the sand. Whatever the form of the abacus, Vasumitra's reference implies the existence of a notation that took account of positional value.

The same is true of the zero, the use of which in India is known from literary references predating the earliest written examples. The zero forms part of the positional system of numeration. Originally it seems to have been a gap in a column resulting from the absence of a figure or marker in the space reserved for an order of the power of ten. This is shown by the use of one of the words meaning empty, çûnya or kha. The word kha occurs in a treatise on metrics by Pingala, in which he sets forth a rule for turning binary numbers into decimal numbers. Pingala's dates are unknown, but quotations from his works are found from the third century A.D. onwards, and so he must have lived earlier than that.

That a dot came to be used to indicate an empty space we know from a Sanskrit storyteller, Subandhu, who probably lived in the sixth century A.D. To denote the zero Subandhu used the compound noun cûnya-bindu, literally "empty point", in other words a dot indicating an empty space in a column.

The zero itself appears in a deed of gift, carved on copper plates, from King Devendravarman of Kalinga (Orissa, in eastern India). The document is dated in letters and figures: "samvacchara-çatam trir-âçîte (100) 83 shravane masi dine vimçati 20 utkîrnnam", literally "carved a hundred and eighty-three years (100) 83 (having passed) the twenty day 20 in the month of Shravana". The number 183 is written as three signs, the sign for a hundred and then the figures 8 and 3. The number 20 is written with the figure 2 and a zero in the form of a small circle. The period specified in this document began in 498 A.D., so that it dates from the year 681 A.D.

Positional notation, and the zero in the form of a big dot or small circle, are found in inscriptions in southeast Asia, at Sambor (Cambodia) and Kota Kapur (Malaysia), where the earliest records go back to the seventh century A.D. The scripts used in these countries are all derived from Indian scripts, and their system of writing numbers is undoubtedly the Indian system. All these documents show that by the late seventh century the positional system and the zero were in general use not only in India but in all the countries to which Indian civilization had spread as well.

Notation using nine digits and a zero seems to have quickly taken the lead for inscriptions, but it never completely superseded the old system, which survived until recently in manuscripts, and in southern India even in early twentieth century-printed books.

Figure 2. Number names in Sanskrit			
eka	1	çata	100
dvi	2	sahasra	1000
tri	3	ayuta	10 000
catur	4	niyuta	100 000
pañca	5	prayuta	1 000 000
shat	6	arbuda	10 000 000
sapta	7	nyarbuda	100 000 000
ashtan	8	samudra	1 000 000 000
nava	9	madhya	10 000 000 000
daça	10	anta	100 000 000 000
		parârdha	1 000 000 000 000

Words standing for numerals

A mixed notation, in which features of the old system are combined with or alternate with characteristics of positional notation, was also known and used in India. In this system number names are replaced by words with numerical connotations. For example, two is replaced by "eyes", "arms", "wings", or "twins", four by "oceans" (there being four oceans in Indian geographical mythology), ten by "fingers", thirty-two by "teeth", hundred by "human life-span", zero by "empty space", and so on. These words are arranged as they would be in speech, so that in a compound number the lowest numerals come first. In other words, the order is opposite to that used in writing. For instance, the number 4,320,000 is pronounced khaca-tushka-rada-arnavâh, which literally means "tetrad of empty spaces-teeth-oceans," or 0—0—0—0—32—4.

This example is taken from the *Sûrya-siddhânta,* an astronomical text which takes account of data observable in the fourth century A.D. It is one of the earliest records of this mixed notation, which enjoyed great popularity throughout the history of Sanskrit literature. Even among mathematicians and astronomers it seems to have been the preferred method of expressing numbers. Its advantage was that it allowed variation of vocabulary. Sanskrit has ten or so common words for eyes, whereas there is no synonym for the number 2. Sanskrit technical and scientific literature was usually written in verse, so that authors needed to command a wide vocabulary in order to find words to fit the requirements of prosody.

It would be a mistake to regard this mixed notation as a transitional stage between the old oral system and the pure positional system. It was an artificial method adopted by authors who were familiar with both systems and used them in their writings.

Economy and lightness

In 662 A.D. a Syriac writer, Severus Sebokt, wishing to show that the Greeks had no monopoly on science, referred to the inventiveness of Indian scholars. The only one of their mathematical skills that he mentioned was their system of reckoning using nine digits. Severus Sebokt's comment points to the greatest advantage of this system, its economy. By reducing the symbols needed for the notation of all numbers to ten—nine digits and a zero—the system achieves the ideal of economy and efficiency. Indian intellectuals were well aware of the advantages of economy. They had a technical term for it—laghava or "lightness"—and have cultivated it since Antiquity in various fields of thought.

Article 25   *The New York Times,* April 16, 1998

Ancient Hindu Festival Thrives in Computer-Age India

By JOHN F. BURNS

HARDWAR, India, April 14—The rushing grey-green waters of the Ganges were as chilly as they have been in years today as A. K. Sharma stripped to his underwear, plunged into the shallow edge of India's holiest river and raised cupped handfuls of water towards the rising sun.

But Mr. Sharma, a 48-year-old engineer, was jubilant. After journeying 250 miles from his home in Agra, the city of the Taj Mahal, Mr. Sharma, his wife and two children joined millions of Hindu pilgrims who traveled to Hardwar from across India in the last three months to join in what is billed here as the world's biggest religious festival.

After an exhausting day on chaotic roads and a night in a dusty tented camp, Mr. Sharma had timed his bathing well. As he made his way through the dense crowd of worshipers pressing towards the river, less than two hours remained to the most propitious moment of the most propitious day in the Hindu calendar, as determined by astrological calculations that underpin what is known here as the kumbh mela.

The mela, or festival, is a rotating rite chroniclers say has been observed at Hardwar every 12 years since the second millennium B.C.

As India rushes into the age of technology, launching communications satellites, developing nuclear weapons and enthusiastically embracing the Internet, the passion for the ancient rituals among the country's 700 million Hindus shows no sign of flagging.

The Hardwar mela is believed to have drawn the largest crowds ever to converge on this city in the lee of the Himalayan foothills. By some accounts as many as 10 million people have come since January. In 1989, a kumbh mela at Allahabad, on the lower reaches of the Ganges, drew as many as 30 million.

The phenomenon has delighted many Indians, who yearn to guard their ancient traditions even as they seek to modernize what had been one of Asia's most creaky economies.

"Our technological know-how is very well, but our ancients were understanding things much better," Mr. Sharma said. Motioning towards the hubbub along the Ganges and the dozens of brightly-hued temples dotting the escarpment, he added: "Something is there, something which I am not exactly knowing, something which is hidden; something which I may not be able to prove technically, but which I know to be there in my soul."

Ritual bathing and spiritual renewal at the Ganges.

According to ancient Hindu scriptures, bathing at Hardwar at the time of the kumbh mela, or at Allahabad, Nasik and Ujjain, the other cities on the north Indian plain that host the mela at three-year intervals, is the supreme act of worship, worth 10 million dips in the Ganges at less propitious times.

Some Hindus believe that dipping at a kumbh mela will guarantee eternal salvation, a release from the cycle of birth, death and reincarnation. Others believe that the mela washes away all sins, cleanses the soul, or earns the blessings of the Hindu deities for a marriage or business venture, or for relief from illness.

There were many pilgrims with disabilities here this week. One man in his 30's, paralyzed in both legs by polio, arrived at the most holy spot along the riverbank, known as the brahmakund, after dragging himself by his arms from a camp more than 10 miles away, a journey he said had taken him 20 hours.

The origin of the kumbh melas lies in a Hindu legend involving a struggle between gods and demons for control of a kumbha, or clay pitcher, filled with the nectar of immortality churned from the bottom of the oceans. According to the legend, one god seized the pitcher and circled the earth for 12 days—12 years in earthly time—spilling drops of nectar at four places on earth that are the sites of the kumbh melas and at eight places in the heavens.

According to early records, including an account in the 7th century A.D. by a Chinese traveler, Hsuang Tang, the melas served from ancient times as grand gatherings of Hindu holy men, the sadhus, swamis, sanyasis, gurus and yogis of the time.

Associated Press

Throngs of Hindus bathed in the Ganges this week during the kumbh mela, a major festival at Hardwar, in northern India. Millions of pilgrims gathered at the holy site, one of four where it is celebrated.

"When the stars were in a particular position, the sadhus simply followed the great rivers to their confluence and stayed there until others, from all directions, joined them," according to Rajesh Bedi, who wrote a 1991 book on the sadhus, itinerant holy men who renounce all wordly goods. "Then they discussed the state of the body politic, the economic condition of the people and philosophical and theological questions."

The ascetic sadhus still dominate the festivals, setting up vast encampments near the river where they pray, practice yoga, perform their rites, read from Hindu scriptures, chant mantras and hold discourses with the common pilgrims. For urban Hindus, in particular, the sadhus, many of whom still live lives of renunciation in the forests and mountains, are a focus of profound fascination and respect.

Although India is instinctively entrepreneurial, Hindu beliefs have engendered an abiding respect for those who abjure the material world; exploiting this politically was part of the genius of Mohandas K. Gandhi, the independence

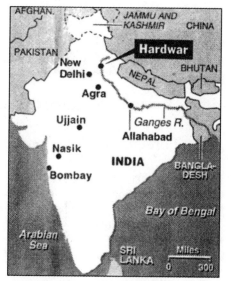

The New York Times

Hardwar is the site of this year's kumbh mela, a major festival.

leader, a London-trained barrister who led the struggle against British rule in the accoutrements of the sadhu, with a cotton loincloth and a wooden stave. These days, Indians who once followed

Gandhi are as likely to be found at melas chanting the praises of near-naked sadhus, as the crowds did everywhere at Hardwar.

Men like Mr. Sharma, the engineer from Agra, and their wives, lined the riverbanks today as more than 60,000 sadhus, organized into monastic orders called akharas, marched across pontoon bridges to the bathing ghats, terraced areas flanked by temples at the heart of the city. The crowds tossed garlands of marigolds and shouted "We bow to you, o holy men!" "We kiss your feet!" and "Long Live Lord Ram!".

The sadhus and their leaders, many of them carried to the ghats in gaily-colored palanquins shaded from the sun by gold and crimson parasols, waved back regally.

But not all sadhus, or their supreme leaders, known as shankaracharayas, are what they once were. Few shankaracharayas arrive these days atop richly caparisoned elephants or camels; many came in air-conditioned cars, and were borne to the rivers on thrones mounted atop cars and trucks. According to Indian newspapers, their numbers include many charlatans, more interested in money, power and women.

Not for the first time at a kumbh mela, rivalries between monastic orders known as the akharas erupted in violence. On March 28, a pitched battle flared between two orders, the Niranjani and the Juna, after members of one group delayed evacuating the most sacred of the bathing ghats. The fighting, involving ceremonial swords, staves and trishuls—trident-like staffs—left more than 100 sadhus and policemen injured. Several policemen were thrown into the Ganges, and several ashrams burned down.

Indeed, animosities threatened to scuttle the heart of the festival. Unable to agree on which group should occupy the central ghat at 12.10 P.M. on Tuesday, the moment astrologers had set as marking the correct alignment of Jupiter, Saturn, the earth and the moon, the two orders

threatened to fight again. A police force of 30,000 moved special units with automatic rifles, flak jackets and riot helmets in to surround all 13 akharas in their camps, lifting the siege only hours before the astrologically propitious moment.

Even then the Juna, having ceded precedence at the ghat, boycotted the procession to the river, along with three other allied akharas. This left the Niranjani to march to the river in triumph, headed by hundreds of stark naked Naga sadhus, the warrior-like holy men who constitute a kind of commando force of their own. The Juna leaders charged that India's new Government, headed by the Hindu nationalist Bharatiya Janata Party, had manipulated the negotiations in favor of the party-linked Niranjani.

The festival was rated a success for the Hindu nationalists who control the

Government in Delhi and the state government of Uttar Pradesh and were responsible for the management of the festival. Contrary to the state's reputation elsewhere in India as a crucible of the country's ills, Uttar Pradesh ran the event with uncharacteristic efficiency, re-building 100 miles of roads, laying 50 miles of water piping to the tented camps, and re-building bathing ghats. Most important, the police avoided a repeat of the disasters that marred previous Hardwar melas, including a stampede in 1986 in which at least 60 people died.

But not all the warrior-like holy men appreciated the police controls. "We have asked them not to carry pistols and other firearms during the processions to the river," said J. P. Sharma, the official responsible for managing the mela. "We have kindly requested them to carry only religious symbols."

Article 26

The Washington Post, October 5, 1998

Inspiring Devotion—and Fear

In Afghanistan, the puritanical militia enforces Islam for better or worse

By Pamela Constable, *Washington Post* Foreign Service

KANDAHAR, Afghanistan

Are you sure you want to take the risk" The Pakistani border official, about to stamp the exit visa, stops with his hand in midair. "Those people are not educated. They may act before they think. And you might suffocate under one of those veils." He grins darkly, then tosses back the stamped passport.

Across the border lies Afghanistan, a country nearly destroyed by two decades of warfare, sunk in such primitive poverty that the World Bank no longer attempts to measure its economy and ruled by the Taliban, a puritanical Is-

lamic militia. The Taliban, recognized by only three nations as a government, has provoked widespread international outrage by its Draconian enforcement of its version of Islamic law.

Few Westerners are allowed in Afghanistan today, and all but a handful of foreign relief workers have been evacuated since August, when terrorists suspected of operating from Afghanistan bombed the U.S. embassies in Kenya and Tanzania-and the United States struck back with cruise missile attacks on suspected terrorist camps in the Afghan hills.

An American reporter and a Pakistani photographer are about to embark on a

500-mile journey through Taliban territory that will reveal why many Afghans have welcomed the country's radical new rules-and why many others have come to fear them.

In Jalalabad, a devout Muslim physician secretly arranges tutoring for hi daughter, banned from school by the Taliban. Kabul, the once-cosmopolitan capital, seems like an Orwellian ghost town where no woman's face is eve seen and no man dares appear beardless Along the desert highway, cars procee at a camel's pace around endless bomb craters, the legacy of two decades of wa against Soviet invaders and among riva Afghan militias. And in Kandahar, loca ethnic traditions are so conservative that the Taliban's medieval ethos seems right at home.

The famed Khyber Pass is a crowded, muddy footpath, and no one notices us in the two-way stream of traffic: donkeys laden with grapes, children bent under loads of scrap metal, hustlers and herders and holy men.

The assuring sense of anonymity does not last long, however

Not 15 minutes after we climb into a taxi driven by a jovial, chattering man named Habib, we reach the first Taliban check-point. Habib yanks a Muslim skullcap onto his head as a stern young man in a black turban approaches us, a Kalashnikov rifle across his shoulder. He peers at our faces, examines our documents, roughly rummages through the glove compartment and back seat. Finally he waves us on with his rifle.

AS WE PULL AWAY, WE NOTICE A cluster of long black ribbons waving prettily from a utility pole. It is a decoration we are to see at dozens of Taliban checkpoints along the road. We ask Habib what the turbaned man was looking for. "Music cassettes," he explains. "If they find any, they rip them apart right there and hang them from the poles."

The other passengers are a shoemaker from Jalalabad, a city about 50 miles ahead, and a doctor visiting his family in a village along the way. Their responses to questions about the Taliban are much like those we will hear from many ordinary Afghans, at first.

"They have brought us peace and security," says the cobbler. "The people are happy. Islamic law is so beautiful. There is no more corruption."

The doctor says he was once a soldier in the *jihad,* or holy war, against Soviet occupation in the 1980s. "We had to walk hundred of miles, there were no beds and little food, but we were glad to do it for Islamic state."

The Taliban—a home-grown religious militia that seized Afghanistan's capital, Kabul, two years ago-has vowed to create a pure Islamic society free from crime, vice and Western influence. After years of civil war, many Afghans welcomed them and the sense of order they brought to the country. But for many middle-class Afghans-teachers who are no longer allowed to teach, doc-

tors who have no place to practice medicine, women who never wore a *burqa* veil and men who never grew a beard-the Taliban's harsh restrictions have begun to chafe, especially since economic and social conditions also have continued to deteriorate.

Even some devout Muslims who conscientiously follow *sharia,* or Islamic law, are spooked by the Taliban's totalitarian means of enforcing it. Once they feel comfortable with a foreigner, they bring out their hidden Hindi music tapes

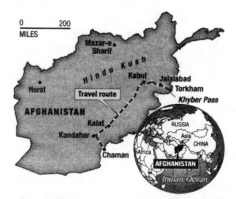

BY JOHN ANDERSON—THE WASHINGTON POST

or short-wave radios, complain bitterly that their daughters are prohibited from attending school, or confide that they are in desperate need and feel abandoned by the authorities.

At dusk we reach Jalalabad, where the physician and the shoemaker bid a polite farewell. Habib, taking a deep breath, turns and asks if we would "like to meet some other people." Soon we are entering a refugee camp at the edge of town, a maze of mud huts where ragged children swarm around the car. Many have sores on their faces and arms.

In a small, cave-like room, a gaunt young doctor named Abdul sits at a table with his only equipment: scissors, gauze, iodine and a dusty microscope. He says there are 50,000 refugees from civil conflict zones in the camp, that many have eye diseases and almost half the children have malaria, but that few families can afford treatment.

"The children have nothing to do all day but run in the streets. There is no school, no clinic, no work," the doctor says. "Nobody cares about these people, and most of the foreign aid groups have gone away."

Later, over rice and kebabs in a restaurant swarming with flies, the doctor confides that he is also worried about his own family. He earns the equivalent of only $6 a month, and the school his sons were attending has closed. His daughter is being taught secretly by a woman in her home.

"Look, I am Muslim, everyone in this country is Muslim by birth. We go to the mosque because we want to," Abdul says. "If people think the Taliban have brought Islam to Afghanistan, they are wrong. They have brought something else, and they are implementing it by force."

Asked about his beard, he says he never wore one until 1996. "If I were to cut it off now," he adds, "they would throw me in prison until it grew back."

As we drove toward Kabul the next day, the desert begins and the highway becomes increasingly pockmarked with craters. One-legged beggars, maimed by land mines, stand by the roadside with arms outstretched. Every few miles, the over turned hulks of Russian tanks litter the stony slopes like the carcasses of huge horseshoe crabs. In every village, warnings with crude depictions of mines are painted on every building.

The entry to the capital is another checkpoint festooned with black ribbons. As ordered, we report directly to the Foreign Ministry, where an official ticks off a list of rules for foreign journalists: no photographs of people, no interviews with women, no visits to private homes. We must stay in a government-run hotel and be accompanied at all times by a government driver and interpreter. The total cost for their services is about $100 per day, payable only in cash dollars.

Once a cosmopolitan capital, Kabul lies in ruins from years of bombing and shelling. Half the population, once more than a million, has fled to other parts of the country or across the borders as refugees. The Taliban, preoccupied with fighting its armed opponents in the countryside and disdainful of the "foreign influence" that once pervaded Kabul, has done almost nothing to rebuild the city. The government is virtually dysfunctional except for the Taliban moral police who cruise the streets in pickup trucks, detaining men whose beards are too short and women whose faces are not covered.

Even at midday, the city seems oddly silent. There is little traffic; teams of donkeys or men strain to pull heavily laden carts. There is a 10 p.m. curfew, but by nightfall almost every shop will be shuttered, every street empty except for Taliban policy pickup trucks. With television, movies and music banned, only the soft sounds of muezzins' voices calling worshipers to prayer disturb the night.

TEL IS A HAUNTED 500-ROOM HILL-top palace in which we are the only guests. Once it was the city's social center. Now the carpet and jewelry boutiques are long closed, the grand salons locked. The "staff members" follow our every move, lingering outside our rooms and surprising us around corners.

At one point we try to leave for dinner in Habib's car, but a guard runs after us, shouting that we are forbidden to do so. The next morning, the driver appears in the lobby, badly shaken. He tells us he was taken to the hotel basement by two men and questioned closely about us, our driver from the border, whom we met and what they told us. Reluctantly we agree to let him go, feeling as if we have lost our only friend in Taliban territory.

For the rest of our stay in Kabul, we play cat-and-mouse with out interpreter, a pleasant medical student named Sayed who confides that the Taliban police don't like his longish haircut, but who quickly insinuates himself into every conversation we strike up and who periodically reminds us in a gentle voice that if we don't follow the rules, we can be immediately escorted to the border.

Despite his presence, however, a number of Afghans are willing to express their frustrations with Taliban rule and to confess certain surreptitious deviations from the official line. In a once-popular appliance shop, the manager complains that a recent government order required him to remove all stereo equipment; in the last week, he says, he has sold only one tea flask. In a school-supply store, where slide rules and notebooks are gathering dust, the owner complains mildly that he must walk far, several times a day, to find a mosque. Then he frowns and adds, "Please be careful what you write. If you say I am unhappy, the Taliban won't like it."

In a market stall that sells cassettes of Koran recitations and Taliban political chants (the latter invariably decorated with drawings of rifles or rocket launchers), a question about Western music draws a swift array of responses. "It's a sin," declares one teenager. "I like Michael Jackson," says his friend, and they both giggle.

And in the office of an agency whose job is to clear minefields and warn the populace about the dangers of thousands of land mines still buried across the country, the director confesses his frustration that women are not permitted to attend public mine-awareness lectures with men. "The only way we can reach them in some areas is to drive by apartment buildings with loudspeakers," he says with a brief frown. "But we try our best."

The only opportunity to speak with women comes at a hospital run by the International Committee of the Red Cross, where war-disabled workers make thousands of artificial limbs for mine victims and other handicapped Afghans. In the women's ward, patients and staff members remove their burqas upon entering, with evident relief.

A beautiful young woman named Suhaila, waiting for her nephew to be treated, says she was an elementary school teacher before the Taliban came, and misses it very much. "Now we have only my husband's income, and I am forgetting a lot of my lessons," she says. "People without education might as well be blind." She never wore a burqa before 1996, she says, but has since gotten used tot he stifling garment. "If we don't wear it, they will beat us," she points out matter-of-factly.

"They" are the police agents of the Amar-bil-Maroof Nahi-anil-Munker, the Ministry for the Propagation of Islamic Orders and the Discouragement of Islamic Prohibitions-informally known as the department of virtue and vice. The deputy minister is a mullah in a black turban with ham-size hands named Maulwi Qualmuddin, who answers a foreigner's question with polite contempt.

"The burqa is very, very important to maintain a society that is free of corruption," he says, and his ministry seeks to promote "dignity" for women by sheltering them from men in public. The

practice is nothing new in rural areas, where, he notes, "we couldn't detach women from their burqas." The only problem is in Kabul, where certain "foreign influences" once were allowed to infect the culture.

On the other hand, Qalmuddin asserts, the ban on women's education and work is only a temporary measure that will end once the Taliban has defeated its internal armed enemies and can devote its energy to social issues. But Afghan women will clearly continue to be "protected" from the world of men. In Western societies, he lectures, women are used by men when young and discarded when old. "In Islam," the stern mullah declares with pride, "we shelter women for life."

HEAT AND DUST, HEAT AND DUST. The road rises and falls; the car lurches upward and plummets into impossible gullies of frozen sand. The 300-mile highway leading south from Kabul to Kandahar, once a model of American engineering that could be traveled in five hours, is now an agonizing obstacle course that the most seasoned Afghan truckers can barely navigate in 22 hours.

Short stretches of pavement sheer off abruptly into jagged craters gouged by Russian bombs and Afghan antitank mines. In many spots, so many alternative tracks have been forged along-side that the road loses itself in the wasteland. The taxi driver swerves and brakes, dodges and skids. For two days-with one three-hour napping break on a hard café floor-time passes in a haze of fine grit, nauseating jolts and blinding sun.

The landscape is barren and empty except for periodic clusters of tents pinioned to the rocky slopes: the camps of nomadic shepherds. Their flocks amble along the silent highway, followed by small boys with wooden staffs. From nowhere appears a turbaned old man on a bicycle, or a caravan of camels led by women with deeply creased faces and swirling, filthy skirts.

It is on this part of the journey that the depth of Afghanistan's economic exhaustion and despair sinks in. In villages along the way, people draw water by hand from wells, plow behind cattle with wooden blades, stand by the highway smoothing holes with a shovel and hoping travelers will pay them a few cents. Small children work all day herding goats, washing dishes, selling fruit. Families walk dozens of miles a day, looking for a few shrubs for their emaciated animals to graze.

It is also along this tortuous stretch of road that the Afghan tradition of hospitality seems most poignant. At every stop to wash off the dust, people invariably offer cups of tea and dishes of sweets. At a roadside café in the town of Kalat, the owner refuses to let us pay for lunch. He shows us his prized short-wave radio, then points with distaste to a handwritten sign taped to the wall. It is a notice advising women to wear veils, men to wear beards and all Afghans to avoid music and drugs. It is signed by a local chief of the Amar-bil-Maroof. "I had to grow a beard too, but my wife doesn't like it," he says with a laugh.

His name is Zaher, and he was once a teacher Now there are no public schools, so be bought the café and reluctantly enrolled his 10-year-old son in a *madrassa,* or Islamic studies center, because it is "the only place he can go." The local Taliban authorities are "well-behaved" in the area, he says, "but they cannot meet the people's real demand-to · end this terrible poverty. We all try to be good Muslims, but that is something not even Islam can cure."

Late at night, grimy and bleary-eyed, we reach the city of Kandahar. To our astonishment, the bazaars are teeming with customers, bright with lantern light and bursting with produce. Melons and pomegranates are neatly piled, lamb carcasses swing from ropes, flats of just-baked roti bread are spread out invitingly.

Compared with the paranoia and ghostliness of Kabul, the first impression of Kandahar is one of freewheeling, relaxed urbanity. The impression is dead wrong.

Kandahar is the birthplace and headquarters of the Taliban movement, and within two days it becomes easy to un-

derstand why. To a large extent, the city's more modern and educated residents fled long ago, across the border with Pakistan to the city of Quetta or beyond. To a large extent, those who remained are not only Muslims, they are ethnic Pashtun folk of rural origins like the Taliban, deeply conservative in their social values and behavior. The large majority are illiterate.

Here, there is no need for a curfew, and it is fashionable among young men to adopt the Taliban mode of dress: black or white turbans, baggy trousers and robes, casually slung rifles. The day before we arrived, we are told, two murderers two murderers were executed by a Taliban firing squad in a local stadium, and several thousand people came to watch.

Women, of course, are rarely seen and never heard; on brief shopping excursions they scurry quietly along the sidewalks, anonymous behind billowing sky-blue or pine-green burqas.

"Our traditions are even more strict than Islam," explains a young man named Abdullah, who sells burqas in a shop that his grandfather opened 70 years ago. "Our women like to wear the burqa because every glance has a cost."

Abdullah, 21, was married in 1996 to a girl who was chosen by his parents. In accordance with local custom, they first met on their wedding night. They are very happy, he says, and have a 1-year-old son.

"Every people should live in accordance with their own customs, and the Taliban are the system we want," he says "If you have a tradition of so-called freedom in your country, that's fine, but we have our own traditions."

In another bazaar, our interpreter locates a cousin named Said who sells shampoo and tomato paste; the man promptly invites us for lunch at his modest, mud-walled home. In a cool room lined with rugs, we eat rice and vegetables with his father and sons, talking about duck hunting and pilgrimages to Mecca. When we have finished, the left-

overs are gathered up in a tablecloth and taken outside for the women to eat.

"Our life hasn't changed at all since the Taliban came," says Said. "It has always been our habit to wear turbans; without them we feel naked. About 90 percent of us wore beards; now the other 10 percent wear them too. And our women have traditionally been at home. So you see there was little that needed to be changed."

THE TALIBAN OFFICIALS WE MEET are less formal than their counterparts in Kabul; their offices are moldy and collapsing after years of urban warfare, but their manner is casual and open. We are quickly granted interviews with two chief Taliban spokesmen, who answer questions with soft-spoken patience. At the local Foreign Ministry office, an aide repeatedly assures us we are welcome in the city.

In the bazaars, we approach several different rank-and-file Taliban members, who seem surprised but happy to talk. One describes himself as an "ordinary soldier. I patrol the street looking for criminals and making sure other Taliban deal with the people correctly. We are very proud to serve the people, and we don't want any member to discredit us."

Still, it is hard to ignore the stares in the street, or the knowledge that only a few weeks ago, hundreds of thousands of ordinary people mobbed the streets here after a U.S. missile attack on alleged terrorist camps in Afghanistan, chanting anti-American slogans and calling for the death of President Clinton.

On our way out of the country, when we spot the green and white Pakistani flag at Chaman we are suddenly flooded with relief. Night is falling fast, and we have another three hours' drive before reaching Quetta. But when the dapper, officious Pakistani immigration official invites us in for tea while he inspects our passports, we accept without a moment's hesitation.

Article 27   *Newsweek,* December 6, 1999

The Holy Men of Heroin

Afghanistan has been ruined by war. But it does one job better than
anyplace else in the world: produce opium.

BY JEFFREY BARTHOLET AND STEVE LEVINE

ZUBER HAS A GAZE THAT'S A LITTLE too steady. Taken together with his bushy black beard, shaved head and tan *shalwar kamiz*—the pajamalike clothes that Afghan men wear—the effect is unsettling. He looks like one of those Afghans who's seen too much war. But Zuber's ghosts have a different origin. Until a month ago the 30-year-old Afghan worked at an opium-processing factory in Nangarhar province that every day produced up to 220 pounds of morphine base—the main ingredient in heroin. He says the place was bubbling with steam from boiling vats of opium gum. "Whether you like it or not, you're breathing it," says Zuber, who recently checked into a rehabilitation clinic in Peshawar, Pakistan. "When you get home, after the opium wears off, your legs and arms begin to ache, and so you start eating or smoking opium to relieve the pain." The clinic Zuber now calls home has 20 beds and a waiting list with 3,000 names. Some addicts have scars on their heads where they once sliced open their scalps to rub heroin into the wounds. They thought that was the most direct route to their brains.

Afghanistan, wrecked by 20 years of war and now ruled by Islamic radicals, has one perverse claim to success. Thanks to this year's bumper poppy crop, the country has become the world's undisputed leader in the production of opium. The United Nations estimates that Afghanistan accounted for an astonishing three quarters of global output in 1999, eclipsing the Golden Triangle region of Burma, Laos and Thailand. Afghan heroin is sold in neighboring Pakistan, which has nearly 2 million addicts, and also in Iran, Central Asia and Russia. As much as 90 percent of the heroin used in Europe originates in Afghanistan. Although most of the heroin sold in the United States comes from Colombia, American officials worry that increased quantities of Afghan drugs will find their way here.

This presents policymakers in Washington and other capitals with a dilemma. How do you combat drug production in a country that, even if you ignore the heroin trade, already is treated like a pariah? The Islamic Taliban militia, which administers roughly 85 percent of Afghanistan, claims that it would like to cooperate with drug-eradication efforts, but it lacks credibility. The government is recognized by only three countries: Pakistan, Saudi Arabia and the United Arab Emirates. It practices what the West calls "gender apartheid" by severely subjugating women, including forbidding them from working and attending school. Its forces have committed human-rights abuses against minorities, including roundups of ethnic Hazaras, some of whom have disappeared. And it harbors Islamic extremists like Osama bin Laden, the alleged ringleader behind the bombings of two U.S. embassies in Africa last year that killed 224 people.

Intense diplomatic pressure on the Taliban hasn't had much impact. In July, Washington banned all U.S. commerce with Afghanistan because of the Taliban's refusal to turn over bin Laden. When that failed, the U.N. Security Council two weeks ago ordered a freeze on overseas accounts of Taliban leaders and imposed a ban on its airline. The Taliban remains unyielding. "We will never hand over Osama bin Laden," scoffed Wakil Ahmad Muttawakil, the Taliban's foreign minister, in response to the sanctions. "He will remain free in defiance of America."

The Taliban can afford to be defiant, in part, because the opium trade provides it with both income and political leverage. To bring the trade to an end, Taliban mullahs argue, the United Nations should recognize the Taliban as a legitimate government and help it find alternatives. In the meantime, by allowing opium production, the Taliban improves economic conditions in areas under its control, and attracts needed tax revenue to prosecute the war against its rivals.

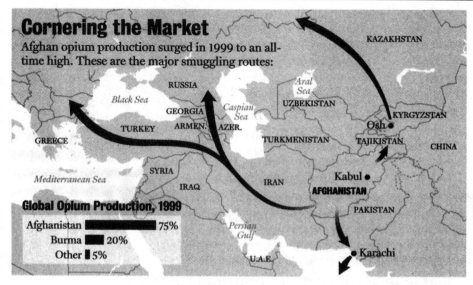

Cornering the Market

Afghan opium production surged in 1999 to an all-time high. These are the major smuggling routes:

Global Opium Production, 1999

Afghanistan	75%
Burma	20%
Other	5%

SOURCE FOR OPIUM PRODUCTION: UNDCP. GRAPHIC BY GUILBERT GATES—NEWSWEEK

For the record, Taliban officials correctly argue that poppy cultivation was part of the Afghan landscape long before the Taliban forced its rivals out of Kabul in 1996. The regime has its own drug czar, it outlaws drug use and it occasionally makes a show of destroying poppy fields or closing labs. Most recently it ordered farmers to cut poppy cultivation by 30 percent. It also admits to imposing a 10 percent *usher*—or religious tax—on the poppy crop. But officials argue that poppies are not a drug, and say the tax is no different from that charged on, say, wheat. Moreover, they insist they cannot afford—politically—to crack down on farmers. "We are against poppy cultivation, narcotics production and drugs," says Abdul Hakeem Mujahid, the Taliban representative in the United States. "But we cannot fight our own people. They are the sole source of our authority."

That's only a half-truth. The fuller version is that the Taliban also earns taxes directly not just from poppy farmers, but from heroin labs. Zuber, the addict who now lives in a Peshawar rehabilitation clinic, says that his lab packed morphine base into bundles that were taxed at about $55 per kilogram (2.2 pounds) by the Taliban. The daily tax revenue at that lab alone could amount to $5,500 in peak season—and the facility was one of 20 or 25 in the vicinity. NEWSWEEK has also examined photographs of official tax receipts from the heroin labs. "Criminal elements, religious elements and official elements are all connected in the heroin trade like rice and honey," says a law-enforcement agent for a Western government who has done undercover work in Afghanistan.

Opium is traded at large bazaars in Afghanistan that are the treacherous domain of criminal syndicates. One of the more notorious is located in the town of Sangin, a three-hour drive west of the Taliban capital at Kandahar. "Sangin is known as a dangerous place," says Bernard Frahi, head of the U.N. drug-agency office in Islamabad, who visited

the market town in October. "It is known for people going in and not coming out." Of about 500 shopkeepers crowded along one main street and two or three footpaths off it, he says, almost half sell opium. In front of their shops are scales, and inside they keep wet opium in plastic bags and dry opium stacked in large cakes. "One trader told me he sold 28,000 kilos [61,600 pounds] of opium last year," says Frahi—earning the merchant gross revenue of about $132,000.

Even more dangerous than the opium markets are the border areas with Iran, Tajikistan and Pakistan, where smugglers sometimes battle with border guards. Iran is fighting what amounts to a war of attrition—by Tehran's count, drug traffickers have killed more than 2,650 Iranian security personnel since 1983. In early November more than 30 Iranian guards were killed in a single battle with a drug convoy.

Some suspect the Taliban of an ulterior motive in its drug policy: poisoning "infidels." But Afghan drugs are harming at least as many Muslims as non-Muslims. In Pakistan, addicts either shoot up or "chase the dragon" by smoking opium, and Iran has a swelling population of more than 1 million drug abusers. Although addiction is a problem in parts of Afghanistan, it's not widespread, so opium farmers don't often see the human damage of their trade. "Afghanistan is a poor, landlocked country," says Ghulam Hazrat, who once worked as a high-school literature teacher, but now grows opium poppies. "In these past 20 years, the land wasn't tilled right. Schools didn't operate. The roads became bad. The only thing we have is opium." Somewhere far down the road—in Tehran or Paris or one of a thousand other places—Hazrat's gain will become another man's horror.

Scientific American, November 1999

The
Grameen Bank

A small experiment begun in Bangladesh
has turned into a major new concept in eradicating poverty

by Muhammad Yunus

Over many years, Amena Begum had become resigned to a life of grinding poverty and physical abuse. Her family was among the poorest in Bangladesh—one of thousands that own virtually nothing, surviving as squatters on desolate tracts of land and earning a living as day laborers.

In early 1993 Amena convinced her husband to move to the village of Kholshi, 112 kilometers (70 miles) west of Dhaka. She hoped the presence of a nearby relative would reduce the number and severity of the beatings that her husband inflicted on her. The abuse continued, however—until she joined the Grameen Bank. Oloka Ghosh, a neighbor, told Amena that Grameen was forming a new group in Kholshi and encouraged her to join. Amena doubted that anyone would want her in their group. But Oloka persisted with words of encouragement. "We're all poor—or at least we all were when we joined. I'll stick up for you because I know you'll succeed in business.

Amena's group joined a Grameen Bank Center in April 1993. When she received her first loan of $60, she used it to start her own business raising chickens and ducks. When she repaid her initial loan and began preparing a proposal for a second loan of $110, her friend Oloka gave her some sage advice: "Tell your husband that Grameen does not allow borrowers who are beaten by their spouses to remain members and take loans." From that day on, Amena suffered significantly less physical abuse at the hands of her husband. Today her business continues to grow and provide for the basic needs of her family.

Unlike Amena, the majority of people in Asia, Africa and Latin America have few opportunities to escape from poverty. According to the World Bank, more than 1.3 billion people live on less than a dollar a day. Poverty has not been eradicated in the 50 years since the Universal Declaration on Human Rights asserted that each individual has a right to:

A standard of living adequate for the health and well-being of himself and of his family, including food, clothing, housing and medical care and necessary social services, and the right to security in the event of unemployment, sickness, disability, widowhood, old age or other lack of livelihood in circumstances beyond his control.

Will poverty still be with us 50 years from now? My own experience suggests that it need not.

After completing my Ph.D. at Vanderbilt University, I returned to Bangladesh in 1972 to teach economics at Chittagong University. I was excited about the possibilities for my newly independent country. But in 1974 we were hit with a terrible famine. Faced with death and starvation outside my classroom, I began to question the very economic theories I was teaching. I started feeling there was a great distance between the actual life of poor and hungry people and the abstract world of economic theory.

I wanted to learn the real economics of the poor. Because Chittagong University is located in a rural area, it was easy for me to visit impoverished households in the neighboring village of Jobra. Over the course of many visits, I learned all about the lives of my struggling neighbors and much about economics that is never taught in the classroom. I was dismayed to see how the indigent in Jobra suffered because they could not come up with small amounts of working capital. Frequently they needed less than a dollar a person but could get that money only on extremely unfair terms. In most cases, people were required to sell their goods to moneylenders at prices fixed by the latter.

This daily tragedy moved me to action. With the help of my graduate students, I made a list of those who needed small amounts of money. We came up with 42 people. The total amount they needed was $27.

I was shocked. It was nothing for us to talk about millions of dollars in the classroom, but we were ignoring the minuscule capital needs of 42 hardworking, skilled people next door. From my own pocket, I lent $27 to those on my list.

Still, there were many others who could benefit from access to credit. I decided to approach the university's bank and try to persuade it to lend to the local poor. The branch manager said, however, that the bank could not give loans to the needy: the villagers, he argued, were not creditworthy.

I could not convince him otherwise. I met with higher officials in the banking hierarchy with similar results. Finally, I offered myself as a guarantor to get the loans.

In 1976 I took a loan from the local bank and distributed the money to poverty-stricken individuals in Jobra. Without exception, the villagers paid back their loans. Confronted with this evidence, the bank still refused to grant them loans directly. And so I tried my experiment in another village, and again it was successful. I kept expanding my work, from two to five, to 20, to 50, to 100 villages, all to convince the bankers that they should be lending to the poor. Although each time we expanded to a new village the loans were repaid, the bankers still would not change their view of those who had no collateral.

Because I could not change the banks, I decided to create a separate bank for the impoverished. After a great deal of work and negotiation with the government, the Grameen Bank ("village bank" in Bengali) was established in 1983.

From the outset, Grameen was built on principles that ran counter to the conventional wisdom of banking. We sought out the very poorest borrowers, and we required no collateral. The bank rests on the strength of its borrowers. They are required to join the bank in self-formed groups of five. The group members provide one another with peer support in the form of mutual assistance and advice. In addition, they allow for peer discipline by evaluating business viability and ensuring repayment. If one member fails to repay a loan, all members risk having their line of credit suspended or reduced.

The Power of Peers

Typically a new group submits loan proposals from two members, each requiring between $25 and $100. After these two borrowers successfully repay their first five weekly installments, the next two group members become eligible to apply for their own loans. Once they make five repayments, the final member of the group may apply. After 50 installments have been repaid, a borrower pays her interest, which is slightly above the commercial rate. The borrower is now eligible to apply for a larger loan.

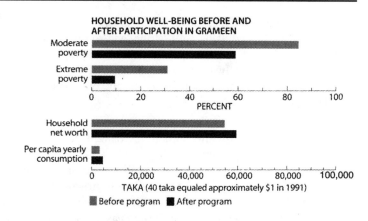

HOUSEHOLD WELL-BEING BEFORE AND AFTER PARTICIPATION IN GRAMEEN

TAKA (40 taka equaled approximately $1 in 1991)

■ Before program   ■ After program

The bank does not wait for borrowers to come to the bank; it brings the bank to the people. Loan payments are made in weekly meetings consisting of six to eight groups, held in the villages where the members live. Grameen staff attend these meetings and often visit individual borrowers' homes to see how the business—whether it be raising goats or growing vegetables or hawking utensils—is faring.

Today Grameen is established in nearly 39,000 villages in Bangladesh. It lends to approximately 2.4 million borrowers, 94 percent of whom are women. Grameen reached its first $1 billion in cumulative loans in March 1995, 18 years after it began in Jobra. It took only two more years to reach the $2-billion mark. After 20 years of work, Grameen's average loan size now stands at $180. The repayment rate hovers between 96 and 100 percent.

A year after joining the bank, a borrower becomes eligible to buy shares in Grameen. At present, 94 percent of the bank is owned by its borrowers. Of the 13 members of the board of directors, nine are elected from among the borrowers; the rest are government representatives, academics, myself and others.

A study carried out by Sydney R. Schuler of John Snow, Inc., a private research group, and her colleagues concluded that a Grameen loan empowers a woman by increasing her economic security and status within the family. In 1998 a study by Shahidur R. Khandker an economist with the World Bank, and others noted that participation in Grameen also has a significant positive effect on the schooling and nutrition of children—as long as women rather than men receive the loans. (Such a tendency was clear from the early days of the bank and is one reason Grameen lends primarily to women: all too often men spend the money on themselves.) In particular, a 10 percent increase in borrowing by women resulted in the arm circumference of girls—a common measure of nutritional status—expanding by 6 percent. And for every 10 percent increase in borrowing by a member the likelihood of her daughter being enrolled in school increased by almost 20 percent.

Not all the benefits derive directly from credit. When joining the bank, each member is required to memorize a list of 16 resolutions. These include commonsense items about hygiene and health—drinking clean water, growing and eating vegetables, digging and using a pit latrine, and so on—as well as social dictums such as refusing dowry and managing family size. The women usually recite the entire list at the weekly branch meetings, but the resolutions are not otherwise enforced.

Even so, Schuler's study revealed that women use contraception more consistently after joining the bank. Curiously, it appears that women who live in villages where Grameen operates, but who are not themselves members, are also more likely to adopt contraception. The population growth rate in Bangladesh has fallen dramatically in the past two decades, and it is possible that Grameen's influence has accelerated the trend.

In a typical year 5 percent of Grameen borrowers—representing 125,000 families—rise above the poverty level. Khandker concluded that among these borrowers extreme poverty (defined by consumption of less than 80 percent of the minimum requirement stipulated by the Food and Agriculture Organization of the United Nations) declined by more than 70 percent within five years of their joining the bank.

To be sure, making a microcredit program work well—so that it meets its social goals and also stays economically sound—is not easy. We try to ensure that the bank serves the poorest: only those living at less than half the poverty line are eligible for loans. Mixing poor participants with those who are better off would lead to the latter dominating the groups. In practice, however, it can be hard to include the most abjectly poor, who might be excluded by their peers when the borrowing groups are being formed. And despite our best efforts, it does sometimes happen that the money lent to a woman is appropriated by her husband.

Given its size and spread, the Grameen Bank has had to evolve ways to monitor the performance of its branch managers and to guarantee honesty and transparency. A manager is not allowed to remain in the same village for long, for fear that he may develop local connections that impede his performance. Moreover, a manager is never posted near his home. Because of such constraints—and because managers are required to have university degrees—very few of them are women. As a result, Grameen has been accused of adhering to a paternalistic pattern. We are sensitive to this argument and are trying to change the situation by finding new ways to recruit women.

Grameen has also often been criticized for being not a charity but a profit-making institution. Yet that status, I am convinced, is essential to its viability. Last year a disastrous flood washed away the homes, cattle and most other belongings of hundreds of thousands of Grameen borrowers. We did not forgive the loans, although we did issue new ones, and give borrowers more time to repay. Writing off loans would banish accountability, a key factor in the bank's success.

Liberating Their Potential

The Grameen model has now been applied in 40 countries. The first replication, begun in Malaysia in 1986, currently serves 40,000 poor families; their repayment rate has consistently stayed near 100 percent. In Bolivia, microcredit has allowed women to make the transition from "food for work" programs to managing their own businesses. Within two years the majority of women in the program acquire enough credit history and financial skills to qualify for loans from mainstream banks. Similar success stories are coming in from programs in poor countries everywhere. These banks all target the most impoverished, lend to groups and usually lend primarily to women.

The Grameen Bank in Bangladesh has been economically self-sufficient since 1995. Similar institutions in other countries are slowly making their way toward self-reliance. A few small programs are also running in the U.S., such as in inner-city Chicago. Unfortunately, because labor costs are much higher in the U.S. than in developing countries—which often have a large pool of educated unemployed who can serve as managers or accountants—the operations are more expensive there. As a result, the U.S. programs have had to be heavily subsidized.

In all, about 22 million poor people around the world now have access to small loans. Microcredit Summit, an institution based in Washington, D.C., serves as a resource center for the various regional microcredit institutions and organizes yearly conferences. Last year the attendees pledged to provide 100 million of the world's poorest families, especially their women, with credit by the year 2005. The campaign has grown to include more than 2,000 organizations, ranging from banks to religious institutions to nongovernmental organizations to United Nations agencies.

The standard scenario for economic development in a poor country calls for industrialization via investment. In this "top-down" view, creating opportunities for employment is the only way to end poverty. But for much of the developing world, increased employment exacerbates migration from the countryside to the cities and creates low-paying jobs in miserable conditions. I firmly believe that, instead, the eradication of poverty starts with people being able to control their own fates. It is not by creating jobs that we will save the poor but rather by providing them with the opportunity to realize their potential. Time and time again I have seen that the poor are poor not because they are lazy or untrained or illiterate but because they cannot keep the genuine returns on their labor.

Self-employment may be the only solution for such people, whom our economies refuse to hire and our taxpayers will not support. Microcredit views each person as a potential entrepreneur and turns on the tiny economic engines of a rejected portion of society. Once a large number of these engines start working, the stage can be set for enormous socioeconomic change.

Applying this philosophy, Grameen has established more than a dozen enterprises, often in partnership with other entrepreneurs. By assisting microborrowers and microsavers to take ownership of large enterprises and even infrastructure companies, we are trying to speed the process of overcoming poverty. Grameen Phone, for instance, is a cellular telephone company that aims to serve urban and rural Bangladesh. After a pilot study in 65 villages, Grameen Phone has taken a loan to extend its activities to all villages in which the bank is active. Some 50,000 women, many of whom have never seen a telephone or even an electric light, will become the providers of telephone service in their villages. Ultimately, they will become the owners of the company itself by buying its shares. Our latest innovation, Grameen Investments, allows U.S. individuals to support companies such as Grameen Phone while receiving interest on their investment. This is a significant step toward putting commercial funds to work to end poverty.

I believe it is the responsibility of any civilized society to ensure human dignity to all members and to offer each individual the best opportunity to reveal his or her creativity. Let us remember that poverty is not created by the poor but by the institutions and policies that we, the better off, have established. We can solve the problem not by means of the old concepts but by adopting radically new ones.

The Author

MUHAMMAD YUNUS, the founder and managing director of the Grameen Bank, was born in Bangladesh. He obtained a Ph.D. in economics from Vanderbilt University in 1970 and soon after returned to his home country to teach at Chittagong University. In 1976 he started the Grameen project, to which he has devoted all his time for the past decade. He has served on many advisory committees: for the government of Bangladesh, the United Nations, and other bodies concerned with poverty, women and health. He has received the World Food Prize, the Ramon Magsaysay Award, the Humanitarian Award, the Man for Peace Award and numerous other distinctions as well as six honorary degrees.

Further Reading

GRAMEEN BANK: PERFORMANCE AND SUSTAINABILITY. Shahidur R. Khandker, Baqui Khalily and Zahed Khan. World Bank Discussion Papers, No. 306. ISBN 0-8213-3463-8. World Bank, 1995.

GIVE US CREDIT. Alex Counts. Times Books (Random House), 1996.

FIGHTING POVERTY WITH MICROCREDIT: EXPERIENCE IN BANGLADESH. Shabidur R. Khandker. Oxford University Press, 1998.

Grameen Bank site is available at www.grameenfoundation.org on the World Wide Web.

Article 29　　　　　　　　　　　　　　　　　*The World Today*, November 1993

Bhutan: The Dilemmas of a Small State

John Bray

Bhutan is the last Himalayan Buddhist kingdom to retain its independence. It is nearly the same size as Switzerland and, with only 600,000 inhabitants, is among the world's smallest states. However, it is sandwiched between two of the largest: India and China. Traditionally isolated both by geography and as a deliberate political strategy, it is now pursuing a policy of cautious modernisation. Many of Bhutan's dilemmas are common to other developing countries: how to balance tradition with modernity; how to stimulate popular participation without creating instability; how to promote economic growth without damaging the environment. In addition it faces the special problems of a small, landlocked state which depends heavily on India and at the same time wishes to preserve the independence and integrity of its decision-making.

In the Bhutanese government's view, all these issues are linked to the most important question of all: how to preserve the country's culture and identity. In the government's view, this identity is now challenged not only by the normal proc-

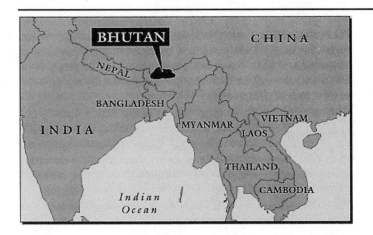

esses of social and political change but also by the special difficulties of absorbing a growing population of Nepali origin. According to official estimates, Nepalis now make up some 28 per cent of the total population, but Nepali dissidents claim that this figure should be 50 per cent or even higher. In the late 1980s the Bhutanese authorities took steps to curb the number of illegal immigrants in the south of the country. Since then at least 85,000 Nepalis from Bhutan have taken refuge in camps in Nepal. The camp-dwellers insist that they have a right to Bhutanese citizenship and have been persecuted in their home country; the authorities in Thimphu, the capital, dismiss both these claims. Bhutan therefore finds itself caught up in a damaging human rights controversy which has soured its reputation as a haven of premodern tranquillity. This article examines the choices that Bhutan will have to make—and the contradictions that it faces—as it struggles to sustain its culture and independence into the next century.

Bhutan's origins

Unlike many more recently emerged nations in Asia and Africa, Bhutan can claim a continuous existence as a separate polity for over three centuries. The country traces its origins to the mid-seventeenth century when a Tibetan monk, Shabdrung Ngawang Namgyal, united the area within its present borders. The Shabdrung, as he is generally known, was a leader of the Drukpa Kagyudpa sect of Tibetan Buddhism as distinct from the 'Yellow Hat' Gelugpa sect which dominated Lhasa politics. The 'Druk' in the sect's name means 'Dragon', and the local name for the country is 'Druk Yul' or 'Land of the Dragon'. The indigenous Buddhist population, most of whom live in the north of the country, are known collectively as 'Drukpas'.

Buddhism has acted as a unifying force, but there has always been considerable cultural variety. There are 18 distinct indigenous languages. The two most important are Dzongkha, which is spoken in the west of the country and has become the new national language, and Sharchop, which is the *lingua franca* of the eastern districts. The third major language is Nepali, which is widely spoken throughout the country but especially in the south.

The first Nepali settlers entered southern Bhutan—with official encouragement—in the late nineteenth century. They quickly assumed an important economic role, first as cultivators and later as businessmen, teachers and civil servants. In 1958 the government granted citizenship to those who could prove residence in Bhutan. Henceforth Bhutan's Nepalis were to be known officially as 'Lhotshampas' (southerners), and for the next three decades the country provided what appeared to be a model of racial integration. Lhotshampas benefited from the government's education programme, and by 1990 made up 39 per cent of Bhutan's civil servants.

The political system

Bhutan has never been through a major revolution, and its political institutions are therefore the product of a long process of evolution and adaptation. The question it now faces is whether these institutions can be adapted to the demands of modern statehood.

The emergence of the monarchy is a comparatively recent development. Until the early twentieth century the country was ruled by a diarchy of lay and religious rulers. The first King, Sir Ugyen Wangchuk, was crowned only in 1907—with the blessing of the British. The present King, Jigme Singye Wangchuk, is the fourth, and ascended the throne in 1972 at the age of 17. The monarchy is based on a contract with the people and has never held absolute power. The King himself has expressed doubt whether it will continue to be an appropriate institution for Bhutan in the twenty-first century. However, there is general consensus that the monarchy acts as a vital political focus to unite the country. The King is a serious-minded and hard-working ruler: he is genuinely revered.

Bhutan's legal system is founded on customary law and on a code established by the Shabdrung which itself is based on Buddhist ethics. However, the third King, Jigme Dorje Wangchuk (1952–72), began a series of reforms to modernise the legal framework. These reforms included the introduction of a National Assembly (Tshogdu), which consists of 105 elected lay members, 12 clergy and 37 senior civil servants. The King participates in the Assembly sessions, which normally take place twice a year. He has no legal right of veto, but in practice the Assembly members defer to his views. The King's views are more liberal than those of the average MP, particularly on the present Lhotshampa crisis. Bhutan's present political system therefore provides a balance between traditional deference to authority and popular consultation.

External links

Under the terms of a treaty signed in 1910, Bhutan agreed to accept British advice in its external relations and in return secured a promise of non-interference in the country's internal affairs. In 1949 Bhutan signed a further treaty confirming the main principles of this arrangement with the newly independent government of India. This relationship has worked to both sides' advantage. New Delhi values Bhutan as a convenient buffer between India and China and has trained its defence forces. Indian support helped deter aggression from China, which in the 1950s claimed Bhutan, along with Tibet, as part of its territory.

Over the last 25 years Bhutan has sought to diversify its foreign contacts. In 1971 it joined the United Nations, and it is an active member of the South Asian Association for Regional Cooperation (SAARC). However, the shortage of trained manpower imposes a practical constraint on Bhutan's diplomacy: it maintains embassies in only five countries and has full diplomatic relations with no more than 20. Most of these are either near neighbours or key aid partners. Bhutan has never had formal diplomatic relations with either the former Soviet Union or with the United States—though it is now considering opening an embassy in Washington.

In recent years the potential threat from the north appears to have diminished. Bhutan and China have held a series of meetings on the demarcation of their 470km-long common border; the ninth such meeting took place in Thimphu in July 1993. It is understood that the main sources of controversy have been settled but that the two sides find it convenient to meet regularly without going so far as to exchange ambassadors.

India remains by far the most important of Bhutan's foreign partners. For example, India continues to finance 40 per cent of Bhutan's government expenditure and receives 90 per cent of Bhutan's exports. Indian engineers built most of Bhutan's roads and Indian soldiers continue to influence the country's defence policy.

Bhutan's foreign policy has always been pragmatic, with clearly defined aims. In spite of the constraints imposed by its landlocked position between India and China, it has so far succeeded in asserting its independence while maintaining effective contact with neighbours and aid donors. The broad direction of its foreign policy—including the close link with India—is unlikely to change in the foreseeable future.

Economic development

King Jigme Dorje Wangchuk began Bhutan's economic modernisation programme in the 1950s partly because he believed that failure to do so would undermine his country's long-term chances of survival. Bhutan's small size, and the fact that it began the development process relatively late, have brought both advantages and disadvantages.

Bhutan's smallness means that the higher echelons of authority are more accessible than they might otherwise be. Furthermore, the country's planners are in a position to learn from the mistakes of other countries who launched their development programmes earlier. Its other advantages include ample natural resources—notably timber—and a substantial potential for hydroelectric power. Unlike other countries in the region, Bhutan is free from the pressures of over-population, and this gives it a certain freedom of manoeuvre.

The disadvantages of Bhutan's small size include its inability to make economies of scale. For example, the national airline Druk Air has recently expanded its fleet from one airliner to two. The second airliner cost $20m, and its purchase therefore made a major impact on the country's hard-currency reserves, now estimated at $90m. These two aircraft require a large team of technicians and airport staff who inevitably are fully engaged for relatively short periods in any given week.

A much-quoted comment by the King states that 'gross national happiness' is more important than 'gross national product'. His aim is to improve his subjects' standards of living without introducing the social problems which have soured the development process elsewhere in South Asia. Government planners place much emphasis on the virtues of sustainability, decentralisation and—more recently—privatisation. While making the most of aid from a variety of government and non-government sources, they hope in the long term to ensure their country's self-reliance.

Bhutan's efforts to encourage self-reliance have succeeded to the extent that it is able to finance all recurrent government expenditure from tax income and export receipts. However, internal sources will finance no more than only 30 per cent of the current seventh five-year plan. As noted above, India provides 40 per cent, and the remaining 30 per cent comes from other aid donors.[1] One of the most important projects involving India is the Chhukha hydroelectric scheme: almost all the electricity produced by the scheme is exported to India, and further similar projects are planned as a future source of foreign exchange.

Tourism is another source of foreign exchange. However, the government imposes strict limits on tourism in line with its determination to preserve the national culture from harmful outside influences. Only 2,748 tourists visited Bhutan in 1992, and they were each obliged to pay some $200 per day. Bhutan evidently is seeking maximum income from minimum cultural pollution.

Although Bhutan has made considerable economic progress, it continues to depend heavily on foreign expertise in several fields. For example, in 1991, 36.1 per cent of all primary school teachers were non-Bhutanese citizens, as were 43 per cent of the teachers in junior high schools and 54.7 per cent in senior high schools. At a more mundane level, most road and construction workers come from India and Nepal. Bhutan will continue to require substantial inputs of foreign expertise—and muscle-power—for the foreseeable future.

Developing a 'modern' culture

The Bhutanese government is acutely conscious that economic development is bringing about social changes which challenge the country's traditional culture—or cultures. It has responded by taking steps to instil a unified sense of national identity.

In particular, it is promoting the use of Dzongkha, the western Bhutanese language which traditionally is spoken in eight out of the country's 20 districts and derives ultimately from Tibetan. Throughout Bhutan the traditional written language has been classical Tibetan (*chos-skad*), the language used to translate the Buddhist scriptures. However, *chos-skad*'s complexity and its remoteness from Bhutan's spoken languages made it impractical for day-to-day use. The government has therefore appointed a team of scholars to develop Dzongkha as a written language. English remains the language of instruction in Bhutanese schools because of its international importance. However, Dzongkha is a compulsory subject and the Dzongkha Development Commission has now prepared a series of textbooks for use at all levels. Since 1989 the government has discontinued the teaching of Nepali in schools on the ground that children found it confusing to learn three languages at once.

Alongside its propagation of Dzongkha, the government has also promoted the *Driglam Namzha,* which is translated as 'traditional values and etiquette'. The aspect of *Driglam Namzha* which has received most attention has been the dress code. All Bhutanese citizens are expected to wear national dress on official occasions and when visiting *dzongs*—the fortress/monasteries which serve as government offices in much of Bhutan. For men, traditional dress consists of the *gho,* while women are expected to wear the *kira.* Both are robe-like garments associated with the Buddhist north of the country.

This policy glosses over the extent of Bhutan's traditional cultural variety: traditionally the *gho* has been far from universal even in the Drukpa north. The dress code has proved particularly controversial among the Nepali/Lhotshampa population in the south of the country, where quite different cultural traditions prevail.

Tensions in the south

Two events outside Bhutan appear to have influenced Thimphu's policy on the Lhotshampas. The first was India's annexation of Sikkim in 1974. Sikkim's political association with India had always been closer than Bhutan's, but the two kingdoms nevertheless had much in common. Like Bhutan, Sikkim had experienced large-scale Nepali migration. By 1974 the Nepali population far outnumbered the indigenous Lepchas and Bhotias in Sikkim, and it was the Nepalis rather than the other two communities who called for integration with India. Many Bhutanese believed that India's annexation set a worrying precedent for their own country.

The second event was the mid-1980s Gurkha National Liberation Front (GNLF) agitation in Darjeeling which called for the creation of a Nepali-speaking state within the Indian union. New Delhi resisted the creation of a separate state but sanctioned the establishment of a semi-autonomous Hill Council. This episode again highlighted the growing political power of Nepali-speakers outside Nepal—and in a region immediately adjacent to Bhutan.

In 1985 the Bhutanese government passed a new Citizenship Act. The Act defined the requirements for citizenship more rigidly than before and defined seven categories of residents and non-residents from 'F1' (full citizen) to 'F7' (non-national). The new legislation defined 1958—the date of the previous Citizenship Act—as the cut-off point for citizenship. Lhotshampas had to provide documentary evidence that they—or both parents—had resided in the country since 1958. Some who had been provided with citizenship certificates under previous legislation now found that these were considered void.

In 1988 the government conducted a formal census operation in southern Bhutan with a view to detecting illegal immigrants. The census caused considerable disquiet in the south because of the way in which it was conducted. Many Lhotshampas who had previously believed their status to be secure now felt under threat.

Meanwhile, the government made greater efforts to enforce the *Driglam Namzha* regulations, particularly the dress code, as part of its national integration policy. It appears that officials in the south enforced the regulations even more strictly than the government intended, so that Lhotshampas were obliged to wear the *gho* and the *kira* whenever they went to the market and not just on special occasions.

In response to these pressures, a group of Lhotshampas formed the People's Forum for Human Rights in 1989 and the Bhutan People's Party (BPP) in 1990. The BPP began to stage public protests, and these culminated in a series of mass demonstrations in southern Bhutan in September and October 1990. Some 18,000 people joined in protests in nine different places to the extent that the government feared that it faced an open revolt.

Terrorists and refugees

The events of 1990 mark a turning-point in what has become known as the 'southern problem'. Since then, the battle lines have been clear. On the one side the government claims that Bhutan faces a threat to its survival. On the other, Lhotshampa dissidents claim that they face a deliberate policy of persecution to drive them from the country. From the government's point of view, the main threat stems from 'anti-nationals' or '*ngolops*' who since 1990 have launched a series of terrorist attacks, mainly on government targets. By March 1993 the Bhutanese government had reported 56 killings in the terrorist campaign, 35 rapes, 201 kidnappings and 510 armed robberies, though it has been suggested that many of these incidents may have been the work of ordinary criminals rather than dissidents.[2]

The Lhotshampas themselves have suffered most—both as a result of direct attack and because of the disruption of development initiatives. By the end of 1990, 76 schools in the south were closed down, though many have since re-opened. According to government figures, terrorists have destroyed over 200 installations, including 29 schools, 12 health units, 14 water supply projects and 8 power pylons.

Meanwhile, thousands of Lhotshampa refugees have fled to Nepal. By July 1993 there were 85,000 refugees in Nepali camps, and several thousand more were thought to be staying elsewhere in Nepal and northern India. This exodus naturally has caused tensions between Bhutan and Nepal—which can ill afford to support the refugees. Meetings between Bhutanese and Nepali leaders held in 1991 and 1992 failed to find the basis of a common approach to the problem. The main points at issue have been the identity of the refugees and their reasons for leaving Bhutan.

Until now the Bhutan government has claimed that the overwhelming majority of refugees are either former illegal immigrants or else ex-Bhutanese nationals who have sold their property and registered their departure with local officials, thus forfeiting their right to citizenship. It offers several reasons to explain these emigrants' wish to leave—including pressure from 'anti-national' relatives who have already left, and coercion from the BPP. One theory suggests that the BPP and its allies plan to muster 100,000 refugees in Nepal in the hope that this will discredit Bhutan abroad and that aid donors will force it to change its policies.

The refugees themselves claim that they left as a result of deliberate government pressure. One particular episode illustrates the claims and counter-claims by the two sides.[3] In May 1992 terrorists shot and killed Chime Dorji, the Sub-Divisional Officer (SDO) of Geylegphug. According to Lhotshampa refugees now in Nepal, Chime Dorji's successor called a meeting of villagers and told them to 'go back to their own country', whether they were 'F-1' or 'F-7'. The King himself later heard that 400 families from the district had applied to leave the country. He appealed in person for them to stay and promised an enquiry into the SDO's threats. However, most of the 400 families had already left by the time the investigation team came to make its enquiries, and the SDO was exonerated.

Questions for the future

In July 1993, Bhutan and Nepal agreed to set up a ministerial-level joint committee to determine the different categories of people in the Nepali refugee camps; to arrive at a mutually acceptable agreement on the approach to each of these categories; and thus provide the basis of a solution to the current crisis. This appears be a diplomatic breakthrough, but it remains to be seen whether the two sides will have the political will to implement the agreement objectively. The Nepali government, which is distracted by many other pressures, cannot afford to seem negligent of the interests of fellow-Nepalis in need. Equally, the Bhutanese government faces pressure from its Drukpa constituents not to make concessions to people who are said to have demonstrated their disloyalty simply by leaving the country.

India's role will remain crucial, either overtly or behind the scenes. Bhutan's problems are on a small scale by comparison with India's—for example in Assam, where the number of alleged illegal immigrants is counted in millions. Perhaps partly for this reason, India has so far eschewed public involvement in the Lhotshampa controversy, although it is indirectly implicated since the refugees must have passed through India on their way to Nepal. In August 1993, shortly before an official visit to Thimphu, the Indian Prime Minister, Narasimha Rao, confirmed that India considers the refugee issue to be a bilateral affair between Bhutan and Nepal.

Whatever happens at the Nepal–Bhutan joint committee, Bhutan will continue to face a problem of national integration. Here the King's personal leadership will be vitally important. His approach to the 'southern problem' has been consistently conciliatory. For example, since 1990 he has granted amnesties to over 1,500 people who were detained for 'anti-national activities'. He has continued this policy in the face of speeches in the National Assembly suggesting that this approach was too gentle.

There is no indication that the King is about to change his conciliatory policy, but the popular tensions of the last three years have, if anything, widened the differences of perception between the Drukpa and Lhotshampa communities. Both sides believe that they are fighting for their survival, and both will lose out unless they recognise their common interest in creating a modern state which genuinely recognises unity in diversity.

NOTES

1. Karma Ura, 'Development and decentralisation in modern Bhutan'. Paper presented at the conference on 'Bhutan: a traditional order and the forces of change'. School of Oriental and African Studies (SOAS), University of London, March 1993.

2. Kinley Dorji, 'Bhutan's current crisis'. Paper presented at the SOAS conference on Bhutan.

3. The incident is discussed, from rival points of view, in the June, July and August editions of *Kuensel*, Bhutan's national newspaper; and in the July/August edition of *Himal*, published in Kathmandu.

Article 30   *The Economist*, May 13, 2000

Letter from Maldives

Not sinking but drowning

MALE, MALDIVES

HOW do you keep paradise afloat? The Maldivians urgently want to know. Their ocean country is made up of more than a thousand coral islands strewn across the turquoise waters of the equatorial Indian ocean. Buoyed by good weather, good location and lots of tourism, the country's 250,000 or so citizens lead comfortable lives. Yet for how much longer, nobody knows. The sea around them is rising.

The problem of greenhouse gases may sound nebulous in Maidstone or Miami. But to the people of Maldives it is a clear and present danger. The noisy tea shops of Male, the capital, are full of men (no women: this is an Islamic country) who can tell you all about the early signs of impending disaster. Fishermen hawking their catch at the market complain of the decline in live bait. Hotel owners lament that the warming of the sea has bleached the life, and pretty colours, out of much of the famous coral.

And in case anyone should gaze at the clear sky or sparkling water and wonder if life wasn't so bad after all, Abdul Gayoom, the president of the Maldives and Asia's longest-serving ruler, is never silent for long on the threat that global warming poses to his fellow citizens and to the island's tourism. He uses his grip on the local press to keep the dangers close to the front of everyone's mind. Nor do his anxieties stop at his own country's coral. He is world spokesman for low-lying islanders everywhere.

Engineering is one answer, for Maldives at least. To combat the surge in storms and waves, the government has built what locals call the Great Wall of Male: a concrete barrier 1.8-metre (6 ft) high that partly rings the capital. Set

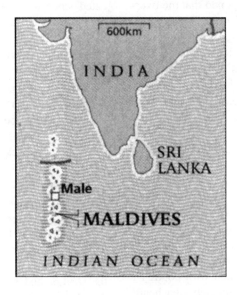

just off shore, it was designed to absorb wave energy and spare Male further damage. More ambitious is Hulhumale, an artificial island, higher than Male, that officials say they are building nearby. Sceptics mock. But the plan is to house perhaps half the country's present population there, eventually.

Most of the Maldives coral is less than a metre above sea level. So a sea-level rise of three-quarters of a metre this century, which many who study climate think it reasonable to expect, would wipe the country out. Even a less fearsome 20-centimetre rise, combined with bigger waves, could wreak havoc.

William Allison, a scientist who lives in Male, explains it as follows. Global warming threatens coral in several ways. Rising seas are not bad in themselves. They give coral more upward growing room. But coral flourishes in water of around 22°C. A warmer atmosphere threatens to heat the local ocean to more than that, killing the coral. Another danger is carbon dioxide. When too much

of this gas dissolves in sea water, corals build skeletons only with the greatest difficulty. A final worry is that hotter temperatures will increase the scale and frequency of storms.

It sounds grim. But Robert Mendelsohn of Yale University has a cheery, get-in-your-boat solution. Not that he thinks low-lying islanders are exaggerating. Their reefs and beaches could well be submerged, in his view. But burning less oil to keep air cool so ice stays ice and the seas don't warm is too expensive and roundabout a way to meet the danger, Mr Mendelsohn thinks. Wouldn't it be cheaper, he asks, for Maldivians, and those like them, to move?

On cost, he may be right. But people like their homes. Particularly Maldives homes. There was a time when the Maldivians were more nomadic. Life was not always so idyllic. In the past, when storms destroyed one island habitat, they would move to another. Nowadays, they would rather stay if they can. Even so, one government idea is to gather the people of the smaller islands on to three bigger ones, and defend these behind sea walls.

This is not without regret. The country's environment minister talks fondly of small-island life, particularly its sense of community, which he feels is missing in the bustle of Male. Yet the outliers may not have a choice. "We simply cannot have 200 inhabited islands, one with 60,000 people and others with 200, vying for the same expensive defences and services!" In consequence, he explains, the government wants "to consolidate services into three regional hubs."

Mural defences have drawbacks of their own. The coral that forms the islands is porous, making them in effect giant sponges. If the ocean continues to rise, before long the salt water will begin to seep through from under the walls. Quite apart from that, the cost can be astonishing. Someone has calculated that the Great Wall of Male cost $13,000 per linear metre to build.

It is interesting to know how Maldives could afford this. As an official explains, the Japanese government was generous enough to pay for it. He hesitates. Yes? He goes on: the aid was linked to a contract award for a Japanese firm, which used patented technology. To extend or repair the wall, the official complains, they must buy from the firm at outrageous prices. "These rich countries pollute the atmosphere," he says as

a flash of anger displaces his jovial smile, "and then they profit from it."

Making and unmaking paradise

It sounds wrenching: peaceful denizens of a simple land in harmony with their environment, paying for others' wastefulness. Is it so simple? Oil-guzzlers in rich countries do have something to answer for. But not all Maldives' troubles can be laid at their door. Like most paradises, Maldives is to a large extent artificial. Development made the harsh coral habitable. Development brought the hotels (over 80 at last count). And development is bringing problems, familiar and less familiar.

Jetties and harbour breakwalls have weakened natural sea defences. They

channel sand to deep water while landfills extend the coastline to the vulnerable deepwater verge. The Great Wall of Male was probably needed only because the island's natural wave buffer, its wide, flat reef, was filled in to house a booming population.

People take their toll in other ways. Male's residents have made such a call on the underlying aquifer that the ground water is now laced with salt. Their fresh water (and soft drinks) reach them by way of desalinisation plants. Even fresh air is getting scarce. The city of Male has terrible traffic jams and people idle their engines even when standing still just to run the air conditioning. How do you keep paradise afloat? How do you keep paradise paradise?

Article 31

World Today, February 1, 2000

Front line, Fault line

The hijacking at the turn of the year of an Indian Airlines jet by opponents of India's administration of Kashmir, has focussed attention again on an increasingly dangerous fault line. As the crisis ended in Kandahar, Afghanistan, the five hijackers disappeared, with three militants whose release from Indian custody they had secured, into an area that some regard as a zone of chaos.

Mohan Malik

IN THEIR RECENT BOOK, *Anticipating the Future*, Barry Buzan and Gerald Segal visualised the area west of India—Pakistan, Afghanistan and parts of Central Asia—becoming a 'zone of chaos' by 2030. The signs of this are already visible. -The Afghanistan-Pakistan area is now the main centre of Islamism, drug trafficking, the illicit trade in small arms and international terrorism.

The last decade has seen the growth there of religious and fundamentalist organisations and terror outfits masquerading as 'holy warriors' and 'freedom fighters; causing death and destruction.

Fanatical Islamists, reportedly led by Osama bin-Laden and linked to drug trafficking networks, have long enjoyed the military support of Afghanistan's Taliban militia and Pakistan's armed forces. Their cross-border operations have increasingly blurred the distinction between 'regulaars' and 'irregulars' The roots of Islamic terror, from Algiers to Xinjiang and Chechnya and Daghestan to Kashmir, can be traced to this area.

The Pakistani army—and the Taliban-backed—armed intrusion into Indian administered Kashmir last May was as much an extension of the twodecade-old

Afghan conflict as a direct consequence of the power struggle between Pakistan's civilian government and its militarist authoritarian power structure.

The Kashmir misadventure was followed by the October military coup in Islamabad that deposed the popularly elected Prime Minister, Nawaz Sharief. The coup further shattered any hopes ofthe restoration of the Lahore process of dialogue, begun last February between India and Pakistan. This had been derailed in May by the Kashmir conflict.

MILITARY MORASS

The coup has been widely perceived in the West as the last desperate military attempt to prevent Pakistan's slow slide into the ranks of 'failed states' However, notwithstanding some attempts at positive spin—the appointment of scholars/ academics like Maleeha Lodhi and Akbar Ahmed as the regime's envoys in Washington and London; the projection of Musharraf as the upright and patriotic General who came to the rescue of a beleaguered state and as the 'saviour of democracy'- the sad reality is that the military's role and policies have largely contributed to Pakistan's current morass.

Militarism and democracy are like oil and water; they have never mixed and never will. As the examples of Burma and Indonesia demonstrate, the virus of militarism in politics is not only detrimental to strengthening nationhood, but also adversely affects state and civil society, endangering democratic pluralism and civil liberties.

The military coup itself is a reflection of the failing state phenomenon experienced first in Afghanistan and now in Pakistan. It has already set in motion new geopolitical alignments in Southwest Asia.

AFGHANISTAN-PAKISTAN NEXUS

Far from being a solution to Pakistan's current woes, General Pervez Musharraf is part of the problem. A veteran of the Afghan conflict, he is to a great extent responsible not only for the establishment of close links between the Taliban militia and Pakistani army, but also for the Afghanisation of the Kashmir dispute and the Talibanisation of Pakistan.

Pakistan has long sought to use Afghanistan as a buffer against Iran, as a conduit for Central Asian trade and as a strategic space vis-ah-vis India. In the process, it has alienated its neighbours to the east and west.

Iranian-Pakistani ties have been strained over their support for opposing sides in the Afghan civil war, with Islamabad backing the Sunni Muslim Taliban militia, which controls most of Afghanistan, and Iran—along with Russia—supporting the ousted Rabbani

government and the Nor-them Alliance. India has always interpreted the Pakistani military's victory in installing a Taliban regime in Kabul as having inflated its ambitions and whetted its appetite. Despite the imposition of UN sanctions against Afghanistan, Musharraf has signalled no change in Islamabad's Afghanistan policy. He needs to appease the radical Islamic forces within Pakistan who support the Taliban, and have a history of destabilising governments that they dislike. Without military, diplomatic and economic support from Pakistan, however, the Taliban's days in power would be numbered.

Islamabad also feels indebted to the Taliban for giving sanctuary to the Pakistanbacked Kashmiri militants who are fighting the Indian army. As one senior Pakistani bureaucrat told the Far Eastern Economic Review in November, 'Unfortunately, our policy towards Afghanistan has become intimately linked to our policy to Kashmir. It's difficult to see how we can disengage from one without harming the other.'

That the Pakistani military leadership has been working hand in hand with guerrilla fighters and hardened Afghan mercenaries is no secret. At the height of the 1999 Kashmir conflict, General Musharraf allowed full military honours for slain fighters from the Harkatul-Mujahideen—an organisation on the US State Department's list of terrorists.

Pakistan's military establishment believes that a pliable Taliban regime in Afghanistan to the west, now provides the strategic depth it has long sought vis-h-vis its much larger neighbour to the east. For instance, in the event of a full-scale war with India, Pakistan's military assets potentially including nuclear-armed aircraft and missiles—could be deployed in Afghanistan's mountainous terrain.

In the calculations of some Pakistani strategists, should India decide to strike deep inside Afghan territory, it would lead to a wider war (jihad) between Islamic countries and predominantly Hindu India. However, the very thought of Pakistani nukes in Taliban-controlled territory ought to send shivers down the spines of Pentagon analysts.

POWERFUL CAUSE

From the regional security viewpoint, it should be noted that two of the three wars in South Asia took place when Pakistan was under a military dictator— General Ayub Khan in 1965 and General Yahya Khan in 1971. Likewise, the 1999 Kashmir battle was masterminded by none other than General Musharraf

Interestingly, when the Indian Prime Minister Atal Behari Vajpayee went to Lahore last February, General Musharraf, along with his counterparts in the Navy and Air Force, publicly defied his Prime Minister's orders to be present at

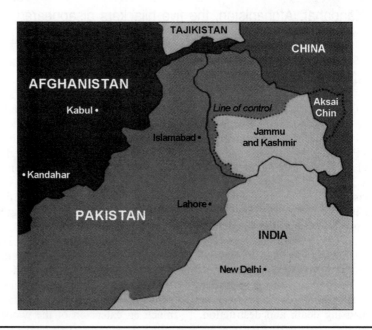

the welcoming ceremony. They preferred to be with their friend, the visiting Chinese Army Chief, who happened to be in Islamabad.

General Musharraf is said to have embarked upon the Kashmir misadventure without Sharief's consent or knowledge. After all, Kashmir is the cause that keeps the military in a powerful, privileged position. This, in turn, acts as the glue that binds the Pakistani state together.

Any permanent peace with India, which could turn the present Kashmir Line of Control into the regular border, is not looked on kindly by the Pakistan military as it would reduce its status, power and budget. It could even lead to the withering of the Pakistani state. A few, weeks before the coup, General Musharraf told the BBC that even a settlement of the Kashmir issue would not usher in regional peace.

It is significant that the military coup, although rooted in the US-manoeuvred withdrawal of Pakistani troops from the icy heights in Indian administered Kashmir, followed an open rift between civilian (Sharief) and military (Musharraf) authorities over American pressure to break the Taliban-army nexus and halt the country's rapid descent into anarchy,

General Musharraf believes that the military adventures in Afghanistan and Kashmir were 'great successes betrayed by a weak civilian government, and that the army was being robbed of the opportunity to consolidate its territorial gains.

After each conflict with India—in 1965, 1971 and 1999—there has been a political upheaval leading to the overthrow of the Pakistani ruler. Repeated attempts by the civilian leadership to marginalise the military over key strategic subjects such as Kashmir, nuclear capability and Afghanistan have always backfired.

With the man responsible for derailing the Lahore peace process now firmly entrenched in power, the chances of reconciliation between New Delhi and Islamabad and wider regional peace have faded.

CHINA'S CAIN?

Recent developments signal waning US influence on its erstwhile ally. During the Cold War, Pakistan's delusions of grandeur as a strategic counterweight to non-aligned India and as a frontline state against the 'evil' Soviets, were nurtured and nourished by British and American cold-warriors.

Washington turned a blind eye to Pakistan's quest for nuclear weapons as the country had become a willing conduit for clandestine CIA funds and weaponry for the Afghan mujahideen. The mujahideen, which the US supported against the former Soviet Union, has now transformed itself into a multinational, hydra-headed, Islamic monster.

Still, the United States is unlikely to abandon Pakistan, despite its propensity for aberrant behaviour and the likelihood of it becoming a failed state. The Clinton administration, while pressing for the return of civilian rule, has stressed that it is not going to walk away from Pakistan, given the United States' range of regional and global interests. Convinced that worse will follow if General Musharraf fails to control the situation, the US and some Western countries are not averse to dropping a lifeline to the military regime.

Pakistan is also kept afloat by China and the oil-rich Arab States. The removal of the pro-Western Sharief regime has left Beijing in a stronger position. The need to sustain good relations with Pakistan is now linked to the rise of Islamic extremism in Xinjiang, and other parts of China. Friendly ties with Islamabad could limit the flow of disruptive Islamic ideas from Afghanistan and Pakistan.

LOOSE NUKES

Though Pakistan is no stranger to military coups, what is worrying this time is that it is now an overt nuclear weapon state. While the military has charge of the nuclear weapons, it now holds them without even the pretence of elected civilian control.

To make-matters worse, the military is no longer a unified institution. Since the mid-1980s, well-organised groups of Islamic zealots have penetrated its core middle and lower ranks, and it is now split into pro- and anti-Western factions. Those elements that want to use Islam and nuclear weapons for a politically ag-gressive role, and as bargaining chips, are gaining influence.

There is also some concern that Pakistan's economic crisis could lead it to transfer either nuclear know-how or weapons to states like Saudi Arabia or Iran. Pakistan's economy is propped up by loans from the International Monetary Fund and World Bank.

General Musbarrafs first overseas trip was to Saudi Arabia. This raised eyebrows in the region because not long before, the Saudi Defence Minister Sultan Bin Abdul Aziz had visited the highly secret Pakistani nuclear facilities at Kahuta, The Tadla complex and the uranium enrichment plan. The minister also met Dr AQ Khan, head of Pakistan's nuclear weapons programme.

There is growing speculation that the Saudis have offered to help salvage Pakistan from bankruptcy in return for sharing nuclear technology. Saudi Arabia is also looking for replacements for mediumrange ballistic missiles, bought from China in 1988, which are nearing the end of their operational life. Islamabad might be tempted to provide medium-range solidfuelled Chinese M-11 or Ghauri missiles to Riyadh in return for financial assistance. The missile nexus between Pakistan and North Korea is already well known.

DESTABILISING

Failed states, characterised by ungovernability, decaying infrastructure, corruption, chaos, violence, and a no-holdsbarred contest for power, have become a source of post-Cold War instability. Fragmentation often destabilises neighbouring countries. It may be followed by a rise of suppressed nationalism, ethnic or religious violence, humanitarian disasters, major regional crises, and the spread of dangerous weapons.

Signs that Afghanistan's today could be Pakistan's tomorrow are clearly visible. Its cities are infested with Islamic and drugtrafficking militias and the country is awash with arms and overwhelmed by sectarian violence. Should the central government lose effective control, Pakistan would descend into chaos and create instability for the whole of Southwest and Central Asia. The region thus faces, for the first time, the prospect of a failing, if not failed, state with weapons of mass destruction. Such a state may not behave like a responsible, rational, nuclear weapon power—an essential prerequisite for successful nuclear deterrence.

As the Soviet Union's case shows, the disintegration of a nuclear power is particularly fraught with dangers. Weapons of mass destruction may fall into the hands of separatists or religious fanatics. In conditions of civil war and internal chaos, nuclear materials or facilities could conceivably be used as bargaining chips in a struggle for internal power, or to obtain leverage with external forces.

A Talibanised, militarised and nuclearised Pakistan acting as a rogue state would not bode well for regional security. There have already been geopolitical realignments. The warming of Indo-US relations since last year's Kashmir conflict is a case in point.

Just as Pakistan was the frontline state against Soviet expansion, India is now seen as the frontline state against the new threats to international security.

The Narco-Nuclear-Fundamentalist-Terrorist menace in Southwest Asia could threaten the whole of Central Asia, including parts of Russia and China.

For its part, Beijing now has to weigh up the dangers for its security of a weak, unstable Pakistan. China's support for Russia's military offensive in Chechnya indicates that Beijing sees Moscow's assertiveness in Central Asia as increasing its own security against Islamist forces. In the long term, Beijing may have to rethink its alliances in Asia—they all happen to be weak, failing states: Pakistan, Burma and North Korea.

Washington has a great deal at stake in Pakistan and retains significant economic leverage. The United States' moves to counter China's growing influence strengthen Islamabad's negotiating position.

CHANGES NEEDED

Although the military regime in Pakistan has committed itself to resurrecting the state by reviving the bankrupt economy, curbing corruption, preserving civil

liberties and ending the ethnic and sectarian violence, its chances of success are not very bright because it has not implemented radical policy changes.

These changes would include: breaking the Taliban-army nexus; delinking Afghanistan from Pakistan's India policy; an end to the military sponsorship of militant factions in Afghanistan and Kashmir; a quick return to the barracks; a peaceful negotiated settlement of the Kashmir dispute; and an expansion of economic and trade links in South and Central Asia.

As long as real power is exercised by the army, the mullahs and the feudal lords in the name of Islam, jihad and Kashmir, there will be no peace in the region.

Dr Mohan Malik is Director of the Defence Studies Programme at Deakin University in Victoria, Australia.

Article 32   *New York Times,* September 11, 2000

Rebels Without a Childhood in Sri Lanka War

By CELIA W. DUGGER

PALALI, Sri Landa, Sept. 9—Renuka, a 13-year-old wisp of a girl, said she is afraid she will be scolded because she chose not to swallow her cyanide capsule.

Recruited at age 11 by ethnic Tamil rebels to fight for a separate state, she lay wounded on the front lines of Sri Lanka's civil war six days ago, surrounded by the blasted bodies of three other insurgents who were on duty with her when mortar fire hit their sentry post.

But rather than kill herself to avoid capture as her superiors in the Liberation Tigers of Tamil Eelam had ordered, Renuka said she wrapped her bloody chest in a sarong and waited for the soldiers from the Sri Lankan Army. "I didn't want to die," she said in a thin, quavering voice during an interview at an army detention camp here. "And I'm not going back to the L.T.T.E. They will threaten me and scold me and ask why I didn't take the cyanide."

Two years ago the Tigers met in northern Sri Lanka with Olara A. Ottunu, the United Nations official charged with trying to halt the use of an estimated 300,000 child soldiers worldwide. They promised him that they would stop recruiting children under 17 and sending anyone under age 18 into battle. But evidence emerging from the recent carnage in Sri Lanka's 17-year war with the separatist rebels strongly suggests that they have continued using children in their battle to win a homeland for the country's mostly Hindu Tamil minority in the north and east of the country.

Renuka and Malar Arumugam, another 13-year-old girl soldier captured by the army, gave accounts of their years with the Tigers in interviews through an independent Tamil translator. Malar, an orphan who said she was recruited at age 8, remains fiercely loyal to the Tigers, whom she regards as her family. She wept angrily when she spoke of what she called atrocities against Tamils by the Sri Lankan and Indian armies.

In contrast, Renuka, who said she left her impoverished family to join the Tigers largely because she was hungry and knew they would feed her, wants nothing more to do with the rebels. The Tigers refused to let her see her parents, and she believes that the rebel fighters abandoned her when she was wounded in battle.

The girls' stories could not be independently verified, though their wounds and scars were consistent with their accounts, as were the circumstances of their confinement. Army officials, happy to score propaganda points against the Tigers, readily agreed to allow Renuka, still in their custody, to be interviewed. Her last name was withheld by The New York Times out of concern that the rebels would punish her for turning against them.

A district magistrate in Jaffna permitted an interview with Malar, who unlike Renuka is still a true Tiger believer. Captured in July, she is now in judicial custody and is incarcerated in the run-down jail in Jaffna. Officials stood listening to both interviews.

One other thing also suggests that the Tigers are using child soldiers: the youthfulness of the rebel dead found after a Sept. 3 battle here on the Jaffna peninsula. Six of the 36 dead rebels whose bodies were picked up by the Sri

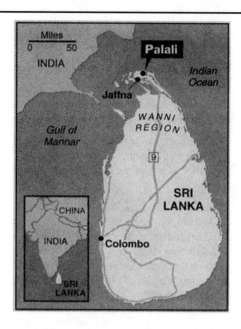

Lankan Army and returned to the Tigers appeared to have been girls between ages 12 and 16, said an international official who inspected them, but asked that the organization not be identified to preserve its ability to function in Jaffna.

Officials at the Jaffna Teaching Hospital, where the bodies were taken, declined to comment, but a hospital worker who saw the dead said, "Most of them were young, but you can't say whether they were 12, 14 16, 18 or 20. They were small-made." For the past year, human rights groups have alleged that the Tigers are still using child soldiers. In July, the United Teachers for Human Rights in Jaffna charged that the rebel group was rounding up an increasing number of boys and girls in its push to retake the Jaffna peninsula, a northern spit of land that had long been its stronghold.

The United States has classified the Tigers as a terrorist organization, but Canada and Great Britain, with substantial Tamil communities, have not banned the group, which raises money from the nearly one million Sri Lankan Tamils living abroad.

A man who identified himself as A. Shanthan, in the group's London branch, said he was not a spokesman for the organization and could not comment on the girls' stories. He said he would try to get an answer to faxed questions in coming days, though it was difficult for him to reach Tiger leaders in Sri Lanka.

The girls' stories had much in common, though Renuka was timid and soft-spoken, while Malar was defiant and angry. Both said they came from poor backgrounds, joined the Tigers without telling their families and received heavy indoctrination and arms training in Tiger camps.

Renuka hobbled out of the detention center, dressed in a polka-dotted hospital gown. She whimpered as she lowered herself into a chair shaded by a tree in the parking lot. Doctors had operated the day before to remove shrapnel from her chest.

She said she grew up in the desolate northern reaches of the country known as the Wanni. Her father was unemployed and she, her sister and her parents survived on the bit of money a relative in Colombo sent them every now and then. Often they went hungry.

Tiger soldiers came to her school every month on recruiting drives from the time she was in the 6th grade, she said. The children were gathered in the school's main hall as men and women in battle fatigues told them it was their duty to join the Tigers and help save the Tamil people from the approaching Sri Lankan army.

One day when she was in the 7th grade, Renuka told her parents she was going shopping, but instead went to a Tiger camp. She was hungry, she said, "and we all knew that they give meals."

As it turned out, she was well fed, but said she quickly regretted her choice. She pleaded to see her parents, but was told she could only have a visit after she had fought on the front lines. During the next two years, she said she and many other children were drilled in the Tiger view of history, the Tiger vision of a Tamil homeland and the Tiger cult of martyrdom. They learned to lob a grenade and dive for cover and to fire a machine gun on the run.

She was assigned to an all-female fighting group and dispatched a month ago to a battlefront east of the city of Jaffna. Early in the morning of Sept. 3, the Sri Lankan army began a deafening assault. Thousands of rounds of mortar fire rained down. Within hours, everyone in her sentry post was dead except her.

"The L.T.T.E. took me," she said of the Tamil rebel group. "They didn't let me see my parents. When I was injured, they didn't come to help me. I ask myself, 'Who are they?' "

Unlike Renuka, Malar, her short, curly hair pulled back by a headband, said she is still a true believer. According to her account, she was born in the Mannar district in northwestern Sri Lanka. Her father died of a heart attack when she was 3 and her mother went into the hospital when she was 6 and never returned. She moved in with her uncle, an unmarried farm laborer. Often, they had little to eat, she said.

When she was 8, she said, a woman from the Tigers came and told her the rebels would educate and care for her. "I thought it was better to go with the L.T.T.E. sister because of our poverty," she said. "I also wanted to contribute to freedom."

She was trained with 50 other girls, most of them orphans like her. They underwent years of ideological indoctrination in Tiger schools. She once caught a glimpse of the secretive, reclusive rebel leader, Velupillai Prabhakaran, and said, "We treat him as our god."

Last year, at age 12, she volunteered to go to war. "I wanted to save the country," she said. She was eventually sent to the eastern coast of the Jaffna peninsula, carting a Chinese-made submachine gun.

In July, during a routine sweep, army soldiers tossed a grenade into her bunker. "Eleven of us girls were in the bunker," she said as hot angry tears streaked down her cheeks. "Ten died in front of me. The military removed the girls' clothes and fired rounds into the bodies."

She lives now in a jail cell with Dayalani Balasubramaniam, 22, who joined the jailhouse conversation to say she had become a Tiger cadre when she was 16. The young woman held out her warped hands, the fingers curving at odd angles. She said soldiers had broken the bones with batons and left the fingers to heal without setting them. Human rights groups say the torture of rebel suspects is not uncommon.

The girl and the young woman, sharing a dark, dank cell, seemed to bolster each other's resolve to stay true to the cause. With their jailers listening, Miss Balasubramaniam declared she was still worked up to fight because of the army's bombing and shelling.

Malar fiercely echoed her words. "I feel the same," she said.

Article 33   *The Economist*, October 7, 2000

The war the world is missing

The Tamil Tigers' struggle in Sri Lanka is one of the longest-running wars. But as the island prepares to go to the polls, both sides are losing interest in suing for peace

EVEN by the standards of divided countries, Sri Lanka seems to be two different places. Most of the island is a lush land of palm-fringed beaches, tea gardens and pop-music radio stations that sound as if they are being beamed from New Jersey. The insurrection by the island's Tamil minority, which has claimed 60,000 lives and is dragging on into its 18th year, seems relevant only from time to time. Even bombs in the capital, Colombo, have the far-away quality of motorway accidents.

Not so in Trincomalee on the east coast. There, checkpoints are thicker on the ground than traffic lights. Although the army controls the town, there are "uncleared" areas barely 32km (20 miles) away in the hands of the dreaded separatist army, the Liberation Tigers of Tamil Eelam. From these areas the Tigers can strike inside "cleared" Trincomalee. On October 2nd a suicide bomber, presumably one of theirs, killed 21 people, including a candidate aligned to the ruling party, at a rally near the

town for next week's election. Such operations have the virtue, from the Tigers' point of view, of stirring a cocktail of overreaction and discrimination by the authorities that, in turn, feeds separatism among the local Tamils.

A visiting journalist hears a torrent of grievance. There are complaints about cordon-and-search operations by the security forces; there are tales of beatings, murder and reprisal. A woman says that the security forces murdered her brother, then refused to release his body unless she signed a statement saying he had belonged to the Tigers. She refused. The fishermen of Pattanatheru, a village nearby, lament security restrictions on where they can fish and their debts to Sinhalese *mudalalis* (proprietors), whom they repay by turning over their catch at cut-rate prices. Banks will lend money to fishermen from the Sinhalese majority, but not to them, they say.

Sri Lanka's government claims that there is scant support among ordinary Tamils for the Tigers, who are a vicious terrorist group as well as an astoundingly successful army. But although the Sri Lankan army has become somewhat less brutal, it has not improved enough and the police are less reformed. For that reason, the Tamils of Trincomalee seem to regard the Tigers as their defenders. "It is because of them that we are surviving," says one young Tamil.

The prospects for narrowing the divide look dim. Sri Lanka is scheduled to hold a parliamentary election on October 10th. It is likely either to prolong the current set-up, a government obedient to the president, Chandrika Bandaranaike Kumaratunga, who was re-elected to a six-year term in December 1999, or to produce gridlock: a parliament without an overall majority or one dominated by the opposition United National Party (UNP). Although the two main parties offer contrasting proposals for settling the conflict, there is little expectation that either will bring peace.

Why peace eludes Sri Lanka is something of a puzzle. Compared with the Arab-Israeli dispute or the struggle over Kashmir between India and Pakistan, the obstacles seem small. Hardliners do not have much parliamentary clout in Sri Lanka. The two biggest political parties, though they disagree over detail, both say they will talk about any compromise, short of granting the Tamils an independent state. In contrast with the insurgents in Kashmir, who are backed by Pakistan, the Tigers have no outside state behind them. Unlike India, Sri Lanka has accepted international involvement in its dispute: a Norwegian envoy is conveying messages between the antagonists. Nor is there ethnic rancour of the sort that has frustrated peace in the Balkans. Sinhalese and Tamils seem able, by and large, to forgive each other for the excesses of their leaders.

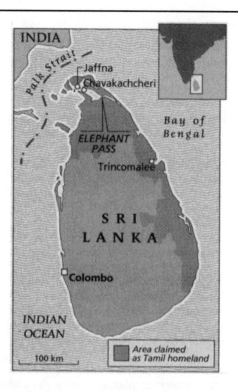

So why is nobody dusting off the Nobel peace prize? The answer lies in two finely-poised struggles: for political mastery in Colombo and, more important, for military mastery in the northeast, the Tamils' prospective homeland. The first has frustrated a consensus between the UNP and the ruling People's Alliance on what sort of offer the government should make to the Tamils, who are about 13% of the population. Mrs Kumaratunga presented her ideas to parliament as a draft constitution that would have devolved some powers of the highly centralised state to the regions, including the north-east. She withdrew it in August, when it emerged that Ranil Wickremesinghe, the UNP's leader, would not support it. The mutual loathing between president and opposition leader has little to do with principle.

Whether the flailing about in Colombo will achieve anything depends on another protagonist, Velupillai Prabhakaran, the Tigers' leader. Mr Prabhakaran's ambition is to set up Eelam, a sovereign Tamil homeland. With an armed force of 7,000–8,000 he has captured, the Tigers claim, 70% of Eelam (though a far smaller share of its population), from an army ten times the size. In Colombo it is said that he tells new recruits that they have the right to kill him if he settles for anything short

of Eelam. His followers are thought to have murdered many Tamils less fanatical than he is, along with leaders who have dared to negotiate with him, including an Indian prime minister and a Sri Lankan president. Mrs Kumaratunga has little reason to love a man who was presumably behind a bomb that nearly killed her during the last presidential campaign. They and the opposition leader form a Bermuda Triangle of hatred and suspicion in which peace efforts have so far disappeared.

The economic damage

It is a Sri Lankan clich to observe that the Sinhalese majority has many of the complexes of a minority. One reason is that, although they outnumber Tamils in Sri Lanka, they are outnumbered by Tamils just across the Palk Strait in the Indian state of Tamil Nadu. There is thus a sense that the Sinhalese language and Buddhism, the religion of most people who speak it, is under threat from a Tamil juggernaut with a beachhead in Sri Lanka. A second reason is that the British, who ruled Sri Lanka until 1948, treated Tamils, especially those of the Jaffna peninsula, as an elite. They were Sri Lanka's best-educated people and got more than their fair share of plum government jobs.

Soon after independence, the Sinhalese began to claim what they regarded as the majority's rightful place in Ceylon, as it then was. The then prime minister, S.W.R.D. Bandaranaike, Mrs Kumaratunga's father, championed a policy of making Sinhalese the country's sole official language and Buddhism the state religion. Tamils found themselves on the wrong end of racial-preference policies in favour of Sinhalese and Muslim applicants to universities. These disabilities, coupled with unemployment among the young, provoked violence in the Tamil-majority Jaffna peninsula, and horrific counter-violence in the Sinhalese south in 1983. Separatism and war have raged since.

This has cost Sri Lanka dear. It was, and in many ways remains, a model developing economy, with rates of literacy, fertility and life-expectancy closer to those of Europe than to those of other South Asian countries. It was the first economy in the region to liberalise, in

1977. Despite the shocks of war, the economy grew at a respectable average rate of 4.7% between 1980 and 1999. This year GDP is expected to grow by 5–5 1/2%.

Yet it could have been so much better. Saman Kelegama, head of the Institute of Policy Studies in Colombo, guesses that forgone investment, lost tourism, military spending, the loss of workers to death and emigration and other costs of the war amount to 200% of 1999's GDP. In a Sri Lanka at peace, the economy could grow at an average annual rate of 8%, thus absorbing the 140,000 people who enter the workforce each year. Unemployment—among both Sinhalese and Tamil young people—has been a primary cause of Sri Lanka's bloodshed. Young men (and women) from country villages join one army or the other for lack of anything else to do. An estimated 700,000 people have left for southern Sri Lanka or abroad, where they have become a mainstay of the Tigers' finances. A similar number are displaced from their homes in and near the north-east by shifting lines of battle.

The ferocity of war masks progress both in policy and in Sinhalese thinking about the conflict. No longer does a crude majoritarianism prevail. Sinhalese has lost its privileged status in the constitution, if not always in day-to-day life. Sri Lanka recognises Tamil as an official language. The Tamils' handicap in getting university places is largely gone. What remains is their resentment and insecurity, which can be mollified only by giving them political autonomy.

What price devolution?

At the moment, there is no autonomy for the north-east except where the Tigers rule. But the main political parties now express few inhibitions about devolving powers to the regions. The foreign minister, Lakshman Kadirgamar, says the government wants a solution "on federal lines", using a word that was, and in Sinhalese nationalist circles still is, taboo. The government's strategy is to placate moderate Tamils and pummel the Tigers into accepting a deal.

Unfortunately, Mrs Kumaratunga's ideas for constitutional reform meshed with no one else's. They offered too little devolution to satisfy even non-Tiger

Tamils, but enough to antagonise Sinhalese nationalists and many of the Buddhist clergy, who want no weakening of the unitary state. One function of the election will be to test how much support nationalists can muster at the ballot box.

Nor is devolution in itself a magic answer. A permanent merger of the Northern and Eastern Provinces, for example, is something most Tamils would insist on. The president's constitutional draft wriggles out of this by subjecting a merger of the provinces to a referendum in the eastern portion after ten years. This ridiculous-sounding fudge is a response to a serious problem. Although the north is almost entirely Tamil, the east has big populations of Sinhalese and Muslims, most of whom speak Tamil but see themselves as a separate ethnic group and have often allied with the Sinhalese. They might vote to secede from the northern province. Trincomalee is almost evenly divided among the three groups. Although professing love for their neighbours, the native Tamils point out that, in the 1881 census, the district's population was just 4% Sinhalese. Colonisation by chauvinist governments brought their share of the population to 34% a century later. Their fate would be uncertain in a Tamil-run, and especially a Tiger-run, north-east.

Mrs Kumaratunga means to reintroduce her constitutional draft, or a modified version, to the new parliament. It will make little difference. The People's Alliance is unlikely to win the two-thirds majority required to pass it. The president has threatened to turn parliament into a constituent assembly, which could pass the new constitution by majority vote. Sri Lanka's constitution authorises her to do no such thing. Mahinda Samarasinghe, an influential opposition MP, warns of "3.6m people taking to the roads" if she tries. Nor would it impress the Tigers, who say the devolution package "fails to address the key demands or the national aspirations of the Tamil people."

Some people think the UNP's more accommodating line—an offer of an "interim council" to run the north-east with a leading role for the Tigers while a final solution is worked out—has a better chance of ending hostilities. That

presumes that the Tigers will be less bloody-minded, and simply less bloody, than they have ever been before. Even if he becomes prime minister after the election, Mr Wickremesinghe will have a hard time persuading the president of that.

In the Tigers' lair

Would any solution acceptable to most Sinhalese and Muslims also satisfy Mr Prabhakaran? In theory, possibly. The Tigers are committed to the "Thimpu principles", among them the Tamils' right to self-determination and to a homeland with territorial sovereignty. Most Sri Lankans, the government included, regard these as tantamount to secession; but some, such as Rohan Edirisinha, a leading constitutional lawyer, think they may be compatible with belonging to a Sri Lankan federation. The Tigers have hinted that they think so, too. In rejecting Mrs Kumaratunga's proposals, Anton Balasingham, the Tigers' "theoretician", seemed to back "radical structural reforms" to the Sri Lankan constitution, implying that there could be room for Eelam within it.

What prevents compromise, apart from Mr Prabhakaran's fanaticism, is what might be called a dynamic stalemate between the two armies. That is the result of the Tigers' astounding potency and the Sri Lankan army's refusal to lose decisively.

Since 1987, when India unwisely intervened to keep a "peace", the Tigers have evolved from a band of 1,000–2,000 cadres into a force of 7,000 capable of operating "at all five spectra of conflict", according to a military analyst. They have a field army equivalent to three brigades, armed with artillery, armour, radios with encryption devices and other paraphernalia, which now fights on the Jaffna peninsula. They have a 1,000-cadre guerrilla force in the Eastern Province, which specialises in ambushes and mortar attacks. They have a terrorist outfit, which sends suicide bombers to Colombo and blows up electricity transformers. They have a global propaganda network of websites, broadcasters and newspapers, and a diplomatic wing. All this is paid for with contributions, mostly from expatriate Tamils, and profits from businesses, such as restaurants and shipping. The government guesses that the Tigers take in $80m a year.

In 1995 the Tigers lost the city of Jaffna, the main town of the peninsula, to the Sri Lankan army after talks with Mrs Kumaratunga broke down. Since then they have had a string of successes, gaining swathes of territory in the north, in April overrunning Elephant Pass, the disused but heavily defended land link between the peninsula and the rest of the island, and then very nearly recapturing Jaffna, which might have prompted a declaration of independence.

What the Tigers "liberate", they rule. The apparatus of the Sri Lankan state remains, but it takes orders from and is supplemented by the Tigers. People familiar with the uncleared areas (and well disposed to the Tigers) talk of them almost as Tamil havens. The Tigers, they say, make sure that teachers show up to teach at state schools, and pay them to give extra lessons. Mr Prabhakaran himself is said to set demanding standards for the number of students who must pass state exams. The government sends in food and supplies (too little, complain the Tamils); the Tigers supervise their distribution. Villages have boxes into which Tamils can post petitions and suggestions, which they say go directly to Mr Prabhakaran. To them he is Talaivar, the leader.

Yet there are credible reports that the Tigers can be as brutal to their own people as they are to their enemies. Amnesty International, a human-rights group, said last year that the Tigers have "recruited children as combatants on a large scale", sometimes forcibly. Neutral observers say the Tigers have also shelled Tamil civilians during their offensives, as has the Sri Lankan army. The lack of provisions in the uncleared areas is partly the Tigers' fault, claims the government: they commandeer the lorries for weeks at a time, disrupting supplies. The Tigers know that grumbling about provisions is likely to be directed at Colombo.

The army fights back

After nearly losing Jaffna, and with an election looming, Mrs Kumaratunga pulled the armed forces together. She spent about $350m on new weaponry, including devastating multi-barrel rocket launchers and MiG-27 fighter-bombers, and established a joint-operations headquarters, which brings all armed forces, including the police, under a single command. In September the army began to make some progress, notably with the recapture of the peninsula's second-biggest town, Chavakachcheri, a deserted pile of rubble by the time the soldiers moved in.

Sri Lanka's demoralised army (a fifth of its troops have deserted) is feeling stirrings of hope, and the government is optimistic that a series of reversals will squeeze the Tigers' morale and money. Mr Kadirgamar, the foreign minister, says that the flow of money to the Tigers ebbs when they suffer defeats. In April and May they "went around Europe saying Eelam is around the corner." The army's recent victories have quietened that boast. Sri Lanka and India stepped up their co-operation, says Mr Kadirgamar, tightening a "naval cordon" that is reducing the flow of arms to the Tigers.

The government thinks that only a series of defeats will persuade Mr Prabhakaran to negotiate for something less than full independence. It has yet to break his spirit. The Tigers this week launched the fourth phase of their "Unceasing Waves" offensive, which may be intended to fulfil their pledge to recapture Jaffna this year. The battle for the peninsula may be coming to a head.

Meanwhile, says Mr Kadirgamar, "not much is happening" with Norway's efforts at mediation. The Tigers have made it clear that they have "no interest in talking about peace." For the moment, that goes for both sides: both the government and the Tigers believe they have more to gain from war.

Credits

Page 86 Article 1. From *Harvard International Review,* Summer 1996. © 1996 by Harvard International Review. Reprinted by permission.

Page 90 Article 2. From *The Wilson Quarterly,* Summer 2000. © 2000 by Stephen P. Cohen. Reprinted by permission.

Page 98 Article 3. From *The Atlantic Monthly,* September 2000. © 2000 by Robert D. Kaplan. Reprinted by permission.

Page 108 Article 4. This article first appeared in *History Today,* September 1997. © 1997 by History Today, Ltd.

Page 113 Article 5. This article first appeared in *History Today,* September 1997. © 1997 by History Today, Ltd.

Page 118 Article 6. From *World Watch,* July/August 1998. © 1998 by the Worldwatch Institute. Reprinted by permission.

Page 126 Article 7. Reprinted by permission of *The New Republic,* September 25, 2000. © 2000 by The New Republic, Inc.

Page 133 Article 8. From *Harvard International Review,* Winter 1998/1999. © 1998 by Harvard International Review. Reprinted by permission.

Page 135 Article 9. This article appeared in *The World & I,* August 1998. *The World & I* is a publication of The Washington Times Corporation. © 1998.

Page 139 Article 10. From *Far Eastern Economic Review,* January 20, 2000. © 2000 by Review Publishing Company Limited. Reprinted by permission.

Page 141 Article 11. From *Far Eastern Economic Review,* September 14, 2000. © 2000 by Review Publishing Company Limited. Reprinted by permission.

Page 143 Article 12. From *Far Eastern Economic Review,* August 24, 2000. © 2000 by Review Publishing Company Limited. Reprinted by permission.

Page 146 Article 13. From *Populi,* June 1998. © 1998 by WFS, Women's Feature Service.

Page 148 Article 14. From the *New York Times,* May 9, 1999. © 1999 by The New York Times Company. Reprinted by permission.

Page 151 Article 15. From *Commonweal,* October 8, 1999. © 1999 by the Commonweal Foundation (1-888-495-6755). Reprinted by permission.

Page 154 Article 16. From the *Wall Street Journal,* September 21, 1999. © 1999 by Dow Jones & Company. All rights reserved.

Page 156 Article 17. From *Education About Asia,* Fall 1996. © 1996 by *Education About Asia.* Reprinted by permission.

Page 159 Article 18. This article appeared in *The World & I,* October 1996. *The World & I* is a publication of The Washington Times Corporation. © 1996.

Page 163 Article 19. From the *New York Times,* May 11, 1998. © 1998 by The New York Times Company. Reprinted by permission.

Page 165 Article 20. From *Ms.,* September/October 1998. Reprinted by permission of *Ms.* magazine. © 1998.

Page 167 Article 21. Reprinted with permission from *The Christian Science Monitor,* May 13, 1998. © 1998 by The Christian Science Publishing Society. All rights reserved.

Page 169 Article 22. This article appeared in *The World & I,* October 1996. *The World & I* is a publication of The Washington Times Corporation. © 1996.

Page 173 Article 23. Reprinted with permission from *The Economist,* May 27, 2000. © 2000 by The Economist, Ltd. Distributed by The New York Times Special Features.

Page 175 Article 24. Reprinted with permission from the *UNESCO Courier,* November 1993, pp. 30-33.

Page 178 Article 25. From the *New York Times,* April 16, 1998. © 1998 by The New York Times Company. Reprinted by permission.

Page 180 Article 26. From *The Washington Post,* October 5, 1998. © 1998 by The Washington Post. Reprinted by permission.

Page 184 Article 27. From *Newsweek,* December 6, 1999. © 1999 by Newsweek, Inc. All rights reserved. Reprinted by permission.

Page 186 Article 28. Reprinted with permission from *Scientific American,* November 1999. © 1999 by Scientific American, Inc. All rights reserved.

Page 189 Article 29. From *The World Today,* November 1993. Reprinted by permission of *The World Today.* © 1993.

Page 194 Article 30. Reprinted with permission from *The Economist,* May 13, 2000. © 2000 by The Economist, Ltd. Distributed by The New York Times Special Features.

Page 195 Article 31. From *The World Today,* February 1, 2000. Reprinted by permission of *The World Today.* © 2000.

Page 198 Article 32. From the *New York Times,* September 11, 2000. © 2000 by The New York Times Company. Reprinted by permission.

Page 200 Article 33. Reprinted with permission from *The Economist,* October 7, 2000. © 2000 by The Economist, Ltd. Distributed by The New York Times Special Features.

Sources for Statistical Reports

U.S. State Department, *Background Notes* (2000).

CIA *World Factbook* (2000).

World Bank, *World Development Report* (2000/2001).

UN *Population and Vital Statistics Report* (January 2001).

World Statistics in Brief (2000).

The Statesman's Yearbook (2000).

Population Reference Bureau, *World Population Data Sheet* (2000).

The World Almanac (2000).

The Economist Intelligence Unit (1999).

Glossary of Terms and Abbreviations

Asoka A Mauryan emperor in northern India from 268 to 232 B.C. Overcome with remorse about deaths caused by his military conquests, he abandoned warfare as an instrument of imperial power and adopted the Buddhist Dharma as the standard for his rule. He enforced this expectation in a series of edicts carved into stones and pillars throughout his kingdom. His example is recognized today in the adoption of the lion capital on one of his pillars as the insignia of the Republic of India.

Babur The first of the Moghul emperors, who engaged in a military conquest of northern India from 1526 to 1529. It was during his brief reign that the Babri Mosque was built in Ayodhya, purportedly on the site of an earlier Hindu temple, the destruction of which, in December 1992, led to communal riots across India. Akbar, the greatest of the Moghul monarchs, who ruled from 1556 to 1605 and completed the Moghul conquest of northern India, was Babur's grandson.

Bharatiya Janata Party (BJP) "Indian Peoples Party" grew as a Hindu nationalist party out of the heartland of the Gangetic Plain during the 1980s to become the only party to challenge Congress Party hegemony on a national level. It attained leadership in Parliament in 1998, but only through the support of a 19-party coalition.

Bindi A small, red cosmetic circle in the middle of the forehead, worn by women as a sign that they are marriageable or married. It is not usually worn by girls or by widows.

Brahmin The priestly community, ranked highest on the varna caste scale.

Buddhism A religious faith that started in India in the sixth century B.C. by Siddhartha Gautama, who renounced his royal heritage to seek enlightenment for the salvation of all humankind. The attainment of Nirvana (his death) is placed at 483 B.C. This faith extended throughout Asia in two major traditions: Theravada ("Teaching of the Elders") to Sri Lanka and Southeast Asia; and Mahayana ("Great Vehicle") to China and Japan. Tibetan Buddhism is a subset of the Mahayana tradition. Theravada has been called Hinayana ("Lesser Vehicle") by Mahayana Buddhists to distinguish that tradition from their own.

Chola A Tamil dynasty centered in the Tanjavur District of the current state of Tamil Nadu, which dominated that part of south India from A.D. 880 to 1279. The temples built and the bronzes cast under the patronage of the Chola kings remain some of the most beautiful and cherished works of Indian art.

Congress Party As the successor of the Indian National Congress in 1935, it led the new Republic of India to independence in 1947 and remained in control of the country for 45 years as the majority party in India's Parliament. The party split in 1969 but has rallied around the descendants of its first prime minister, Jawarhalal Nehru. His granddaughter-in-law, Sonia Gandhi, was elected president of the party in 1998.

Dalits The "broken" or "oppressed"; this is the name preferred by those traditionally known as scheduled castes, outcastes, or untouchables, members of the lowest-rank communities in the classical caste system, below the four ranks of priests, rulers, citizens, and laborers on the varna social scale. Mahatma Gandhi, deeply concerned about removing their oppression, called them *Harijans,* children of God.

Dharma Translated as "law, justice, duty, cosmic order," the moral standard by which society and an individual's life are ordered and given meaning.

Dhoti A single piece of cloth tied as a garment by men around the lower portion of their bodies.

Green Revolution An upsurge in agricultural production that followed the introduction of high-yielding hybrids of rice and grains, developed by the Rockefeller Foundation in Mexico and the Philippines, into South Asia during the 1950s and 1960s.

Harappa and Mohenjo Daro The two largest cities excavated during the 1930s in the Indus River Valley to reveal an ancient urban culture that began around 3000 B.C. It flourished for 1,000 years and then inexplicably disappeared.

Hindi The prevalent language and literature of northern India.

Hindu One who follows the faith of Hinduism.

Hinduism The dominant religion of India, emphasizing Dharma, with its ritual and social observances and often mystical contemplation and ascetic practices.

Indian National Congress An association of educated Indians and sympathetic Europeans who gathered in Bengal in 1885 to seek admission for qualified Indians into the British Indian Civil Service. In the early twentieth century, this association became the bearer of the independence movement of the subcontinent from British colonial rule. Following the establishment of a provisional government in 1935, it evolved into the Congress Party.

Islam A religious faith started in Arabia during the seventh century A.D. by the prophet Mohammad.

Jain A religious faith started in India by Mahavira in the sixth century B.C. Its primary teachings include the eternal transmigration of souls and the practice of nonviolence toward all living creatures.

Jajmani A barter system of economic activity in the village, in which villagers provide their services on a regular basis to particular land owners—their patrons—in exchange for fixed portions of the annual harvest.

Jati An extended kinship group, usually identified with a traditional occupation, that defines the parameters of accepted marriage relationships. It is the unit that is ranked in the hierarchical social (caste) structure of a village and that moves within that structure.

Koran The sacred scripture of the Islamic faith, the teachings of Allah (God) as revealed to His prophet Mohammad in the seventh century A.D.

Ladakh The easternmost and highest region of the state of Kashmir-Jammu, inhabited mostly by Buddhists.

Lama A leader of a Tibetan Buddhist monastic community (sangha).

Lok Sabha and Rajya Sabha The two houses of Parliament in the Republic of India: "The House of the People" has 545 members elected directly by voters on the district level; "The Council of States" has 250 members, 12 appointed by the president and 238 elected by state legislatures.

Mahabharata The Great Epic of India, with more than 90,000 stanzas, composed around the third century B.C. The longest poem in the world, it is the story of five brothers' struggle to wrest their father's kingdom from their cousins. This epic contains the *Bhagavad Gita,* a discourse between one of the brothers, Arjuna, and his charioteer, Krishna, on the eve of the culminating battle with their cousins, when Arjuna is overcome by concerns about appropriate behavior and quality of life.

Mahar A depressed (untouchable) community in the state of Maharashtra, which converted to Buddhism in October 1956 as an initiative to free themselves as a community from the social burden of untouchability, under the leadership of Dr. B. R. Ambedkar.

Mahatma Literally "great souled one"; a title given to Mohandas Gandhi by Rabindranath Tagore in 1921 and adopted by the people of India to express their belief in Gandhi's saintliness.

Mandala An intricate visual symbol developed in the Tibetan Buddhist tradition, revealing elaborate patterns of many shapes and colors, intended to lead its creator and observer into supranormal levels of consciousness.

Moghuls Islamic invaders of Turkish descent who established the longest dynastic imperial rule in the Great Central Plain of South Asia, from A.D. 1526 to 1857.

Mohajirs "Immigrants"; those Muslims who moved from their homelands in India at the time of partition in 1947 to settle in Pakistan. Because they have retained many of the customs as well as the language (Urdu) of their former homes, even today they remain a distinctive community and political force, as the Mohajir Quami Movement (MQM) in Pakistan.

Monsoon An annual torrential rainfall, which normally begins during the month of June, when the prevailing winds shift to the west, gather clouds with water from the Arabian Sea, and deluge the subcontinent with rain as the clouds rise over the Himalayan Mountains. The dramatic shift from the torrid dry heat of late spring to this stormy wet season and the lush growth that it provides has an immense impact on the economies, the literature, and the consciousness of South Asian peoples. Raja Rao gives a brief, gripping description of the coming of the monsoon on page 50 of his novel *Kanthapura* and in his notes, pages 215–216.

Mujahideen Militant tribal leaders in Afghanistan who joined in alliance to protect their authority as local warlords from national and foreign (Soviet) incursion.

Muslim One who submits to the supreme will of Allah (God), as revealed to the prophet Mohammad; one who practices Islam. Sometimes spelled Moslem.

Nirvana Literally, "blowing out, extinguishing"; the ultimate enlightenment of Buddhism: departure from the relentless transmigratory cycle of births and deaths into nothingness.

Pali One of many regional Indo-European languages (called Prakrits) spoken in the northern plains region of South Asia following the Aryan Invasion (ca. 1700 B.C.) and before the evolution of the subcontinent's modern languages, following the twelfth century A.D. It was the language in which the earliest documents of the Buddhist faith were composed in northern India.

Panchayat Literally, "council of five." This traditional leadership of elders in the jati kinship group was adopted in the Panchayat Acts in state legislatures during the 1950s as the appropriate form of democratically elected village government in the Republic of India.

Parsi A member of the Zoroastrian faith, the ancient religion of Persia. Most of the Parsis in South Asia live in Bombay (Mumbai) and Karachi.

Pathans Tribal peoples in the northwest corner of the subcontinent who speak the Pushtu language.

Punjab Translated as *panch* ("five") and *ap* ("water"), designates the land in the western portion of the Great Central Plain through which the five rivers forming the Indus River System flow. The province that had this name during the British Indian Empire was divided between India and Pakistan in 1947.

Purana "Tradition," a genre of Sanskrit religious texts of different sects of Hinduism from the Classical Period (A.D. 300 to 1200), setting forth their primary myths and teachings; also the accounts in local languages of the sacred significance of religious sites, temples, places of pilgrimage, etc.

Rabindranath Tagore An outstanding Bengali poet and educator (1861–1941), whose collection of poems, *Gitanjali,* published in English translation in 1912, won the Nobel Prize for Literature.

Raj Translated as "rule" or "king," a term that designates political sovereignty. (The word *reign* comes from the same Indo-European root.) Raj is used with British to identify the British colonial government in India; it is used with *maha* ("great") to identify rulers of the Indian princely states; and it is used with *swa* ("self") to mean self-rule or independence. Swaraj also has the connotation of self-discipline, which is an important aspect of Mahatma Gandhi's concept of independence.

Ramayana An epic Sanskrit poem, composed around the second century A.D. and attributed to Valmiki, describing the ordeals of the ideal prince Rama. Most of the text describes his ultimately successful quest for his faithful wife Sita, who was abducted by the demonic King Ravana.

Rg Veda The first of the four Vedas, which are the earliest and most sacred of the writings of the Hindus. Around 1000 B.C., it was compiled into an anthology of 10 books containing 1,028 hymns.

RSS Rashtriya Swayamsevak Sangh, an organization founded in 1925 to train Hindus to seek independence from the British Raj by whatever means necessary and to further Hindu nationalistic objectives. Recognized as a militant alternative to Mahatma Gandhi's nonviolent movement, it is today a significant political force within the Bharatiya Janata Party (BJP).

Salt March An act of nonviolent civil disobedience (*satyagraha*) led by Mahatma Gandhi in 1930. He and his followers marched from his *ashram* at Sabarmati 241 miles to Dandi on the coast to evaporate salt from the sea, in order to protest the British tax on salt.

Salwar Kameez Salwar is a pajama-like trouser; Kameez is a loose-fitting, long-sleeved blouse that extends below the hips. This attire is more common for women than the sari in the wheat-growing portion of the subcontinent.

Sangha A Buddhist community of holy men and women who follow the Buddha's path called Dharma. The Buddha, Dharma, and Sangha are called the "three jewels of the Buddhist faith."

Sanskrit Translated as "made together, formed, perfected," as descriptive of the classical language of India as structurally perfected.

Sari A woman's garment, a single piece of cloth 6 yards long, which she wraps around her waist, pleats across the front, and drapes over her shoulder. Simple in design and graceful in appearance, it is worn by those of all walks of life, with only the quality of the material and the pattern changing to meet the occasion.

Satyagraha Literally, "holding the truth," the name that Mahatma Gandhi adopted while in South Africa to describe his nonviolent civil protest against the South African government's oppression of the people from India. Gandhi's translation of this term as "soul force" affirms that, even early in his public career, he understood such action to be primarily religious and only secondarily political.

Shiva Literally, "auspicious"; the name of God in one of the two main sects of Hinduism: Shaivism (from Shiva) and Vaishnavism ("followers of Vishnu").

Sitar, Vina, and Sharod Traditional stringed instruments used to play classical Indian music. The vina, upon which south Indian, or Karnatic, music is performed, is the oldest. The other two, more prevalent in the north of the subcontinent, evolved during Moghul times to perform music that reveals the Persian and Middle Eastern influences of that period.

Sufi A person of the Islamic faith who affirms through religious discipline and mystical experience the spiritual union of self with God.

Taliban "Seekers of religious knowledge"; members of a militant and exceptionally conservative freedom force named after the Pathan students of Islam from Kandahar who started a fundamentalist crusade to free Afghanistan from foreign and modern corruptions of their faith and traditional way of life.

Varna Originally translated as "class," later as "color"; the fourfold division of classical Indian society, ranked on a purity–pollution scale: priests, rulers, citizens, and laborers. The untouchables and tribals are a fifth group, known as outcastes, ranked below the laborers.

Vellalas Among Tamil-speaking peoples, the dominant landholding and cultivating communities, similar to the Jat communities in the Hindi-speaking regions of the subcontinent.

Vishnu Receiving somewhat minor attention as a solar deity in the *Rg Veda,* Vishnu became recognized as Supreme Lord of the universe, its creator and preserver during the classical period (A.D. 300–1200). He is worshipped widely throughout Hinduism through His incarnations (*avatars*), of whom Rama and Krishna are the most prevalent.

Yoga A highly disciplined set of exercises to identify, nurture, and develop different parts of one's natural body, breathing, nervous system, and consciousness. Practice of this discipline leads to the integration of one's total self—physical, mental, and spiritual, the unconscious as well as the conscious.

Bibliography

GENERAL WORKS

Bina Agarwal, *A Field of One's Own: Gender and Land Rights in South Asia* (Cambridge: Cambridge University Press, 1994).

F. R. Allchin et al. *The Archaeology of Early Historic South Asia: The Emergence of Cities and States* (Cambridge: Cambridge University Press, 1995).
A survey of archeological research done in South Asia.

A. L. Basham, *The Wonder That Was India* (Columbia, MO: South Asia Books, 1995).
A comprehensive introduction to classical India.

Ashish Bose, ed., *Population Transition in South Asia* (Columbia, MO: South Asia Books, 1992).

Myron L. Cohen, *Asia, Case Studies in Social Sciences* (Armonk, NY: M. E. Sharpe, 1992).
A Guide for Teaching, Columbia Project on Asia in the Core Curriculum.

W. T. deBary, ed., *Sources of Indian Tradition* (New York: Columbia University Press, 1988).
Translations of primary texts from the Vedic Period to independence.

Joseph Elder, ed., *Lectures in Indian Civilization,* Dubuque, IA: 1970).
A syllabus and supporting materials for a survey course on India and Pakistan.

Ainslie T. Embree and Carol Gluck, eds., *Asia in Western and World History* (Armonk, NY: M. E. Sharpe, 1993).
A Guide for Teaching, Columbia Project on Asia in the Core Curriculum.

Roger Jeffery and Alaka M. Basu, *Girls' Schooling, Women's Autonomy and Fertility Change in South Asia* (New Delhi: Sage, 1996).

Veena Jha, Grant Hewison, and Maree Underhill, *Trade, Environment, and Sustainable Development: A South Asian Perspective* (New York: St. Martin's Press, 1997).

Ann Leonard, *Seeds: Supporting Women's Work in the Third World* (New York: Feminist Press, 1989).
Chapters on Credit Organization in Madras, India; Non-craft Employment in Bangladesh; and Forest Conservation in Nepal.

Todd Lewis and Theodore Riccardi, *The Himalayas: A Syllabus of the Region's History, Anthropology, and Religion* (Ann Arbor, MI: Association of Asian Studies, 1995).

Satu Limaye, *South Asia and the United States After the Cold War* (New York: The Asia Society, 1994).

Barbara Stoler Miller, ed., *Masterworks of Asian Literature in Comparative Perspective* (Armonk, NY: M. E. Sharpe, 1993).
A Guide for Teaching, Columbia Project on Asia in the Core Curriculum.

Gowher Rizvi, *South Asia in a Changing International Order* (Troy, NY: Sage Publishing, 1993).

Francis Robinson, ed., *The Cambridge Encyclopedia of India, Pakistan, Bangladesh, Sri Lanka, Nepal, Bhutan, and the Maldives* (Cambridge: Cambridge University Press, 1989).

Joseph Schwartzberg, *A Historical Atlas of South Asia* (New York: Oxford University Press, 1992).

Robert H. Taylor, ed., *Asia and the Pacific*, 2 vols. (New York: Facts on File Publications, 1990).
Brief articles on every Asian country, with supplementary essays on topics of development, education, communication, and so on.

NATIONAL HISTORIES AND ANALYSES

Afghanistan

N. D. Ahmad, *Survival of Afghanistan: A Historical Survey of the Afghanistan Crisis* (Rockwell, TX: KBA Publishing, 1992).

Louis Dupree, *Afghanistan* (Princeton, NJ: Princeton University Press, 1973).

Edward R. Girardet, *Afghanistan: The Soviet War* (New York: St. Martin's Press, 1986).

Ralph H. Magnus and Eden Naby, *Afghanistan: Marx, Mullah, and Mujahid* (Boulder, CO: Westview Press, 1992).

William Maley and Fazel H. Saikal, *Political Order in Post-Communist Afghanistan* (New York: International Peace Academy, 1992).

Louis Palmer, *Adventures in Afghanistan* (Los Altos, CA: Institute for the Study of Human Knowledge, 1990).

Myron Weiner and Ali Banuazizi, eds., *The Politics of Social Transformation in Afghanistan, Iran, and Pakistan* (Syracuse, NY: Syracuse University Press, 1993).

Bangladesh

Craig Baxter, *Bangladesh: A New Nation in an Old Setting* (Boulder, CO: Westview Press, 1984).

Dilara Choudhury, *Bangladesh and the South Asian International System* (Chicago: Kazi Publications, 1992).

Amiul H. Faraizi, *Bangladesh: Peasant Migration and the World Capitalist Economy* (New York: Apt Books, 1993).

Rokeya Sakhawat Hossain, *Sultana's Dream* (New York: The Feminist Press, 1988).
A Bengali Muslim writer on purdah and her dream of its reversal.

Bosse Kramsjo, *Breaking the Chains: Collective Action for Social Justice Among the Rural Poor in Bangladesh* (New York: Intermed Technology Development Group of North America, 1992).

Beth Roy, *Some Trouble With Cows: Making Sense of Social Conflict* (Berkeley, CA: University of California Press, 1994).

Abu N. M. Wahid, ed., *The Grameen Bank: Poverty Relief in Bangladesh* (Boulder, CO: Westview Press, 1993).

Bhutan

Tom O. Edmunds, *Bhutan: Land of the Thunder Dragon* (New York: Viking Penguin, 1989).

A. C. Singh, *Bhutan: Ethnic Identity and National Dilemma* (New York: Apt Books, 1991).

Narendra Singh, *Bhutan, A Kingdom in the Himalayas* (New Delhi: S. Chand, 1985).

India

Bina Agarwal, *A Field of One's Own: Gender and Land Rights in South Asia* (Cambridge: Cambridge University Press, 1994).

Geoffrey Ashe, *Gandhi* (Chelsea, MI: Scarborough House, 1969).

Jonah Blank, *Arrow of the Blue-Skinned God: Retracing the Ramayana Through India* (Boston: Houghton Mifflin, 1992).

Joan Bondurant, *Conquest of Violence* (Princeton, NJ: Princeton University Press, 1988).

Sumantra Bose, *The Challenge in Kashmir: Democracy, Self-Determination and a Just Peace* (New Delhi: Sage, 1997).

Paul Brass, *The Politics of India Since Independence* (Cambridge: Cambridge University Press, 1990).

Leslie J. Calman, *Toward Empowerment: Women and Movement Politics in India* (Boulder, CO: Westview Press, 1992).

Sharat Chandra, *Population Pattern and Social Change in India* (Columbia, MO: South Asia Books, 1992).

Barbara Crossette, *India: Facing the Twenty-First Century* (Bloomington, IN: Indiana University Press, 1993).

Dennis Dalton, *Mahatma Gandhi, Nonviolent Power in Action* (New York: Columbia University Press, 1995).

Narendra K. Dash, *Encyclopaedic Dictionary of Indian Culture* (Columbia, MO: South Asia Books, 1992).

Steve Derne, *Culture in Action: Family Life, Emotion, and Male Domination in Banaras, India* (Albany: State University of New York Press, 1995).

Jean Dreze and Amartya Sen, eds., *Indian Development: Selected Regional Perspectives* (Delhi: Oxford University Press, 1997).

———*India: Economic Development and Social Opportunity* (Delhi: Oxford University Press, 1995).

Diana Eck, *Darshan—Seeing the Divine Image in India* (New York: Columbia University Press, 1995).

Ainslie Embree, *Utopias in Conflict: Religion and Nationalism in Modern India* (Berkeley, CA: University of California Press, 1990).

Eric Ericson, *Gandhi's Truth* (New York: Norton, 1970).

Geraldine Forbes, *Women in Modern India: The New Cambridge History of India* (Cambridge: Cambridge University Press, 1996).

Mohandas K. Gandhi, *An Autobiography: The Story of My Experiments With Truth* (Boston: Beacon, 1957).

Zoya Hasan, ed. *Forging Identities: Gender, Communities and the State* (New Delhi: Kali for Women, 1994).

John Stratton Hawley and Donna Marie Wulff, *Devi: Goddesses of India* (Berkeley, CA: University of California Press, 1996).

Thomas Hopkins, *The Hindu Religious Tradition* (Belmont: Dickenson, 1971).

S. M. Ikram, *Muslim Civilization in India* (New York: Columbia University Press, 1964).

Doranne Jacobson, *India: Land of Dreams and Fantasy* (Columbia, MO: South Asia Books, 1992).

Ashok Kapur and A. Jeyaratnam Wilson, *The Foreign Policy of India and Her Neighbors* (New York: St. Martin's Press, 1996).

David Knipe, *Hinduism, Experiments in the Sacred* (New York: Harper, 1990).

Donald Lopez, Jr., *Religions of India in Practice* (Princeton, NJ: Princeton University Press, 1995).

David Ludden, ed., *Contesting the Nation: Religion, Community, and the Politics of Democracy in India* (Philadelphia: University of Pennsylvania Press, 1996).

V. S. Naipaul, *India: A Million Mutinies Now* (New York: Viking, 1992).

Kirin Narayan, *Mondays on the Dark Night of the Moon: Himalayan Foothill Folktales* (New York: Oxford University Press, 1997).

Jawaharlal Nehru, *The Discovery of India* (New York: John Day, 1946).

Jean-Luc Racine, ed., *Peasant Moorings: Village Ties and Mobility Rationales in South India* (New Delhi: Sage, 1997).

Raja Rao, *Kanthapura* (New York: New Directions, 1963).
   A novel describing the impact of Mahatma Gandhi on a south Indian village.

Lloyd and Suzanne Rudolph, *The Modernity of Tradition* (Chicago: University of Chicago Press, 1984).

Jadunath Sarkar, *India Through the Ages* (New York: Apt Books, 1993).

Tanika Sarkar and Urvashi Butalia, ed., *Women and Right Wing Movements: Indian Experiences* (London and New York: Zed Books, Ltd. 1995).

S. N. Sharma, *Personal Liberty Under Indian Constitution* (Columbia, MO: South Asia Books, 1991).

Thomas Spear and Romilia Thapar, *A History of India*, 2 vols. (Baltimore, MD: Penguin, 1965).

M. N. Srinivas, *Social Change in Modern India* (Berkeley, CA: University of California Press, 1969).

Mark Tully and Zareer Masani, *From Raj to Rajiv, 40 Years of Indian Independence* (New Delhi: Universal Book Stall, 1988).

Peter van der Veer, *Religious Nationalism: Hindus and Muslims in India* (Berkeley, CA: University of California Press, 1994).

John C. B. Webster, *A History of the Dalit Christians in India* (San Francisco: Mellen Research University Press, 1992).

William and Charlotte Wiser, *Behind Mud Walls* (Berkeley, CA: University of California Press, 1989).
   A classic description of an Indian village in 1930 and 1960, with a new chapter on 1984.

Stanley Wolpert, *India* (Berkeley, CA: University of California Press, 1991).

———*Nehru, A Tryst With Destiny* (New York: Oxford University Press, 1969).

R. C. Zaehner, *Hinduism* (New York: Oxford University Press, 1970).

Heinreich Zimmer, *Myths and Symbols in Indian Art and Civilization* (New York: Harper, 1946).

Maldives

Mark Balla, *Maldives and Islands of the East Indian Ocean: A Travel Survival Kit* (Oakland: Lonely Planet Publishing, 1993).

Camerapix, *Maldives* (Edison, NY: Hunter Publishing, 1993).

Ursula and Luithui Phabnis and Ela Dutt, *Maldives: Winds of Change in an Atoll State* (New Delhi: South Asian Publishers, 1985).

Nepal

Lok R. Baral, *Nepal: Problems of Governance* (New York: Advent Books, 1993).

Monica Connell, *Against a Peacock Sky* (New York: Viking, 1992).

Kirkpatrick, *An Account of the Kingdom of Nepal* (Columbia, MO: South Asia Books, 1986).

Bruce M. Nevin, *The Mountain Kingdom: Portraits of Nepal and the Gurkhas* (Cincinnati, OH: Seven Hills Book Distributors, 1991).

Leo E. Rose and John T. Schulz, *Nepal: Profile of a Himalayan Kingdom* (Boulder, CO: Westview Press, 1980).

Andrea M. Savada, ed., *Nepal and Bhutan: Country Studies* (Washington, D.C.: Library of Congress, 1993).

Prem R. Uperty, *Political Awakening in Nepal: The Search for a New Identity* (Columbia, MO: South Asia Books, 1992).

Eden Vansittart, *Notes on Nepal With an Introduction by H. H. Risley* (Columbia, MO: South Asia Books, 1992).

Pakistan

Prabha Arun, *Pathway to Pakistan* (Columbia, MO: South Asia Books, 1992).

Benazir Bhutto, *Daughter of Destiny, An Autobiography* (New York: S & S Trade, 1990).

Shahid Javed Burki, *Pakistan: The Continuing Search for Nationhood* (Boulder, CO: Westview Press, 1991).

Attar Chand, *Pakistan: In Search of Modernization* (Columbia, MO: South Asia Books, 1992).

Surendra Chopra, *Pakistan's Thrust in the Muslim World: India as a Factor* (Columbia, MO: South Asia Books, 1992).

Ayesha Jalal, *Democracy and Authority in South Asia: A Comparative and Historical Perspective* (Cambridge: Cambridge University Press, 1995).

Jamal Malik, *Colonialization of Islam: Dissolution of Traditional Institutions in Pakistan* (New Delhi: Manohar, 1996).

Mokhdum E. Mushrafi, *Pakistan and Bangladesh: Political Culture and Political Parties* (Columbia, MO: South Asia Books, 1992).

Richard Reeves, *Passage to Peshawar* (New York: Simon & Schuster, 1984).

Abdul Quddus Syed, *Cultural Patterns of Pakistan* (Chicago: Kazi Publications, 1989).

Sri Lanka

Kingsley De Silva, *Problems of Governing Sri Lanka* (New York: Advent Books, 1993).

Pradeep Jeganathan and Qadri Ismail, *Unmaking the Nation: The Politics of Identity and History in Modern Sri Lanka* (Colombo: Social Scientists' Association, 1995).

E. F. Ludowyk, *The Footprint of the Buddha* (London: George Allen & Unwin, 1958).

James Manor, ed., *Sri Lanka in Change and Crisis* (New York: St. Martin's Press, 1984).

Walpola Rahula, *History of Buddhism in Ceylon* (Colombo: M. D. Gunasena, 1956).

Mohan Ram, *Sri Lanka: The Fractured Island* (New York: Penguin, 1990).

S. J. Tambiah, *Sri Lanka, Ethnic Fratricide and the Dismantling of Democracy* (Chicago: University of Chicago Press, 1991).

Ananda Wickremeratne, *Buddhism and Ethnicity in Sri Lanka: A Historical Analysis* (Columbia, MO: South Asia Books, 1995).